A Cold War in the Soviet Bloc

A
COLD WAR
IN THE
SOVIET BLOC

Polish–East German Relations,
1945–1962

Sheldon Anderson

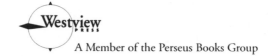

A Member of the Perseus Books Group

Copyright © 2001 by Westview Press, A Member of the Perseus Books Group

Published in 2001 in the United States of America by Westview Press, 5500 Central Avenue, Boulder, Colorado 80301-2877, and in the United Kingdom by Westview Press, 12 Hid's Copse Road, Cumnor Hill, Oxford OX2 9JJ

Find us on the World Wide Web at www.westviewpress.com

Library of Congress Cataloging-in-Publication Data
Anderson, Sheldon R., 1951–
    A Cold War in the Soviet Bloc : Polish–East German relations : 1945–1962 / Sheldon Anderson.
      p. cm.
    Includes bibliographical references and index.
    ISBN 0-8133-3783-6 (pb)
    1. Poland—Foreign relations—Germany (East). 2. Germany (East)—Foreign relations—Poland. 3. Poland—Foreign relations—1945–1989. I. Title.

DK4185.G3 A53 2000
327.4380431—dc21

                                                                    00-063305

The paper used in this publication meets the requirements of the American National Standard for Permanence of Paper for Printed Library Materials Z39.48-1984.

10   9   8   7   6   5   4   3   2   1

PERSEUS
POD
ON DEMAND

For Woody

Contents

Illustrations

Acknowledgments

I am deeply indebted to many people who contributed to the completion of the book. I would like to thank the archivists at the Archiwum Akt Nowych and the Archiwum Spraw Zagranicznych in Warsaw, and the Stiftung Archiv der Partei und Massenorganizationen and the Archiv des Aussenministerium der DDR in Berlin. Thanks to their efficiency and cooperation, I was able to complete my research in a timely manner. I would also like to thank the Deutsche Akademische Austauschdienst (DAAD), the Kennan Institute of Advanced Russian Studies, and Miami University for their generous grants to facilitate my research in Poland, Germany, and Washington D.C.

The book would not have been possible without the gracious hospitality of my good friends in Warsaw, Macek and Basia Roszkowski, and Peter Meitz in Berlin, all of whom made my European research visits so comfortable and enjoyable.

I would like to give a special thanks to Professor Tom Taylor, who took his precious time to read and critique the manuscript.

Last but not least, I am forever grateful to my wife, Kristie, for enduring long periods of separation while I did research in Europe, and for her patience and understanding as I worked on the manuscript.

Abbreviations

I have used the German and Polish abbreviations with the exception of commonly translated cases, such as FRG.

ADN   Allgemeiner Deutscher Nachrichtendienst (General German News Service)
CC   Central Committee
CDU   Christlich-Demokratische Union (Christian Democratic Union)
CPSU   Communist Party of the Soviet Union
CzCP   Czechoslovak Communist Party
DBD   Demokratische Bauernpartei Deutschlands (German Democratic Peasant Party)
DWK   Deutsche Wirtschaftskommission (German Economic Commission)
ECSC   European Coal and Steel Community
FDGB   Freier Deutscher Gewerkschaftsbund (Free German Trade Union)
FDJ   Freie Deutsche Jugend (Free German Youth)
FDP   Freie Demokratische Partei (Free Democratic Party)
FRG   Federal Republic of Germany (Bundesrepublik Deutschland)
GDR   German Democratic Republic (Deutsche Demokratische Republik)
KC   Komitet Centralny (Central Committee of the PPR/PZPR)
KPD   Kommunistische Partei Deutschlands (Communist Party of Germany)
KPP   Komunistyczna Partia Polski (Communist Party of Poland)
KRN   Krajowa Rada Narodowa (National People's Council)
KVP   Kasernierte Volkspolizei (People's Police in Barracks)
LDP   Liberale Demokratische Partei (Liberal Democratic Party)
LPG   Landwirtschaftliche Produktionsgenossenschaft (Agricultural Production Co-operative)
NDPD   National-Demokratische Partei Deutschlands (National Democratic Party of Germany)
NEP   New Economic Policy
NVA   Nationale Volksarmee (National People's Army)

PPR	Polska Partia Robotnicza (Polish Workers' Party)
PPS	Polska Partia Socjalistyczna (Polish Socialist Party)
PRP	People's Republic of Poland (Polska Rzeczpospolita Ludowa)
PSL	Polskie Stronnictwo Ludowe (Polish Peasants' Party)
PZPR	Polska Zjednoczona Partia Robotnicza (Polish United Workers' Party)
SD	Stronnictwo Demokratyczne (Democratic Party)
SDKPiL	Social Democracy of the Kingdom of Poland and Lithuania
SED	Sozialistische Einheitspartei Deutschlands (Socialist Unity Party of Germany)
SL	Stronnictwo Ludowe (Peasants' Party)
SMAG	Soviet Military Administration in Germany
SPD	Sozialdemokratische Partei Deutschlands (Social Democratic Party of Germany)
URM	Urząd Rady Ministrów (Bureau of the Council of Ministers)
ZK	Zentralkomitee (Central Committee of the SED)
ZMS	Związek Młodzieży Socjalistyczny(Socialist Youth Union)
ZSL	Zjednoczone Stronnictwo Ludowe (United Peasants' Party)

Abbreviations Used for
Archival References

German Archives

BRD AA   Bundesrepublik Deutschland, Politisches Archiv des
               Auswärtigen Amtes (Federal Republic of Germany, Po-
               litical Archive of the Foreign Office), Bonn.
BRD BfGDF   Bundesrepublik Deutschland, Bundesministerium für
               gesamtdeutsche Fragen (Federal Republic of Germany,
               Federal Ministry for All-German Questions)], Koblenz.
BRD BKA   Bundesrepublik Deutschland, Bundeskanzleramt (Fed-
               eral Republic of Germany, Federal Chancellor's Office),
               Koblenz.
DDR MfAA   Deutsche Demokratische Republik, Ministerium für
               Auswärtige Angelegenheiten, Politisches Archiv des
               Auswärtigen Amtes (German Democratic Republic.
               Ministry for Foreign Affairs, Political Archive of the
               Foreign Office), Berlin.
DDR MfAuIH   Deutsche Demokratische Republik, Ministerium für
               Aussenhandel und Innerdeutschen Handel (German
               Democratic Republic, Ministry for Foreign Trade and
               Inner-German Trade), Potsdam.
DDR MR   Deutsche Demokratische Republik, Ministerrat (Ger-
               man Democratic Republic, Council of Ministers), Pots-
               dam.
SED ZK   Sozialistische Einheitspartei Deutschlands, Zen-
               tralkomitee (Socialist Unity Party, Central Committee),
               Berlin.

Polish Archives

KWKzK   Komitet Współpracy Kuturalnej z Zagranicą (Commit-
               tee for Cultural Cooperation with Foreign Countries),
               Warsaw.

MSZ   Ministerstwo Spraw Zagranicznych (Ministry of For-
             eign Affairs), Warsaw.
MZO   Ministerstwo Ziem Odzyskanych (Ministry of Recov-
             ered Territories), Warsaw.
PZPR KC   Polska Zjednoczona Partia Robotnicza, Komitet Cen-
             tralny (Polish United Workers' Party, Central Commit-
             tee), Warsaw.
URM BP   Urząd Rady Ministrów, Biuro Prezidialne (Bureau of
             the Council of Ministers, President's Office), Warsaw.

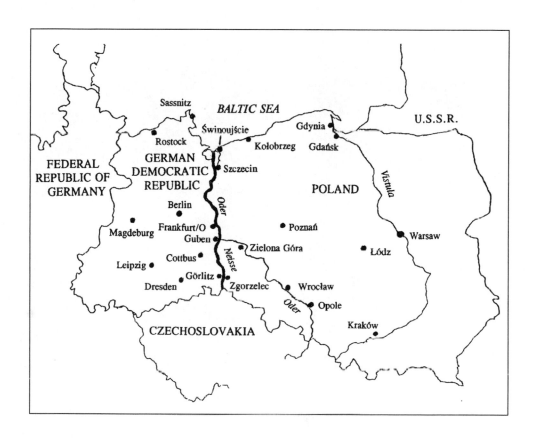

FEDERAL
REPUBLIC OF
GERMANY

GERMAN
DEMOCRATIC
REPUBLIC

POLAND

U.S.S.R.

CZECHOSLOVAKIA

BALTIC SEA

Sassnitz

Świnoujście

Rostock

Kołobrzeg

Gdynia

Gdańsk

Szczecin

Vistula

Berlin

Oder

Frankfurt/O

Magdeburg

Guben

Poznań

Warsaw

Zielona Góra

Łódz

Neisse

Leipzig

Cottbus

Görlitz

Dresden

Zgorzelec

Wrocław

Oder

Opole

Kraków

Introduction

The alliance of the two nations [German and Polish] is . . . not by any means a beautiful dream, a charming illusion; no, gentlemen, it is an inevitable necessity resulting from the common interests of the two nations.

—*Friedrich Engels, 1847*[1]

I crossed the Oder-Neisse border for the first time in 1987 on an overnight train from Hanover to Warsaw. As the train approached Frankfurt/Oder around midnight, I was aroused from my sleep by a phalanx of gruff East German border guards and customs agents. They took over three hours to check documents and comb the train from top to bottom for stowaways and contraband. I had experienced many close inspections and long delays on trips between West and East Germany, but the East Germans seemed to be even more vigilant along their border with Poland than they were on their western border, across which sat enemy NATO troops.

The incident prompted me to ask my East German and Polish friends about their impressions of relations between the German Democratic Republic (GDR) and the People's Republic of Poland (PRP). On the one hand, the East Germans responded that interstate relations were cordial and emphasized their government's constructive political, cultural, and economic efforts to bring the two peoples together. On the other hand, they often harbored old prejudices; that is, the Poles were lazy, disorganized, and untrustworthy. Many complained about Poles who crossed the border to buy up scarce East German consumer goods.

The Poles also had ambiguous opinions about the East Germans. Although some criticized the East Germans' arrogance, dogmatism, and slavish adherence to Stalinism, they begrudgingly respected the GDR's economic and technical achievements. But the Polish attitude can be summarized in the old saying *Jak świat światem, nie będzie Niemiec Polakowi bratem* (As long as the world is whole, no German will be a brother to a Pole).[2]

This filial reference is an apt metaphor for East German-Polish relations after World War II. The East Germans and Poles were like siblings born into the Soviet family: No matter how much they quarreled, they could not leave it. They curried favor with the paternal center while pursuing conflicting national interests. The result was a "cold war" of misunderstanding and distrust. Like the Cold War between the Soviet Union and the United States, there were times of détente and times of crisis, but in the end the East German and Polish communist parties had irreconcilable national differences. Furthermore, the illegitimacy of the East German and Polish communist governments precluded an honest reconciliation between their peoples.

This study seeks to fill several gaps in the history of East German-Polish relations in the context of the Cold War. Much has been written about relations between the Soviet Union and Eastern Europe after World War II; but scholars have paid relatively little attention to East European communist party relations and treated them as though they were always dictated by Moscow. Marxist historians of Soviet bloc relations told an incomplete and slanted story of close cooperation and friendship; Polish and East German historians such as Eugeniusz Gajda and Werner Hänisch simply imitated vacuous party propaganda promoting fraternal friendship and mutual socialist goals.[3]

When the United States adopted a policy of containing Soviet expansionism after the war, Western policy makers and scholars propagated the idea that the Kremlin was running a monolithic communist movement. The communist takeovers in Eastern Europe by 1948, the victory of the communists in China in 1949, Mao Zedong's alliance with Josef Stalin, and the North Korean invasion of the South in 1950 confirmed this perception.

Throughout the Cold War, Western Europe and the United States based their security policy and defense spending on a confrontation with the Soviet bloc countries. Western policy makers assumed, as perhaps they had to assume, that if war broke out the communist states would constitute a cohesive fighting force. The geopolitical world was simplified into a bipolar system that either ignored or downplayed differences within the two opposing blocs.

In the mid-1960s, Zbigniew Brzezinski was one of the first scholars to argue that relations within the communist world were more complicated than that. He contended that national interests in Eastern Europe still had an important role to play in interparty relations:

> The Communist camp as a collective entity is guided by purposes which are said to reflect its collective interest. At the same time, within these dominant, universal objectives there are also the specific, particular interests of

the component units. Occasionally, and almost inescapably, a clash between the universal and particular takes place, and much of the history of relations between Communist states has to be written in terms of such conflicts.[4]

In the 1970s, several scholars took up Brzezinski's call for serious studies of Soviet bloc relations. Roger Kanet noted that historians usually focussed on the deviation of satellite foreign policy from Moscow's, while ignoring the foreign policy differences between the satellites themselves.[5] In the case of East Germany, Peter Merkl wrote that "East German foreign policy for many years has been ignored by Western scholars and even journalists on the assumption that it was unlikely to be much more than a mere instrument of Soviet foreign policy."[6] Political scientist Peter Marsh agreed: "An interpretation of East German foreign policy . . . as one consistent development towards the role of most trusted supporter of the Soviet Union would be grossly simplistic."[7]

There is also a dearth of histories on Polish foreign policy after World War II. In the mid-1970s, James F. Morrison identified a general need for foreign policy studies of the East European countries, and Poland specifically. He also noted that analysts had mainly focused on the means that the Soviet Union used to control its satellites' foreign policies.[8]

Recent works on Soviet foreign policy toward Eastern Europe have suggested that the communist parties enjoyed greater latitude than many Western scholars and policymakers previously thought. Vladislaw Zubok and Constantine Pleshakov confirmed that Soviet control over their East European allies was haphazard; they argued that Stalin had no master plan for the communization of the area or designs for a separate socialist German state.[9] Norman Naimark and Inessa Iazhborovskaia corroborated this view of Soviet policy in Eastern Europe and Germany as unplanned and reactive, although the German Communist Party (KPD/SED) was more tightly controlled.[10]

Despite much new evidence to the contrary, the simplistic view of the bipolar world persists. In his 1999 study of the postwar Europe, Marc Trachtenberg wrote:

> People still think of the Cold War as a simple two-sided conflict, a kind of gigantic arm wrestle on a global scale. But this view, I believe, is profoundly mistaken. A purely bipolar system would have been quite stable: Soviet power and American power would have balanced each other so completely that the risk of general war would have been minimal. But we know the Cold War was a serious conflict.[11]

Until 1989, the biggest obstacle to writing an accurate history of relations between the communist parties in Eastern Europe was a lack of archival evidence. Using previously classified Polish and East German communist party and foreign ministry documents, my research seeks to build on the works of those who have argued that the Polish and East German communists pursued conflicting national interests first and foremost. As Brzezinski pointed out, "The Polish Communist preached and practiced a fanatical national hatred somewhat out of step with the doctrinal concepts of relations between nationalities."[12]

German historian Franz Sikora, in his study of Polish-East German relations, also concluded that their shared communist community did not, in his words, "lead to a disappearance of the average Pole's prejudice and distrust of Germans or to their trust in a long lasting understanding with their neighbor to the west."[13]

Given the centuries of conflict between Poles and Germans (especially those Germans of the Brandenberg-Prussia area that comprised a large part of the Soviet zone), continued enmity between them was hardly surprising, regardless of their political affiliation. Nazi Germany's long occupation and thorough devastation of Poland in World War II was the latest and most awful chapter in this confrontation. Sikora argued that the Poles did not really want "reconciliation" [Versöhnung] with the Germans after the war; the Poles' rapid and often harsh expulsion of Germans from Poland only exacerbated their mutual hatreds.[14] The expellees from Poland represented over one-fifth of the population in the Soviet zone in the late 1940s. It was indeed a mighty task for the parties of the Polish and German Left to convince the masses, as well as their own party members, that Poles and Germans shared a common socialist destiny. Many communist leaders did not believe their own propaganda on this point.

The ebb and flow of East German-Polish relations obviously depended on their patronage from the Soviet Union and the contingencies of the Cold War. The Kremlin ultimately determined the fate of the satellite parties, and the freedom that Moscow allowed the parties often fluctuated with the state of Soviet relations with the West. Although the Polish and East German communists could not stray too far from Moscow's foreign-policy line, they promoted their respective national interests whenever possible. There are notably few references in the Polish and East German communist party and foreign ministry archives to Moscow's directives regarding their relations, although much of what was said was undoubtedly left unrecorded.[15]

Guidance and patronage from the Soviet Union did not bring the Polish and East German communists any closer. On the contrary, they were less trusting of each other because of their competition for Moscow's favor, a situation that the Soviets used to their own advantage. Because Lenin's motto, "Nationalist in form and socialist in content" had not really resolved the intense national rivalries in the Soviet Union, the Soviet leadership found the tried and true imperial policy of *divide et impera* expedient in maintaining their disparate and far-flung empire.

It is not the purpose of this study to chronicle all the economic, cultural, and political ties between Poland and East Germany from 1945 to 1962. I have intentionally focussed on those issues that were persistently contentious; First was the dispute over Poland's administration of German territories east of the Oder and Western (Lusacian) Neisse border. In 1946, the SED adopted a platform calling for a revision of the border, but finally had to recognize the Oder-Neisse line in 1948. The Polish communists knew that the Soviets had forced the East Germans to adopt this position; repeated manifestations of revisionism in the SED and the GDR made this all too clear.

Second, the two parties could not reach a consensus on policy toward the West, particularly West Germany. The SED claimed that it was conducting a socialist foreign policy in line with the Soviet Union and supportive of workers everywhere. Poland adopted a more realistic, less idealistic policy. Walter Ulbricht insisted that Warsaw follow his lead on the German question, and frequent confrontations occurred over Poland's unilateral attempts to develop political and economic ties to the FRG and West Berlin. In 1957, friction developed over a Polish plan to create a nuclear-free East Central Europe (including the FRG), in part because it was not an East German idea.

Third, the East German and Polish communists were in open conflict over Marxist-Leninist ideology and the correct road to socialism. The two parties quarreled over censorship, collectivization, church policy, tourist traffic, cultural affairs, and many other domestic policies. The East German communists often compounded ideological differences by adopting an arrogant and condescending demeanor toward their Polish comrades. British historian Mary Fulbrook has characterized German communism as having "a Prussian complexion,"[16] which, according to Polish scholar Lesław Koćwin, featured "dogmatism, intolerance, and chauvinism."[17]

I have deliberately included numerous official reports on cultural exchanges to illustrate the animosity that existed on party, government, and unofficial levels. The sheer number of such incidents is evidence of the communists' utter failure to develop better personal relationships. Many exchanges seemed to do more harm than good in breaking down old stereotypes and promoting genuine friendships. Much to the embarrassment of both communist régimes, many of their own officials, as well as the average citizen, preferred to make contacts with West Germans.

The most serious ideological rift came in 1956. After being expelled from the party in 1949, Władysław Gomułka returned to power on a platform that directly challenged the tenets of Stalinism. Fearful that the

PZPR's reforms would destabilize the GDR, the SED cut off many cultural exchanges, shored up border controls along the Oder-Neisse, and instituted visa requirements for Poles. Although Gomułka eventually proved to be a loyal Warsaw Pact partner and even supported the military intervention into Czechoslovakia in 1968, Ulbricht never forgot that Gomułka was the product of a potentially dangerous reform movement.

Fourth, bitter disputes arose time and time again over trade. In the early postwar years, the SED vehemently opposed paying reparations to Poland. Although trade grew significantly in the first few years after the GDR was founded in 1949, it did not reach the levels that the East Germans wanted. The SED repeatedly accused the Poles of conducting a foreign economic policy that was inimical to the interests of the GDR and the socialist camp, especially when Poland's trade with capitalist countries increased in the mid-1950s. The Polish communists were not persuaded by East German arguments that the GDR had to achieve a standard of living comparable to that of capitalist West Germany. As trade negotiators on both sides recognized, the muddled trade situation also had negative political ramifications.

Finally, friction steadily grew over the status of the Germans in Poland. Many wanted to emigrate, but the Polish authorities were reluctant to allow the GDR to act as the Germans' sole representative. The Polish government often favored Bonn's interests in regard to these Germans, but the East Germans viewed this as an unacceptable deviation from socialist solidarity.

I have employed a loose chronological narrative whenever possible, but some recurring disagreements over the Oder-Neisse border, trade, and German repatriation from Poland are addressed in separate chapters. Chapter 1 introduces the interwar links between the Polish and German communists, and postwar relations in the context of the communist takeover in Poland and the German communist movement in the Soviet zone. Chapter 2 examines the Oder-Neisse problem from 1945 to the creation of the GDR in 1949. When the SED openly campaigned for a border change in 1946, it confirmed Polish suspicions that the German communists were nationalists in Marxist clothes. Although the SED eventually had to recognize the border, many party members remained steadfastly opposed to it.

Chapter 3 covers the period from 1949 to the turmoil in the Soviet bloc following Stalin's death in 1953. Disputes had to be hidden to maintain the illusion of unity in Stalin's empire; relations between the SED and the PZPR were correct, but plagued by persistent ideological debates and trade squabbles.

Chapter 4 is devoted to a closer examination of economic relations and the problem of German refugees from Poland and of Germans who remained there. Disagreements over these subjects in the early postwar period contributed to the general feeling on both sides that national interests trumped socialist solidarity.

Chapter 5 examines the period after Stalin's death in 1953 to 1956, when the Kremlin's more liberal New Course allowed the Poles to raise many of these outstanding issues in public. Much to their consternation, however, the SED again broached the subject of a border revision.

I have devoted four chapters to the volatile events surrounding Khrushchev's secret speech in 1956, Gomułka's return to power in October of that year, and the SED's denunciation of Gomułka's policies in 1957, when relations reached their lowest point. Chapter 6 deals with the impact of Khrushchev's de-Stalinization on relations between the two parties; the SED's rejection and the PZPR's acceptance of de-Stalinization set the tone for East German-Polish relations for several years. Chapter 7 takes a closer look at the SED's reaction to Gomułka's return; how Ulbricht tried to build a firewall against the reforms of the Polish October; and Gomułka's ideas about a national road to socialism. Writer Wolfgang Harich's arrest and imprisonment on charges of conspiring with Polish intellectuals revealed Ulbricht's determination to avoid an "East German October."

Chapter 8 returns to the problems of trade and the Germans in Poland in the context of the Ulbricht-Gomułka rivalry. Chapter 9 covers the serious lack of foreign policy coordination between the two Warsaw Pact partners as well as the first face-to-face meeting between Ulbricht and Gomułka in the summer of 1957.

Aside from the Oder-Neisse border, the most sensitive issue for Polish-East German relations was GDR's role in the question of German unification. Chapter 10 focuses on the disagreements over the Polish foreign minister's plan for denuclearizing East Central Europe, the so-called Rapacki Plan. Chapter 11 examines the many domestic-policy differences that continued to undermine the relationship in the late 1950s as well as the impact of the Berlin crises and the East German leader Walter Ulbricht's cool reception in Warsaw in 1958. This second meeting between Ulbricht and Gomułka did not clear the atmosphere. The pride of the East German communists in their stable political situation and relatively successful economy was readily apparent in the early 1960s. Chapter 12 describes the ongoing ideological debates between the SED and the PZPR over agricultural policy, trade, religious and artistic freedom, and the East Germans' constant sermonizing about the virtues of their road to socialism. Chapter 13 recounts Gomułka's reluctant acceptance of the Berlin Wall in 1961 and the uneasy détente that developed after his third meeting with Ulbricht in the fall of 1962.

Notes

1. Karl Marx and Friedrich Engels, *Collected Works*, vol. 6: 1845–1848 (Moscow: Progress Publishers, 1976), p. 389. Quoted from Engels's speech in London on November 29, 1847, to mark the seventeenth anniversary of the Polish uprising of 1830.

2. Quoted from Ines Mietkowska-Kaiser, "Zur brüderlichen Zusammenarbeit zwischen polnischen und deutschen Kommunisten und Antifaschisten nach dem Sieg über den deutschen Faschismus (1945–1949)" (On the fraternal cooperation between the Polish and German Communists and anti-fascists after the victory over German fascism, 1945–1949), *Jahrbuch für Geschichte der sozialistischen Länder Europas* (Yearbook for the history of the socialist countries of Europe) 23, no. 1 (1979), p. 51.

3. Eugeniusz Gajda, *Polska Polityka Zagraniczna, 1944–1971: Podstawowe Problemy* (Polish foreign policy, 1944–1971: Basic problems) (Warsaw: Ministerstwa Obrony Narodowy, 1972); and Werner Hänisch, *Aussenpolitik und internationale Beziehungen der DDR, 1949–1955* (The foreign policy and international relations of the GDR, 1949–1955) (Berlin: Staatsverlag der DDR, 1972).

4. Zbigniew Brzezinski, *The Soviet Bloc: Unity and Conflict* (New York: Frederick A. Praeger, 1961), p. ix; see Gabriel Fischer, "Nationalism and Internationalism in Hungary and Rumania," *Canadian Slavonic Papers*, no. 1 (1968). The Romanian deviation from the Warsaw Pact has been documented. Fischer concluded that national interests played, in his words, "a substantial role in shaping and reshaping relations among socialist countries"; see also Yannis Valinakis, "Diversity in the Warsaw Pact: Bulgarian and Rumanian Security Perceptions," *Balkan Studies*, no. 1 (1984). Valinakis also revealed the widely divergent security interests of Bulgaria and Romania and the lack of strategic policy coordination on the Warsaw Pact's southern flank.

5. Roger Kanet, "Research on East European Foreign Policy: Other Needs, Other Areas, New Directions," in Ronald H. Linden, ed., *The Foreign Policies of East Europe: New Approaches* (New York: Praeger, 1980), p. 313.

6. Peter H. Merkl, *German Foreign Policies, West and East: On the Threshold of a New European Era* (Santa Barbara, Calif.: ABC-Clio, 1974), p. 90.

7. Peter Marsh, "Foreign Policy Making in the German Democratic Republic," in Hannes Adomeit, ed., *Foreign Policy Making in Communist Countries* (London: Saxon House, 1979), p. 106; see also Wilhelm Bruns, *Die Aussenpolitik der DDR* (The foreign policy of the GDR) (Berlin: Colloquium Verlag, 1985), p. 14. Bruns also found that researchers had limited knowledge of relations between the Socialist Unity Party of Germany (SED) and the other communist parties in Eastern Europe.

8. James F. Morrison, "The Foreign Policy of Poland," in James Kuhlmann, ed., *The Foreign Policies of East Europe: Domestic and International Determinants* (Leyden, Netherlands: A. W. Sijthoff, 1978), p. 129.

9. Vladislaw Zubok and Constantine Pleshakov, *Inside the Kremlin's Cold War: From Stalin to Khrushchev* (Cambridge: Harvard University Press, 1996).

10. Norman Naimark, *The Russians in Germany: A History of the Soviet Zone of Occupation, 1945–1949* (Cambridge: Harvard University Press, 1995); and Inessa

Iazhborovskaia, "The Gomułka Alternative," in Norman Naimark and Leonid Gibianski, eds., *The Establishment of Communist Régimes in Eastern Europe, 1944–49* (Boulder: Westview Press, 1997).

11. Marc Trachtenberg, *A Constructed Peace: The Making of the European Settlement 1945–1963* (Princeton: Princeton University Press, 1999), p. viii; see also Leonid Gibianski, "The Soviet-Yugoslav Conflict and the Soviet Bloc," in Francesca Gori and Silvio Pons, eds., *The Soviet Union and Europe in the Cold War, 1943–53* (New York: St. Martin's Press, 1996), pp. 222–245.

12. Brzezinski, *The Soviet Bloc*, p. 53.

13. Franz Sikora, *Sozialistische Solidarität und nationale Interessen* (Socialist solidarity and national interests) (Cologne: Verlag Wissenschaft und Politik, 1977), p. 100. Sikora's work is based on press reports and public documents; see also Lesław Koćwin, *Polityczne determinanty polsko-wschodnioniemieckich stosunków przygranicznych 1949–1990* (Political determinants of Polish-East German relations on the border) (Wrocław: Wydawnictwo Uniwersytetu Wrocławskiego, 1993), p. 13. Koćwin agrees with this view in his recent work on the political determinants of Polish-East German relations: "The development of bilateral cooperation of the former PRP and the GDR did not take a uniform course, in spite of certain propaganda, because it often confronted difficulties and impediments."

14. Sikora, *Sozialistische Solidarität und nationale Interessen*, p. 99.

15. See Hope Harrison, *Bulletin: Cold War International History Project*, no. 2 (fall 1992), p. 12. Harrison points out that the Soviets often did not allow anyone to take notes of their discussions with the SED.

16. Mary Fulbrook, *Anatomy of a Dictatorship: Inside the GDR, 1945–1989* (Oxford: Oxford University Press, 1995), p. 31.

17. Koćwin, *Polityczne determinanty polsko-wschodnioniemieckich stosunków przygranicznych 1949–1990*, p. 10.

1

"There Are No Good Germans": The Myth of Proletarian Internationalism, 1945–1949

There are no good Germans . . . a German communist is always and above all a German who places German interests above the international solidarity of the proletariat.

—**The Polish West Institute in Poznań**[1]

It would be a formidable task for any Polish government, let alone a communist one, to reconcile the Polish people with their neighbors to the west and east. World War II was the latest and most tragic chapter in a long history of conflict between Russians and Poles and between Germans and Poles. For centuries, Poles had resisted the German *Drang Nach Osten* and Russian expansionism. Polish national identity was linked to the early modern commonwealth that stretched from the Baltic Sea to the Black Sea and its heroic struggles against the Germans, Russians, and Swedes. Poland stood as a Catholic outpost between Prussian Protestantism and Russian Orthodoxy, but the weak Polish state finally succumbed to the late eighteenth-century partition between Prussia, Austria, and Russia. Poland's resurrection after World War I lasted less than a generation: Germany and the Soviet Union overran the Polish state in September 1939.

Poland endured the longest and harshest occupation of the countries that fought Nazi Germany. The Germans destroyed the Polish state, pillaged the economy, and eviscerated the intelligentsia and political parties. Poland lost 300,000 men in battle and 6 million civilians, among them almost 3 million Polish Jews. Tens of thousands of Poles perished in the Soviet Union; Poles who survived those brutal six years were left with a country in ruins. Much of the great city of Warsaw was obliterated.

With the Soviet Red Army's entry into East Central Europe at the end of World War II, German and Polish communists were obligated to put relations between their two peoples on a new footing. As this verse from the old communist anthem "The Red Regiment of Warsaw" professed, the enemy of the working classes would not be any one nation, but the capitalist class as a whole:

> Our enemy is not a foreign people,
> whether defeated or victor,
> our enemy are those, who hold the whip
> the foreigner, or your own oppressor.[2]

According to Marxist-Leninist theory of socialist internationalism, the Polish communists would jettison all vestiges of Polish bourgeois-romantic nationalism, Polish Catholicism, and any sentimental attachment to Polish territories annexed by the Soviet Union. The German communists, for their part, were bound to reject nationalist calls for the return of German territories occupied by Poland after the war.

Communism had shallow roots in Poland. There was much truth to Stalin's analogy likening communism in Poland to a saddle on a cow. The pantheon of communist founders did not inspire the patriotic, Catholic, and often anti-Semitic Poles; Marx was a German and a Jew, and Lenin was a Russian. With the exception of Rosa Luxemburg, Poland had not produced prominent communist leaders. Luxemburg was a Jew and committed internationalist, even to the point of opposing a Polish state. The forerunner of the Polish Communist Party (KPP), the Social Democracy of the Kingdom of Poland and Lithuania (SDKPiL), was founded in 1899 and reflected Luxemburg's orthodox Marxist views. The party had few followers.[3]

The Polish Socialist Party's (PPS) nationalist appeal outflanked the KPP for support among the Polish working and peasant classes. The PPS promoted a patriotic, evolutionary social democracy. Fearing a right-wing government takeover in 1926, the KPP supported the PPS and Józef Piłsudski's May coup d'état. This so-called "May error" was among the reasons Stalin cited for exterminating virtually the entire KPP leadership and dissolving the party in 1938. Some 5,000 Polish communists were executed.[4] Postwar Foreign Ministry official Marian Naszkowski later remembered his shock at hearing the news of the KPP's demise:

> A party that had done so much to awaken the revolutionary spirit of the masses, a party that had led mighty working-class brigades to war with capitalism, with fascism, could not be a fraud. . . . Shaken to the depths of our souls, accepting, with pain, with bitterness, the 'truth' about our leaders'

treachery, not for a moment did we doubt our idea or the rightness of our movement, our party. That gave thousands of Communists the strength to live through the difficult times that had arrived. That was the basis for the resurrection of the party later on."[5]

Under the watchful eye of the Soviet secret police, Polish communism returned in 1942 as the Polish Workers' Party (PPR). Without Stalin's knowledge or approval, Władysław Gomułka was elected secretary general in German-occupied Warsaw in November 1943. Stalin formed the Union of Polish Patriots in Moscow to ensure his control over the PPR. These "Muscovite" Poles, among them Bolesław Bierut, Jakub Berman, Hilary Minc, and Stanisław Radkiewicz, formed the core of the party leadership after the war.

From its inception in 1944, the PPR dominated the Polish Provisional Government of National Unity. Gomułka muted Marxist revolutionary goals in an attempt to form a national front with the PPS, the intelligentsia, and the peasantry. When this strategy failed to gain broader popular support, the PPR gradually coopted the other political parties or drove them underground. Under pressure from the Western Allies to fulfill the Yalta agreements, the Soviets allowed some members of Stanisław Mikołajczyk's opposition Polish Peasant Party (PSL) into the government in the spring of 1945, but they had no real power. After the phony elections in January 1947, the PPR was the master of the political scene. Mikołajczyk fled the country in November.[6] The PPR had some latitude to decide domestic policy in the early postwar period, but there was never any doubt that Moscow ultimately determined Poland's political future.[7]

The Prospects for German Communism

The German communists had a stronger base in the German working class. Germany's defeat in World War I, the failure of capitalism to solve the ills of the interwar economy, the demise of the Weimar Republic in the 1930s, and the disaster of the National Socialist period gave the party some ideological ammunition to promote communism in postwar Germany. Monarchism, democracy, and fascism had failed Germany, and the German communists could claim to have fought them all. Now the party stood ready to construct a truly "democratic" socialist state, one founded on Marxist-Leninist-Stalinist principles.[8]

Unlike the KPP, the German Communist Party (KPD) survived its exile in the Soviet Union before the war, although almost three-quarters of the membership had been jailed. Those who spent the war in the Soviet Union were Stalin's lackeys; the KPD's association with the Soviet occupation authorities further tarnished its image. Many Red Army soldiers inflicted their revenge on the German people, and the Soviets wantonly extracted reparations from their zone. Although the KPD registered numerous protests with the Soviet military administration, most Germans viewed the KPD as a collaborator with the Soviet occupiers, not as champion of German interests.

The SPD's more moderate socialism had much broader appeal in postwar Germany. Because the KPD and the SPD were bitter enemies during the Weimar period, the KPD initially spurned cooperation with the SPD. The Soviet occupation authorities forced the KPD and SPD to form the Socialist Unity Party (SED) in April 1946. The other parties in the anti-fascist National Front, the CDU and the LDP, were also coopted. After the elections of October 1946, in which the SED fared poorly in competition with the SPD in Berlin, the Soviets no longer allowed free elections in its zone.

The Soviets did not immediately hand over power to their protegés, however. Stalin did not think that his plans to exploit Germany's economy (including the Ruhr) and to bring about the eventual communization of the entire country would be served by a hasty communist takeover in the Soviet zone.[9] Even if Stalin did not want a division of Germany initially, his undemocratic tactics to consolidate communist control in the Soviet zone and Poland contributed to the emerging Cold War.[10]

The German and Polish Communists Before 1945

There was historical precedent for cooperation between the Polish and German Left before 1945, but by the end of the war ties to the past were threadbare.[11] Luxemburg and fellow Poles Julian Marchlewski and Leo Jogiches helped found the KPD in 1918, and Jogiches led the party for a short time. When the KPP was outlawed in 1919, the KPD provided indispensable support; the Polish communists reciprocated when Adolf Hitler seized power in Germany in 1933.[12] Many German communists escaped the Nazis through their underground connections to the KPP, which operated clandestinely in several Polish cities with large German populations, Gdańsk and Zabrze among them. A few Polish and German Leftists also developed friendships during their incarceration in Nazi concentration camps.[13]

Wilhelm Pieck, the first secretary of the KPD after World War II, was one of the few German communists left to continue this tradition.[14] A veteran of the communist movement in Germany for nearly half a century, Pieck had been a close confidant of many of the Polish communists in the SPD before World War I. Pieck studied under Luxemburg at the party

school in Berlin, and staunchly defended her against revisionists in the
party who rejected her orthodox Marxist positions.[15] During the war,
Pieck helped Marchlewski publish his works in Berlin; in the early 1920s
the two worked together at the communist party school in Moscow.

Pieck narrowly escaped with his own life the day radical right-wing
nationalists shot Luxemburg in Berlin in January 1919. Jogiches was as-
sassinated five months later.[16] When Marchlewski died in 1925, the old
Polish guard in the KPD was gone. Pieck gave the eulogy at Marchlewski's funeral; the placement of his funereal urn next to the graves of
Luxemburg and Karl Liebknecht at the cemetery in Berlin-Friedrichs-
felde was one of the few symbols left of Polish-German communist solidarity in the early twentieth century.[17]

The PPR had reason to be suspicious of collusion between the KPD
and the Soviet Union at Poland's expense. Since the partition of Poland
in the late eighteenth century, the Germans and Russians had often set
aside their differences to repress Polish national aspirations. Even the
Bolshevik Revolution in Russia in 1917 had not changed that; in 1922 and
1926, the Weimar Republic and the Soviet Union signed cooperative
agreements that were in part directed against the new Polish state.

The most egregious anti-Polish agreement was the Nazi-Soviet Pact of
August 1939. The KPD declared that "the German people welcome the
non-aggression pact between the Soviet Union and Germany because
they want peace." The KPD went so far as to profess that the pact
strengthened ties between the German and Soviet people.[18] Pieck characterized Poland's defeat in 1939 as a victory of German workers over the
Polish gentry.[19] He said that the vanquished Polish government was a
"reactionary structure" anyway.[20] Ignoring the Nazi-Soviet partition of
Poland, the KPD condemned the war as an imperialist conflict. The party
criticized Great Britain for allegedly declaring war on behalf of the Polish
landowning class, and praised the work of the CPSU (Communist Party
of the Soviet Union) among the workers in the Soviet-occupied Polish areas of Ukraine and Belarus.[21]

Walter Ulbricht, who led the SED from 1949 to 1971,[22] defended the
Nazi-Soviet Pact in a way that seemed to accept Hitler's aggression
against Poland. He blamed the war on British imperialists instead:

> The German people and all those nations that have been incorporated into
> the German state are faced with a decision: to choose not English capitalism,
> prolongation of the war, and another Versailles, but the Soviet Union, peace,
> national independence, and friendship among all nations. The workers,
> farmers, and intelligentsia of Germany, Austria, Czechoslovakia, and
> Poland will be the staunchest supporters of the Soviet-German Pact and the
> sworn enemies of the English plan.[23]

This was heavy historical baggage for the PPR to carry. Until Khrushchev's de-Stalinization in the mid-1950s, the Polish communists could not openly question Stalin's liquidation of the KPP. They also had to deny that Stalin had secretly partitioned Poland with Hitler in 1939. The Nazi-Soviet Pact was, as the Polish communists were forced to declare at the time, ostensibly "an element of peace, the result of the Soviet Union's consistent peace policy."[24] The PPR was also saddled with the task of convincing Poles to accept the loss of Poland's eastern territories to the Soviet Union. The party had to follow the line that the Nazis, not the Soviets, had massacred thousands of Polish army officers at the Katyn Forest in 1940, and had to ignore Stalin's failure to aid the Warsaw Uprising against the Germans in 1944. Among those left to fight the Germans in Warsaw had been the PPR's own "People's Guards."[25]

The PPR's Anti-German Propaganda

The PPR consciously used nationalist propaganda in its struggle for power in Poland in 1945, and stubbornly defended Poland's national interests against Germany.[26] Having lived through the brutal five-year German occupation, Gomułka had little sympathy for German political parties. He did not see an old ally in the KPD; he saw instead a party that had embraced Luxemburg's internationalism, obsequiously sanctioned Stalin's liquidation of the KPP, and approved of the partition of Poland in 1939. After the war, Gomułka declared that "the German horse must have its legs broken regardless of whether that horse is ridden by a Nazi or a Social Democrat."[27] As Minister of the Recovered Territories, Gomułka had a hand in the ruthless expulsion of the Germans from Poland.[28]

The PPR promoted a new pan-Slavism instead of the unity of working classes across national lines. On March 16, 1945, a big headline in the PPR organ *Głos Ludu* (Voice of the People) proclaimed "Slav Solidarity" in Eastern Europe, and stressed Poland's political and economic cooperation with Czechoslovakia, Yugoslavia, Bulgaria, and the Soviet Union.[29] Gomułka told a Warsaw audience in April 1946 that Poland now had friendly relations with the Soviet Union and the other Slavic nations, adding that "without this alliance we would never have been able to defeat Germany or include Gdańsk within the borders of the Polish state."[30] On July 15, *Głos Ludu* celebrated the anniversary of the Polish victory over the Teutonic Knights at the Battle of Grunwald in 1410 with the headline, "Through the Unity of the Slav Nations—To Victory."[31]

The Polish government announced that it would base its foreign relations with any country, communist or not, first on that country's policy toward Germany. In April 1946, Edward Ochab, one of the Muscovites, called for solidarity with France and the Anglo-Saxon powers for the defense of Poland against its biggest threat—"German imperialism."[32] The PPR counted on Czechoslovakia as a partner in this struggle, even though until February 1948 it had a democratically elected coalition government and a noncommunist president, Edvard Beneš. Although Prague and Warsaw had numerous disagreements after the war,[33] *Głos Ludu* called for a united front with Czechoslovakia against German revanchism, warning that "the mortal enemy to the life and liberty of both [Poland and Czechoslovakia] is still lurking—Germany."[34] Poland signed a Treaty of Friendship and Mutual Assistance with Czechoslovakia in 1947, and with all the other East European states by 1949. Poland did not have a similar treaty with the GDR until 1967.[35]

The Polish government also promoted the principle of collective German guilt for the crimes of the Nazi régime. During the Nuremberg trials in the fall of 1946, Polish officials criticized former British Prime Minister Winston Churchill for arguing that Germany as a whole should not be punished for the war.[36] The PPR barely recognized the existence of any "progressive" German political elements—such as the KPD and the SPD. Polish authorities rejected offers of cooperation from the German Leftists in the former German territories.[37] Foreign Minister Zygmunt Modzelewski declared that the Poles did not have confidence in any of the German political parties, including the KPD. The Polish West Institute in Poznań issued this blanket statement: There are no good Germans ... a German communist is always and above all a German who places German interests above the international solidarity of the proletariat.[38]

For the first year after the war, the Polish communist press paid little attention to the German political scene.[39] Reports that did appear were usually critical of the Germans, including the German Left.[40] *Głos Ludu* barely mentioned the fusion of the KPD and the SPD into the SED in April 1946,[41] knowing that the new party was a machination of Soviet occupation policy. The Polish Military Mission in Berlin underscored this fact: "No activity [for the creation of the SED] was to be seen from the masses, but instead [their] passive and loyal submission to the orders of the party organs."[42]

The Polish communists were outraged that the KPD (and later the SED) welcomed former Nazis into its ranks, and alleged that some were assuming important party posts. Ulbricht later acknowledged to Gomułka that the ex-Nazis had been recruited because the party was failing to attract new members. Ulbricht pointed out that many of the German communists had lost connections to the movement during their years in Nazi prisons; by the end of the war, many had become members of the SPD or the CDU.[43]

The Polish communists adroitly used anti-German propaganda to strengthen their popular support. They accused Mikołajczyk's PSL of befriending the German occupiers during the war and of supporting neo-Nazi underground groups in Poland. In the summer of 1946, the PPR tried to undercut the PSL by holding a referendum on three constitutional reforms. Mikołajczyk encouraged his followers to vote "no" on the first proposition to abolish the Senate. Gomułka declared that any Pole who voted against any of the three propositions "helps Germany against Poland." He called the PSL the party of *"drei mal nein"* (three times no), purposely using the German phrase to imply that the party was infiltrated by German agents.[44] Wincenty Rzymowski of the Polish Democratic Party (SD)[45] urged Poles to vote for the propositions to show domestic unity for the new "historical Piast border" with Germany. He declared Germans living in Poland would not be allowed to vote.[46]

One of the SED's primary objectives was to establish itself as an equal among the communist parties in Eastern Europe, but the party was slow to gain acceptance. The SED was not invited to Szklarska Poręba for the first meeting of Cominform in September 1947, and was not informed until October that the meeting had taken place. .[47] According to West German sources, the Poles and Czechoslovaks expressed reservations about including the SED in any future Cominform meetings.[48]

Gomułka had serious misgivings about the Soviets' "two camp" policy announced at this first Cominform meeting; the policy would eventually preclude cooperation with the West and increase Soviet control over the bloc parties. He did agree that "when two antagonistic blocs—imperialist and democratic—have crystallized on the world scale, the problem of tactics to be adopted by communist Parties in particular countries cannot be treated as merely a domestic problem for each Party separately, but must be the object of concern and discussion by all the Parties." Gomułka had no qualms about using the principle of socialist solidarity to circumscribe the freedom of the SED, however.[49] He again slighted the German communists by declaring that "Slav solidarity" was one of the foundations of Polish foreign policy.[50] When the Polish United Workers' Party (PZPR) was formed in December 1948, the new party organ *Trybuna Ludu* (People's Tribune) published congratulatory letters from the French, Czechoslovak, Greek, Soviet, Hungarian, and Italian Communist parties, but nothing from the SED.[51]

The SED Promotes Socialist Solidarity with Poland

Confronted with so many other serious problems after the war, the SED had little time to conduct a concerted campaign to improve relations with the Poles. The SED's primary incentive for developing ties to Poland after the war was economic rather than political or cultural. The loss of the vital industrial center of Silesia to Poland had direct economic implications for the Soviet zone, and the SED repeatedly asked the Poles to increase exports, primarily much-needed coal.

The SED leadership knew how difficult it would be to change anti-Polish sentiments in the Soviet zone, especially among the German refugees from Poland. Many Germans viewed the subjugation of Poles as natural and proper; to them, the typical Pole was ignorant, lazy, and backward. In March 1947, a representative of the East German *Kulturbund* conceded to the officers at the Polish Military Mission that "most German people are not aware of the responsibility and guilt that falls on the German people as a result of the war. Among other things this ignorance is the main cause of the continued reluctance of the German people for relations with the Polish people." He said that Germans lacked any knowledge of Polish culture, and had no interest in learning about it. They adhered to the old adage that "what is to the east of Germany is low and uncultured." Most Germans still thought that Chopin was French and Copernicus was German.[52]

Two years after the war, a Polish officer at the Polish Military Mission in Berlin observed that SED functionaries knew next to nothing about the political situation in Poland.[53] Ulbricht told the German press that "Germans still had a lot to learn about democratic Poland."[54] He acknowledged that Soviet-zone journalists needed to pay more attention to Polish political and economic achievements, but suggested that the Poles reciprocate by publicizing the accomplishments of the Germans in the Soviet zone.[55] A year later, SED functionaries were still telling Polish officers at the mission that it would be a huge undertaking to eradicate anti-Polish attitudes, even among party members.[56] The SED also acknowledged that there were "deep-seeded nationalist prejudices [of the German working classes] against the Polish people."[57]

The SED did not have enough instructional materials to conduct a serious campaign to overcome East Germans' ignorance of Poland. In April 1947, the editor of the *Leipziger Zeitung* wrote a letter to the PPR Central Committee requesting honest information on the reconstruction of Poland and life in the country in general.[58] That fall, the SED leadership ordered its press services to devote more coverage to Poland,[59] but it was not until the end of December 1947 that the SED issued its first bulletin about Poland.[60] The Polish Military Mission repeatedly urged the Polish Foreign Ministry to provide the SED with more propaganda, but the Polish government had other priorities.[61] Until 1948, the main SED newspaper, *Neues Deutschland* (New Germany), virtually ignored German-Polish relations and devoted more coverage to developments in Czechoslovakia. The newspaper generally portrayed the Czechoslovaks in a more favorable light.[62]

When Moscow tightened the reins on the satellite parties in 1948, the Polish and East German press began to promote the idea that the SED and Polish communists were ushering in a new era in Polish-German relations. In the suspicious atmosphere of the times, however, there was little objective reporting on either side. Few East Germans or Poles, including party members, believed in this propaganda. In March, the Polish journal *Nowe Drogi* vigorously criticized two Polish authors for writing a book emphasizing the continuity of German territorial expansionism in the twentieth century. The journal attacked the authors for ignoring the new political developments in the Soviet zone and the differences between Soviet and U.S. policy in Germany. They were accused of harboring "hyper-anti-German" attitudes.[63]

In June, the SED resolved to increase press coverage of all important political, economic, and cultural events in Poland and to develop more cultural exchanges.[64] Later that summer, the party opened the Helmut-von-Gerlach Society in Berlin to provide Germans with reading materials and exhibits about Poland.[65] *Głos Ludu* reported in the fall that the SED was intensifying its campaign against nationalism and anti-Polish attitudes in the Soviet zone. Ulbricht acknowledged the presence of a strong nationalist element in the SED and the trade unions, and declared that anti-Polish attitudes were dangerous and unacceptable.[66]

Although the Polish press still devoted more coverage to the western zones in 1948, Polish officials were quick to point out oversights in East Germany's reporting on Poland. For example, when *Neues Deutschland* failed to publish an important parliamentary speech by Premier Józef Cyrankiewicz in June, Polish diplomats in the Polish Military Mission told Rudi Wetzel, the head of the SED's press department, that the omission was an expression of the SED's general anti-Polish stance. According to the Poles, the SED press spent too much time emphasizing the threat from the West rather than reminding readers of the strength of the new people's democracies. Wetzel told Grotewohl and Pieck that the SED press should pay closer attention to such important speeches in order to cultivate what Wetzel termed "the weak seedling of German-Polish relations."[67]

Gomułka's Fall and the Stalinization of Party Relations

The fallout from Stalin's expulsion of Yugoslav leader Josip Broz Tito from Cominform in 1948 soon reached the other communist parties in Eastern Europe. Each party engaged in a witch hunt of alleged "Titoists": Those who supported national roads to socialism, or simply opposed Stalinist methods, were ousted, imprisoned, or executed. The capriciousness of the purges, however, put every communist in the cross hairs. The communist leaders in Eastern Europe now worked under the strain of slavishly adhering to Moscow's directives.

Tito's ouster and the heightened East-West tensions during the Berlin blockade in the summer of 1948 was a boon to the political fortunes of the SED, but signalled an end to the PPR's limited independence from Moscow. When Stalin demanded greater ideological and political conformity from the communist parties in 1948, the SED easily fell into line. The SED had already embarked on an economic transformation of the zone that closely followed the Stalinist model,[68] and the prospect of a more permanent division of Germany served the party's short-term political goals. Pieck and Ulbricht knew that there was no democratic way for the SED to take power in a united German state.[69] The SED underwent purges and recantations, but the top party leadership remained largely intact.[70]

Blind devotion to anything Russian was anathema to the Polish people, and the Polish communists never fully adopted Stalinist policies. Gomułka tried steer a course that recognized the Soviet Union's geopolitical interests in Poland while advancing a Polish-style communism that would ensure the greatest possible independence from the CPSU. For the first few years after the war, Stalin tolerated Gomułka's attempts to create a suitable socialist path for Poland;[71] Poles maintained many of their religious, cultural, and economic freedoms.[72]

Gomułka told a plenary session of the PPR Central Committee in June 1948 that "both for the PPS and the PPR the independence of Poland is a supreme consideration, to which all others are subordinated."[73] He defended Tito's national road to communism, and rejected the notion that the Yugoslav leader was a threat to Soviet leadership of the international communist movement. He opposed Tito's excommunication from Cominform, warning that communist unity would suffer.[74] That was enough for Stalin; in the fall, the Muscovites denounced Gomułka and his faction. In contrast to the purges in the Bulgarian, Hungarian, Romanian, and Czechoslovak parties, however, the Polish communists did not execute their own. Gomułka was arrested but never brought to trial. A few years later, Bierut told Khrushchev, "To tell you the truth, I myself don't know what the charges are and why he's in jail."[75]

Bierut replaced Gomułka as party secretary, and Cyrankiewicz took over leadership of the PPS from Edvard Osóbka-Morawski, in part because Osóbka-Morawski was opposed to the unification of the two parties. In December 1948, the PPR and the PPS merged to form the PZPR. The Stalinist die had been cast for the Polish Left.[76]

At first the SED took a wait-and-see attitude toward Gomułka's ouster; but in an article in the November issue of the party's ideological journal, *Einheit*, Karl Peters issued the obligatory condemnation by accusing the deposed Polish leader of deviating from a consistent Marxist-Leninist line and of coddling bourgeois-nationalists.[77] After the PPR-PPS merger, SED Politburo member Hermann Matern declared that "never again will Poland be a reactionary springboard and the base of counterrevolutionary war provocations against the Soviet Union." But in a condescending tone he concluded that "the reactionaries in Poland tried to develop anti-Russian and anti-Bolshevik attitudes and use [them] to come to power. This too created vacillations and deviations among the leading comrades in the PPR, like Gomułka." Matern paid the usual tribute to the "great Soviet Union" for ensuring Poland's security and "happy future."[78]

Ulbricht's visit to Poland in October 1948 was the first face-to-face meeting between a high-ranking SED functionary and the top Polish leadership. The SED viewed the trip as a turning point in relations with the Polish communists. Ulbricht recalled later that it was not easy to address a crowd in Warsaw, a city that had been destroyed by the Germans. He tried to reassure the Poles that the SED had abandoned any hopes of revising the Oder-Neisse border: "For us the question of the Polish-German border has been definitively settled."[79] Ulbricht exaggerated the level of trust that he had developed with Polish officials, however, claiming that Cyrankiewicz was fully satisfied that the SED had overcome its revisionist tendencies.[80] Ulbricht said that his delegation had "succeeded in winning the trust of the Polish comrades for our party and our party leadership." He concluded that it was now up to the SED to keep that trust.[81]

The Poles gave Ulbricht a rather lukewarm reception.[82] Cyrankiewicz declared, "We cannot imagine the victory of socialism without the victory of the SED in Germany,"[83] but he cautioned Ulbricht that only "the first step has been taken."[84] Fearing popular demonstrations against Ulbricht's visit, *Głos Ludu* did not cover it until after Ulbricht had returned to Berlin.[85] The Polish Military Mission in Berlin viewed Ulbricht's pronouncements as a positive sign for the direction of the SED's foreign policy and reported that the SED had made it a top priority to quash its members' ideas about revising the Oder-Neisse border. But the Polish officers at the mission, mindful of Stalin's demand for communist party fealty, warned that "even in the central organs [of the SED] not everyone speaks candidly about what they think [about the border]."[86] Moreover, the SED's illegitimacy gave the Poles pause about the party's ability to eliminate the German people's opposition to the Oder-Neisse border, let alone their negative attitudes toward Poles.

The SED leadership knew that much work had to be done to convince its constituents of the need for friendly relations with Poland.[87] Ulbricht acknowledged that "unfortunately in the past the German workers' movement was unable to overcome reactionary elements."[88] In a letter to the PPR thanking the Poles for inviting Ulbricht to Poland, Pieck conceded that there was still considerable nationalist sentiment in the ranks of the SED.[89] *Trybuna Ludu's* correspondent in Berlin, Stanisław Brodzki, also said that the SED's main task was to redress the historical corruption caused by Nazism and social democracy of the German working class.[90]

Both parties now publicly proclaimed the dawning of a new era in Polish-German relations. At the PZPR's unification congress in December, Cyrankiewicz extended a warm welcome to SED delegate Franz Dahlem, whom he remembered as "my comrade from the concentration camp in Mauthausen." Cyrankiewicz praised the efforts of the SED leadership to combat social democratic, reformist, and other un-Marxist ideas in the party, and lauded the SED's campaign to convince the masses of the need for good relations with Poland. Dahlem replied that "as socialist-internationalists, as German workers, we feel deeply bonded to the working class and the working masses of Poland. We are most vitally interested in the strength of the People's Republic of Poland."[91]

The Polish delegation also took home a favorable impression of the SED party congress in January 1949. Edward Ochab observed that there was a new fresh air of trust between the SED and the PZPR: "We want to enlighten [the Polish working class] that under the leadership of the SED the true democratic, anti-imperialist forces are assembling to create a united, peaceful, democratic Germany that we have always wanted for a neighbor."[92]

Trybuna Ludu reported that the audience's reaction was "especially warm" when Pieck stressed the need for cooperation with the other nations of Eastern Europe, especially Poland.[93] The newspaper even commended the SED for changing the nationalistic, anti-Polish attitudes in the German working classes[94] and lavished praise on the party for eliminating the influence and power of Hitlerites, nationalists, and industrialists.[95] Brigadier General Jakub Prawin, the head of the Polish Military Mission, told *Nowe Drogi* in 1949 that the working classes in the Soviet zone had developed a new attitude toward the Soviet Union; he said that the SED had done much to improve relations with the people's republics, particularly with Poland.[96]

Pieck led another SED delegation to Poland in September 1949. Ulbricht reported that his talks with Cyrankiewicz and the Polish Minister of Industry Hilary Minc were conducted in a friendly tone. He maintained that Cyrankiewicz was now satisfied that the SED had quelled opposition to the border within the party.[97] But the relative importance of Pieck's visit to each side was revealed in the coverage it received in the SED and the PZPR press. *Neues Deutschland* devoted several extensive front-page articles to the visit, interpreting it as a significant breakthrough for the recognition of the SED as a legitimate communist party. *Trybuna Ludu* made only brief mention of the talks.[98]

Relations between the two communist parties seemed to have done a volte-face by 1949, but it was a thin facade of communist solidarity rather than a genuine rapprochement; in the oppressive and suspicious atmosphere of Stalin's empire, the parties' propaganda had a hollow ring. Before Stalin's split with Tito and the breakdown of allied cooperation in Germany in 1948, neither party had made a concerted effort to reconcile their differences. For the first few years after the war, Polish communists not only ignored their German counterparts but exploited Poles' hatred of all Germans to attract adherents to the party. The SED was preoccupied with its relations with the Soviet authorities and with consolidating its power in the Soviet zone. The Soviets did not actively foster closer relations between the Polish and German communists either, for friction between them increased their dependency on Moscow. In Stalin's empire, a genuine friendship between the communist parties, let alone the peoples, was impossible.

The Poles possessed more diplomatic leverage than the German communists in the early postwar period, but Tito's expulsion from Cominform and the subsequent purges in the Soviet bloc parties changed the dynamic of PZPR-SED relations. The committed Stalinists and Soviet satraps in the SED saw their fortunes on the upswing, culminating in the formation of the German Democratic Republic in October 1949. Until Stalin's death in 1953, Ulbricht's confidence grew, as did his resolve to promote East German interests in his dealings with the Poles.

Neither the postwar communist government in Poland nor the SED in the Soviet zone had any legitimate claim to power. As a result, relations between the Polish and German communists were also artificial, conducted with the knowledge that Moscow might purge them at any time. The East Germans had misgivings about Polish and Russian Slavic solidarity and the possibility that Moscow would support a demilitarized, neutral, and democratic Germany. The SED knew that it had no chance of winning a free election. Meanwhile, the Polish communists worried that a closer relationship between the SED and the CPSU could result in a revision of the Oder-Neisse border. The German communists' unwillingness to recognize the permanence of the border in the early postwar period cast a pall over relations with the Polish communists for years to come.

Notes

1. Quoted in Franz Sikora, *Sozialistische Solidarität und nationale Interessen* (Socialist solidarity and national interests) (Cologne: Verlag Wissenschaft und Politik, 1977), pp. 101–102.

2. Quoted from a letter from Polish communist veterans to the SED Central Committee on the tenth anniversary of the founding of the GDR, October 1959, SED ZK, Walter Ulbricht Papers, NL 182/1244.

3. Luxemburg's closest confidant in the party was Leon Jogiches, who was born in Wilno to a wealthy Jewish family. Another founder was the infamous Bolshevik inquisitor Feliks Dzierżyński. The SDKPiL and the left-wing Socialists formed the Polish Communist Workers' Party in 1918. It was renamed the Polish Communist Party (KPP) in 1925.

4. See M. K. Dziewanowski, *The Communist Party of Poland: An Outline of History* (Cambridge, Mass.: Harvard University Press, 1976), pp. 118–119, 150–151. Stalin also alleged that virtually the entire KPP was infiltrated with agents of the Polish intelligence service.

5. Quoted in Roy A. Medvedev, *Let History Judge: The Origins and Consequences of Stalinism* (New York: Vintage Books, 1971), p. 220.

6. See M. K. Dziewanowski, *Poland in the Twentieth Century* (New York: Columbia University Press, 1977), pp. 162–164. Gomułka's native communist group included Zenon Kliszko, Marian Spychalski, and Władysław Bieńkowski; and Anita Prazmowska, "The Soviet Liberation of Poland and the Polish Left, 1943–1945," in Francesca Gori and Silvio Pons, eds., *The Soviet Union and Europe in the Cold War, 1943–53* (New York: St. Martin's Press, 1996), p. 76; and John Coutouvidis and Jaime Reynolds, *Poland 1939–1947* (New York: Holmes and Meier, 1986), pp. 185–197.

7. See Coutouvidis and Reynolds, *Poland 1939–1947*, p. 315; see also Nikita Khrushchev, *Khrushchev Remembers: The Glasnost Tapes* (Boston: Little, Brown, 1990), p. 116. In these memoirs, Khrushchev maintains that Stalin was not responsible for Gomułka's arrest: "I knew for a fact, I heard it from Stalin, that he did not order Gomułka's arrest; on the contrary, he even voiced doubts about the arrest. He trusted Gomułka."

8. Manfred Wilke, "Kommunismus in Deutschland und Rahmenbedingungen politischer Handelns nach 1945" (Communism in Germany and the contingencies of political exchange), in Manfred Wilke, ed., *Anatomie der Parteizentrale: Die KPD/SED auf dem Weg zur Macht* (Anatomy of the Central Party Office: The KPD/SED on the road to power) (Berlin: Akademie Verlag, 1998), pp. 24–25.

9. See R. C. Raack, "Stalin Plans His Post-War Germany," *Journal of Contemporary History* 28 (1993), pp. 55, 66.

10. See Wilfried Loth, *Stalins ungeliebtes Kind: Warum Moskau die DDR nicht wollte* (Stalin's unloved child: Why Moscow did not want the GDR) (Berlin: Rowohlt, 1994); and Wilfried Loth, "Stalin's Plans for Post-War Germany," in Francesca Gori and Silvio Pons, eds., *The Soviet Union and Europe in the Cold War, 1943–53* (New York: St. Martin's Press, 1996), p. 24. Loth argues that Stalin did not intend to birth his "unloved child," the GDR: "Stalin really pursued the democratization of Germany under the auspices of the four powers and that he only ended up with a separate Socialist state as a result of the incompetence of the Communists to play the democratic game"; see also Alexander Dallin, "Stalin and the Prospects for Post-War Europe," in Francesca Gori and Silvio Pons, eds., *The Soviet Union and Europe in the Cold War, 1943–53* (New York: St. Martin's Press, 1996), p. 189. Dallin adds that Stalin's long-term goal was a communist Germany, even if he would accept a democratic Germany for the time being: "There is nothing in the record to sustain the argument that, in the long run, Stalin wanted a 'bourgeois-democratic' government anywhere anytime—surely not in the Soviet

Union, surely not in Eastern Europe, and surely not in Germany;" Michail M. Narinskii, "The Soviet Union and the Berlin Crisis," in Francesca Gori and Silvio Pons, eds., _The Soviet Union and Europe in the Cold War, 1943–53_ (New York: St. Martin's Press, 1996), p. 59. Narinskii concurs with Loth, arguing that Stalin gradually warmed to the idea of a separate East German state in reaction to the Truman Doctrine, the Marshall Plan, and other seemingly threatening moves by the West; see also John Lewis Gaddis, _We Know Now: Rethinking Cold War History_ (Oxford: Clarendon Press, 1997), p. 119.

11. "Left" refers to the communist and socialist parties, the Communist Party of Germany (KPD), the Socialist Party of Germany (SPD), the Polish Workers' Party (PPR), and the Polish Socialist Party (PPS). The KPD and SPD united in 1946 to form the Socialist Unity Party (SED), and the PPR and PPS merged into the Polish United Workers' Party (PZPR) in 1948. Because the KPD and PPR dominated these new parties, the terms _Polish communists_ and _German communists_ will be used to characterize the Left in each country, with the exception of where differentiation with the socialists is necessary.

12. Internal memo, undated, unsigned, SED ZK, Hermann Axen Office, IV 2/2.035/159. In 1955, Hermann Axen wrote that "during the Weimar Republic the German Communist Party always saw its duty to support the struggle of the illegal Polish Communist Party."

13. Heinrich Gemkow, "_Gemeinsame Traditionen der revolutionären deutschen und polnischen Arbeiterbewegung 1917/18 bis 1945_" (Common traditions of the revolutionary German and Polish Workers' Movement 1917/18 to 1945), in _Beiträge zur Geschichte der Arbeiterbewegung_ (Contributions to the history of the workers' movement) 16, no. 1 (1974), pp. 19, 27. For example, postwar PPS leader Józef Cyrankiewicz was imprisoned in Mauthausen with German communist Franz Dahlem. Adam Rapacki, Poland's foreign minister in the 1950s, and Jan Izydorczyk, the Polish chief of mission in the GDR in the early 1950s, also shared cells with German communists during the war. This cohabitation did not necessarily mean that they befriended each other; German political prisoners were among the most privileged inmates, and were often used to guard other prisoners.

14. During KPD leader Ernst Thalmann's internment in a Nazi prison from 1935 to 1944, Pieck acted as chairman of the Central Committee. Pieck spent most of the Nazi period in Moscow, and after the Nazis executed Thalmann in 1944, Pieck became head of the party.

15. Luxemburg's profession of a strict Marxist-Leninist internationalist foreign policy was similar to the one espoused by the SED after World War II. Luxemburg opposed a separate Polish state and any social democratic notions of a nonviolent, democratic means to socialism. She alienated many Polish and German communists with these views. See Elzbieta Ettinger, _Rosa Luksemburg: Ein Leben_ (Rosa Luxemburg: A life), (Bonn: Verlag J.H.W. Dietz, 1990), pp. 203–204. She writes that "the more Rosa Luxemburg stood up for 'revolutionary Marxism' the more she was isolated. The Polish tradition of heroism and martyrdom and the German tradition of conforming and conservatism were unreconcilable."

16. Heinz Vosske, _Wilhelm Pieck: Biographischer Abriss_ (Wilhelm Pieck: Biographical Abstract) (Berlin: Dietz Verlag, 1975), pp. 46–47. Karl Liebknecht was also interrogated at the Eden Hotel and shot the same day.

17. On the twenty-fifth anniversary of Marchlewski's death on March 22, 1950, Pieck presented a Polish delegation with Marchlewski's ashes, which they took back to Poland.

18. Declaration of the KPD Central Committee, September 23, 1939, SED ZK, Wilhelm Pieck Papers, NL 36/496.

19. George L. Flemming, "The Polish Eagle Looks West," *East Europe* 16, no. 10 (1967), p. 18.

20. Wilhelm Pieck notes, October 22, 1939, SED ZK, Wilhelm Pieck Papers, NL 36/496.

21. KPD circular, October 21, 1939, SED ZK, Wilhelm Pieck Papers, NL 36/496; see Horst Duhnke, *Die KPD von 1933 bis 1945* (The KPD from 1933 to 1945) (Cologne: Kiepenheuer u. Witsch, 1972), pp. 333–351.

22. Carola Stern, *Ulbricht: A Political Biography* (New York: Frederick Praeger, 1965), p. 31. Ulbricht became a member of the KPD Politburo in 1929, and was the party's representative to the Communist International in Moscow in the late 1920s, and again during World War II. Ulbricht had the reputation of being a humorless, efficient, and dogmatic apparatchik, acquiring the derogatory moniker "Comrade Cell" for his work in party organization. During his years in the Soviet Union, Ulbricht developed closer ties to the Czechoslovak Communist Party (CzCP) and its chief, Klement Gottwald, than to the Polish communists. Pieck also served with Gottwald on the political secretariat of the Communist International in the 1930s and 1940s. As a result, the KPD enjoyed better relations with the CzCP after the war than it did with the PPR.

23. Stern, *Ulbricht*, p. 207. Ulbricht's article appeared in *Die Welt*, a Comintern paper published in Sweden.

24. KPP note on the German-Soviet Non-Aggression Pact, November, 1939, SED ZK, Wilhelm Pieck Papers, NL 36/496.

25. See Norman Davies, *God's Playground: A History of Poland, Volume II: 1795 to the Present* (New York: Columbia University Press, 1982), pp. 544–548.

26. See M. K. Dziewanowski, *Poland in the 20th Century* (New York: Columbia University Press, 1977), p. 164. Dziewanowski observes that the Kremlin accepted a Polish national road to communism in 1945: "They apparently calculated that toleration of nationalistic slogans was one means of weakening the Polish popular opposition to Communism during the crucial takeover period." Although the Polish communists began to change this propaganda in 1948, this campaign had a long-term negative impact on the SED's relations with Poland.

27. Quoted in Georg W. Strobel, *Deutschland-Polen: Wunsch und Wirklichkeit* (Germany-Poland: Wish and reality) (Bonn: Edition Atlantic Forum, 1969), p. 14. Born in the Austro-Hungarian province of Galicia, Gomułka attended a German school where he acquired a working knowledge of German. When the Soviets occupied Lwów in the fall of 1939, he fled to his home town of Krosno, where he took his chances with the German occupiers.

28. This ministry administered the German territories occupied by Poland in 1945.

29. *Głos Ludu* (Voice of the People), March 16, 1945, p. 1. Although the non-Slavic countries in Eastern Europe, Romania and Hungary, would eventually become part of the Soviet bloc and the Warsaw Pact, they had supplied Hitler with several divisions for the attack on the Soviet Union in 1941.

30. Władysław Gomułka, *O problemie Niemieckim* (On the German problem) (Warsaw: Książka i Wiedza, 1984), p. 39.

31. *Głos Ludu*, July 15, 1946, p. 4.

32. *Głos Ludu*, April 30, 1946, p. 6.

33. For a thorough discussion of Polish-Czechoslovak relations in the immediate postwar period, see Marek Kamiński, *Polsko-Czechosłowackie Stosunki Polityczne, 1945–1948* (Polish-Czechoslovak political relations, 1945–1948) (Warsaw: Państwowe Wydawnictwo Naukowe, 1989); see also Andrzej Pączkowski, "The Polish Contribution to the Victory of the 'Prague Coup' in February 1948," *Bulletin: Cold War International History Project*, no. 11 (winter 1998), p. 141. The disputed area of Tesin (Czieszen) Silesia was one of the main issues dividing the two countries until 1947, when Stalin brokered a compromise.

34. *Głos Ludu*, June 25, 1946, p. 4; and *Głos Ludu*, August 26 1946, p. 4; see Hans Georg Lehmann, *Der Oder-Neisse-Konflikt* (The Oder-Neisse conflict) (Munich: C. H. Beck, 1979), p. 58. Relations between the Polish and Czechoslovak governments were in reality rather tense after the war, especially in April 1946 when the Czechoslovak government claimed small border areas in Polish Silesia. The Polish government responded by sending troops to the area, and the Czechoslovak government relented.

35. Alfons Klafkowski, *The Polish-German Frontier After World War II* (Poznań: Wydawnictwo Poznańskie, 1972), p. 91.

36. See *Głos Ludu*'s reports on the Nuremberg trials in September, 1946.

37. Norman Naimark, *The Russians in Germany: A History of the Soviet Zone of Occupation, 1945–1949* (Cambridge: Harvard University Press, 1995), p. 147.

38. Quoted in Sikora, *Sozialistische Solidarität und nationale Interessen*, pp. 101–102.

39. See *Głos Ludu* from May 1945 to April 1946.

40. See, for example, *Głos Ludu*, October 22, 1946, p. 2. The newspaper carried just two small articles on the victory of SPD in Berlin and the SED in the rest of the Soviet zone.

41. See *Głos Ludu*, April 23, 1946, p. 2. In this issue was a small article from the TASS news agency titled "Progress in the Work of German Democracy"; see also *Głos Ludu*, April 25, 1946.

42. Polish Military Mission Report, May 2, 1946, MSZ, 6/671/42.

43. Erwin Weit, *Ostblock intern: 13 Jahre Dolmetscher für die polnische Partei- und Staatsführung* (East bloc intern: 13 Years as interpreter for the Polish Party and State leadership) (Hamburg: Hoffmann und Campe Verlag, 1970), pp. 225–226. According to Weit, who was Gomułka's interpreter in 1950s and 1960s, these former Nazis were even more loyal to Ulbricht because he could use their past to incriminate them.

44. Jan Gross, "War as Revolution," in Norman Naimark and Leonid Gibianski, eds., *The Establishment of Communist Régimes in Eastern Europe, 1944–1949* (Boulder: Westview Press, 1997), p. 34; see also *Głos Ludu*, May 7, 1946, p. 5.

45. The SD, along with the Polish Socialist Party (PPS) and the United Peasant Party (ZSL), collaborated with the PPR in the provisional government.

46. *Głos Ludu*, June 30, 1946, pp. 3–4, 8; see also Strobel, *Deutschland-Polen: Wunsch und Wirklichkeit*, p. 13.

47. Loth, *Stalins Unbeliebtes Kind*, p. 104. Loth argues that the Soviets did not invite the SED because it was not a communist party; see also Naimark, *The Rus-*

sians in Germany, p. 305; and Giuliano Procacci, ed., *The Cominform: Minutes of the Three Conferences, 1947/1948/1949* (Milan: Giangiacomo Feltrinelli, 1994), p. 37; and Erich W. Gniffke, *Jahre Mit Ulbricht* (Years with Ulbricht) (Cologne: Verlag Wissenschaft und Politik, 1966), p. 264.

48. Press and Information Service of the Federal Government, June 17, 1950, BRD AA, Department 2, vol. 437; see also Alfred Schickel, *Deutsche und Polen: Ein Jahrtausend gemeinsame Geschichte* (Germans and Poles: A thousand years of common history) (Bergisch Gladbach, Germany: Gustav Lübbe Verlag, 1984), p. 245.

49. Anna Di Biagio, "The Marshall Plan and the Founding of the Cominform, June-September 1947," in Francesca Gori and Silvio Pons, eds., *The Soviet Union and Europe in the Cold War, 1943–53* (New York: St. Martin's Press, 1996), p. 217; and Raina, *Gomułka*, p. 70.

50. Procacci, ed., *The Cominform*, p. 61.

51. *Trybuna Ludu*, December 16, 1948, p. 1.

52. Lewandowski notes of meeting with Weiner, March 1, 1947, PPR KC, 295/XX–70.

53. Przebój-Jarecki notes, March 1, 1947, MSZ, 6/711/46.

54. Report on Ulbricht's press conference in Berlin, October 23, 1948, PPR KC, 295/VII–69.

55. Meller notes of meeting with Ulbricht and Prawin, March 15, 1947, PPR KC, 295/XX–70.

56. See the letter from the SED Press Information Department to Meller, April 26, 1948, PPR KC, 295/XX–70.

57. Letter from the SED Party School Karl Marx to the PPR Central School in Łódz, September 27, 1948, PPR KC, 295/XX–70.

58. Dr. Hermann Ley to the PPR Central Committee, April 18, 1947, PPR KC, 295/XX–71.

59. Protocol No. 13 of the meeting of the Central Secretariat, November 10, 1947, SED ZK, IV 2/2.1/144.

60. Ostap Dłuski to Gomułka, December 15, 1947, PZPR KC, 295/XX–72; see also *Głos Ludu*, September 23, 1947, p. 1.

61. H. Meller to Grosz, February 16, 1948, PPR KC, 295/XX–72.

62. See *Neues Deutschland* (New Germany) from April 1946 to December 1947.

63. *Nowe Drogi* (New Paths), March 1948, p. 209. The book was Janusz Pajewski and Włodzimierz Głowacki's *Analogie rewizjonizmu niemieckiego* (Analysis of German revisionism) (Poznań, 1947).

64. Appendix No. 4 to Protocol No. 82 of the meeting of the Central Secretariat, June 7, 1948, SED ZK, IV 2/2.1/205.

65. In March 1950, its name was changed to the Deutsch-polnische Gesellschaft für Frieden und gute Nachbarschaft (German-Polish Society for Peace and Good Neighborliness).

66. *Głos Ludu*, September 23, 1948, p. 1; and *Głos Ludu*, October 10, 1948, p. 3.

67. Wetzel to Pieck, Grotewohl, et al., June 26, 1948, SED ZK, microfilm FBS 339/13487.

68. Wilfried Loth, "Stalin's Plans for Post-War Germany," in Francesca Gori and Silvio Pons, eds., *The Soviet Union and Europe in the Cold War, 1943–53* (New

York: St. Martin's Press, 1996), p. 33. By the spring of 1948, 40 percent of all industrial production in the Soviet zone had been de-privatized.

69. See Naimark, *The Russians in Germany*, p. 299. Even Otto Grotewohl, the former SPD leader who was now in a leadership position in the SED, recognized that
there was no alternative but to kowtow to Stalin. During his first visit to Moscow in
January 1946, Grotewohl fawned over the Soviet leader: "Comrade Stalin is the
greatest socialist in the world, Comrade Stalin is the father of the world."

70. See Ann L. Phillips, *Soviet Policy toward East Germany Reconsidered: The Post-
war Decade* (New York: Greenwood Press, 1986), p. 40. Ackermann first elucidated
the KPD's idea of a "German Road to Socialism" in December 1945, and it was
not until 1948 that the SED rejected Ackermann's theory. He recanted in September of that year. Paul Merker was expelled from the SED in 1950, Ackermann and
Franz Dahlem in 1953. Ackermann was rehabilitated in 1956.

71. Khrushchev, *Khrushchev Remembers: The Glasnost Tapes*, p. 116.

72. Dziewanowski, *The Communist Party of Poland*, p. 207.

73. Quoted in Dziewanowski, *Poland in the Twentieth Century*, p. 166.

74. Raina, *Gomułka*, pp. 74–75.

75. See Nikita Khrushchev, *Khrushchev Remembers: The Last Testament* (Boston:
Little, Brown, 1974), p. 197. Gomułka was purged from the PZPR in 1949, and arrested in 1951. Five years later, he returned to lead the party.

76. Marian Spychalski, Zenon, Kliszko, and Władysław Bieńkowski were other
prominent leaders purged. See Zbigniew Brzezinski, *The Soviet Bloc: Unity and
Conflict* (Cambridge: Harvard University Press, 1967) p. 61. Brzezinski claims that
one of the reasons for Gomułka's fall was that he was the only prominent communist leader in Eastern Europe to oppose the formation of Cominform in 1947;
see also Iazhborovskaia, "The Gomułka Alternative," p. 126. She writes that
Stalin had not been consulted on Gomułka's election to head the PPR in November 1943, and was opposed to Gomułka's commitment to collective decisionmaking in the party, and to his attempt to make an honest connection between a national communist party and the masses; see also Leonid Gibianski, "The
Soviet-Yugoslav Conflict and the Soviet Bloc," p. 227. For several years the Foreign Policy Department of the CPSU had been filing critical reports on Gomułka's
attempts to put a Polish, rather than a Soviet, cast on the communist system.
Now his unwillingness to slavishly follow the Soviet model was used against
him; see also Gniffke, *Jahre mit Ulbricht*, p. 340.

77. *Einheit* (Unity) 3, no. 11 (November 1948), p. 1066.

78. *Neues Deutschland*, January 1, 1949, p. 6; see also Sikora, *Sozialistische Solidarität und nationale Interessen*, pp. 116–117. Sikora calls Matern's lecture to the
Poles typical of the SED's "arrogance" (*Überheblichkeit*).

79. Report of Ulbricht's press conference in Berlin, October 23, 1948, PZPR KC,
group PPR KC, 295/VII–69.

80. *Neues Deutschland*, October 26, 1948, p. 2.

81. Report on Ulbricht's trip to Poland, SED ZK, meetings of the party leadership, October 20–21, 1948, IV 2/1/55.

82. Sikora, *Sozialistische Solidarität und nationale Interessen*, p. 116. Sikora writes
that Dahlem's visit was much more thoroughly reported in the Polish press than
Ulbricht's "somewhat toneless visit."

83. Unsigned memo, October 20, 1948, SED ZK, Walter Ulbricht Papers, NL 182/1245.

84. *Neues Deutschland*, November 21, 1948, p. 3.

85. *Głos Ludu*, October 24, 1948, p. 1.

86. Meller to the Polish Foreign Ministry, October 29, 1948, PZPR KC, group PPR KC, 295/XX–70.

87. *Neues Deutschland*, November 21, 1948, p. 3.

88. Report of Ulbricht's press conference in Berlin, October 23, 1948, PZPR KC, group PPR KC, 295/VII–69.

89. Pieck, et al., to the PPR Politburo, November 20, 1948, PZPR KC, group PPR KC, 295/XX–70.

90. *Trybuna Ludu*, February 11, 1949, p. 3.

91. *Trybuna Ludu*, December 17, 1948, p. 4; and December 18, 1948, pp. 8–9.

92. Notes on Ochab's visit, unsigned, undated, ca. October 1948, SED ZK, Walter Ulbricht Papers, NL 182/1245.

93. *Trybuna Ludu*, January 27, 1949, p. 1.

94. *Trybuna Ludu*, January 26, 1949, p. 4.

95. *Trybuna Ludu*, October 4, 1949, p. 3.

96. *Nowe Drogi*, March-April 1949, p. 127.

97. Ulbricht speech, October 22, 1949, SED ZK, Wilhelm Pieck Papers, NL 36/441.

98. See *Trybuna Ludu* and *Neues Deutschland* for the first week of September, 1949.

2

The Controversy over the Oder-Neisse Border, 1946–1949

Poland no longer wants to be a soccer ball that is kicked around from place to place.

—*Wladyslaw Gomulka, 1946*[1]

The primary obstacle to better relations between the Polish and German communists after World War II was the loss of German territories to Poland. The equivocation of the KPD, the SPD, and the SED on recognizing the permanence of the Oder-Neisse border undermined Polish confidence in the German Left. That they shared an internationalist ideology that theoretically transcended their national differences did not seem to matter; the border was still relevant.

The conflict between Poland and Germany over Upper Silesia after World War I was a prologue to the dispute over the Oder-Neisse border. Rosa Luxemburg had rejected the notion of nation-states, national borders, and even the resurrection of a Polish state.[2] In 1918, Pieck was also opposed to drawing the Polish-German border on strictly national lines. He promoted Polish and German working-class solidarity in the quest for a general victory of communism in East Central Europe. In the fall of 1922, shortly before the plebiscite that would determine the final border, Pieck wrote an open letter to the Poles calling for cooperation against nationalist agitators: "We would like the Polish and German workers from the border areas to come together, fraternize as members of the proletariat, and investigate and prevent the criminal plans of reactionary nationalists and their agents."[3]

After the plebiscite, Pieck criticized the nationalists' appeals to the workers in both countries, but he blamed German exploitation of Polish workers for the extreme character of Polish nationalist propaganda.[4] He urged German and Polish workers to unite in a revolutionary cause against the industrial magnates in Upper Silesia.[5] The KPP and the KPD finally agreed to a border drawn along ethnic lines on January 29, 1933, the day before Adolf Hitler became chancellor of Germany.[6]

At the Yalta conference in February 1945, British Prime Minister Winston Churchill and U.S. President Franklin Roosevelt tentatively agreed to Stalin's demand for a Polish-German border on the Oder and Western Neisse Rivers. At first, the Polish Provisional Government hesitated to make a legal claim to the German territories. The Poles did not want to set a precedent to change Poland's 1937 borders; such a change could mean the permanent loss of the eastern territories now occupied by the Soviet Union.[7] By the time the Allied leaders met again at Potsdam in July, however, the Polish government had established an administration in the German territories; the expulsion of Germans was underway. The Allies confirmed at Potsdam that Poland would occupy the territories until a final peace treaty with Germany.[8]

The Western Allies raised no objection to the Soviet Union's annexation of Belarus and Western Ukraine; the Polish government ceded the territories to the Soviet Union on August 16, 1945. Now Warsaw stood firmly behind the Yalta and Potsdam agreements as Poland's legal claim to the Oder-Neisse border.[9] The government turned its energies to the administration and development of the Western Territories,[10] in part to create a fait accompli before the Allies completed a German peace treaty.[11]

The KPD, like all the German political parties, was adamantly opposed to the new border. At first, the party avoided making public statements in the hope that the establishment of Leftist governments in Germany and Poland would aid a revision of the Oder-Neisse line. The KPD often referred to the Soviet zone as "Central Germany" *(Mitteldeutschland)*, with the implication that an "East Germany" was yet to be reclaimed from Poland. Such references elicited vehement protests from the Polish Military Mission in Berlin.[12]

The KPD was in a compromised position, of course, because its political patron, the Soviet Union, had drawn the border in the first place. The party organ *Deutsche Volkszeitung* (German People's Newspaper) avoided discussion of the border or conditions in the German territories lost to Poland. Several articles did appear about the German refugees who were pouring in from Poland and Czechoslovakia, but without mentioning that most had been expelled.[13]

The KPD tried to absolve itself and its working-class constituents of responsibility for the lost territories by arguing that Hitler, with the support of non-communist German elements, had gambled them away. Pieck, whose own hometown of Guben[14] on the Neisse River was now a divided city, blamed Hitler for the plight of the German refugees from

Poland: "We understand what it means when the German people in the east lose a piece of their land. There is no one who does not deeply regret that it was possible for Hitler to gamble criminally with the existence and the future of the German people."[15]

The KPD leaders hoped that a free exchange of goods between the former German territories and Germany was one way to make the new border irrelevant, but the Polish government was in no mood to cooperate. The PPR ignored requests from the KPD to deliver more goods from these territories. Ulbricht rejected the idea that Germany could not prosper within the new borders: however: "This is the old *(Lebensraum)* argument with which Hitler prepared the war. But from it came catastrophe for Germany; as a result of the war of conquest Hitler lost the territories east of the Oder and the Neisse forever."[16]

The KPD rejected Poland's historical claims to the territories; if the Allies decided to sign a final peace treaty with Germany, the party wanted to use this as an argument to call for a return of the territories to Germany. For the time being, the KPD wanted to leave historical claims out of it. *Deutsche Volkszeitung* wrote that "any reference to [Germany's] historical rights is senseless, because historical events have repeatedly shown that the main cause of the bloody wars of conquest has been the *'Drang nach Osten'* policy of German imperialists and militarists."[17]

The KPD's qualified acceptance of the new border with Poland did not reflect the opinion of most of the German communists and socialists in Germany, however. Social Democratic Party leader Otto Grotewohl was unequivocally opposed to the Oder-Neisse line; in August 1945 he told an SPD gathering in Leipzig that the border was provisional. When he angrily attacked the Polish government for its obdurate border and reparations policies, he charged that "the nationalistic demands of our eastern neighbor, Poland, have increased immeasurably."[18] Grotewohl, in rejecting Ulbricht's argument that Germany could live without this *Lebensraum* in the east, maintained that the lost territories were vital to the industrial and agricultural well-being of the country. He warned Soviet officials that the Oder-Neisse border would be the cause of a future Polish-German conflict, and would jeopardize the Soviet Union's long-term security.[19] Moscow saw things differently; as long as the Red Army occupied part of Germany, there was little possibility of another German war of aggression. At this point, the tension between the German and Polish communists made them that more dependent on the Soviet Union.

Poland's Claims to the Oder-Neisse Border

Most Poles supported the Oder-Neisse border, especially given the slim chance that Poland would recover its eastern territories.[20] Poles justified the acquisition of German land on moral, strategic, economic, and historic grounds. As a victim of German aggression and a victorious ally, the Poles regarded the German territories as just compensation for the human and material damage that Poland had suffered during the war. Polish officials argued that Germany's economic and military potential would be decisively weakened by ceding Silesia and Pomerania to Poland. These territories would also give Poland a stronger and more balanced agricultural and industrial economy.[21]

Polish officials were offended when the Germans, including German Leftists, suggested that Poland could not make efficient economic use of the German territories. The Germans often alleged that the slow economic development in the territories was typical of the "Polish economy," a pejorative term that Germans had long used to stereotype Polish backwardness, disorganization, and inefficiency.[22]

Poland's historical claim was founded on the presence of medieval Piast empire on both sides of the Oder River. Gomułka often referred to the Oder-Neisse line as the "new Piast border." A popular slogan in Poland after the war was *"Nad Odra-Nysa Łużycką—Byliśmy, Jesteśmy, Będziemy"* (On the Oder-Lusacian Neisse—we were, we are, and we will be).[23] In February 1945, *Głos Ludu* proclaimed that "Silesia was and will be Polish," adding that it was "the spirit of all Poland, the power of Poland."[24] Schoolteachers taught that towns such as Wrocław and Szczecin were originally Polish,[25] and the government alluded to Poland's historical rights by creating a new Ministry of Recovered Territories.[26]

The PPR even claimed that areas to the west of the Oder-Neisse border were inhabited by Slavs, not Germans. Writing in *Głos Ludu*, Stefania Osinska pointed out that when the Germans conquered the Oder-Neisse area in the tenth century, it was inhabited by Slavs known as Lusatian Sorbs. She estimated that there were about 275,000 Lusatian Sorbs living in the Soviet zone of Germany, and said that they had cheered the Polish army on its way to Berlin at the end of the war. Some had carried placards that read, "A Slav nation lives here, the Lusatian Sorbs." She exhorted Poles to remember their Slav kinsmen across the border: "Poland has regained its independence. Our brothers in the west beyond the Oder and Neisse remain in captivity."[27]

Poles not only supported the new western border, but most wanted the Germans out of Poland. At Yalta, Churchill initially objected to the forced removal of the Germans, but Stalin argued that most of them were fleeing from the advancing Red Army anyway. Churchill did not press the issue.[28] By removing the Germans as quickly as possible, the majority of them in the first year after the war, the Polish authorities made sure that Poland was not susceptible to German ethnic claims to the Western Territories.[29] The government immediately Polonized the area by resettling Polish refugees from the eastern territories.[30] Although estimates vary, by

1950 approximately 11,600,000 Germans had left Poland, 4,300,000 going to the Soviet zone; 3,800,000 to the British zone; 3,300,000 to the American zone; and 150,000 to the French zone.[31]

In September 1945, *Głos Ludu* wrote that "all Poland is of the opinion that there is no place for the Germans in these territories, and that they should be expelled from them as soon as possible." The newspaper even criticized the government for not deporting them faster.[32] Gomułka eschewed proletarian internationalism by declaring that "we must expel all the Germans because countries are built on national lines and not on multinational ones."[33] When he promised that no "enemy or foreign" elements would be allowed to live in Poland, he meant the Germans.[34]

The SED Rejects the Oder-Neisse Line

After the SED was formed in April 1946, the PPR hoped that Pieck and Ulbricht would prevail upon the party to recognize the Oder-Neisse border. But the SED adopted a position that more closely reflected Grotewohl's and the SPD's blunt revisionism. Although the SED could not promote national interests as openly as the Poles, the party's stubborn opposition to the new Polish-German border confirmed what the Polish communists feared the most—that the ghost of Rapallo and the Nazi-Soviet Pact would return in the form of a deal between the Stalin and the SED to revise the border in Germany's favor.

The SED's first manifest to the German people did not mention foreign policy or the Polish-German border.[35] In August, however, the SED declared that a communist German government that was untainted by the Nazi's crimes against Poland and that contributed to the reconstruction of Europe would be able to undo the unfortunate results of Hitler's war, namely, the loss of German territories to Poland.[36] The new organ of the SED, *Neues Deutschland*, made a deliberate reference to Pieck's birthplace to show that the SED sympathized with the refugees from Poland: "If the workers of Guben, in the spirit of strictest democracy, work with all their might for reconstruction, then they can hope that one day the part of the city of Guben on the other side of the Neisse will again be placed under German administration."[37]

Former SPD member Max Fechner, now deputy chairman of the SED, openly speculated that the Soviets would revise the Oder-Neisse border because Germany was more important to them than Poland.[38] The PPR was worried about Grotewohl's and Fechner's revisionism, which reflected the view of the majority SPD-wing of the SED.[39] When Fechner told a meeting of SED leaders that a Soviet officer had informed him the border would be revised in Germany's favor, Polish officials were incredulous that no one present had raised an objection.[40] The Polish Military

Mission in Berlin repeatedly attacked the SED for not recognizing the permanence of the Oder-Neisse border; the mission kept Warsaw well informed of the situation.[41]

The CDU in the Soviet zone[42] also went on record as opposing the Oder-Neisse line. In May, CDU Vice President Ernst Lemmer told the top officer at the Polish Military Mission, Jakub Prawin, that he supported a border that ran from the west of Kołobrzeg through the middle of Silesia, then to the east of Legnica to the Polish-Czechoslovak border. Lemmer thought that the disputed territory to the west of this line could be resolved in bilateral negotiations, but the Poles rejected the proposition outright.[43]

The SED indirectly challenged the Oder-Neisse line by objecting to a loss of German territory in the West. Shortly before their merger in April, the KPD and the SPD flatly rejected French proposals to sever the Rhein-Ruhr-Saar region from Germany. They joined the CDU and the LDP in issuing a statement calling for the integrity of Germany's western border as guaranteed in the Potsdam agreements.[44] Ulbricht contradicted his previous renunciation of *Lebensraum* in the east by defending Germany's 1937 border in the west: "Germany cannot live without the Ruhr, the Rheinland, and the Saar."[45] Pieck also told a Cologne audience that Germany should not lose more territory.[46] In August, the SED issued a statement supporting Germany's western border because Poland already occupied German territory. The party added that the Potsdam agreements did not sanction Poland's annexation of German lands.[47]

Polish officials thought that if the Western Allies moved Germany's western boundary eastward, justifying Poland's occupation of German territory would be easier. Foreign Minister Zygmunt Modzelewski argued that the reduction of German territory would contribute to the security of Europe by weakening Germany forever: "[Germany's] borders of peace run along the Oder and the Rhein."[48] Many French and Soviet officials agreed.

Pieck knew that the SED's revisionist stance was contributing to anti-Soviet sentiment in the zone, but he did little to stop it. The millions of refugees from the former German territories were a constant source of nationalist backlash. After visiting the British zone in early August, Pieck told *Neues Deutschland* that he saw great danger in appeals to nationalist sentiment, but he still left the door open for a revision of the Oder-Neisse line.[49] Bruno Koehler, the head of the SED's Central Press Service, told Prawin that the SED would do everything possible to represent the interests of the German people at a future peace conference. He added that his party recognized that Poland was developing socialism, in which case the border question would be less significant.[50]

Koehler was certainly not speaking for the German people or the majority of the SED membership. In August, SED functionary Walter Bartel warned Pieck of tendencies among party members to support "reactionary machinations" in regard to the Oder-Neisse question, and recommended that the SED leadership clarify the party's position.[51] But Pieck continued to hedge. Faced with a barrage of criticism from Kurt Schumacher's SPD that the SED was not doing enough to defend German interests, Pieck carefully formulated his call for a border revision in Marxist terms: Germany must "gain the trust of other nations by eliminating aggressive forces and through democratic [socialist] consolidation. Then the Allied powers will have understanding for the vital needs of our people when it comes to the final determination of the border."[52]

The SED leadership even hoped that the Soviets might change the Oder-Neisse line in connection with a return of Poland's eastern territories. Pieck and Grotewohl speculated that the Soviets would return the oil basin around Lwów to Poland and then revise the German-Polish border, but Stalin had no such plans. During a visit to Moscow in June, Stalin gave the Polish leadership assurances that Poland's borders were permanent, in part because of the ethnic faits accomplis created by the expulsion of Germans from the Western Territories, and the resettlement there of Poles from Belarus and Ukraine. Stalin told the Poles that the Oder-Neisse border was "entirely settled." Nonetheless, Polish officials wondered why the Soviet occupation authorities were not censoring the SED's revisionist statements.[53]

The Soviets knew that if the SED was forced to recognize the border, the party's chances at the polls would be hurt. During the election campaign in the Soviet zone in the fall of 1946, the SED joined the other German parties in making open appeals for a revision of the Oder-Neisse border.[54] At a gathering of SED functionaries on September 10, Fechner repeated what he and Grotewohl had said many times before: The eastern border was "only provisional."[55] According to the Polish Military Mission, Fechner and other SPD elements in the SED had convinced Pieck to adopt a clearer revisionist stance. Previously, Pieck had been more circumspect in his statements about the border, but now he rejected the Oder-Neisse line outright. He told the SED youth organization, Free German Youth (FDJ), "After the SED gains the complete trust [of the Soviets], the Soviet administration will retract the Oder and Neisse border and return to Germany those areas that are really German. . . . The SED has certain information that this will happen."[56]

On September 6, the SED received indirect support for a border revision when U.S. Secretary of State James Byrnes declared in a speech in Stuttgart that Germany's borders would not be determined until the Allies had signed a peace treaty with Germany. Churchill had already declared his opposition to Poland's western border in his "Iron Curtain" speech in May, which Gomułka had condemned as "encouragement for

German imperialism."[57] Now Byrnes' statement found echo throughout the SED's campaign. In a stump speech in Schwerin, Pieck contended that the "final settlement" meant a border revision in Germany's favor.[58] At rallies in Guben and Cottbus on September 13, he reiterated that once Germany had developed a "democratic" character, in other words a socialist government led by the SED, the Allies might revise the border.[59] In Berlin two weeks later, Grotewohl declared that "recently the position of the SED on the eastern border has been clearly and definitively laid out. . . . The SED is fighting for a sensible settlement of all borders and the unity of Germany."[60]

Grotewohl even speculated that the differences between the occupying powers might cause the Soviets to move the border in Germany's favor.[61] Fechner continued to rail against the "provisional" border, promising that the SED would oppose a reduction in German territory at the peace conference.[62]

The PPR organ *Głos Ludu* immediately ran a series of angry denunciations of Byrnes and the German parties who supported a revision of the Oder-Neisse border, including the SED. On September 7, *Głos Ludu* ran a huge front page headline that read, "Byrnes Defends Germany: Attack on Poland's Right to the Recovered Territories."[63] Successive issues condemned the enthusiastic German reaction to Byrnes' speech. The newspaper appealed to the other Slavic countries to protect Poland's interests, even making the dubious claim that the Oder-Neisse border was essential for "all Slavs." And as if to remind readers of Germany's imperialist past, *Głos Ludu* referred to Germany as the "Reich" (*Rzesza*). No mention was ever made of solidarity with the German communists or the German working class.[64]

Polish leaders squelched the notion that Poland would give up one inch of the Western Territories. President Bolesław Bierut stated unequivocally that the "recovered territories on the Oder, Neisse, and Baltic are Polish now and will always be Polish."[65] Gomułka announced that the "Slavic" border in the west was final, reiterating that Poland had a historical right to the area. He remarked bitterly that "Poland no longer wants to be a soccer ball that is kicked around from place to place." Despite Gomułka's intention to develop socialism in Poland on his own terms, he called for close relations with the Soviet Union as the sole guarantor of the Oder-Neisse border.[66] Władysław Bieńkowski, one of Gomułka's close confidants in the PPR, branded Germany as Poland's "mortal enemy"; concerning Poland's foreign policy, he warned, "Our friends will be judged by their relations to Germany." The PPS declared that if the great powers stood on the side of Germany in the border issue, all Poland would unite against them.[67]

Poles across the political spectrum joined in censuring Byrnes, even the opposition Polish Peasant Party (PSL), which had the diplomatic support of the United States. A PSL member of the Polish National Council put it this way: "Whoever is with the Germans is against us, be it Byrnes, Churchill, or anyone else."[68]

Polish officials were shaken by Byrnes' remarks and disappointed by Pieck's frank revisionism; they were baffled by the failure of the Soviet occupation authorities' to stop the SED's propaganda. No consistent policy was coming from the Soviet Military Administration in Germany (SMAG), although some Soviet officers acknowledged that the SED's nationalist appeals were crossing the line. Colonel S. I. Tiul'panov reported to Moscow that allowing the SED to lobby for a border change was a risky policy: "We run the danger of allowing the party to revert to extreme nationalism."[69]

The Soviets tried to reassure the Poles that the border was final. Soviet Foreign Minister Vyacheslaw Molotov said that the Polish administration of the German areas east of the Oder-Neisse Rivers had been sanctioned at Potsdam, and that it was a fait accompli that had little chance of being reversed at a future peace conference. He repeated that it would be cruel to resettle the 2 million Germans who had moved out of these territories and the 1 million Poles who had moved in. Molotov concluded that "all that remains is to wish the Polish friends success in their huge reconstruction efforts in the Western Territories."[70]

Molotov's statement had no impact on blunting the SED's revisionism, however. Although Soviet officials in Germany told the Poles that they did not support the SED's position, they made no move to stop it. Aware that the SED's chances at the polls would suffer if the party recognized the border, the Soviets tolerated this propaganda, even though it was contributing to a growing animosity between the SED and the PPR. As long as Soviet troops remained in Germany and the Soviet Union controlled the political fate of both communist parties, this duplicitous policy served Soviet interests in consolidating political control of the zone.[71]

When the SED received only 20 percent of the vote in the elections in Berlin, where the party had to compete with the SPD and the other parties from the Western zones, Polish officials pointed out that the SED's nationalist appeals and revisionism had failed miserably.[72] They warned that the SED's propaganda was exacerbating old German nationalist prejudices. *Głos Ludu* criticized the SED for succumbing to "German chauvinist pressure"[73] and for its "shameful solidarity with the revisionist campaign." The newspaper admonished the SED for misleading the German working class, and cautioned the party not to become "a tool of a resurrected German imperialism."[74] The Polish Military Mission even concluded that the SPD, better than the SED, understood that blatant national appeals would ultimately hurt Germany's chances for a border revision.[75]

The SED's nationalist propaganda also estranged the party from the other communist parties in Eastern Europe. In early 1947, the Polish Foreign Ministry noted that the SED remained isolated, and that especially the Czechoslovak and Yugoslav communist parties were critical of the East German communists.[76] *Głos Ludu* published numerous articles about Yugoslavia and Czechoslovakia and their support for the Oder-Neisse border, but virtually ignored political developments in the Soviet zone. In 1947, the newspaper still excluded the SED from the socialist camp, publishing such headlines as "All Slavdom Stands in Defense of Poland's Western Border."[77]

Caught between the dictates of the Soviet occupiers and the demands of the German people, the SED had no way out of its political bind. Schumacher's SPD attacked the SED relentlessly for being "too little German" in fighting for Germany's 1937 borders.[78] Even the KPD, which was still operating in the Western zones, encouraged the SED to pressure the Soviets for a border revision.[79] And the SED's partner parties in the Soviet zone, the LDP and the CDU, maintained their openly revisionist positions.[80]

Polish diplomats understood the SED's dilemma, but nonetheless insisted that the party recognize the existing border. In April 1947, Prawin informed Modzelewski that if the SED took this position it would lose union support in Berlin to the SPD.[81] Modzelewski criticized the Polish press for exaggerating the possibility of losing the Western Territories, and for poisoning relations with the Germans. At a press conference in November 1946, a reporter asked Modzelewski about the final delineation of the border around Świnoujście. Modzelewski replied that an international committee was studying small changes in the border, but refused further comment. Another reporter drew parallels between the current status of Świnoujście and Szczecin with the precarious geopolitical position of Gdańsk and Westerplatte in the interwar period, reminding Modzelewski that German agitation for the return of Gdańsk was the pretext for attacking Poland in 1939. Modzelewski said that moving the border about five kilometers in Poland's favor was likely, but he refused to elaborate.[82]

The SED Officially Recognizes the Oder-Neisse Border

The Soviet occupation authorities at last began to clamp down on the SED's overt revisionism in 1947. Pieck, Ulbricht, and Grotewohl visited Stalin and Molotov in Moscow in January to ask for small corrections in the Oder-Neisse line, but Stalin gave them an unqualified "no."[83] Vladimir Semjonov, the political adviser to the SMAG, told Prawin that the "SED's unclear position on the Polish-German border matter protracted a crisis in the SED as well as impeded the possibility of developing closer relations between the SED and the PPR." Semjonov and Prawin agreed to warn the SED of the dangers of another world war if they retained illusions of revising the border.[84] In February, the Polish

Military Mission reported that Pieck, Ulbricht, and even Grotewohl were now moving toward "the right attitude in the border matter."[85] *Głos Ludu*, which had been notably critical of Grotewohl, quoted him as saying that the Potsdam agreements delineating Germany's border with Poland "form a good basis for the future peace treaty."[86]

The first face-to-face meeting between Polish army officers in the Polish Military Mission and SED leaders took place at the mission on February 28, 1947. Prawin wrote Warsaw that the Germans expected the Poles to have a "rigid hatred" of them, but were surprised by the Poles' invitation and the officers' openness and hospitality. Prawin added that the Germans were especially grateful for the meeting because up to that point their only contact with foreign officials had been with the Soviet occupation authorities. The East Germans viewed the meeting as an opportunity to end the SED's isolation from the other communist parties.[87] Paul Merker cautioned, however, that until the two sides had developed greater personal trust, they should refrain from discussing substantive issues. One Polish officer was unconvinced that the Germans' passive attitude was sincere, but believed it an unwillingness to discuss the Oder-Neisse border.[88]

The Polish officers were most interested in gleaning the Germans' candid opinions about that very issue. The Poles knew that even if the SED leaders publicly accepted the loss of German territory to Poland as a war reparation, in private they still believed the loss was a temporary situation.[89] Prawin told Ulbricht in no uncertain terms that the SED's revisionism, no matter what the reason, had to be abandoned: "The German people's chauvinism finds its reflection in the political line of the party [SED], making cooperation between our parties impossible. What is worse, the SED position does not aim to cure the German people, but exacerbates its chauvinist sickness." Ulbricht conceded that the SED's present position was tactical. He pointed out that the SPD and other parties had defeated the SED in the Berlin elections by relentlessly criticizing the SED for not demanding a border change from the Soviet occupiers. He added that if the SED recognized the border now, and then the Allies agreed to elections for an all-German government, the party would be saddled with an unpopular position. Prawin had no sympathy for this line of thinking.[90]

The SED hoped for a definitive decision on Germany's political future and the Oder-Neisse border at the conference of Allied foreign ministers in Moscow in April 1947. Shortly before the meeting, Franz Dahlem declared that "the final delineation of the border, whether the border should run east or west of the Neisse, is still open. . . . The SED is as little responsible as any other German party for the eastern border that was decided in 1944."[91]

But by this time cooperation between the Soviet Union and the Western Allies in the Allied Control Commission was breaking down. The

United States and Great Britain responded to the Soviets' reparations policy and refusal to send promised foodstuffs to the Western zones by creating the Bizone in January 1947. Two months later, U.S. President Harry Truman decided to aid the anti-communist governments in Turkey and Greece, laying the groundwork for the emerging U.S. policy of containing Soviet expansionism. The foreign ministers' meeting in Moscow failed to reach an agreement on Germany; in July the Soviets rejected the Marshall Plan, which included the controversial reconstruction of the Western zones of Germany. As the Allied positions hardened that spring, a final settlement on Germany seemed remote.

Relations between the SED and the PPR appeared to be improving. For the first time, Polish officials promoted the idea that there were some "progressive" Germans, namely, the German communists. In April, Gomułka told *Głos Ludu* that "all of the German parties are continuing the spirit of fascism and imperialism among the Germans, *except the SED*." Gomułka stopped short of praising the party for recognizing the Oder-Neisse border, which it had not yet done, but said that the SED was the only party that was not actively campaigning against it.[92] On May Day 1947, *Głos Ludu* ran an editorial applauding several SED leaders for stating that they rejected border changes. The newspaper called this a sign that the SED now understood that recognizing the Oder-Neisse border was an "indispensable platform for strengthening the democratic [socialist] forces in Germany."[93]

But Pieck was still performing a delicate balancing act between the Polish and Soviet demands on the one hand, and the national interests of the SED membership and the Soviet zone population on the other. Most East Germans rejected the Oder-Neisse border outright. In May, Prawin told Pieck that his government was disappointed in the SED's persistent and opportunistic use of the border issue. He asked the SED leader whether there was truth to the rumor that the SED, in meetings with the Soviets in Moscow, had proposed a border change. Although Stalin and Molotov had told Pieck in January that there would be no changes in the border, Pieck now told Prawin that there might be some very small border rectifications in Germany's favor, but no major ones. Once again, Prawin left the meeting disappointed.[94]

The debate over the Oder-Neisse line continued to rage within the SED. In July, the Polish Ministry of Public Security reported that both the SPD and KPD wings of the party thought it was time the SED took a "concrete, clear, and precise position in reference to the eastern border." The old SPDers still maintained, according to the ministry, that "the land [beyond the Oder-Neisse] was German and that the Germans [there] had been wronged." Pieck and the other former KPD leaders were more realistic; lacking support from the Soviet Union, Pieck now sought to smooth relations with Poland by recognizing the border essentially as it was.[95]

At the SED congress in September, Grotewohl declared that his position in favor of a border revision had not changed, and that the present border was unjust because it had been drawn "without the participation and consent of any prominent leaders of German society." To gain support in local and zonal elections, Grotewohl called for a "tough position" in favor of revising the border. For tactical reasons, Grotewohl supported the payment of reparations for the war, but then argued that Germany could better afford to pay them if the Allies returned the German territories.[96]

In January 1948, the French linked their occupation zone with the British and American zones to form the Trizone. The Soviets walked out of the Allied Control Commission in March, and, in response to a currency reform in the Western zones in June, they blockaded the land routes from the Western zones to Berlin. The unification of Germany appeared to be a remote possibility, and the SED became more confident that the Soviets would continue to support the party's grip on power in the zone. The SED's immediate political future no longer depended on popular support.

Although it is unclear to what extent the Soviets pressured the SED to accept the Oder-Neisse line, the SED leadership undoubtedly drew its own conclusions from the breakdown of Allied cooperation in Germany.[97] The SED cast its lot with the other East European communist parties, which, after the Czechoslovak communist coup in February, controlled all the governments in the region. The SED had to accept the present border as final.[98] At the Second Peoples' Congress in Berlin in March 1948, Pieck declared that "the Polish-German border would not undergo any changes." Now Grotewohl agreed as well. The Polish Military Mission reported that some of the leaders from the SED's partner parties, such as Otto Nuschke (CDU) and Wilhelm Külz (LDP), made similar statements supporting the Oder-Neisse line, but without Pieck's "decisive tone."[99]

In May 1948, Georgi Dertinger, who led the CDU in the Soviet zone, told the Polish Military Mission that the leaders of his party understood that the border issue was settled. He suggested, however, that it would be easier for the German people to accept the loss of the territories if the Poles delivered agricultural goods to the German people, and especially to the Soviet zone. Mission officers informed Dertinger that if the CDU publicly declared its support of the Oder-Neisse border, the Polish people would not be opposed to trade with Germany.[100]

During meetings of the Soviet bloc foreign ministers in Warsaw in June 1948, the Polish delegation demanded that the SED accept the Oder-Neisse border, and promised that trade with the Soviet zone would then follow.[101] Franz Dahlem assured them that the SED was not considering changes in the border agreed upon at Potsdam.[102] Much to the Poles' satisfaction, the foreign ministers issued a declaration stating that the Oder-Neisse border was "immovable" and a "frontier of peace."[103]

In July, *Głos Ludu* reported that the SED had at last recognized the border.[104] On September 30, the newspaper carried a huge front page headline that read, "Walter Ulbricht Confirms: There Cannot Be Any Discussion about a Revision of the Oder-Neisse."[105] Ulbricht used the Polish formulation that the Oder-Neisse line was the "border of peace";[106] he called the lost territories a center of twentieth-century German aggressive wars against Poland: "As Germans we cannot deny that twice in the last 25 years Germany attacked Poland from the pincers of East Prussia and Silesia. The cause was the dominance of the reactionary forces in Germany, which had particularly strong support in East Prussia and Silesia."[107]

Overt revisionism was still rampant in the SED, however. At a workshop for East German journalists at the Brandenburg SED Party School, one reporter pointed out that "Comrade Pieck declared in 1945, and again in 1946, that the last word had not been spoken in regard to the Oder-Neisse border. . . . Why do you [the SED leadership] suddenly say that the decision is final?" Another journalist asked why Germans had been stripped of their possessions and summarily expelled from Poland after the war. One reporter stated out loud what the SED could not say in public; namely, that the SED's recognition of the Oder-Neisse border was temporary and tactical: "Well, of course today we cannot do anything else, today we have to swallow it, but sometime in the future, when we become stronger, this border will not be maintained."[108]

This kind of talk made Polish officials jittery; with East-West tensions on the rise, they did not rule out the possibility that the Soviets would make a deal with the SED to change the border. In 1948, the Polish Foreign Ministry investigated a rumor circulating in the Western zones that the Soviets intended to force the Poles to give up Silesia between the Neisse and the Oder and thus return Wrocław (Breslau) to Germany.[109] Although the rumor was groundless, Ulbricht told a Polish diplomat that he disagreed with the Polish argument that the former German territories were economically indispensable to Poland but unimportant for Germany. The diplomat reported that when he suggested that such an economic argument could be used to justify German claims to the Western Territories, "Ulbricht indignantly rejected such an interpretation." Ulbricht cited his many statements that the border was final. He acknowledged that although the SED had succeeded in eliminating the most dangerous elements from the party, many "reactionaries in masked forms" remained. As for Grotewohl's persistent revisionism, Ulbricht assured the Poles that Grotewohl could no longer count on the support of his old comrades from the SPD in the central organs of the SED. Ulbricht pointed out, for instance, that Fechner had been demoted from deputy chairman of the SED to the lesser position of president of the Central Administration of Justice.[110]

Much to the dismay of Polish officials, however, the East German communists did not rule out a border revision. In November 1948, the SED proposed a peace treaty that would unify Berlin and establish one central, democratic German government.[111] Although the resolution called for a treaty based on the Yalta and Potsdam agreements, which recognized Polish administration of the German territories east of the Oder-Neisse border, the border was not directly mentioned.[112] In May 1949, Nuschke, now chairman of the CDU, told a French newspaper that "Germany and Poland . . . must work together in all areas. The problem of their borders must be settled in the same spirit of freedom loving cooperation."[113]

The Polish government did not consider the Polish-German border a "problem"; it refused to resolve other political or economic issues with the Soviet zone until the SED formally recognized the border. The SED leadership no longer tolerated open revisionism in the party in 1949, although many members remained unreconciled to the border.[114] At the SED Party Congress in January, Pieck said that recognition of the border was a prerequisite for German-Polish understanding.[115] On January 26, *Trybuna Ludu*, the new organ of the PZPR, covered Pieck's statement and his promise to cooperate with the other countries in Eastern Europe, especially Poland. The newspaper observed that the audience reaction to Pieck's statement was "especially warm" and that "the SED shows Germany the way to peaceful cooperation with Poland."[116] In February, the Polish political journal *Nowe Drogi* quoted Pieck as saying that "recognition of the border on the Oder and Neisse as the border of peace and the fight against all revisionist influences are the first conditions for understanding with the Polish nation."[117]

The SED was gradually gaining a modicum of trust from the Polish communists. *Trybuna Ludu*'s Berlin correspondent, Stanisław Brodzki, declared that the SED's recognition of the border in the face of opposition from the other German parties was "a courageous political act."[118] In July 1949, the Polish Military Mission praised the SED for its hard work in promoting the Oder-Neisse border as a matter of world peace, in contrast to the continued revisionism of the political parties operating in the Western zones.[119]

The Poles still had lingering doubts about the SED's sudden change of heart, however, because they suspected that the Soviets had ordered an end to the SED's revisionism. They were fully aware that many SED members did not accept the party's official position. To further consolidate control over the former German territories and preclude a change in the border, the Polish government dissolved the Ministry of Recovered Territories at the end of 1948 and formally integrated the territories into the Polish state.

When the Federal Republic of Germany was formed in September 1949, and preparations for an East German state were underway, once again the Polish government feared the Western Allies would renounce the Potsdam agreements. Warsaw sent the Allies a diplomatic note emphasizing that the Potsdam agreements provided the basis for the security of Europe, and that Poland supported the political and economic unity of Germany. The demarche brought no response.[120] The Polish-German border remained a recurring source of friction between the Poles and East Germans long after the creation of the GDR in October and its formal recognition of the Oder-Neisse line in 1950.

Notes

1. Władysław Gomułka, *O problemie Niemieckim* (On the German problem) (Warsaw: Książka i Wiedza, 1971), p. 105.

2. Rosa Luxemburg, *Gesammelte Werke: Band 1: 1893 bis 1905* (Collected Works: Volume 1: 1893 to 1905) (Berlin: Dietz Verlag, 1990), pp. 50–51.

3. Pieck letter to the Poles, undated, ca. September, 1922, SED ZK, Wilhelm Pieck Papers, NL 36/536; see Peter Wozniak, "Blut, Erz, Kohle: A Thematic Examination of German Propaganda on the Silesian Question During the Interwar Years," *East European Quarterly* 28, no. 3 (September 1994), p. 323. One of the Polish nationalist slogans was, "Whoever is stupid as a fool, votes yes for the Germans on Sunday."

4. Pieck speech to the Prussian State Parliament, October 4, 1922, SED ZK, Wilhelm Pieck Papers, NL 36/386.

5. Wilhelm Pieck, *Gesammelte Reden und Schriften. Band II: Januar 1920 bis April 1925* (Collected speeches and writings. Volume II: January 1920 to April 1925) (Berlin: Dietz Verlag, 1959).

6. Franz Sikora, *Sozialistische Solidarität und nationale Interessen* (Socialist solidarity and national interests) (Cologne: Verlag Wissenschaft und Politik, 1977), p. 106.

7. Wacław Barcikowski memo from the Legal Commission of the Settlers' Committee in Olsztyn, ca. spring, 1945, PZPR KC, Bolesław Bierut Archive, 254/IV-1.

8. The peace treaty between Germany and the Allies was finally signed in 1990.

9. See Article IX of the Potsdam Agreement. The Oder-Neisse border remained in legal limbo until a reunited Germany recognized the border in 1990.

10. The term *Western Territories* will be used to denote the German territories of 1937 east of the Oder and Neisse Rivers.

11. Legal opinion by Dr. Bolesław Walewski, September, 1945, PZPR KC, Bolesław Bierut Archive, 254/IV-1.

12. *Deutsche Volkszeitung* (German People's Newspaper), March 21, 1946, p. 2. The headline on this day read "Central Germany Greets Wilhelm Pieck."

13. See *Deutsche Volkszeitung*, October 17, 1945, p. 2; and August 4, 1945, pp. 1–3.

14. The German half of the city was later renamed Wilhelm Pieck Stadt.

15. Henry Krisch, "Vorstellungen von künftiger aussenpolitischer Orientierung in der SBZ bis 1947 und ihre Auswirkungen auf die spätere Aussenpolitik der DDR (Concepts of the future foreign policy orientation in the Soviet occupation zone to 1947)," in Hans Adolf Jacobsen, Gerd Leptin, Ulrich Scheuner, and Eberhard Schulz, eds., *Drei Jahrzehnte Aussenpolitik der DDR* (Three decades of the foreign policy of the GDR) (Munich: R. Oldenbourg Verlag, 1979), p. 48.

16. Walter Ulbricht, *Die Entwicklung des deutschen volksdemokratischen Staates, 1945–1958* (The development of the German Peoples' democratic state, 1945–1958) (Berlin: Dietz Verlag, 1961), p. 25.

17. *Deutsche Volkszeitung*, August 7, 1945, p. 1.

18. Quoted in Sikora, *Sozialistische Solidarität und nationale Interessen*, p. 107.

19. Krisch, "Vorstellungen von künftiger aussenpolitischer Orientierung in der SBZ bis 1947 und ihre Auswirkungen auf die spätere Aussenpolitik der DDR," pp. 43–45.

20. See Sarah Terry, *Poland's Place in Europe: General Sikorski and the Origins of the Oder-Neisse Line, 1939–1943* (Princeton: Princeton University Press, 1983). Evidence shows that Władysław Sikorski, head of the Polish government-in-exile in London until his death in 1943, understood that if the Germans lost the war the Soviet Union would probably annex the eastern territories of interwar Poland, and therefore he supported the Oder-Western Neisse border for Poland.

21. See Hans Georg Lehmann, *Der Oder-Neisse-Konflikt* (The Oder-Neisse conflict) (Munich: C. H. Beck, 1979), p. 41. The Polish delegation at Potsdam pointed out that the area lost in the east was larger than the Western Territories. The area of prewar Poland was 388,000 square kilometers, and postwar Poland was approximately 309,000 square kilometers.

22. Prawin to the Polish Foreign Ministry, September 24, 1946, MSZ, 6/668/42.

23. Letter from Stefan Krzywicki to Jan Izydorczyk, November 1, 1959, PZPR KC, group Izydorczyk 473/29.

24. *Głos Ludu*, February 21, 1945, p. 3.

25. Memorandum from the President's Office of the Council of Ministers to Władysław Ferenc, June 5, 1946, URM PB, file 70.

26. Władysław Gomułka headed this ministry.

27. *Głos Ludu*, July 29, 1946, p. 7. Jakob Kaiser of the CDU asserted that only a few thousand Lusatian Sorbs were living in Germany. The true number was about 70,000; see Gerald Stone, *The Smallest Slavonic Nation: The Sorbs of Lusatia* (London: The Athlone Press, 1972), p. 184.

28. See Diane Clemens, *Yalta* (New York: Oxford University Press, 1970), p. 193.

29. Dr. Bolesław Walewski to the PPR, September, 1945, PZPR KC, Bolesław Bierut Archive, 254/IV–1Z; Anthony Kruszewski, *The Oder-Neisse Boundary and Poland's Modernization: The Socioeconomic and Political Impact* (New York: Praeger Publishers, 1972), p. 16. Kruszewski points out that the most of the 7.6 million Germans who had lived in the territories now occupied by Poland left before being expelled; see also Phillip Bühler, *The Oder-Neisse Line: A Reappraisal under International Law* (Boulder: East European Monographs, 1990), p. 104. According to Bühler, approximately 4 million Germans from Poland first settled in the Soviet zone of Germany.

30. See Lehmann, *Der Oder-Neisse-Konflikt*, p. 57. According to Lehmann, the Polish government's territorial aims went beyond the Oder-Neisse border to a line 30 miles west of the Oder.

31. Bolesław Wiewióra, *The Polish-German Frontier from the Standpoint of International Law* (Poznań: Wydawnictwo Zachodnie, 1959), pp. 133–134; and Norman Naimark, *The Russians in Germany: A History of the Soviet Zone of Occupation, 1945–1949* (Cambridge: Harvard University Press, 1995), p. 149.

32. *Głos Ludu*, September 16, 1945, p. 3.

33. Quoted in Naimark, *The Russians in Germany*, p. 146.

34. *Głos Ludu*, January 1, 1946, pp. 12–13.

35. SED manifest to the German people, April 22, 1946, PZPR KC, group PPR KC, 295/XX–70.

36. "The SED and the Eastern Question," unsigned, August 12, 1946, SED ZK, Wilhelm Pieck Papers, NL 36/743.

37. *Neues Deutschland*, May 7, 1946, p. 2.

38. Polish Military Mission report, May 2, 1946, MSZ, 6/671/42.

39. *Głos Ludu*, September 24, 1947, p. 1. According to SED figures, about 700,000 (47 percent) of the 1,295,000 party members were from the KPD, the rest from the SPD.

40. Information on the SED's position on the eastern border of Germany, July 30, 1946, PZPR KC, group PPR KC, 295/VII–69.

41. Prawin report of meeting with Arthur Pieck, April 23, 1946, MSZ, 6/668/42.

42. The CDU was one of the SED's coalition partners in the National Front, along with the Liberal Democratic Party (LDP), the National Democratic Party of Germany (NDPD), and the Democratic Peasants' Party of Germany (DBD).

43. Prawin report of a meeting with representatives of the German cultural community, May 19, 1946, MSZ, 6/668/42.

44. *Deutsche Volkszeitung*, April 9, 1946, p. 2. Pieck signed for the KPD, Grotewohl for the SPD, Jakub Kaiser for the CDU, and Wilhelm Külz for the LDP.

45. Ulbricht quoted in Krisch, "Vorstellungen von künftiger aussenpolitischer Orientierung in der SBZ bis 1947 und ihre Auswirkungen auf die spätere Aussenpolitik der DDR," p. 48.

46. *Głos Ludu*, August 27, 1946, p. 2.

47. "The SED and the Eastern Question," unsigned, August 12, 1946, SED ZK, Wilhelm Pieck Papers, NL 36/743.

48. *Głos Ludu*, April 30, 1946, p. 4.

49. *Neues Deutschland*, August 6, 1946, p. 3; see also PPR memo, unsigned, undated, PZPR KC, group PPR KC, 295/VII–70.

50. Special report by Prawin, September 24, 1946, MSZ, 6/668/42.

51. Bartel notes for Wilhelm Pieck, August 15, 1946, SED ZK, Wilhelm Pieck Papers, NL 36/743.

52. PPR memo, undated, unsigned, PZPR KC, group PPR KC, 295/VII–70.

53. Chromecki notes of meeting between Foreign Minister Olszewski and Garreau (French Ambassador to Poland), September 5, 1946, PZPR KC, group PPR KC, 295/VII–264.

54. Polish Military Mission report, September 24, 1946, MSZ, 6/668/42.

55. Special report by Prawin, September 24, 1946, MSZ, 6/668/42.

56. Polish Military Mission report, September 2, 1946, MSZ, 6/671/42.

57. Gomułka, *O problemie Niemieckim*, p. 99. See Lehmann, *Der Oder-Neisse-Konflikt*, pp. 70–109, for a thorough discussion of the Western Allies' deliberations on the Polish-German border.

58. *Neues Deutschland*, September 14, 1946, p. 1.

59. Speech by Wilhelm Pieck, September 13, 1946, Wilhelm Pieck Papers, NL 36/743.

60. *Neues Deutschland*, October 1, 1946, p. 1.

61. Polish Military Mission report, October 1, 1946, MSZ, 6/671/42; Krisch, "Vorstellungen von künftiger aussenpolitischer Orientierung in der SBZ bis 1947 und ihre Auswirkungen auf die spätere Aussenpolitik der DDR," p. 43; see also Naimark, *The Russians in Germany*, p. 288. Naimark states that "the Soviets dismissed Grotewohl's resistance to acceptance of the finality of the Oder-Neisse border with Poland as a sign of his petit bourgeois past."

62. *Neues Deutschland*, September 14, 1946, p. 1.

63. *Głos Ludu*, September 7, 1946, pp. 1–2. The newspaper devoted its first two pages to attacks on Byrnes' speech.

64. *Głos Ludu*, September 8, 1946, p. 3; and *Głos Ludu*, September 10, 1946, p. 2.

65. Stenographic Records of the National People's Council (KRN), September 20, 1946, p. 14.

66. Gomułka, *O problemie Niemieckim*, pp. 99, 112, 114.

67. Stenographic Records of the National People's Council (KRN), September 22, 1946, pp. 290, 349.

68. Stenographic Records of the National People's Council (KRN), September 22, 1946, p. 302.

69. S. Tiul'panov report, September 16, 1946, *Bulletin: Cold War International History Project,* no. 4 (1994), p. 32; see also Gaddis, *We Now Know*, p. 119.

70. *Neues Deutschland*, September 18, 1946, p. 1.

71. Special report by Prawin, September 24, 1946, MSZ, 6/668/42.

72. The Social Democrats received 49 percent of the vote in Berlin. In the rest of the zone, where the SPD was not active, the SED won 47 percent of the vote.

73. *Głos Ludu*, October 13, 1946, p. 4.

74. *Głos Ludu*, October 29, 1946, p. 3.

75. Polish Military Mission report, November 9, 1946, MSZ, 6/671/42.

76. Notes on the SED in Berlin, January 3, 1947, MSZ, 6/711/46.

77. *Głos Ludu*, February 9, 1947, p. 4.

78. H. Meller report (Polish Military Mission), March 18, 1947, PZPR KC, group PPR KC, 295/XX–72.

79. Article in the *Westdeutsches Volks-Echo* (West German People's Echo), March 4, 1947, in SED ZK, Wilhelm Pieck Papers, NL 36/743.

80. See J. Marecki notes of meeting with Arthur Leutenant, February 28, 1947, PZPR KC, group PPR KC, 295/XX–70.

81. Prawin to Modzelewski, April 17, 1947, MSZ, 6/711/46.

82. Press conference with Modzelewski, November 18, 1946, MSZ, 15/230/22.

83. Naimark, *The Russians in Germany*, p. 301.

84. Prawin notes of a meeting with Semjonov, February 8, 1947, MSZ, 6/699/45.

85. Prawin to Olszewski, February 18, 1947, MSZ, 6/711/46.

86. *Głos Ludu*, February 16, 1947, p. 2.

87. Prawin to Modzelewski, March 4, 1947, MSZ, 6/711/46.

88. Przebój-Jarecki notes of a meeting with German politicians, March 1, 1947, MSZ, 6/711/46.

89. Ibid.

90. Meller notes of a meeting between Ulbricht and Prawin, March 15, 1947, PZPR KC, group PPR KC, 295/XX–70; see also Wiesław Dobrzycki, *Granica Zachodnia w polityce polskiej 1944–1947* (The western border in Polish politics, 1944–1947) (Warsaw: Państwowe Wydawnictwo Naukowe, 1974), p. 188. Dobrzycki writes that the SED did not recognize the Oder-Neisse border for domestic political reasons, fearing that the other German parties would label the SED the "party of capitulation."

91. *Neues Deutschland*, April 2, 1947, p. 1; see also Sikora, Sozialistische Solidärität und nationale Interessen, p. 108; and Naimark, *The Russians in Germany*, p. 302.

92. *Głos Ludu*, April 21, 1947, p. 1.

93. *Głos Ludu*, May 1, 1947, p. 6.

94. Meller notes of meeting between Pieck and Prawin, May 2, 1947, PZPR KC, group PPR KC, 295/XX–70. At this meeting Pieck mentioned the island of Uznam near Świnoujście for a possible border revision.

95. Ministry of Public Security to Berman, July 16, 1947, PZPR KC, group PPR KC, 295/VII–72.

96. Report on Grotewohl's speech to the Sixth Plenum of the SED Central Committee, undated, PZPR KC, group PPR KC, 295/XX–3.

97. See Ralf Badstübner, "Die sowjetische Deutschlandpolitik im Lichte neuer Quellen" (The Soviet policy toward Germany in light of new sources), in Wilfried Loth, ed., *Die Deutschland Frage in der Nachkriegszeit* (The German question in the post-war period) (Berlin: Akademie Verlag, 1994), pp. 114–123.

98. "Agricultural Policy in the New Poland," from the SED Press Service, May 11, 1948, SED ZK, Otto Grotewohl Papers, NL 90/483.

99. Prawin to the Polish Foreign Ministry, undated, ca. March, 1948, MSZ, 6/767/54.

100. Meller notes of a meeting with Dertinger, May 14, 1948, MSZ, 6/767/54.

101. *Neues Deutschland*, June 27, 1948, p. 3.

102. Notes on the German press, undated, ca. June 1948, PZPR KC, group PPR KC, 295/XX–3; see also Gottfried Zeiger, *Die Haltung von SED und DDR zur Einheit Deutschlands, 1949–1987* (The attitude of the SED and the GDR toward the unification of Germany, 1949–1989) (Cologne: Verlag Wissenschaft u. Politik, 1988), p. 14.

103. Viktoria Vierheller, *Polen und die Deutschland-Frage 1939–1949* (Poland and the German question, 1939–1949) (Cologne: Verlag Wissenschaft und Politik, 1970), p. 140.

104. *Głos Ludu*, July 16, 1948, p. 2.

105. *Głos Ludu*, September 30, 1948, p. 1.

106. Meller to the Polish Foreign Ministry, October 29, 1948, PZPR KC, group PPR KC, 295/XX–70. Ulbricht called it the *"Friedensgrenze."*

107. Walter Ulbricht, "The Foundations of German-Polish Friendship," ca. January, 1949, MSZ, 10/470/49.

108. Georg Kraus notes, October 26, 1948, SED ZK, Walter Ulbricht Papers, NL 182/1245.

109. Wierna to Modzelewski, May 25, 1948, MSZ, 6/767/54; see also Patrick Kenney, "Polish Workers and the Socialist Transformation," in Norman Naimark and Leonid Gibianski, *The Establishment of Communist Régimes in Eastern Europe, 1944–49* (Boulder: Westview Press, 1997), p. 146–147. Kenney notes that the Soviet army encouraged this fear by shipping materials and factories from Wrocław back to the Soviet Union. Furthermore, some older Germans returned to Wrocław temporarily after the war, and some Germans worked in industry there.

110. Meller notes of meeting with Ulbricht, December 8, 1948, MSZ, 6/767/54.

111. See Loth, "Stalin's Plans for Post-War Germany," p. 29. The Soviets were as yet unwilling to form a separate socialist state and precipitate the permanent division of Germany. In December 1948, the Soviets rejected a SED proposal to form a provisional government and accelerate the socialist revolution in the Soviet zone.

112. Protocol No. 130 of the SED Central Secretariat, November 15, 1948, SED ZK, IV 2/2.1/248.

113. Zuckermann to Grotewohl, May 17, 1949, SED ZK, Otto Grotewohl Papers, NL 90/483; see Norman Naimark, "The Soviets and the Christian Democrats, 1945–1949," in Francesca Gori and Silvio Pons, eds., *The Soviet Union and Europe in the Cold War, 1943–53* (New York: St. Martin's Press, 1996), pp. 37–56. Soviet military commander Colonel S. I. Tiul'panov forced Jakob Kaiser out of the CDU in December 1947, and Ernst Lemmer out of the LDP in 1948.

114. See Krisch, "Vorstellungen von künftiger aussenpolitischer Orientierung in der SBZ bis 1947 und ihre Auswirkungen auf die spätere Aussenpolitik der DDR," p. 48; and Fischer, "Aussenpolitische Aktivität bei ungewisser sowjetischer Deutschland-Politik (bis 1955)," p. 70.

115. Vierheller, *Polen und die Deutschland-Frage 1939–1949*, p. 141. The Polish delegation to the congress was made up of Politburo member Edward Ochab, Central Committee member Dorota Kluczyńska, and the head of the PZPR Central Committee's Foreign Affairs Department, Ostap Dłuski.

116. *Trybuna Ludu*, January 26, 1949, p. 4; and *Trybuna Ludu*, January 27, 1949, p. 4; see also Sikora, *Sozialistische Solidarität und nationale Interessen*, p. 117.

117. *Nowe Drogi* (3/1, January-February 1949), p. 265.

118. *Trybuna Ludu*, February 12, 1949, p. 3.

119. Polish Military Mission report to Modzelewski, July 1, 1949, MSZ, 15/113/111.

120. Sikora, *Sozialistische Solidarität und nationale Interessen*, p. 119.

3

The Myth of the Stalinist Brotherhood, 1949–1954

I do not believe in the democratic Germans [in the GDR].. . . Germans were, are, and will be our enemy.

—Warsaw train porter to Polish journalist Stanisław Brodzki, 1949[1]

The Soviet blockade of Berlin was a diplomatic blunder and a propaganda setback for the Soviet Union and Stalin's long-range plans to expand communist influence in Germany. Stalin had calculated that the Western allies would leave Berlin, but the blockade only fortified their resolution to stay; furthermore, it hastened the formation of the West German state, a development Stalin had been trying to prevent.[2]

The Polish communists had mixed feelings about the division of Germany. They did not necessarily want a unified Germany or a new peace treaty that reversed the Potsdam decisions on the Polish-German border, but an artificial East German state was not a genuine guarantee of the status quo either. Furthermore, a Socialist German state legitimized the SED's status within the Soviet bloc, a situation the Poles had resisted. The SED leaders hoped that an official recognition of the Oder-Neisse border would enhance their standing with Poland and the other communist states.

Poland recognized the German Democratic Republic on October 18, 1949, and in November the two countries exchanged diplomatic representatives.[3] According to the public posturing of the Polish and East German communists, a new state of neighborliness and good will now characterized their relations. *Trybuna Ludu* declared that "a new Germany has been born on our western border, one that offers its hand to us in cooper-

From left to right: Otto Grotewhol and Józef Cyrankiewicz signing the Zgorzelec agreement recognizing the Oder-Neisse border, Zgorzelec, Poland, July 6, 1950. (Photo courtesy Stiftung Archiv der Parteien und Massenorganisationen der DDR im Bundesarchiv, reprinted with permission)

ation."[4] Polish reporter Stanisław Brodzki commented that the Soviets were giving the Germans an opportunity to carry on the tradition of Marx, Engels, and Liebknecht; he added that "on the foundation of this tradition—and only this tradition—are built the bridges of friendship across the Oder and Neisse."[5]

The fatuous propaganda extolling eternal East German-Polish friendship was typical in Stalin's empire. Bureaucrats and party members worked under a cloud of suspicion and mistrust. Officials did not have the courage to address directly the many unresolved issues that divided the PZPR and the SED; many of their reports were misleading.[6]

Nothing symbolized this false sense of Polish-East German friendship better than the GDR's recognition of the Oder-Neisse border. Otto Grotewohl, the head of the new East German government, had bitterly opposed the new border with Poland after the war. Now he proclaimed that "the Oder-Neisse border is for us a border of peace, which makes possible a friendly relationship with the Polish people."[7] In a preliminary agreement signed in Warsaw on June 6, 1950, an East German delegation led by Walter Ulbricht committed the GDR to the present border. The two sides also initialed accords on economic and cultural cooperation. Ul-

From left to right: GDR President Wilhelm Pieck and PRP President Bolesław Bierut in Warsaw, December 1950. (Photo courtesy Stiftung Archiv der Parteien und Massenorganisationen der DDR im Bundesarchiv, reprinted with permission)

bricht concluded that "there are no more problems between the German and Polish people which cannot be resolved in a peaceful manner." Cyrankiewicz had little in common, personally or ideologically, with a hard-liner like Ulbricht, but nonetheless Cyrankiewicz agreed that a period of closer, friendly cooperation had begun.[8] Bruno Leuschner was gratified that President Bolesław Bierut, whom Leuschner called "the most prominent representative of the Polish people," trusted the SED's leadership of the so-called "progressive Germany." Leuschner added that the talks were conducted in a "truly sincere and cordial atmosphere."[9] *Neues Deutschland* greeted the border accord with a huge front-page spread,[10] and for several days the agreement was page-one news in *Trybuna Ludu*.[11]

GDR President Wilhelm Pieck reviewing Polish troops in Warsaw, December 1950. (Photo courtesy Stiftung Archiv der Parteien und Massenorganisationen der DDR im Bundesarchiv, reprinted with permission)

On July 6, 1950 Grotewohl and Foreign Minister Georgi Dertinger met their Polish counterparts, Cyrankiewicz and Stefan Wierbłowski, in the border town of Zgorzelec, where they signed the formal treaty recognizing the Oder-Neisse as the final "border of peace" between Poland and Germany. *Trybuna Ludu* claimed that the agreement ushered in a new era of understanding: "The enthusiasm with which a crowd of people gathered in Zgorzelec, from both sides of the border, welcomed the signing of the agreement, is an expression of the will of both peoples to support mutual relations on friendly principles."[12]

An East German poet dedicated these lines to the event: "The Neisse follows its old course, the Oder flows in its usual bed—but yet it is as if the lazy river had changed its countenance over night. . . . There, where for centuries only anger flourished, through German fault we want to confess, now one will call we Germans neighbor, friend, and comrade. Oh, what a beautiful victory."[13]

East German President Wilhelm Pieck's official visit to Warsaw in December 1950 solidified this new relationship. It was his second visit in a little over two years, but this time he came as a head of state. Overlooking Pieck's opportunistic rejection of the Oder-Neisse border a few years earlier, Cyrankiewicz praised him as "one of the most prominent revolutionaries and anti-fascist fighters." *Trybuna Ludu* lavished compliments on this "devoted friend of Peoples' Poland," writing that "we welcome him with the deepest sincerity, seeing in him the symbol of a new, democratic, peace-loving Germany."[14]

Pieck responded in an equally magnanimous fashion, noting that this was the first time in almost a thousand years that the head of a German state had made a friendly visit to Poland. Pieck evoked the memory of his former Polish comrades in the communist movement: "I feel especially connected to the Polish working class and its party, of course such great political revolutionaries as Julian Marchlewski, Rosa Luxemburg und Leo Jogiches were my friends and comrades in arms. Therefore my visit in Warsaw is an expression of proletarian internationalism, which binds the Polish United Worker's Party with the SED."[15]Upon his departure from the Warsaw railway station, Pieck thanked the Poles for their "great hospitality" and proclaimed, "Long live the great camp of world peace and its ingenious helmsman, our common friend and leader, Generallissimo Stalin!"[16] The Polish communists usually avoided this kind of hyperbole, but all in all the visit was a public relations success.

Bierut reciprocated Pieck's visit by going to Berlin in April 1951. Once again, nothing but kind words were exchanged in public. Bierut thanked the East Germans for their "unusual hospitality and friendship."[17] When Ulbricht went to Warsaw a month later, he solemnly declared that "now there are no more differences between democratic Germans and the Peoples' Poland."[18]

This public show of affection masked the fundamental lack of trust between the Polish and East German communists that had developed after the war. Relations were not what they appeared. The PZPR leadership knew that as long as Stalin stood behind the SED's new overtures toward Poland, no honest partnership was possible.[19] The West German Foreign Ministry speculated that Ulbricht and Grotewohl had received instructions in Moscow in May to recognize the Oder-Neisse border, and Polish officials suspected as much.[20] One eyewitness to the Zgorzelec meeting, Polish diplomat Romuald Spasowski, recalled later that the Soviets eventually had to mediate the serious differences between the two sides concerning the wording of the treaty. He wrote that at the time he had viewed the accord as "a historic victory for peace, for both Poles and Germans. With time, I saw with increasing clarity that it was Soviet foreign policy that was the actual beneficiary there, because the treaty helped their hegemony over Central Europe."[21]

According to former LDP leader Ernst Lemmer, Grotewohl and Dertinger were forced to sign the Zgorzelec agreement instead of Pieck or Ulbricht so that "an old communist" would not be charged with signing away German territory. Lemmer also contended that "the Poles themselves did not take the theatrically staged signing ceremony, behind which stood the will of the Soviets, very seriously." Lemmer alleged that one drunken Polish journalist told Dertinger that no self-respecting Pole trusted a leader who could sign away part of his country.[22]

Most East Germans were of the same mind. The West German press accurately reported that the SED was having serious problems in justifying the treaty to the East German people.[23] The SED leadership still faced the formidable task of reconciling its own party members with the Oder-Neisse border; the East German Foreign Ministry frequently had to admonish its diplomats for using German names for the cities in Poland's Western Territories.[24] The rank and file of the SED's partner parties in the National Front, the CDU and the LDP, remained, in the words of the Polish Military Mission, stridently "chauvinist and revisionist."[25]

Polish officials privately thought the SED leadership was not doing enough to stamp out revisionism in the party. For example, during the visit of a Polish delegation to the Goethe celebration in Weimar in November 1949, an SED functionary was asked when Silesia would return to Germany. His reply echoed Pieck's argument of a few years earlier: "After the signing of the peace treaty and when the Germans show proof of [their] democratic convictions."[26] Two years later, West German officials speculated that the GDR was still banking on a return of Silesia, but Dertinger assured the Polish Chief of Mission, Jan Izydorczyk, that "the Bonn reports relating to Silesia do not have any basis in truth."[27]

Izydorczyk gave Dertinger the benefit of the doubt. Nonetheless, he reported that most GDR officials "lacked arguments confirming its [the border's] legitimacy."[28] Other Polish diplomats observed that the East German communists tried to avoid the issue and that they "were not always up to [answering] questions on the refugee or the Oder-Neisse border issues."[29] In October 1951, Dertinger again had to reassure the Polish government that the SED was not maneuvering for significant changes in the border.[30]

The so-called "border of peace" was far from peaceful; the heavy guard that stood watch on the Oder-Neisse was a powerful symbol of discord over the border. Frequent disputes over territorial fishing rights that had begun shortly after the end of the war continued after the Zgorzelec treaty was signed. In the fall of 1947, the Polish coast guard confiscated several East German boats fishing in the bay near Ueckermünde, south of Świnoujście.[31] Two years later, Polish authorities arrested four more East German fisherman from Ahlbeck for fishing in Polish waters. By September 1950, eight East German fisherman and two of their fishing boats were in Polish custody. The East German government demanded their return, and called for a maritime agreement to prevent future disputes.[32] After repeated entreaties from East Berlin, the Polish authorities released the fishermen and their boats in 1951.[33] Nonetheless, the East Germans continued to fish in Polish waters on the Baltic Sea, and the Polish coast guard stopped three more East German fishing boats in August 1951. The Polish Foreign Ministry informed the East German government that the Polish coast guard would be increasing patrols along the maritime border.[34] Polish diplomats complained that East German boats were still illegally crossing the border near Zgorzelec,[35] and later in the year the Polish government rejected an East German proposal to ease restrictions on this traffic.[36]

If the communists' assertions about the dawning of new epoch in Polish-East German relations were true, the tension along the border did not reflect it. In July 1953, the U.S. international newspaper *Herald Tribune* went so far as to call the Oder-Neisse "Europe's worst border problem." Reporter Gaston Coblentz predicted that after the June 17 uprising in the GDR, "the festering Oder-Neisse situation should breed more hatred for the Soviets. It also stands in the way of complete solidarity between the Polish Reds and German Reds. The Poles still see Germans as enemies— and vice versa." He reported that the border town of Zgorzelec (the site of the Oder-Neisse agreement in 1950) was divided by armed guards and barbed wire, and that East German émigrés from the Polish side of the town could see their old homes across the river. He claimed that they expected to get them back.[37]

Reacting to the *Herald Tribune* article and to similar West German reports, the East German government assured Warsaw that the border was permanent. In response, Bierut wrote Grotewohl that "the border of peace on the Oder and Neisse has established a guarantee of friendly relations between our nations."[38] Frequent anti-Polish demonstrations by the East Germans in the Oder-Neisse area, however, belied Bierut's assertion that the border was a "guarantee." The Polish communists half-heartedly accepted the SED's explanation that such hostile actions against Poles were instigated by Western agents and fascist agitators in the GDR.[39]

East German and Polish officials knew that such allegations were untrue. The SED's Stalinist economic policies and intransigent position on German unification were becoming increasingly unpopular in the GDR. In November, Ulbricht told Izydorczyk in confidence that the SED was having difficulty in overcoming people's chauvinistic and nationalistic attitudes. Ulbricht said that the party needed to instill more political indoctrination, especially in the Guben and Frankfurt areas and eastern Saxony and Lusatia, where popular opposition to the border was particularly strong.[40] At the SED Party Congress in March 1954, Erich Honecker acknowledged that the FDJ had chauvinistic tendencies, especially concerning the Oder-Neisse border.[41]

East German Ambassador to Poland Stefan Heymann filed this report in the summer of 1955: "The Oder-Neisse border is not only misused in West Germany as a means of chauvinistic agitation, but wide circles of the population of the GDR—not only the earlier settlers [from Poland]—do not have a clear conception of this question. . . . An interpretation is often spread that a united Germany will get back the old territories on the other side of the Oder-Neisse." Heymann offered the example of one young woman from an East German collective farm who was asked what she would do in a reunified Germany. She answered, "Then I would go home!" She meant, of course, to her home in Polish Silesia. Heymann concluded that whether or not East Germans were SED members, the Poles simply did not trust them.[42]

Polish officials repeatedly chided the SED for not doing more to stamp out anti-Polish attitudes. The Poles complained that the SED's propaganda was contributing to the belief that the Oder-Neisse border was a temporary result of losing the war.[43] Polish diplomats criticized the SED and its publishing houses for rejecting Polish books on the subject when they referred to Poland's historical presence in the Western Territories.[44] The Polish Embassy reported that "in nearly every public speech, talk, discussion . . . the problem of the border on the Oder and Neisse has not yet been laid to rest. Even the statements of responsible activists in government and society frequently treat the matter of the Oder-Neisse border as 'unjustly decided.'"[45]

The Poles vigorously protested implications that the border was temporary. Some East Germans officials still referred to the GDR as "Middle Germany," as though western Poland was German territory.[46] One official in the Polish Ministry of Trade reported that the East German Embassy in Warsaw often called Lower and Upper Silesia "Poland I" and "Poland II," as if they were not fully integrated into Poland. The official concluded that "this type of reference does not contribute to the strengthening of good neighborly relations."[47]

Poland and the German Problem

The PZPR did not view the creation of two German states in 1949 as a final resolution to the German problem.[48] The Oder-Neisse border and status of West Berlin were ultimately dependent on Moscow's adherence to the Potsdam agreements. As long as there was no peace treaty with a united German state, the Oder-Neisse border was subject to change. Furthermore, the East German state was not recognized by other Western countries, but the Federal Republic of Germany (FRG) was gradually gaining legitimacy in Western Europe as a vital economic and political partner.

In the early 1950s, the Western Allies began to deliberate the rearmament of West Germany. The Polish communists were not as worried about this eventuality as they were about Soviet diplomatic maneuvers to prevent West Germany from joining NATO: a deal, for instance, between the Allies and the German states to unify the country and revise the Oder-Neisse border. The Poles wanted a final peace treaty between the Allies and a legitimate, unified German government that would guarantee the new border. But there were no assurances that the Potsdam agreements would be the basis for negotiations. The SED had more reason to worry; an Allied deal for a united Germany and free elections meant their being relegated to a small and insignificant opposition party.

In October 1950, the foreign ministers of the Soviet bloc countries met in Prague to devise a strategy to block the possible integration of West Germany into NATO and the European Coal and Steel Community [ECSC]. The East Germans were not invited to the formal talks, but came as observers. Dertinger held several meetings with Molotov; these Dertinger regarded as a confirmation of the GDR's legitimacy. He said that the Soviet government was "in complete understanding of our national needs."[49]

The foreign ministers proposed that the four Allies create the "conditions for the formation of a united peace-loving democratic German state." Grotewohl was charged with forming a proposal for a German parliamentary council that would determine the procedures for all-German elections and the future of a neutral, largely demilitarized German state. West German Chancellor Konrad Adenauer rejected the idea, although the overture was probably sincere. Stalin was still not convinced of the long-term efficacy of the GDR; Soviet fears about West Germany's entry into NATO were very real.[50]

The United States and the other Western Allies were in no position to appease Stalin in the early 1950s. The Soviet acquisition of the atomic bomb, overestimates of the Soviet troop strength in Europe, the communist victory in China, and the Korean War made a compromise with Moscow nearly impossible.[51] The "lesson" of Munich informed both sides; the West would not relinquish any part of Germany if it could fall under Soviet influence, and Stalin interpreted Munich as a capitalist deal to provide Hitler with a springboard for a war against the Soviet Union. There was little hope for serious negotiations on Germany; Grotewohl's proposal went nowhere.

In March 1952, while discussions continued over the rearmament of West Germany, Stalin made one last proposal for a unified, neutral, and demilitarized German state. Once again, the Polish government feared that the border with Germany would go back on the negotiating table.[52] Ulbricht and Pieck paid lip service to supporting a unified Germany, but they knew that a change in the status quo threatened the GDR's very existence and the SED's political future. The SED was greatly relieved that the Soviet demarche failed.[53]

The SED took immediate steps to confirm the division of Germany into two states, and to break out of its diplomatic and economic isolation from the non-communist world. The GDR leadership enlisted Poland's support in gaining diplomatic recognition from the non-communist states. Bierut agreed—as long as Poland's interests were not compromised.[54] In early April 1952, Pieck went to Moscow to meet Stalin, who agreed to work on building and supporting the socialist German state. Pieck evoked the Rapallo Treaty as a precedent in Soviet-German cooperation, although he knew full well that a call for a new Rapallo, which was in part an anti-Polish agreement, was an affront to all Poles, communists included.[55]

When the Western powers recognized the sovereignty of the FRG in May 1952, serious discussion began on the FRG's role in the defense of Western Europe. The GDR responded by securing its boundary with the FRG; in August the Soviet Union liquidated its control commission in East Germany and declared its intention to grant sovereignty to the GDR. In October, the GDR's diplomatic missions were upgraded from legations to embassies. Soviet troops remained in East Germany, but the occupation was officially over.[56]

That summer, Ulbricht and the SED resolved to build socialism in the GDR as quickly as possible, in part to prevent a capitalist takeover of East Germany if unification talks convened. The servile SED leaders also wanted to show the Soviets that they were capable of developing a mature socialist state on the Stalinist model. The Soviets cautioned Ulbricht not to push the reforms too fast, however, for fear not only of alienating the East German population but of ending all hope for communism to gain a foothold in the FRG. Molotov remembered that "it turned out that the German comrades began talking at the top of their voices about building socialism without having laid the proper groundwork for it." The plan was a disaster, and by the end of the year Ulbricht was pleading for more Soviet aid. The crisis culminated in the uprising against the SED régime in June 1953 and almost cost Ulbricht his job.[57]

Polish-German "Friendship"

Before the creation of the GDR in 1949, the German and Polish communists made few honest efforts to further people-to-people contacts. In 1950, Grotewohl conceded that "the old prejudice and arrogance of the Germans toward the Poles still exist."[58] The development of genuine partnerships between the communists in Stalin's empire was virtually impossible. No one could be sure who was a Soviet agent or a Western spy. Even the Polish diplomatic corps, which had previously filed more honest reports than the East Germans, now saw ideological deviations and spies everywhere. Shortly before Stalin's death, for example, the Polish Diplomatic Mission in Berlin observed that there were "social-democratic tendencies" in the SED, as well as dangerous influences from foreign agents and bourgeois elements.[59]

It was not the SED's alleged deviations from Marxist-Leninist-Stalinist thought that made the Poles distrust the East Germans. As long as the GDR was the devoted satellite of the Soviet Union, Poles had no more trust in the East Germans than they did in the Russians. Shortly after the founding of the GDR in 1949, a porter at the Warsaw train station probably spoke for most Poles when he told Brodzki that "I do not believe in the democratic Germans [in the GDR].. . . Germans were, are, and will be our enemy." Brodzki commented that most Poles could not distinguish between the criminal Nazi concentration camp commandant [Amnon] Goeth from Płasków and the famous author Goethe from Weimar.[60] Numerous cultural exchanges were developed in the early 1950s to promote East German-Polish friendship, and although some undoubtedly fostered good will and understanding, many had the opposite effect.[61]

Poles were generally more interested in cultural exchanges than the East Germans. Although many Poles stereotyped Germans as coldly efficient, dogmatic, and condescending, they respected German culture, technology, and economic development. The Polish Committee of Cultural Cooperation with Foreign Countries enthusiastically promoted programs to acquaint the East Germans with Polish culture;[62] from October 1950 to May 1951, over 200 Poles made official visits to East Germany, the highest number of Polish visits to another country during this time. Because the East German authorities permitted exchanges only if they were organized and promoted by the SED, only six East Germans went to Poland on official government business during this period, in comparison with 181 Soviets and twelve Czechoslovaks.[63]

Many SED members, especially those in the lower ranks of the party, still held strong prejudices against Poles. These prejudices were evident in various exchanges; for instance, in May 1950, the head of the SED's Economic Department, Willi Stoph, angrily denounced the rude behavior of an East German delegation to the trade fair in Poznań, and criticized an East German newspaper report for calling some of the fair's streets and cultural park a "carnival," which Stoph found demeaning. Stoph said that he was shocked and disappointed by the reporter's "astonishing ignorance." When Bierut visited the East German factory *Leuna-Werken* in 1951, it was difficult for the East Germans to organize a welcome because several thousand German immigrants from Poland worked in the plant.[64] East German officials worried that the workers would ask Beirut embarrassing questions about when the Germans could return to their homes in Poland.[65]

Friction between the East German and Polish diplomats and their respective hosts in Warsaw and Berlin was yet another barrier to better relations. The Polish Diplomatic Mission in Berlin was disappointed in the East German government's lackluster efforts to promote friendship with Poland. East German officials thought that the first "Month of Polish-German Friendship" in the GDR in March 1951 had achieved positive results, but the SED complained about the Polish delegation's lack of political preparation for the celebration. The SED also reported that there were far too many manifestations of East Germans' hostility toward Poles.[66]

In August 1951, Polish diplomats complained about the serious shortage of officials in the East German Foreign Ministry who were responsible for Polish affairs.[67] That same month, Polish diplomats took umbrage when the East Germans breached protocol by sending such middle-ranking SED functionaries as Karl Wloch, the secretary general of the Committee for Cultural Cooperation with Foreign Countries, and Hans Joachim Hertwig, the secretary of the FDJ, to greet a Polish delegation to the Polish Renaissance Festival in Berlin. The Poles were also disappointed when only two SED representatives attended a performance by "Masowsza," the famous Polish dance company.[68]

The discrepancy between the SED's official promotion of international working-class solidarity and the party's policies toward Poland was revealed in the SED's restrictions on casual encounters between Poles and East Germans. The restrictions even applied to government and party officials. At the height of Stalinist repression in late 1952, the East German parliament passed a law requiring the approval of the East German Foreign Ministry for all direct communications between foreigners and East German officials, agencies, and institutions.[69] Dertinger often made personal decisions on the lists of acceptable contact persons for the various East German departments and agencies.[70] As of January 1, 1953, all visa applications for private visits abroad had to be approved by the East German police, the Interior Ministry, and the Foreign Ministry. Articles that the Polish press sent to East German newspapers had to pass muster with the East German Foreign Ministry censors. Foreign Ministry official Fritz Grosse told Polish diplomat Stanisław Dodin that these measures were necessary "to create control and order . . . [and] to hinder the work of our common enemies." Grosse said that the Rudolf Slansky trial was a good lesson for the parties and a reminder to them to be wary of revisionists and western agents.[71]

The Polish diplomats in Berlin soon discovered that the SED was serious about enforcing the new statute. East German officials were careful not to circumvent the law; when they did, they asked the Poles to keep the meetings confidential. After one meeting at the Polish Diplomatic Mission, for instance, Wloch asked the Poles not to mention it to the GDR Foreign Ministry. Word nonetheless got back to the ministry, which sent a note to the Polish mission warning against more unauthorized contacts.[72]

Because the tight restrictions seriously impeded their work, Polish diplomats registered numerous official protests, particularly the activities of the mission's cultural attaché.[73] The mission worried that cooperative propaganda efforts with the East German press would suffer immeasurable damage. Maria Wierna, the director of the East German Department in the Polish Foreign Ministry, called the East German ban on spontaneous contacts "crude."[74] In March 1953, Polish envoy Jan Izydorczyk wrote Warsaw that East German press coverage of Poland had gotten "considerably" worse; of the sixty-three articles the Poles had recently sent to the East German press agencies, only one had appeared in print.[75]

East German diplomats often displayed arrogant and aloof attitudes toward Polish officials. Even the SED recognized the problem. The party's choice for chief of mission, dramatist Friedrich Wolf, protested the assignment, but to no avail.[76] In 1950, an SED report on the work of the East German diplomats in Warsaw found that "the relationship between the diplomatic mission and the responsible authorities in the Ministry of Foreign Affairs of the Republic of Poland leaves much to be desired." According to the report, Wolf and his underlings took little interest in meeting with Polish officials or in fostering personal connections to them.[77] The head of the East German Foreign Ministry's Soviet section, Peter Florin, moved ongoing negotiations on cultural exchanges from Warsaw to East Berlin in order to exclude Wolf from the talks.[78] In the spring of 1951, Wolf resigned before his tour was up.

Polish officials were often no more hospitable to the East German diplomats in Poland. Wolf complained that "it isn't easy for a German living in Poland. You are watched with complete suspicion." Another East German diplomat recalled that Poles reacted negatively to anyone speaking German, including representatives of the new "socialist Germany."[79] According to the West German press, Polish officials rebuffed meetings with the East Germans so many times that the Polish government had to order its bureaucrats to treat the East Germans with "kid gloves."[80] The East German cultural attaché's repeated complaints about the lack of access to Polish Foreign Ministry officials and the PZPR's press section led to her recall to East Berlin in 1950. Other East German diplomats also grumbled about the hardships of serving in Poland; the consulate was inadequate and there was no suitable housing in Warsaw. Like Wolf, many diplomats asked to leave the post.[81]

The East German Foreign Ministry began to question the political reliability of its own diplomats in Warsaw and openly criticized their negative attitudes toward Poles. Some of the lower-ranking diplomats were unhappy with Wolf's successor, Änne Kundermann, in part because her husband, Erich, also worked at the embassy. Kundermann, who had survived the purges in the Soviet Union, was a convinced Stalinist. Horst Grunert, the press attaché, recalled later that Kundermann was incapable of making an honest assessment of life in the Soviet Union under Stalin, even though many of her friends had been victims of the purges; Grunert complained that her preoccupation with embassy security subverted attempts by the diplomats to make contacts with the Poles. Stefan Heymann replaced Kundermann in the fall of 1953. Heymann had previously served as head of the SED's Department of Culture, where, according to Grunert, he had tolerated too much "decadent" and "abstract" art. Heymann helped raise morale at the embassy, but East German diplomats still tried to avoid the assignment.[82]

The malaise that permeated the East German Embassy in Warsaw throughout 1953 was just one example of the SED's failure to forge a new relationship with Poland. Most party and government officials remained indifferent to Poles, if not openly hostile.

The New Course and the June Uprising in the GDR

The power struggle that ensued in the Kremlin after Stalin's death in March 1953 directly affected Soviet bloc relations. The Kremlin gradually loosened its control over the other communist parties in Eastern Europe, and promoted the New Course in political and economic affairs. The CPSU declared its intention to treat the other communist parties as equals, and each country slowly received more freedom to conduct its own foreign economic policy.[83]

Stalin's death also brought hope for a relaxation in the Cold War. The first sign of change came with the end of the Korean War in July. There even appeared to be a possibility for German reunification; for a time the new Soviet leadership seriously debated the future of Germany and Stalin's proposal for a united, nonaligned, and neutral German state.[84] The Polish leadership was also keenly interested in a final resolution to the division of Germany. At the Second Party Congress of the PZPR in March 1954, Bierut declared that "the German problem is the central question of European security" for France as well as for Poland. Bierut went so far as to propose that the historic Polish-French alliance be resurrected.[85] These ideas abruptly ended with West Germany's entry into NATO and the formation of the Warsaw Pact in May 1955.

The mixed ideological messages that were coming out of Moscow in 1953 put the communist parties in the Soviet bloc on edge. The Stalinists worried that their past indiscretions would cost them their jobs, or worse, their freedom or their lives. The first serious test to communist rule in East Germany began on June 17, 1953, with a workers' strike in East Berlin. When the uprising spread to cities throughout the GDR, the Soviet army deployed troops and tanks to suppress it. The Polish government officially approved of the action, and the East German Diplomatic Mission in Warsaw sent a letter to the PZPR thanking the party "for the proof of [your] trust and solidarity that you showed to workers in the GDR in regard to the crushing of the fascist provocation."[86]

Polish diplomats in Berlin echoed the SED's propaganda blaming the demonstrations on foreign agents and provocateurs, but they were genuinely surprised by the extent of the people's disaffection with the SED régime.[87] The Polish mission reported that there was "a serious mood of hostility toward the USSR" in the GDR.[88] Stanisław Dodin construed the events as proof of the strong fascist elements in East Germany. Other diplomats attributed the revolt to the failure of the SED's economic plan for the first quarter of 1953; they warned that the economic situation had not improved much in the second.[89]

Ironically, the June uprising saved the Ulbricht régime, and ended all serious thoughts that Moscow might have had about a new demarche on German unification.[90] Khrushchev later commented that "thanks to the Party [SED] and its leadership, the uprising never got out of hand. As a result of the postwar circumstances which developed in the GDR, we knew we would have to find other ways of establishing East Germany on a solid Marxist-Leninist footing. We knew Stalinism was contrary to Marxism-Leninism."[91]

The Kremlin approved of Ulbricht's campaign to consolidate strict party control over East German politics and society.[92] Ulbricht purged the SED and the East German government of potentially hostile elements, and rather than elevating the other National Front parties to genuine governing partners, the SED subordinated their role even further. The SED made a concentrated effort to undermine the influence of the CDU.[93] Ulbricht told Izydorczyk that, at most, half the German clergy could be won over to socialism anyway, and that they were a barrier to closer cooperation between the SED and the CDU.[94]

Before the June uprising, the Polish Embassy had speculated that Moscow's call for collective party leadership would force the SED to give the CDU and the LDP more important positions in the government.[95] That fall, Poland honored the CDU's top government official, Foreign Minister Georgi Dertinger, for his efforts to improve relations with Poland. Dertinger (CDU) was sacked and arrested on spy charges a few weeks later, an embarrassment for the Poles.[96]

The Polish Foreign Ministry and its diplomats in Berlin were openly critical of the SED's unwillingness to work with the other political parties.[97] Polish journalists accused Ulbricht of disloyalty to Moscow and disregard for the interests of the other people's republics. One newsman concluded that "Ulbricht is viewed in Poland as a man who hates Poland."[98] The PZPR also deplored the SED's purges of such loyal communists as Franz Dahlem, whom Ulbricht accused of adopting "political blindness" to the intrigues of imperialist agents.[99] Even some members of the Soviet diplomatic corps in the GDR expressed disappointment in the SED's policies. One diplomat told Izydorczyk that the East Germans often made policy "without thinking beforehand."[100]

But the PZPR, too, was slow to reform. Polish Cardinal Wyszyński was arrested in September 1953. Only after Józef Swiatło of the Polish Ministry of Public Security defected in December, and his revelations of the ministry's brutal persecution of innocent people became widely known in Poland in the fall of 1954, did the party begin the long and arduous process of self-examination and reform. The PZPR returned Cyrankiewicz to the position of prime minister in March 1954; Bierut kept the title of first secretary of the PZPR.[101] Gomułka was freed in December, and the party reined in its security police.

The SED was so shaken by the June events that the party immediately increased surveillance over the population and took steps to repress liberalizing influences that might emanate from Poland. The SED's central organs remained firmly in charge of all Polish visitors, and the party tightened enforcement of the January 1953 law to restrict direct contacts between foreigners and East German officials.[102] In a meeting at the East German Foreign Ministry, Izydorczyk complained about the time it took for a Pole to obtain a visa to East Germany. Izydorczyk said that the delays were embarrassing for his government because relations with the GDR, a fellow socialist state, were supposed to be friendly.[103]

East German Foreign Ministry official Max Keilson was genuinely surprised when the Polish cultural attaché in East Berlin, Helena Jakubowska, told him that her government had not issued the same kind of restrictions. Jakubowska said that she was having trouble doing her job because of the East German law, to which Keilson replied somewhat disingenuously, "In no case do we have the intention of impeding your work."[104] The East German government intentionally kept Polish officials in the dark about its internal affairs. Polish diplomat J. Burgin told East German Secretary of Security Ernst Wollweber that the Polish government had not been well informed about the events of June 17, or about the SED's recent purges of Wilhelm Zaisser and Rudolf Herrnstadt and their followers. Wollweber promised to work on easing communications with Polish officials, but East German policy did not change.[105] Working conditions for the Polish diplomats became so restrictive that Izydorczyk eventually raised the issue with Grotewohl himself, who replied only that the regulations applied to diplomats from the other peoples' republics as well. Izydorczyk responded that in contrast to the GDR, the Polish government was doing everything it could to cooperate with the East German diplomats in Poland. Grotewohl suggested that the Poles review the policy with the new foreign minister, Lothar Bolz, but he, too, ignored their appeals.[106]

During talks that fall on a plan for cultural exchanges, Polish negotiators again asked the East Germans to ease restrictions on their personal contacts with GDR officials. The Poles argued that they expected the same treatment from the GDR that the Polish government afforded the East German diplomatic representatives in Warsaw, but again the East Germans flatly refused. They said that the law was an internal affair and expected Polish diplomats to respect it.[107]

Polish-East German relations in Stalin's empire were mired in an atmosphere of distrust and paranoia. Stalin's communists were a camorra of sycophants, not an alliance by choice. Loyalty to the CPSU did not foster friendly relations between the satellite parties, nor did it cultivate real understanding between the nationalities of Eastern Europe. Many Polish communists grumbled about the SED's blind obedience to Stalinist orthodoxy; the SED distrusted the PZPR for its alleged social democratic, capitalist, and bourgeois tendencies.

The normalcy and stability that Stalin had brought to communist party relations in the early 1950s broke down after his death. In addition to their greater political autonomy, the satellites soon began to reassert their economic interests. As the political and economic fault lines dividing Europe weakened, the Polish government began to reassess the benefits of its trade with the Soviet bloc.

German repatriation from Poland was also a source of friction between the East German and Polish communists after the war. In the mid-1950s, Bonn began to lobby Warsaw to allow more German emigration. East Berlin demanded equal treatment in this matter, but never got it.

Notes

1. *Trybuna Ludu*, October 26, 1949, p. 3.

2. See Wilfried Loth, "Stalin's Plans for Post–War Germany," in Francesca Gori and Silvio Pons, eds., *The Soviet Union and Europe in the Cold War, 1943–53* (New York: St. Martin's Press, 1996), pp. 26–29; and Loth, *Stalins ungeliebtes Kind: Warum Moskau die DDR nicht wollte* (Stalin's unwanted child: Why Moscow did not want the GDR) (Berlin: Rowohlt, 1994), p. 135; and Nikita Khrushchev, *Khrushchev Remembers: The Last Testament* (Boston: Little, Brown, 1974), p. 192.

3. Polish Military Mission to Warsaw, November 15, 1949, PZPR KC, 237/V–146. In 1950, Karol Tkocz was named the Polish Chief of Mission. Friedrich Wolf represented the GDR in Warsaw. The diplomatic missions were upgraded to embassies in October 1953.

4. *Trybuna Ludu*, October 20, 1949, p. 1.

5. *Trybuna Ludu*, October 11, 1949, pp. 2–3.

6. Aside from some contentious negotiations on trade and repatriation of Germans in Poland (see Chapter 4), most party and government reports on both sides offer little in the way of an honest assessment of relations. Both parties felt the pressure of ever-present Soviet agents. The Soviets even sat in on SED Politburo meetings, and the Polish Minister of Defense was a Soviet citizen, Marshal Konstantin Rokossovsky. It was not until the mid-1950s, when Nikita Khrushchev consolidated his power and the GDR was granted full sovereignty and an army in the Warsaw Pact, that East German officials felt no compunction about criticizing their Polish comrades.

7. *Neues Deutschland*, October 13, 1949, p. 1.

8. Cited in a speech by Friedrich Wolf, October 7, 1950, PZPR KC, 237/XXII–521; see also Horst Grunert, *Für Honecker auf glattem Parkett: Erinnerungen eines DDR-Diplomaten* (For Honecker on the smooth parquet: Memoirs of a GDR diplomat) (Berlin: Edition Ost, 1995), p. 104.

9. Leuschner notes on Ulbricht et al., meeting with Bierut, Minc, Izydorczyk, Wierbłowski, and Dłuski, June 1950, SED ZK, Walter Ulbricht Papers, NL 182/1247.

10. *Neues Deutschland*, June 8, 1950, p. 1.

11. See *Trybuna Ludu*, June 6, 1950, and subsequent issues.

12. *Trybuna Ludu*, July 7, 1950, p. 1.

13. From a poem by Max Zimmering, "Strom des Friedens" (Current of Freedom) quoted in Christa Hübner, "Das Abkommen von Zgorzelec und die politisch-ideologische Arbeit der SED 1950/51" (The Treaty of Zgorzelec and the political-ideological work of the SED, 1950–1951), *Beiträge zur Geschichte der Arbeiterbewegung* (Contributions to the history of the Workers' movement) 23, no. 1 (1981), p. 39.

14. *Trybuna Ludu*, December 19, 1950, p. 1.

15. Pieck speech, December 18, 1950, SED ZK, Wilhelm Pieck Papers, NL 36/449.

16. Pieck speech, December 20, 1950, SED ZK, Wilhelm Pieck Papers, NL 36/449. The SED leadership rarely missed a public opportunity to praise Stalin, but the Polish communists were careful not to inflame the anti-Russian attitudes of the Polish people by stressing the PZPR's relationship with Stalin and the Soviet Union.

17. Bierut speech, April 22, 1951, SED ZK, Wilhelm Pieck Papers, NL 36/451; and Bierut speech, undated, PZPR KC, Bierut file, 254/I–5.

18. Izydorczyk report on "The Origins of the GDR," May 15, 1951, PZPR KC, Izydorczyk file, 473/13.

19. See Alexander Fischer, "Aussenpolitische Aktivität bei ungewisser sowjetischer Deutschland-Politik (bis 1955)" (Foreign policy activity in uncertain Soviet German policy to 1955), in Hans Adolf Jacobsen, Gerd Leptin, Ulrich Scheuner, and Eberhard Schulz, eds., *Drei Jahrzehnte Aussenpolitik der DDR*, 51–84 (Munich: R. Oldenbourg Verlag, 1979), p. 71. Fischer observes that relations between the GDR and Poland did not suddenly improve as a result of the Zgorzelec agreement.

20. Foreign Ministry memo, unsigned, undated, Press and Information Office of the Federal Government, BRD AA, Department 2, vol. 437.

21. Romuald Spasowski, *The Liberation of One* (New York: Harcourt Brace Jovanovich, 1986), p. 293.

22. Ernst Lemmer, *Manches war doch anders: Erinnerungen eines deutschen Demokraten* (Some things were really otherwise: Memories of a German Democrat) (Frankfurt/Main: Verlag Heinrich Scheffler, 1968), pp. 314–315.

23. See the West German newspaper reports in the Press Service and Information Service of the West German Foreign Ministry, June 14, 1950, BRD AA, Department 2, vol. 437.

24. Marten to the GDR Diplomatic Mission in Warsaw, April 26, 1951, DDR MfAA, Warsaw Mission, A3541.

25. Polish Military Mission to the Polish Foreign Ministry, November 15, 1949, PZPR KC, 237/V–146.

26. Ibid.

27. Izydorczyk notes of meeting with Dertinger, October 10, 1951, MSZ, 10/318/36.

28. Izydorczyk to Dłuski, November 5, 1951, PZPR KC, 237/V–146.

29. Wierna to Skrzeszewski, May 14, 1951, MSZ, 10/364/40.

30. Izydorczyk notes of meeting with Dertinger, October 10, 1951, MSZ, 10/318/36.

31. Gebert (Polish Military Mission) to the Ministry of Foreign Affairs, September 9, 1947, URM, MZO, Department of Public Administration, file 134.

32. Freund to the GDR Foreign Ministry, January 7, 1950, DDR MfAA, A10017.

33. Keilson to the GDR Diplomatic Mission in Warsaw, January 9, 1951, DDR MfAA, Warsaw Mission, A3542.

34. Ackermann to the State Secretary for Food and Consumer Industry, September 15, 1951, DDR MfAA, State Secretary, A15627.

35. Izydorczyk to Warsaw, June 11, 1951, MSZ, 10/364/40.

36. See the article in the *Passauer Neue Presse*, (Passau New Press), December 29, 1951, in BRD BfGDF, B137/1055.

37. *International Herald Tribune*, July 12, 1953, in BRD AA, Department 2, vol. 438.

38. Bierut to Grotewohl, July 22, 1953, PZPR KC, Bierut Archive, 254/IV–26.

39. Stanisław Dodin notes of meeting with Ernst Wollweber, October 14, 1953, PZPR KC, 237/V–146.

40. Izydorczyk to Skrzeszewski, November 24, 1953, MSZ, 10/320/36.

41. David Childs, *The GDR: Moscow's German Ally* (London: Unwin Hyman, 1988), p. 39.

42. Heymann to the GDR Foreign Ministry, July 2, 1955, DDR MfAA, Warsaw Embassy, A3670.

43. Józef Knapik to the Polish Foreign Ministry, March 31, 1955, MSZ, 10/369/41.

44. Knapik to the Polish Foreign Ministry, May 5, 1955, MSZ, 10/368/41.

45. Izydorczyk to the Polish Foreign Ministry, April 15, 1954, MSZ, 10/367/41.

46. Wojciecki report on Geneva conference of foreign ministers, November 28, 1955, PZPR KC, 237/V–291.

47. Headquarters of Foreign Trade—Coal and Coke in Stalinograd, to the Polish Ministry of Foreign Trade, June 7, 1954, MSZ, group 10/319/36.

48. Loth, *Stalins ungeliebtes Kind*, p 135. Loth argues that Ulbricht played a major role in convincing a reluctant Stalin to create the GDR.

49. Dertinger report, October 23, 1950, SED ZK, Otto Grotewohl Papers, NL 90/459; and Izydorczyk notes of meeting with Grotewohl, August 23, 1951, MSZ, 10/438/47. At this point, East Germany's national interests could not be voiced too loudly. Dertinger's repeated references to them, along with his CDU credentials, made the Soviets and hard-liners in the SED suspicious of him. Grotewohl told the head of the Polish Diplomatic Mission, Jan Izydorczyk, that Polish officials should avoid discussing any important matters with Dertinger. He was accused of spying and incarcerated in 1953.

50. Gerhard Wettig, "The Soviet Union and Germany in the Late Stalin Period, 1950–3," in Francesca Gori and Silvio Pons, eds., *The Soviet Union and Europe in the Cold War, 1943–53* (New York: St. Martin's Press, 1996), pp. 361–363; and Loth, "Stalin's Plans for Post-War Germany," p. 30. Wettig argues that Adenauer rejected the offer because he did not want SED or Soviet interference in West Germany. Wettig, in contrast to Loth, writes that "the proposal submitted by Grotewohl was clearly not serious offer for negotiations." It is unlikely that Stalin would have given up on the SED and the GDR without some significant concessions in return, such as Western withdrawal from West Berlin and West Germany, but his main goal in the early 1950s was to prevent West Germany's remilitarization, not to hang on to the GDR.

51. See John Lewis Gaddis, *We Now Know: Rethinking Cold War History* (Oxford: Clarendon Press, 1997), p. 123.

52. Ibid., p. 128.

53. Historians differ about the sincerity of Stalin's proposal. See, for example Ann L. Phillips, *Soviet Policy Toward East Germany Reconsidered: The Postwar Decade* (New York: Greenwood Press, 1986), pp. 125–127; and Vladislaw Zubok and Constantine Pleshakov, *Inside the Kremlin's Cold War: From Stalin to Khrushchev* (Cambridge: Harvard University Press, 1996), p. 159. Zubok and Pleshakov, like Gerhard Wettig, argue that Stalin was merely trying to prevent West German integration into a West European defense system, not contemplating a sacrifice of East Germany; see Wilfried Loth, "Die Historiker und die Deutsche Frage: Ein Rückblick nach dem Ende des kalten Krieges," in Wilfried Loth, ed., *Die Deutschland Frage in der Nachkriegszeit* (Berlin: Akademie Verlag, 1994), p. 25; Loth, *Stalins unbeliebtes Kind*, pp. 174–182. Loth views the proposal as a real offer to reunite Germany, and claims that the SED was very concerned that Adenauer would accept the Soviet proposals; see also Eberhard Schulz, "New Developments in Intra-bloc Relations in Historical Perspective," in *Soviet-East European Dilemmas: Coercion, Competition, and Consent*, eds., Karen Dawisha and Philip Hanson (London: Heinemann Educational Books, 1981), pp. 51–52; see also Blankenhorn, et al., report on the acceleration of Polish-German friendship, July 31, 1950, BRD AA, Department 2, vol. 259. There is some question about what the East Germans and Poles knew about the Soviet initiative beforehand. In 1950, diplomats in Bonn hinted that perhaps the Soviets were thinking of reunification plans for Germany, and that they wanted to prepare the Poles and other East Europeans for that

eventuality; Gerhard Wettig, "The Soviet Union and Germany in the Late Stalin Period, 1950–3," p. 366. Wettig contends that the SED was confident that nothing would come of the demarche, and that after Stalin died and Beria raised the possibility of abandoning the GDR, Molotov said that Stalin would never have done that. Wettig says that the note was intended to put pressure on the Adenauer government and destabilize it from the Left; see also Andrei Gromyko, *Memories* (London: Hutchinson, 1989), p. 196. Gromyko later wrote that "no other European government in the post-war period made such a gross political miscalculation. Without doubt, Adenauer lost a historic opportunity"; and Gaddis, *We Now Know*, pp. 124–127. Gaddis asserts that Stalin finally realized in 1952 that his policies had prompted the formation of West Germany, the ECSC, and the Pleven Plan to integrate German soldiers into European units, and therefore took a more compromising approach. But Gaddis agrees with Wettig, Zubok, and Pleshakov that Stalin expected the proposal to be rejected.

54. See Izydorczyk notes of a meeting of the SED Central Committee, March 4, 1952, KC PZPR, 237/XXII–517. In March, 1952, Grotewohl publicly thanked the Poles for their support in the United Nations.

55. Ralf Badstübner, "Die sowjetische Deutschlandpolitik im Lichte neuer Quellen" (The Soviet policy toward Germany in light of new sources), in Wilfried Loth, ed., *Die Deutschland Frage in der Nachkriegszeit* (The German question in the post-war period), 11–28 (Berlin: Akademie Verlag, 1994), p. 129; Gottfried Zeiger, *Die Haltung von SED und DDR zur Einheit Deutschlands, 1949–1987* (The attitude of the SED and the GDR toward the unification of Germany, 1949–1989) (Cologne: Verlag Wissenschaft und Politik, 1988), p. 49; and Phillips, *Soviet Policy Toward East Germany Reconsidered: The Postwar Decade*, pp. 125–127.

56. See Norman Naimark, *The Russians in Germany, A History of the Soviet Zone of Occupation, 1945–1949* (Cambridge: Harvard University Press, 1995) p. 286. Naimark remarks that during the occupation "the Soviets did not help the SED develop a sense of independence and confidence. The self-image of the SED was also poorly served by the need for its leaders to petition repeatedly to the Soviets on a wide variety of material and personnel issues."

57. Albert Resis, ed., *Molotov Remembers: Inside Kremlin Politics. Conversations with Felix Chuev* (Chicago: Ivan R. Dee, 1993), p. 334; Loth, *Stalins unbeliebtes Kind*, p. 226; and Gaddis, *We Now Know*, p. 129.

58. Notes on Stoph and Kling visit to the Poznań Trade Fair, May 7, 1950, SED ZK, microfilm FBS 339/13487; see also *Neues Deutschland*, May 10, 1950, p. 5; and Fischer, "Aussenpolitische Aktivität bei ungewisser sowjetischer Deutschland-Politik (bis 1955)," p. 72.

59. Dodin to Wierna, January 28, 1953, PZPR KC, 237/XXII–517; see also the Educational Institute of Scientific Faculty to Bierut, January 5, 1953, PZPR KC, 237/V–146; and Dodin notes of meeting with Wollweber, October 14, 1953, PZPR KC, 237/V–146. In one case, the Polish Educational Institute of Scientific Faculty in Warsaw criticized a visiting economics professor from the Humboldt University in Berlin, Jürgen Kuczynski, for un-Marxist ideas such as the "possibility of peacefully reforming capitalism." In October 1953, the head of East German security, Ernst Wollweber, told Polish diplomat Stanisław Dodin that Kuczynski was ideologically unreliable.

60. *Trybuna Ludu*, October 26, 1949, p. 3.

61. See Fischer, "Aussenpolitische Aktivität bei ungewisser sowjetischer Deutschland-Politik (bis 1955)," p. 72; and Sikora, *Sozialistische Solidarität und nationale Interessen*, p. 130. The Poles were most interested in technical-scientific agreements as a way of obtaining German "know how"; for a thorough discussion of Polish-East German cultural relations, see Hans-Christian Trepte, "Polish Literature and Culture in East Germany: A Window to the West? *The Polish Review*, no. 1 (1996), pp. 63–72.

62. Committee for Cultural Cooperation with Foreign Countries report for October 1, 1950 to March 31, 1953, URM KWKzZ, N–505/7.

63. Committee for Cultural Cooperation with Foreign Countries report, October 1950 to May 1951, URM, KWKzZ, N–505/7.

64. Notes on Stoph and Kling's visit to the Poznań Trade Fair, May 7, 1950, SED ZK, microfilm FBS 339/13487; see also *Neues Deutschland*, May 10, 1950, p. 5; and Fischer, "Aussenpolitische Aktivität bei ungewisser sowjetischer Deutschland-Politik (bis 1955)," p. 72.

65. Ines Mietkowska-Kaiser, "Zur brüderlichen Zusammenarbeit zwischen polnischen und deutschen Kommunisten und Antifaschisten nach dem Sieg über den deutschen Faschismus (1945–1949)" (On the fraternal cooperation between the Polish and German Communists and anti-Fascists after the victory over German fascism, 1945–1949), in *Jahrbuch für Geschichte der sozialistischen Länder Europas* (Yearbook for the history of the socialist countries of Europe) 23, no. 1 (1979): 49–67, p. 65.

66. Karl Wloch to Ulbricht, April 2, 1951, SED ZK, Walter Ulbricht Papers, NL 182/1247; and Wierna to Skrzeszewski, May 14, 1951, MSZ, 10/364/40.

67. Polish Diplomatic Mission report, August 10, 1951, MSZ, 10/364/40.

68. Polish Diplomatic Mission report, August 24, 1951, MSZ, 10/364/40.

69. (East German) regulation of communications with foreign officials, January 22, 1953, in MSZ, 10/3319/36. Because officials from the East German Ministry of Foreign and Domestic Trade were not covered under these regulations, they enjoyed greater freedom to meet with foreign officials about economic matters.

70. Note of Polish Mission in Berlin, March 17, 1953, MSZ, 10/319/36.

71. Simons notes of meeting between Grosse and Polish diplomats Dodin and Jakubowska, February 19, 1953, DDR MfAA, State Secretary, A15582. Slansky was the Czechoslovak communist executed in 1952.

72. Wierna to Skrzeszewski, January 16, 1953, MSZ, 10/319/36.

73. Simons notes of meeting between Grosse and Polish diplomats Dodin and Jakubowska, February 19, 1953, DDR MfAA, State Secretary, A15582.

74. Wierna to Skrzeszewski, January 16, 1953, MSZ, 10/319/36.

75. Izydorczyk to the Polish Foreign Ministry, March 22, 1953, MSZ, 10/366/40.

76. Grunert, *Für Honecker auf glattem Parkett: Erinnerungen eines DDR-Diplomaten*, p. 96.

77. GDR Diplomatic Mission in Warsaw report, July 28, 1951, SED ZK, microfilm FBS 339/13425.

78. Łobodycz to Wierbłowski on Małecki notes of conversation with Florin in Berlin, August 26, 1950, MSZ, 10/373/41.

79. Wolf to Dertinger, April 14, 1951, DDR MfAA, State Secretary, A15155; and Grunert, *Für Honecker auf glattem Parkett*, pp. 94–96, 109–110.

80. Blankenhorn, et al., report, July 31, 1950, BRD AA, Department 2, vol. 259.

81. M. Łobodycz to Wierbłowski, July 15, 1950, MSZ, 10/313/36.

82. GDR Diplomatic Mission report, December 17, 1953, SED ZK, microfilm FBS 339/13425; and Grunert, *Für Honecker auf glattem Parkett: Erinnerungen eines DDR-Diplomaten*, pp. 99–100.

83. See Khrushchev, *Khrushchev Remembers: The Glasnost Tapes*, p. 116. Khrushchev had a blind spot when it came to the way the Polish Left viewed the CPSU. In his memoirs, he says that the Polish communists were united with the Russians in the struggle against capitalism, even to the point of stating that Felix Dzierżyński, the founder of the Soviet secret police, had the respect of the Polish people: "This all speaks of the fraternal relationship of the Soviet Union to our allies and brothers, the Polish people."

84. See Zubok and Pleshakov, *Inside the Kremlin's Cold War: From Stalin to Khrushchev*, pp. 159–160. After Stalin's death, the Soviet leadership had some serious discussions about the future of the GDR. Beria questioned Ulbricht's leadership and the legitimacy of the East German state itself; see also Marc Trachtenberg, *A Constructed Peace: The Making of the European Settlement 1945–1963* (Princeton: Princeton University Press), 1999, p. 138–139. Dulles posited the idea of a neutral Germany as well, but by 1954 that thinking was over.

85. M. K. Dziewanowski, *Poland in the 20th Century* (New York: Columbia University Press, 1977), p. 238.

86. Letter from GDR Embassy to the PZPR Central Committee, undated, ca. June 1953, KC PZPR, 237/XXII–521.

87. See the Polish Diplomatic Mission reports of June 1953, in MSZ, 10/354/39.

88. Izydorczyk to Wierna, June 30, 1953, MSZ, 23/84/9.

89. Izydorczyk to Wierna, June 22, 1953, MSZ, 10/366/40.

90. See Hermann-Josef Rupieger, "Verpasste Chancen? Ein Rückblick auf die deutschland-politischen Verhandlungen, 1952–1955" (Missed chances? A look back at the German political negotiations, 1952–1955), in Wilfried Loth, ed., *Die Deutschland Frage in der Nachkriegszeit* (The German question in the post-war period) (Berlin: Akademie Verlag, 1994), pp. 207–210; Resis, ed., *Molotov Remembers*, p. 334. Resis quotes Beria when raising the prospect in 1953 of a reunited Germany without the GDR: "Why should socialism be built in the GDR? Let it just be a peaceful country. That is sufficient for our purposes. . . . The sort of country it will become is unimportant"; and Gaddis, *We Now Know*, p. 131, 150. Beria's proposal was one of the pretexts for his arrest on June 26. Gaddis writes, "Having done so, it would have been difficult for any of them [the Kremlin leaders]—at least as long as the succession struggle was under way—to oppose Ulbricht, because that would have suggested association with rebellion and treason. The culture of distrust Stalin had left behind now linked his heirs to an East German leader Stalin himself had never trusted." The Polish communists shared this distrust.

91. Khrushchev, *Khrushchev Remembers: The Last Testament*, p. 193.

92. See Phillips, *Soviet Policy Toward East Germany Reconsidered: The Postwar Decade*, pp. 131–180. Phillips argues that the Soviets eventually decided on the

policy of two Germanies because of the Western allies' unwillingness to bargain on German unification.

93. Łobodycz to Władysław Góralski on a meeting between Dodin and Keilson, February 12, 1954, PZPR KC, 237/XXII–820.

94. Izydorczyk to Skrzeszewski, November 24, 1953, MSZ, 10/320/36.

95. Izydorczyk to Wierna, June 30, 1953, MSZ, 23/84/9.

96. Grunert, *Für Honecker auf glattem Parkett*, p. 91.

97. Łobodycz to Góralski, April 21, 1954, PZPR KC, 237/XXII–820.

98. Von Mende notes on information from Polish journalists, November 12, 1954, BRD BKA, Office for Expellees, B136/6483.

99. Sikora, *Sozialistische Solidarität und nationale Interessen*, p. 142; and Childs, *The GDR*, p. 26. The SED exonerated Dahlem in July 1956.

100. Izydorczyk to Skrzeszewski, March 29, 1954, MSZ, 10/329/37.

101. Bierut had assumed both positions in November 1952.

102. Memo to Hans Lauter (signature unintelligible), March 12, 1953, SED ZK, Department of Fine Literature and Arts, IV 2/906/73.

103. Grosse notes of a meeting with Izydorczyk, June 17, 1953, DDR MfAA, State Secretary, A15582.

104. Helena Jakubowska notes of a meeting with Keilson, November 5, 1953, MSZ, 10/319/36.

105. Dodin notes of a meeting with Wollweber, October 14, 1953, PZPR KC, 237/V–146. Wollweber himself was purged from the party in 1958.

106. Izydorczyk report to Wierna, October 19, 1953, MSZ, 10/319/36. In October 1953, the Polish government raised its diplomatic mission to embassy status.

107. Wierna to Skrzeszewski, November 10, 1953, MSZ, 10/475/49.

4

The Problems of German Repatriation, Reparations, and Trade, 1945–1953

We will not give back one Pole to the Germans . . . and we do not want one German among Poles.

—*Gomułka, November 1946.[1]*

Poland's takeover of German territories after the war immediately spawned disputes over the treatment of German refugees from Poland and the status of the Germans who stayed. If some of the German refugees from Poland did not harbor anti-Polish attitudes before 1945, the loss of their land and the harsh circumstances of their deportation made it likely that they developed them.[2] The non-communist German press attacked the Polish government for the inhumane conditions of the deportations,[3] but Polish officials vehemently denied wrongdoing.[4] After the terrible wartime occupation of Poland, Gomułka, like most Poles, paid no attention to the German complaints.[5] *Głos Ludu* responded to the charges by accusing the German police of "unheard of villainy" and of "bestial assaults" in their treatment of Polish prisoners returning from Germany.[6]

The expelled Germans represented over one-fifth of the population in the Soviet zone by 1946. The KPD and SED faced a nearly impossible task of convincing the expelled Germans of the need for friendly relations with the Polish people and its communist government. The KPD did not directly address the real reasons for the German exodus westward; it referred to them as "settlers" rather than "refugees" or "expellees."[7] The party did not blame the Poles or the Soviets for the Germans' plight; it blamed the German "imperialist monopoly capitalists of industry and agriculture" who had so willingly served Hitler.[8]

Instead of complaining about the refugees' misfortune and alleged mistreatment by the Poles, the KPD urged other Germans to help resettle them.[9] The director of the Central Administration for Refugees in the Soviet zone, Josef Schlaffer, said, "We want to create a new home for these millions, in the political knowledge that we are no less to blame than they are for the terrible pain, the cruel misery, and loss of their homeland."[10] The *Deutsche Volkszeitung* argued that Germans who complained about their present economic situation should remember that Germany had caused millions of French, Russians, Czechs, and Poles to go hungry during the war.[11] As true as this was, it did not ingratiate the communists with the German people.

During his visit to Warsaw in September 1949, Pieck angrily depicted Western propaganda promising the eventual return of the refugees to their homes in Poland as "illusory."[12] Pieck added that those who disseminated these notions wanted to use the Oder-Neisse border as a *causus belli* against Poland.[13] In 1952, Ulbricht declared that "the German people and the German settlers [from Poland] do not want war, however, and they view the Oder-Neisse as the border of peace."[14]

That was patently untrue. Few refugees wanted a new war, but they were by no means reconciled to the loss of the eastern territories. Most would settle for nothing less than a return of Germany's borders of 1937, if not 1914.[15] Their recalcitrant opposition to the SED and its recognition of the Oder-Neisse line complicated Polish-East German relations.

The Problem of the Germans in Poland

Tens of thousands of Germans were still living in Poland in 1946. The Polish government had particular difficulty in expelling the Germans from Silesia because so many had fled from East Prussia and Pomerania to escape the Red Army at the end of the war. In the fall of 1945, the Allies agreed that the Silesian Germans could be deported into the British and Soviet zones, but Polish authorities could not supply enough transports to the British zone. In addition, the Poles wanted to exploit German labor. The Poles valued Germans with technical skills, but most were made to do back-breaking work in the coal, textile, and construction industries.[16] Polish officials tried to replace the Germans with Poles returning from Germany, [17] but many of those Poles either chose not to return or did not possess the necessary skills.[18] The deportation of Germans was also slowed by Polish businesses that preferred to employ German workers at lower wages.[19] In October 1946, *Głos Ludu* reported that 300,000 Germans were still living in the Wrocław province alone.[20]

In August 1946, Polish officials discovered leaflets circulating in Silesia calling on the Germans to petition the Allied Control Council for a restoration of the German-Polish border of 1937.[21] After anti-Polish demonstrations broke out that fall, one Polish official declared that "not one German should be allowed to remain in Poland"[22] *Głos Ludu* predicted in May 1947 that all Germans would soon be out of the country, but tens of thousands remained.[23]

The Polish press vehemently denied German allegations that the Germans in Poland were being mistreated. The Poles said that the Germans fabricated stories about hungry, ill-clad, and homeless German children in the cities of Silesia. Three years after the end of the war, one German newspaper in the British zone charged that there were 20,000 hungry German children in Poland. The Polish Military Mission pointed out that nowhere near that number of German children lived in Poland, let alone hungry children. The mission also denied that Polish authorities were trying to Polonize the Germans.[24] *Głos Ludu* even said that German children were better fed and clothed than Polish children. The newspaper accused the Germans of laziness and drunkenness and of sending their children onto the streets to panhandle.[25] Soviet journalists told an officer at the Polish Military Mission that they, too, were disgusted with the Germans' behavior.[26]

Germans also disputed the Polishness of some indigenous groups that lived in the former German territories.[27] Several separatist movements sprang up in Poland after the war, primarily in Silesia; Gomułka saw these movements as a German attempt to reclaim the territories on an ethnic basis. He said that the Silesians, Kashubians, and Masurians were Poles too, just like the Cracowians. He likened the differences to ethnic groups in Great Britain and warned, "We will not tolerate any weakening of the autochthon-Poles in the Recovered Territories."[28] In November 1946, Gomułka issued assurances to a group of autochthons: "We will not give back one Pole to the Germans . . . and we do not want one German among Poles."[29]

The other German political parties and refugee organizations chastised the SED for not doing enough to represent the interests of the Germans in Poland, but there was little the party could do. The Polish government regarded the status of these Germans as a domestic affair, and told the Germans, including the SED, not to meddle.

The German communists were also powerless to intervene on behalf of the approximately 45,000 German prisoners-of-war in Poland, many of whom were made to work long hours in Polish coal mines,[30] or help reconstruct devastated Polish cities: Warsaw, Cracow, Gdańsk, and Poznań.[31] After visiting a German POW camp in Szczecin in 1949, one SED functionary reported that the German prisoners "often revealed an undisguised hate for the Polish people. . . . The [SED's] policy of friend-ship and peace with the Polish nation, [and] recognition of the Oder-Neisse line as the border of peace is absolutely rejected."[32]

As of August 1949, there were still 10,000 German POWs in Poland.[33] In early December, the head of the Polish Military Mission, Jakub Prawin, promised Ulbricht that most of the prisoners would be released and sent home by Christmas.[34] The last German POW left Poland in April 1950.[35]

Repatriation of the Germans from Poland, 1949–1953

According to official Polish estimates at the end of 1948, approximately 105,700 Germans, or 5.1 percent of the prewar population, still lived in the Western Territories; these Germans comprised only 1.8 percent of the population in the territories.[36] The Polish Ministry of the Recovered Territories found that only a small number of the remaining Germans were specialists, technicians, and other workers with unique and irreplaceable skills.[37]

In December 1949, Prawin informed Ulbricht that the Germans who had families in Germany could leave Poland. According to the Polish Military Mission, of the approximately 130,000 Germans still living in all of Poland in 1949, 15,000 had relatives in the GDR, and 30,000 had family ties in the FRG.[38] Polish Foreign Minister Stefan Wierbłowski advised his government to repatriate in an orderly and humane manner those Germans who wanted to leave Poland, "in order to at least neutralize this element and in this way facilitate the political work of our German friends [in the GDR]."[39]

The SED received hundreds of letters from Germans in Poland complaining of discrimination,[40] but the party was not interested in their fate. Approximately 4 million immigrants from Poland already resided in the GDR, and the SED did not want more. The refugees were bitterly opposed to the SED's policy of reconciliation with Poland, and were a source of uncompromising nationalist opposition to communist rule.[41] Many repatriates soon left the GDR for West Germany, where they agitated against the GDR and the Oder-Neisse border.[42]

The German communists could not afford to ignore the Germans in Poland, however. The East German government had to challenge the FRG's assertion that it was the Germans' legitimate representative abroad. East German officials alleged that Polish authorities were telling the Germans not to go to the GDR because the East German standard of living was much lower than Poland's.[43] East German Chief of Mission Friedrich Wolf also accused Polish authorities of serious abuses against the Germans in western Poland. Wolf asserted that the Germans were not afforded cultural amenities or opportunities to join trade unions and the

PZPR. Premier Cyrankiewicz told Wolf that his government was doing everything it could to give the Germans the same rights as Poles. He said that Polish officials who had committed wrongdoing would be punished, but suggested that the Germans were also guilty of misdeeds. He rejected Wolf's request for official talks on repatriation.[44]

In early January 1950, the East German government offered to take all Germans who wanted to leave Poland; the Polish government flatly rejected emigration on such a large scale.[45] The Poles again agreed to family reunification,[46] but the Polish Parliament passed a law in 1951 declaring that there were no other Germans in Poland who could claim German citizenship. The repatriation transports ended that March.[47] In June, East German Foreign Minister Georgi Dertinger informed Polish Chief of Mission Jan Izydorczyk that the termination of the repatriation transports was creating serious problems for his government, and demanded an explanation. Izydorczyk responded that most of the Germans wanted to go to West Germany, not East Germany, and that they agitated against Poland and the Oder-Neisse border. He said this was causing problems not only for Poland but for the GDR and the Soviet bloc as a whole.[48] Izydorczyk characterized the tone of this discussion as "unpleasant."[49]

During a visit to Poland in July, Ulbricht again raised the repatriation issue. The Polish government agreed to examine individual cases, but rejected a general plan for mass repatriation.[50] An SED report on repatriation concluded that "it is of particular significance that the Polish government is not prepared to negotiate with a GDR delegation over the pressing repatriation matters, although there are a whole series of complicated questions to clear up."[51]

Evidently under some pressure from the Soviet Union, on February 1, 1952, the Polish government signed a new agreement to reunite Germans with their families in the GDR. The operation was supposed to be completed by the end of the year.[52] The East German Diplomatic Mission in Warsaw was delighted with the deal, and wrote the Polish Foreign Ministry that it not only would reduce anti-Polish agitation by the Germans in Poland and the repatriates in the GDR but would have "a definite influence on the solidification of friendly relations between our peoples."[53]

The controversy was far from over. In 1952, the East German government submitted lists of 8,592 persons to be reunited with their families, but by early 1953 only 2,302 had been allowed to leave. When the Poles announced in March that they would not accept more lists, the East German Diplomatic Mission reported that "in no way can it be seen that the problem of reuniting divided families is settled and the protocol of February 1, 1952 fulfilled."[54]

In April 1953, Polish Foreign Ministry official Maria Wierna told the new East German Chief of Mission Änne Kundermann that the last transport of Germans would leave in June. The East Germans protested that Poland could not stop the transports unilaterally, and blamed the Poles for acting too slowly to aid the repatriation.[55] The West German Foreign Ministry observed that there was still "small hope" of emigration to East Germany of Polish Germans who were "old, sick, or had the very next of kin in the Soviet zone. All others can no longer count on their emigration."[56]

The East German government sent a formal note to Warsaw on June 5 protesting Poland's failure to meet the provisions of the repatriation agreement.[57] Polish Foreign Minister Stanisław Skrzeszewski angrily responded that his government was not obligated to repatriate those *Volksdeutsche* and autochthons on the East German lists who held Polish citizenship before September 1, 1939. Skrzeszewski said that most of the approximately 6,000 people on the lists who had been denied emigration fell into that category. In addition, he blamed the East German authorities for not submitting the lists on time. Skrzeszewski wrote that "the [East German] note of June 5, 1953, containing the statement that the Polish-German protocol of February 1, 1952 has not been fulfilled, is without precedence in our relations with the GDR."[58]

A month later, Kundermann confronted President Bierut about Poland's repatriation policy. She characterized Bierut's reception as "rather cool." Kundermann said that her government was not interested in mass transports, but wanted only to repatriate the people on the lists. She complained that no reason had been given for the exclusions. Bierut informed her that the matter was closed: "The submission of lists must also come to an end and cannot be extended to an unspecified time." He said that only individual cases of family reunification would be considered in the future. Bierut agreed to examine the grounds for denying exit visas, and the whereabouts of two other missing lists.[59]

That fall, the Polish government reluctantly agreed to more talks. Hermann Matern and Peter Florin told Polish Foreign Ministry officials Ostap Dłuski and Maria Wierna that East Germans with relatives still in Poland were causing serious political problems for the SED: "Party activists are in a difficult situation because they often have no arguments at all against open questions and attacks on this issue. The impossibility of uniting families is incomprehensible to the people." Matern and Florin pointed out that of the over 12,700 names submitted to the Polish government, only about 4,000 had been permitted to emigrate to the GDR. They contended that it was in the interest of both governments to complete this process as soon as possible. Dłuski and Wierna countered that the mass repatriations had to end so that the remaining Germans could concentrate on building their lives in Poland. They said that every new transport contributed to a "suitcase atmosphere," and reiterated that their government was opposed to repatriating anyone on the East German lists who held Polish citizenship. They noted that of the 12,723 people on these lists, 8,237 held Polish citizenship, and of those, 1,521 had been allowed to emigrate anyway. The Poles added that many of the children on the lists were adults, and that in many cases the Germans' relatives in the GDR were distant relatives, not next of kin. They also said that many of the Germans ultimately wanted to go to West Germany anyway. The Poles pointed out that 4,150 Germans had already emigrated to the GDR, another 1,900 would leave shortly, and an additional 2,500 would probably receive permission to leave. Dłuski and Wierna contended that this total emigration of around 8,500 people "facilitates a definite conclusion to the major difficulties in the GDR resulting from this issue."[60] The repatriations continued well into 1954. According to estimates of the Polish Foreign Ministry, 9,892 Germans were repatriated to the GDR from February 1952 to September 1954.[61]

At the end of October 1953, the Polish government conducted a thorough study of the situation of the estimated 70,000 Germans remaining in Poland.[62] The report characterized their socioeconomic situation as "generally satisfactory" and comparable to the living standards of Poles. The report even found that many Germans enjoyed a higher standard of living than Poles; the report said that German children were happy in school, where they got along reasonably well with Polish children.[63] In other attempts to appease the German population, the Polish government gave Germans the right to vote in parliamentary elections in 1952, and in local elections in 1954. According to Polish sources, a significant number of Germans were becoming more involved in political matters and were generally optimistic about their future in Poland, although many still held negative opinions of Poles and the Polish government. Polish officials blamed some of the anti-Polish, anti-Soviet, and anti-GDR displays on propaganda from the FRG, on families with relatives in the West, and on letters and packages from West Germany.[64]

In the mid-1950s, Warsaw tried to improve relations with Bonn by allowing some of the Germans in Poland to go to the FRG (see Chapter 8). The Poles' disregard for the GDR's interests in this matter contributed to the general decline in relations after Gomułka's return to power in 1956.

Disputes over Reparations and Trade, 1945–1953

Recurring disagreements over trade illustrated that national interests were still paramount in the thinking of the Polish and East German communists. Even after the Soviets formed the Council of Mutual Economic Assistance (Comecon) in 1949, and Western Europe began to direct its trade away from the Soviet bloc, economic cooperation across the Oder-Neisse line never attained the level that the communist propagandists had promised. Each side grumbled that the other was not interested in fully developing mutually beneficial economic ties.

The German communists, along with the other German parties, rejected reparation payments to Poland. The KPD and SED regarded Poland's occupation of German territory as enough payment for the war, but the Polish government expected to receive 15 percent of the reparations from the Soviet zone as stipulated in the Potsdam agreements. In August 1945, the Soviet Union and Poland signed a reparation agreement promising Poland everything from machines to works of art.[65] A Soviet-Polish reparations commission was formed in the fall of 1945, but the Soviet occupation authorities ultimately decided what the Poles received. Shipments to Poland usually fell short of Soviet commitments.[66]

The reparations also held strategic meaning for Poland. The Poles, like the French and the Soviets, wanted to emaciate Germany's industrial capacity so that it could never fight another aggressive war. Gomułka declared that Germany's industrial potential should be completely eradicated, and that Germany's standard of living should be no higher than the rest of Europe's. He said that Poland could not afford to have Germany overtake it economically.[67] After the economic unity of Germany broke down in 1947, and U.S. Secretary of State George Marshall proposed a reconstruction plan for Germany and Europe, Polish Foreign Minister Stefan Wierbłowski again told Allied foreign ministers in London that German economic development should not be allowed to surpass that of its war victims.[68]

The German communists had the almost impossible task of garnering grass roots support while the Soviet occupation authorities were stripping the zone of so many of its vital assets. Many SED members openly expressed their opposition to the reparation payments, but they were powerless to stop them.[69] Few Germans agreed with Paul Merker's explanation that "the reparations which we are obligated to pay are certainly a great burden for the German people, but they do not hinder in any way the normalization of life of the working population. We must merely prevent the trust-and-monopoly bosses from using the reparations output to profit, like after 1918."[70]

In addition to the burden of reparations, many Germans blamed the slow postwar economic recovery on the loss of German territory to Poland, which included Silesia, one of Europe's most important industrial centers. Under the harsh conditions of the Soviet occupation, the SED was hard-pressed to raise the standard of living in the zone without imports of raw materials and agricultural products from Poland. Initially, the East German communists were confident that their ideological affinity to the Polish communists would work in their favor.[71] Bruno Koehler told Prawin that if the Oder-Neisse region was integrated economically, "then the question of the border will not have its past importance. We will have a lively trade in goods from Poland for our factories."[72] At the end of February 1947, the Polish Military Mission predicted that if Poland signed an economic agreement with the Soviet zone, the LDP would probably rethink its rejection of the Oder-Neisse border.[73] The PPR would not compromise, however, and demanded that all the Soviet-zone parties commit to the Oder-Neisse border, with no contingencies.

The SED, however, was initially reluctant to make separate economic agreements with Poland because the party did not want to set a precedent for the eventual division of Germany. In March, Ulbricht informed Prawin that "from a strategic point of view it is not possible to concentrate on an alliance with Poland and Czechoslovakia only . . . [or] to conduct a policy of distancing the Soviet zone from the rest of Germany, because that would put the struggle for the unity of Germany on the back burner." Ulbricht added that the SED had vacillated on recognizing the Oder-Neisse border because the party had been slow to develop an economic recovery plan. Ulbricht told Prawin that to silence critics of the SED's support for the Oder-Neisse border, Germany must expand production three to four times more than was planned at Potsdam. Ulbricht said that the Soviet zone desperately needed the coal and steel that it was no longer getting from the British zone.[74] Prawin later informed Pieck that he saw no connection between an increase in Polish exports and German unification, but agreed that raising the standard of living in the Soviet zone would ultimately contribute to the economic unity of the four zones.[75]

Prawin's superiors in Warsaw were in no hurry to see that happen. The destruction of Poland in the war and the loss of the eastern territories to the Soviet Union made Polish officials reluctant to grant the SED trade concessions; Polish economic plans did not provide for trade with the Soviet zone. Instead, the Polish government made it a priority to integrate the Western Territories into the Polish economy, and fostered Silesia's trade links with Czechoslovakia and Hungary. The PPR conducted an intensive propaganda campaign to promote economic development in the region. In early 1946, *Głos Ludu* wrote that "the Polish Workers' Party is mobilizing all of its forces . . . on the Recovered Territories' front. . . . There is no Poland without the Oder-Lusacian Neisse [border]." The newspaper published numerous articles on the reconstruction of the Western Territories, often accompanied by huge headlines trumpeting such proclamations as "The Recovered Territories: Guarantee of the Strength and Potential of Poland!"[76]

The Synchronization of the Socialist Economies, 1948–1953

The Polish government was keenly interested in Marshall's reconstruction plan for Europe in 1947, but Polish officials were skeptical about Germany's participation. After the Soviets forced Warsaw to reject the plan, the Polish government declared that Poland did not want to be a party to German reconstruction. On July 10, *Głos Ludu* wrote that "Poland, the victim of numerous German attacks, cannot take part in the conference [on the Marshall Plan], whose result might contribute to the revival of German aggression."[77]

The collapse of allied cooperation in Germany was unsettling to the Polish government, however. Poland had much to lose if the Potsdam agreements were no longer regarded as the legal basis for the Oder-Neisse border. When interzonal trade in Germany collapsed in 1948 and the SED leadership began to quash popular opposition to the border, the Polish government considered increasing trade with the Soviet zone.[78]

Given the geographical proximity and existing communications infrastructure, a renewal of prewar trade connections between the Soviet zone and Poland's Western Territories made simple economic sense. The Polish press began to differentiate between the Soviet zone and the rest of Germany; it promoted the SED's plans for economic ties to the Soviet Union and the other socialist countries.[79] But reports on Poland's economic relationships with the Soviet Union and Czechoslovakia still overshadowed coverage about trade with the Soviet zone.[80]

When the Soviets blockaded Berlin in June 1948, the SED stepped up efforts to expand trade with Poland, placing top priority on imports of coal, coke, iron ore, and steel.[81] *Neues Deutschland* reported that "the Polish coal deliveries for Berlin prove that the capitol does not stand alone in its struggle against the throttling of its economy."[82] In July, the head of the German Economic Commission (DWK), Heinrich Rau, told the Poles that "economic cooperation between Poland and the Soviet zone in Germany is one of the basic principles of DWK policy. The commission projects Poland as its main partner in the execution of its economic plans."[83] Following a visit to Poland in October, Bruno Leuschner acknowledged that the SED had to earn the trust of the Poles before it could expect a significant expansion of economic ties:

> Why haven't we received enough coal, any fats, any meat, any steel making equipment, and any coke up to this point? Of course one does not give a trading partner goods that one needs himself, if one is not sure that the friendship is really meant sincerely. First the political step must be taken, then the economic questions will be solved. For example, we should not forget that [Polish] coke production barely satisfies Poland's own needs. If we get coke anyway, that is a gesture of friendship that cannot be valued highly enough.[84]

In a public show of unity, the SED credited their expanding trade connections with Poland for the gradual recovery of the Soviet zone economy. Grotewohl called for a new political and economic relationship with Poland so that East Germany could share in the production from the former German territories.[85] The SED press, which in the past had conspicuously avoided covering Poland's economic development of the Western Territories, now began to reverse that policy. In late August, *Neues Deutschland* predicted that Poland would soon become the Soviet zone's second most important trading partner (behind the Soviet Union), arguing that "in the close cooperation with the new people's Poland there is also a guarantee for achieving a better life in the eastern zone."[86]

In private conversations with the Poles, however, the German communists often expressed their disappointment in the volume of trade, especially the lack of coal and coke imports from Silesia. The Soviets were partly to blame for the shortage of available Polish coal because they were forcing the Polish government to ship so-called "reparation coal" to the Soviet Union at well below world market prices.[87] In addition, the Polish government preferred to export coal and coke to Western Europe (including West Germany and West Berlin), where they commanded a higher price.[88] The Soviet Union and Poland signed a trade agreement in February 1946, but the Soviet zone received none of the 11.4 million tons of coal and coke that Poland exported that year. In 1947, Poland sent all its brown coal exports to the Soviet zone, but only 10 percent of its coke exports.[89]

The Berlin blockade did more economic damage to the Soviet zone than it did to West Berlin. In December 1948, Ulbricht told the Polish Military Mission that the economic situation in the Soviet zone was grave, and pleaded for more imports to boost domestic production.[90] In the spring of 1949, Ulbricht led a delegation to the annual trade fair in Poznań to explore the possibilities of increasing trade with Poland.[91] Poland's trade with the Soviet zone rose significantly in 1949, but only after a drop in demand for Polish coal in Western Europe.[92]

By the time the GDR was formed in October 1949, the Soviet zone of Germany accounted for 10 percent of Poland's exports and 7.5 percent of Poland's imports. In 1950, those figures rose to 15 percent and 11.5 percent respectively, but the East Germans still wanted more Polish coal. The saturated West European coal market and the West's economic embargo forced Warsaw to seek a deal to sell coal and coke in return for East German machines, appliances, raw materials, half-finished goods, and consumer items.[93]

When Ulbricht arrived in Warsaw in June 1950 to sign the Oder-Neisse border agreement, Minister of Industry Hilary Minc and Foreign Trade Minister Tadeusz Gede met the East German delegation at the Warsaw train station. Their presence underscored the importance of a new trade deal to the Poles. Minc told Ulbricht that "there is no doubt that the visit of this delegation to Warsaw will result to a great degree in the resolution of a wide range of economic questions." Before Ulbricht left, he initialed a trade pact.[94]

When the Western Allies announced an end to the state of war with the FRG in 1950, the Soviets admitted East Germany into Comecon. The SED saw political as well as economic benefits of the GDR's membership; the party lobbied for more economic cooperation by arguing that the economic health of the GDR was crucial to the security of the entire Soviet bloc.[95] East Germany sent four trade delegations to Poland in 1952, twice the number of any other Soviet bloc country.[96] In contrast to the problems that the Polish diplomats in Berlin had in making personal contacts with other East German officials, Poland's trade representatives reported that they had easy access to East German trade offices.[97]

Nonetheless, the volume of trade always fell short of expectations. Poland and East Germany were both guilty of delinquent deliveries or outright failures to ship promised goods. Forced by the Western embargo and the logic of their own planned economies to trade primarily within the confines of Comecon, they were hard-pressed to find substitute suppliers. Most of the export shortages were caused by production problems; but in some cases, simple economics dictated that goods be exported elsewhere for higher prices or kept for domestic use.

Neither side trusted that the other was negotiating in good faith. The East Germans questioned Poland's motives for trying to increase trade with West Germany and the other capitalist countries. The SED did nothing to ease Poland's trade with FRG because it was bound to come at the political and economic expense of the GDR.[98] The Poles, however, suspected that the East Germans wanted to develop a special economic relationship with the Soviet Union for political reasons; trade with Poland made more economic sense. Polish officials knew that some of the shortages in promised East German exports to Poland in 1950 were the direct result of an increase in East German deliveries to the Soviet Union.[99]

These shortages resulted in an East German trade deficit of $2 million in 1950 as well as serious bottlenecks in some Polish industries. Polish officials dropped hints about unforeseen political repercussions should the GDR not meet its obligations. The Poles, however, responded positively to Grotewohl's request for more coal in 1950.[100] Wolf warned his superiors that breaking trade agreements would have a detrimental impact on relations with Poland in general: "In my opinion the question is not simply a technical question of trade relations, but of course at the same time also a question of mutual political trust and understanding."[101]

Wolf was right. In the fall of 1950, a shortfall in chemical imports from the GDR forced the Poles to shut down two large factories in Katowice.[102] With their Six-Year Plan in jeopardy, Polish officials insisted that if the GDR could not meet its export requirements on time, the Poles preferred not to include precise delivery timetables in future trade agreements.[103] One Polish trade official told the East Germans that Poland did not have such difficulties with Hungary. He admonished the East Germans to be sure of their ability to make punctual deliveries before entering into more contracts.[104]

Disagreements also arose over the quality of the goods traded. The East Germans complained about receiving coal and coke of poor quality,[105] and the Poles were dissatisfied with the standards of East German consumer items; in 1950, for instance, the Poles returned a shipment of 15,000 watches, most of which were defective, and coffee pots whose covers were so small that they fell into the pot. East German diplomats in Warsaw admitted that East German cosmetics were of such poor quality and so poorly packaged that they could not be put on the Polish market. They also reported that East German butchering machines left the meat black, and that by the time one shipment of graphic machines reached Poland, they were thoroughly rusted through.[106]

Negotiations for a new trade agreement began in March 1951, but it took two months of hard bargaining before an agreement was signed. Izydorczyk blamed the East Germans for refusing to rectify their trade deficit by increasing exports, especially chemicals.[107] Problems resurfaced that summer when the East Germans were unable to deliver promised petroleum products.[108] The Polish government again attributed the shortages to an increase in East German exports to the Soviet Union,[109] and therefore had no compunction about delaying coal and coke shipments to East Germany. East German officials, in turn, complained that some of their factories were idle because of the shortfall of Polish coke and the inferior quality of the coke they did receive. When several appeals from lower-level officials brought no results, Grotewohl wrote a personal letter to Cyrankiewicz in November 1951 requesting more coal. Grotewohl also asked that future trade agreements include high standards for goods.[110] Cyrankiewicz replied that his government was doing everything it could to meet its obligations, but that there was a problem with a new cokery.[111]

Both economies were struggling in the early 1950s. The Polish government ended rationing in 1949, but had to reinstate it in September 1951 as a result of increased defense spending and the over-ambitious industrialization of the Six-year Plan. Collectivization took its toll on the amount of foodstuffs going to market, especially in the former German territories. The West's economic embargo on the Soviet bloc also hurt the socialist economies. The United States ended Poland's most-favored-nation status in 1952.[112]

When the SED embarked on a rapid socialization of the GDR economy in the summer of 1952, energy shortages in East Germany became so serious that Grotewohl sent yet another letter to Cyrankiewicz requesting additional shipments of coal and various heavy industrial goods.[113] No significant increase in Polish exports was forthcoming, however, and the GDR was unable to meet its own export plans for 1953.[114]

There were signs, nonetheless, that trade relations were improving.[115] The East German government praised the Soviet Union and Poland for their economic cooperation, and credited Soviet iron ore and Polish coal for enabling the GDR to produce "steel of peace."[116] In the fall of 1953, the Soviet Union and Poland lifted a heavy burden from the East German economy when they agreed to end reparations;[117] Grotewohl and Pieck sent several personal letters thanking Bierut.[118]

The volume of trade between the two countries jumped 72 percent from 1950 to 1955, but this was largely a result of the growth in their respective economies.[119] The proportion of Poland's trade with the GDR remained the same throughout this five-year period. Imports from the GDR represented 11.5 percent of all Polish imports in 1950, and 15.1 percent in 1954. Exports to the GDR amounted to 14 percent of all Polish exports in 1950, but had dropped to 13 percent by 1954.[120]

The relaxation of Soviet control over the satellites in the mid-1950s allowed Poland to rethink its trade relations with the GDR (see Chapter 8). Poland began to sell more coal and coke to the West, and exports to the GDR dropped. The SED, which no longer considered Poland a reliable trading partner, embarked on a long-term strategy to develop economic ties to the Soviet Union. In economic affairs, the ideological unity of the Polish and East German Marxists was barely evident.

Notes

1. *Głos Ludu*, November 10, 1946, p. 1; and Władysław Gomułka, *O problemie Niemieckim* (On the German problem) (Warsaw: Książka i Wiedza), 1971, p. 120.

2. See Norman Naimark, *The Russians in Germany: A History of the Soviet Zone of Occupation, 1945–1949* (Cambridge: Harvard University Press, 1995), p. 75. He writes, "Orders went out from the Polish communists to expel Germans by whatever means necessary, to ensure incorporation as well as occupation. As a result, the Polish administration of the new territories made little effort to protect local Germans from the depredations of Polish or Russian rapists and thieves. . . . Even the Soviets expressed shock at the Poles' behavior."

3. *Głos Ludu*, April 25, 1946, p. 4; see Hans Georg Lehmann, *Der Oder-Neisse-Konflikt*, (Munich: C. H. Beck, 1979), p. 36. Lehmann characterizes the expulsions in the summer of 1945 as "brutal" and "wild."

4. *Głos Ludu*, January 1, 1946, pp. 12–13.

5. See *Głos Ludu*, March 17, 1946.

6. *Głos Ludu*, February 26, 1946, p. 1.

7. Naimark, *The Russians in Germany*, p. 149.

8. *Deutsche Volkszeitung*, July 24, 1945, p. 1.

9. *Deutsche Volkszeitung*, October 17, 1945, p. 2.

10. *Deutsche Volkszeitung*, November 20, 1945, p. 1; see also *Deutsche Volkszeitung*, November 23, 1945, p. 1.

11. *Deutsche Volkszeitung*, November 17, 1945, p. 3.

12. Pieck speech to the National Unification Congress of the Polish Organization of Fighters for Independence and Democracy, September 1, 1949, SED ZK, Wilhelm Pieck Papers, NL 36/441.

13. Article by Wilhelm Pieck in *Neues Deutschland*, September 6, 1949, in SED ZK, Wilhelm Pieck Papers, NL 36/441.

14. Izydorczyk to Dłuski, February 28, 1952, PZPR KC, 237/V–146.

15. *Głos Ludu*, January 1, 1946, pp. 12–13.

16. *Głos Ludu*, July 17, 1946, p. 2; and August 27, 1946, p. 7; and H. Kotlicki to the Ministry of Recovered Territories, June 14, 1947, PZPR KC, group PPR KC, MZO, file 134; In January 1947, the Polish Military Mission in Berlin sent word to Warsaw of numerous German offers to work on Polish reconstruction projects or to set up special businesses. At this point, the Polish government would not entertain the resettlement of Germans in Poland.

17. Witalis Zielinski notes, undated, URM BP, file 8/179.

18. *Głos Ludu*, March 30, 1946, p. 5.

19. Unsigned letter to the president of the Council of Ministers, December 20, 1945, URM BP, file 8/526.

20. *Głos Ludu*, October 28, 1946, p. 2; on October 31, 1946, *Głos Ludu* reported that 4,237,040 Poles now resided in the "Recovered Territories."

21. Unsigned memorandum to Jakub Berman, August 9, 1946, PZPR KC, group PPR KC, 295/VII–264.

22. Zmichowski to the Council of Ministers, June 11, 1946, URM BP, file 8/184.

23. *Głos Ludu*, May 24, 1947, p. 1.

24. *Głos Ludu*, May 16, 1948, p. 1.

25. *Głos Ludu*, March 19, 1946, p. 6.

26. Leopold Marschak notes of meetings with Loebe, et al., March 1, 1947, PZPR KC, group PPR KC, 295/XX–70.

27. Unsigned memorandum to Berman, August 9, 1946, PZPR KC, group PPR KC, 295/VII–264.

28. *Głos Ludu*, June 23, 1946, p. 3. According to this source, there were between 800,000 and 1 million autochthons in the Recovered Territories, many of whom had been Germanized.

29. *Głos Ludu*, November 10, 1946, p. 1.

30. Alexander Nasielski notes of a press conference in Berlin for returning German prisoners from Poland, November 15, 1948, MSZ, 6/764/54.

31. *Głos Ludu*, September 9, 1945, p. 6; see also Sikora, *Sozialistische Solidarität und nationale Interessen*, p. 122. According to the Potsdam Agreement, the Soviets handed over approximately 40,000 German POWs to Polish authorities. Fifty-one of the sixty POW camps were located in Upper Silesia, where the prisoners worked in the coal mines.

32. Artur Vogt report on his trip to the POW camp in Szczecin, April 1, 1949, SED ZK, Wilhelm Pieck Papers, NL 36/745. This camp was under Soviet control.

33. Herbert Warnke report on a meeting with German officers in a Polish prison camp, June 7, 1949, SED ZK, Wilhelm Pieck Paper, NL 36/745.

34. Georgi Dertinger notes of a meeting with Ulbricht and Jakub Prawin, December 8, 1949, SED ZK, Otto Grotewohl Papers, NL 90/484.

35. Alexander Fischer, "Aussenpolitische Aktivität bei ungewisser sowjetischer Deutschland-Politik (bis 1955)" (Foreign policy activity in uncertain Soviet German policy to 1955), in Hans Adolf Jacobsen, Gerd Leptin, Ulrich Scheuner, and Eberhard Schulz, eds., *Drei Jahrzehnte Aussenpolitik der DDR*, 51–84 (Munich: R. Oldenbourg Verlag, 1979), p. 70.

36. Government report, January 21, 1949, PZPR KC, group PPR KC, MZO, 295/VII–159. The population of the Western Territories (including Gdańsk) was approximately 8,810,000 before the war. The population decreased to 5,739,000 by October 1948, the majority of them Poles from the eastern territories lost to the Soviet Union.

37. Report on activity in the Western Territories, January 21, 1949, PZPR KC, group PPR KC, MZO, 295/VII–159.

38. Dertinger notes of a meeting with Ulbricht and Prawin, December 8, 1949, SED ZK, Otto Grotewohl Papers, NL 90/484; and Dertinger to Wierna, January 2, 1950, MSZ, 10/472/49. Because estimates varied according to how autochthons and Germans who were Polish citizens were counted, it is difficult to verify the number of Germans who remained in Poland.

39. Wierbłowski to Berman, December 30, 1949, MSZ, 10, IV/472/49.

40. See the many letters in SED ZK, Wilhelm Pieck Papers, NL 36/743.

41. Ackermann to Warnke, November 20, 1951, DDR MfAA, Poland Section, A1804; and Simons notes on the GDR's support for the Germans in Poland, October 25, 1951, DDR MfAA, Poland Section, A1811. The German Evangelical Church also lobbied for the Germans in Poland, and many turned to the Swedish and U.S. Embassies in Warsaw for emigration papers.

42. See, for example, the documents on West German efforts to support the Germans in Poland in BRD BfGDF, B137/290.

43. Kuhn to the GDR Minister of Interior, October 6, 1950, DDR MfAA, Main Office, A10068.

44. Notes of meeting between Wolf and Cyrankiewicz, June 5, 1951, MSZ, 10/398/44.

45. Dertinger to Wierna, January 2, 1950, MSZ, 10/472/49.

46. Kuhn to the GDR Ministry of Interior, October 6, 1950, DDR MfAA, Main Office, A10068.

47. Florin to Grotewohl, April 21, 1951, SED ZK, Otto Grotewohl Papers, NL 90/484.

48. Izydorczyk to Wierna, June 11, 1951, MSZ, 10/398/44.

49. Izydorczyk to the Polish Foreign Ministry, June 11, 1951, MSZ, 10/364/40.

50. Simons notes on the GDR's support for the Germans in Poland, October 25, 1951, DDR MfAA, Poland Section, A1811.

51. Unsigned letter to Grotewohl, October 11, 1951, DDR MfAA, State Secretary, A15627.

52. See the documents on the repatriation of Germans, in MSZ, 10/398/44; see also "The Situation of the Germans in the German Eastern Territories under Polish Administration," undated, BRD BfGDF, B137/290.

53. GDR Diplomatic Mission in Warsaw to the Polish Foreign Ministry, June 5, 1953, MSZ, 10/398/44.

54. GDR Diplomatic Mission in Warsaw to the Polish Foreign Ministry, June 5, 1953, DDR MfAA, Main Office, A10068.

55. GDR Diplomatic Mission in Warsaw to the Polish Foreign Ministry, June 5, 1953, MSZ, 10/398/44.

56. Notes on the Germans leaving Poland, July 2, 1952, BRD AA, Department 2, vol. 439.

57. GDR Diplomatic Mission in Warsaw to the Polish Foreign Ministry, June 5, 1953, MSZ, 10/398/44.

58. Skrzeszewski notes on the GDR Diplomatic Mission's note of June 5, 1953, undated, MSZ, 10/398/44.

59. Kundermann notes of meeting with Bierut, July 24, 1953, DDR MfAA, Main Office, A10068. Kundermann told Bierut that 5,000 people on the list had been denied emigration.

60. Notes of meeting between Zambrowski, Dłuski, Wierna, and Matern and Florin in Warsaw, November 2, 1953, MSZ, 10/398/44.

61. Report on the February 1, 1952 repatriation agreement with the GDR, September, 1954, MSZ, 10/398/44.

62. See the documents in BRD BfGDF, B137/1277. The West German government estimated that there were approximately 65,000 Germans left in the Oder-Neisse area, the rest in former East Prussia.

63. Broniatowski notes on the situation of the Germans in Poland, October 29, 1953, MSZ, 10/398/44; see also *Schlesische Rundschau* (Silesian Review), October 15, 1953, in BRD BfGDF, B137/290. The newspaper recommended that West Germans sending packages to Poland leave off the return address; see also the "Report on Assistance for the Territories East of the Oder-Neisse," February 16, 1955, in BRD BfGDF, B137/290. The West German government estimated that West Germans sent about 290,000 packages to Poland every year. The Polish government did not obstruct this traffic because it collected considerable sums of money from custom duties on these packages.

64. Broniatowski notes on the situation of the Germans in Poland, October 29, 1953, MSZ, 10/398/44.

65. Emil Sommerstein (head of the Bureau of War Reparations) to the President of the Polish Council of Ministers, September 14, 1945, URM BP, 8/477.

66. Bureau of War Reparations to the President of the Polish Council of Ministers, October 15, 1947, URM BP, 8/477; and "Report on Reparations," Bureau of War Reparations, May 1, 1947, URM BP, 8/477; see also Vladislaw Zubok and Constantine Pleshakov, *Inside the Kremlin's Cold War: From Stalin to Khrushchev* (Cambridge: Harvard University Press, 1996), p. 147. According to this source, East Germany lost 3,500 plants and factories, 1,115,000 pieces of equipment, and 2 million industrial jobs.

67. Franz Sikora,. *Sozialistische Solidarität und nationale Interessen* (Socialist solidarity and national interests) (Cologne: Verlag Wissenschaft und Politik, 1977), p. 113.

68. Georg W. Strobel, *Deutschland-Polen: Wunsch und Wirklichkeit* (Germany-Poland: Wish and reality) (Bonn: Edition Atlantic Forum, 1969), p. 12.

69. See Naimark, *The Russians in Germany*, p. 296. Naimark quotes Information Officer Sergei Tiul'panov in August 1947: "Direct anti-Soviet speeches at SED

party organization meetings have become almost constant occurrences. At 209 party meetings of production and district groups taking place in Dresden, there were constant provocational speeches."

70. Report on Paul Merker's speech at the Second Congress of the FDGB, April 21, 1947, PZPR KC, group PPR KC, 295/XX–71.

71. Leopold Marschak notes of conversations with Loebe, et al., March 1, 1947, PZPR KC, group PPR KC, 295/XX–70.

72. Prawin to Warsaw, September 24, 1946, MSZ, 6/668/42.

73. Marecki notes of a meeting with Leutenant, February 28, 1947, PZPR KC, group PPR KC, 295/XX–70.

74. Meller notes of a meeting between Ulbricht and Prawin, March 15, 1947, PZPR KC, group PPR KC, 295/XX–70.

75. Meller notes of a meeting between Prawin and Pieck, May 2, 1947, PZPR KC, group PPR KC, 295/XX–70.

76. *Głos Ludu*, June 4, p. 3; see subsequent issues in the summer and fall, 1946; see also Sikora, *Sozialistische Solidarität und nationale Interessen*, p. 126.

77. *Głos Ludu*, July 10, 1947, p. 1.

78. See Christoph Royen, "Osteuropaische Staaten" (East European States), in Hans Adolf Jacobsen, Gerd Leptin, Ulrich Scheuner, and Eberhard Schulz, eds., *Drei Jahrzehnte Aussenpolitik der DDR* (Munich: R. Oldenbourg Verlag, 1979), p. 604.

79. *Głos Ludu*, July 1, 1948, p. 2.

80. See *Trybuna Ludu* from January to June 1948.

81. Appendix No. 4 to Protocol No. 82 of the SED Central Secretariat, June 7, 1948, SED ZK, IV 2/2.1/205.

82. *Neues Deutschland*, June 29, 1948, p. 1.

83. Broniewicz notes for the Polish Ministry of Industry and Trade, July 15, 1948, PZPR KC, group PPR KC, 295/XX–72. On March 15, 1948, the DWK signed a trade agreement with Poland, and then another on September 25.

84. Bruno Leuschner report on his trip to Poland, undated, ca. October, 1948, SED ZK, Walter Ulbricht Papers, NL 182/1247.

85. *Neues Deutschland*, June 27, 1948, p. 4.

86. *Neues Deutschland*, August 29, 1948, p. 4.

87. See M. K. Dziewanowski, *Poland in the 20th Century* (New York: Columbia University Press, 1977), p. 171. From 1945–1947 the Soviets paid $1.25 per ton of coal, but Denmark and Sweden were willing to pay $12 a ton. In 1948, the Soviets paid $14 a ton; the market price in Europe was $18–19. See also Nikita Khrushchev, *Khrushchev Remembers: The Last Testament* (Boston: Little, Brown, 1974), p. 208. During Khrushchev's visit to Warsaw in October 1956, the Poles raised this issue. Khrushchev later asked Mikoyan, "How did this happen? How could we pay our Polish comrades such an unfair price for their coal?" Mikoyan answered, "It was all Stalin's doing."

88. See Sheldon Anderson, "Poland and the Marshall Plan," *Diplomatic History* 15, no. 4 (fall 1991), pp. 473–494.

89. Sikora, *Sozialistische Solidarität und nationale Interessen*, pp. 110, 125. After the Soviet zone no longer received coal from the Ruhr, Polish coal became an essential energy source.

90. Meller notes of meeting with Ulbricht, December 12, 1948, MSZ, 6/767/54.

91. Internal SED memo, May 10, 1949, SED ZK, Walter Ulbricht Papers, NL 182/334.

92. Report on trade between Poland and the Soviet zone, January 1, 1949, PZPR KC, group PPR KC, 295/XX–72.

93. Fischer, "Aussenpolitische Aktivität bei ungewisser sowjetischer Deutschland-Politik (bis 1955)," p. 72; and Sikora, *Sozialistische Solidarität und nationale Interessen*, p. 125.

94. *Trybuna Ludu*, June 6, 1950, p. 1.

95. Michael Kaser, *Comecon: Integration Problems of the Planned Economies* (London: Oxford University Press, 1967), p. 11.

96. PZPR report on delegations to Poland in 1952, March 28, 1953, PZPR KC, 237/V–76.

97. Izydorczyk to Wierna, October 19, 1953, MSZ, 10/319/36.

98. Wierna notes of meeting between Wierbłowski and Wolf, May 6, 1950, MSZ, 10/373/41. In 1950, Polish Foreign Minister Stefan Wierbłowski said that Poland intended to increase its trade with West Germany one way or the other; and Wolf to Dertinger on a meeting with Wierbłowski, May 22, 1950, DDR MfAA, Poland Section, A1812. Wolf reported that Wierbłowski told him that the question of trade with West Germany was still open because Poland would not sign agreements with the Adenauer régime.

99. See Sikora, *Sozialistische Solidarität und nationale Interessen*, p. 126.

100. Wolf notes of meeting with Gede, April 7, 1950, DDR MfAA, Minister's Office, A15155.

101. Wolf to Ackermann, March 20, 1950, DDR MfAA, Warsaw Embassy, Warsaw Mission, A3662.

102. Erben notes of a meeting with Celinska of the Polish Foreign Ministry, September 14, 1950, DDR MfAA, Warsaw Mission, A3662.

103. Letter to Lore Steimer, signature unintelligible, April 20, 1950, DDR MfAA, State Secretary, A15635.

104. Letter from East German trade delegate (signature unintelligible) to Wolf, December 17, 1950, DDR MfAA, Warsaw Mission, A3662.

105. Müller memorandum, December 19, 1949, DDR MfAuIH, DL–2, file 1948.

106. Erben to Ackermann, July 5, 1950, DDR MfAA, State Secretary, A15635.

107. Izydorczyk to the Polish Foreign Ministry, June 11, 1951, MSZ, 10/364/40.

108. Izydorczyk to the Polish Foreign Ministry, August 10, 1951, MSZ, 10/364/40.

109. Izydorczyk to the Polish Foreign Ministry, May 3, 1951, MSZ, 10/364/40.

110. Grotewohl to Cyrankiewicz, November 20, 1951, DDR Ministerrat, DC–20, file 616. The agreement called for Polish exports of 79,000 tons of coke in October, but the Poles sent only 57,429 tons.

111. Cyrankiewicz to Grotewohl, December 8, 1951, DDR MfAuIH, DL–2, file 1948.

112. See R. F. Leslie, et al., *The History of Poland since 1863* (Cambridge: Cambridge University Press, 1980), pp. 319–320.

113. Grotewohl to Cyrankiewicz, November 6, 1952, DDR Ministerrat, DC–20, file 616.

114. Izydorczyk to Wierna, August 12, 1953, MSZ, 10/366/40; see also Zubok and Pleshakov, *Inside the Kremlin's Cold War*, pp. 159–160. The East German economy was in serious difficulty in 1953 in part because the SED was in the process of nationalizing the entire economy on the Stalinist model. Ulbricht repeatedly asked Moscow for economic aid.

115. Izydorczyk to the Polish Foreign Ministry, September 23, 1953, MSZ, 10/366/40.

116. Izydorczyk to Wierna, May 12, 1953, PZPR KC, 237/XXII–517.

117. See *Neues Deutschland*, May 17, 1950, p. 1. The newspaper carried a huge headline on Stalin's note to Grotewohl announcing that the GDR no longer had to pay reparations to USSR or Poland. In truth, Stalin reduced the reparations payments by 50 percent to $3,171 million. Although the Poles had also agreed to this deal, the article did not thank them.

118. Grotewohl to Bierut, September 15, 1953, MSZ, 10/357/39; and Grotewohl to Bierut, December 31, 1953, PZPR KC, Bierut Archive, 254/IV–26; see also Pieck to Bierut, 22 January 1954, PZPR KC, Bierut Archive, 254/IV–26.

119. Analysis of trade with Poland, July 22, 1955, DDR MfAuIH, DL–2, 2392; and notes on trade between Poland and the GDR, July 6, 1961, PZPR KC, 237/V–379. According to the Polish source, the value of trade between the two countries went up about 50 percent from 1950 to 1955, from 660 million (exchange) złotys to 987.6 million złotys.

120. Fischer, "Aussenpolitische Aktivität bei ungewisser sowjetischer Deutschland-Politik (bis 1955)," p. 72; and Royen, "Osteuropaische Staaten," pp. 604–605; see also "The Polish Economy Since World War II," in BRD AA, Department 2, vol. 242.

5

German Remilitarization and the Polish Thaw, 1954–1955

It is well known that there are greater difficulties in relations between Germans and Poles (of course not in relations between our two states) than in relations between Germans and the workers in the other people's democracies.

—East German Ambassador to Poland Stefan Heymann, 1955[1]

Communist party relations in Stalin's empire were frozen in an atmosphere of paranoia and distrust. After Stalin's death, the Kremlin's New Course promised to build stronger communist bonds, but the uprisings in Czechoslovakia and East Germany in 1953, as well as the West's plans to rearm West Germany, prevented significant change in satellite relations. The "thaw" in the Soviet Union did allow for domestic experiments, however. The Ulbricht régime continued down a Stalinist path, and the PZPR began a slow reforming process. Relations between the two parties steadily deteriorated.

When no agreement was reached on German unification at the four-power foreign ministers' conference in Berlin in January-February 1954, the Soviets announced in March that the GDR would be granted full sovereignty. With almost a half million Soviet troops stationed there, this symbolic move had minimal impact on the real political independence of the East German state, but it did bolster the SED's status with the other satellite parties.[2]

The Polish government officially welcomed the Soviet declaration. Ambassador Jan Izydorczyk told the Polish Parliament that in the likelihood of West German remilitarization, East German sovereignty was in "complete agreement with our national interests."[3] In reality, Polish officials were opposed to putting the GDR on an equal basis with the other Soviet bloc countries. They were concerned about the future of their military mission in Berlin and the distinct possibility that East Germany would be armed;[4] in addition, East German officials appeared to be more assertive in promoting East German interests. East German Ambassador Stefan Heymann told a Polish Foreign Ministry official in confidence that the SED Politburo now thought that it was a mistake to wait for Moscow's initiative before making foreign policy. East Berlin launched new efforts to gain diplomatic recognition from such non-aligned states as India, Egypt, and Finland, and sought out new trading partners. Heymann claimed that Yugoslavia was now willing to champion East German interests in the United Nations and in the Economic Commission for Europe.[5]

For years, the East German diplomats in Warsaw had complained about the inadequacy of their embassy building. After Moscow's declaration of East German sovereignty, Heymann told Polish Foreign Minister Stanisław Skrzeszewski that it was time for the GDR to build an embassy that reflected the country's new political importance. Heymann said that East Germany valued good relations with Poland, and that "of course the size and the outside appearance of our embassy also play a role. Therefore our new embassy building is an urgent political necessity." Skrzeszewski replied that no space was available in Warsaw.[6]

Polish diplomats encountered this new East German self-assurance at a banquet at the North Korean Embassy in Berlin in June 1954. Grotewohl promised the North Koreans assistance in rebuilding their war-ravaged country; he then surprised everyone present by suggesting that the representatives of the other peoples' republics, which Grotewohl claimed were better off than the GDR, make the same commitment. Grotewohl embarrassed Polish Ambassador Jan Izydorczyk by asking him point blank, "Well, Jan, will you make such a pledge in the name of the People's Republic of Poland?" Izydorczyk refused to answer. After dinner, Izydorczyk informed Grotewohl that Poland was already giving aid to North Korea, and that he was not authorized to make new commitments. East German security chief Ernst Wollweber later told Izydorczyk that Grotewohl had spoken without Politburo authorization, and that "the whole 'scene' had a strong social democratic aftertaste."[7]

The East Germans could not trumpet their sovereignty too loudly, however. Without recognition from most of the non-communist countries, the GDR still needed Poland to represent its interests abroad.[8] The East German Foreign Ministry observed that

the role that the People's Republic of Poland plays in Europe's collective security is significant for relations between our countries in two ways. Next to the Soviet Union Poland is the strongest country belonging to the peace camp [the Soviet bloc]. Moreover [Poland's] position between the GDR and the Soviet Union makes relations between our countries especially important.[9]

Warsaw's efforts to improve relations with France prompted Heymann to ask Skrzeszewski to promote East German interests in Paris.[10] Ulbricht hoped that if France recognized the GDR, the other Western countries might follow.[11] In the fall of 1954, the East German press gave thorough coverage of Poland's offer to France for a nonaggression and mutual cooperation agreement. East German journalists stressed that the agreement was not directed against Germany, as Bonn argued. But Poland's willingness to represent East Germany abroad had definite limits; the Poles were careful not to complicate their delicate negotiations with France, and officials at the Polish Embassy in Berlin thought the East German press misunderstood the significance of the Polish proposal.[12]

Ulbricht also worried that Poland and the other Soviet bloc countries would now develop closer economic and political ties to West Germany. Heymann publicly praised the Poles for representing the GDR in the United Nations, but in private East German officials were disappointed with Warsaw's lukewarm efforts to promote the GDR as the principal German state. The East Germans flinched every time the Poles ignored the GDR's role in resolving the German problem, and it was becoming apparent that Poland was more interested in improving relations with the FRG.[13] The East German leaders publicly supported Warsaw's overtures to Bonn, but they worried about being outflanked by the other German state. Heymann asked to be informed about new deals with West Germany and any plans to invite West German delegations to Poland. He informed Skrzeszewski that the GDR, not the FRG, represented German interests in other countries.[14]

In response to NATO's decision in October 1954 to bring West Germany into the alliance, the Soviet Union and the satellite countries issued the Moscow Declaration on October 23, 1954. The Soviets proposed all-German elections, an Austrian peace treaty, and nuclear disarmament. Three weeks later, the Soviets declared that

> a policy is being pursued towards Western Germany which is incompatible both with the promotion of peace in Europe and with the national reunification of Germany. The carrying out of the London and Paris Agreements [to bring West Germany into NATO] will mean that the reunification of Germany through free all-German elections is sacrificed to the present plans of resurrecting German militarism, that mortal enemy of the nations of Europe, including the German nation itself.[15]

That fall, representatives of the Czechoslovak, Polish, and East German parliaments met in Prague to discuss West Germany's entry into NATO and Central European security issues in general.[16] The East Germans could not convince the Poles that the NATO alliance posed an imminent danger. The head of the SED's Department of Foreign Affairs, Peter Florin, complained that the Poles did not show interest in strengthening cooperative diplomatic efforts against West German revanchism and militarism. Florin concluded that the Poles ought to be better informed about the serious threat that the Adenauer government posed to the GDR and to peace in Europe.[17]

Heymann reported that serious differences had surfaced among the three delegations over a communiqué to the French Chamber of Deputies protesting the formation of a West German army. Again, the Poles had reservations about jeopardizing their recent efforts to improve relations with France.[18] Heymann was now convinced that Warsaw was ignoring East German interests in favor of better ties to the West.[19]

Some Poles were not at all opposed to having the FRG contained within the Atlantic alliance. Most Poles, including a significant number of PZPR members, thought that a divided Germany was in Poland's best interest.[20] According to the East German Foreign Ministry, "the reservations among the Polish people to a strong, unified Germany are a lot stronger than we usually guessed. . . . The German problem in Poland is not fully viewed correctly, and the meaning and the strength of the GDR is somewhat underestimated."[21]

When the Soviet Union declared an end to the state of war with East Germany in January 1955, Poland dutifully followed suit. In the original draft of Poland's declaration was a warning that if the Western powers and the West German government ratified the Paris treaty to rearm Germany, "the People's Republic of Poland will further strengthen its relations with the GDR and take any measures with the other peace-loving states which will guarantee the security of Poland and other nations." No special mention of the GDR appeared in the final declaration, however, which left Heymann noticeably disappointed: "This deletion has a significant political meaning. I see in this incident more proof that right now the Polish government is still not very enthusiastic about concluding a tripartite pact between the GDR, Poland, and Czechoslovakia."[22]

Heymann speculated that the Polish government did not want a formal pact with the GDR because the Polish people might think that a war with the West was imminent. Polish authorities were already having difficulty convincing people to settle in the Western Territories. In early 1955, Heymann reported that some Polish farmers there were not planting their fields for fear that war would soon break out.[23] He cited several other examples of Poland's disinterest in closer cooperation with East Germany; for instance, the failed Prague conference and the recent disagreements that had surfaced at a meeting of the Foreign Affairs Departments of the SED, PZPR, and CzCP.[24]

In January 1955, *Trybuna Ludu* editorialized that "today we have a situation in which no important German political problem can be resolved in a peaceful way without the German Democratic Republic."[25] Later that month, however, Heymann noted that the newspaper had raised the possibility of a neutral Germany without mentioning the GDR at all. Articles in the Polish provincial press had often ignored the GDR, but this was the first time that *Trybuna Ludu* had adopted, in his words, such "false interpretations of the German question." He thought that *Trybuna Ludu*'s editorials indicated that the PZPR was less supportive of the Moscow Declaration of October 1954 than the other Soviet bloc parties.[26] Although it should have come as no surprise, Heymann exclaimed that "not a few Poles have fears of [German] reunification!"[27] Exaggerating the GDR's legitimacy and importance in resolving the German question, the East German Embassy guessed that "the main reason for this hesitation is that the strength of the GDR is underestimated, so a certain fear exists that our state could be devoured by the Federal Republic."[28]

The East Germans repeatedly told Polish officials that they supported better relations between Poland and the FRG, and promised to assist in that effort. At a meeting between PZPR, SED, and CzCP leaders in January 1955, for instance, the Poles introduced several plans to exchange professional and student delegations with West Germany; the East Germans offered to help the Poles in developing specific contacts.[29] In reality, the East German offers were a pretext for East Berlin to stay abreast of Polish-West German relations, and to prevent agreements that compromised East German interests. The East Germans were concerned about rumors that Poland and West Germany would exchange trade missions and later raise them to diplomatic missions. Ulbricht called this West German ploy a "Trojan horse."[30]

Ulbricht's suspicions were confirmed in February when the West German government offered to discuss a trade agreement with Poland. Cyrankiewicz suggested that the two countries normalize all relations.[31] In an attempt to preempt the trade missions, Foreign Minister Bolz again offered to help economic and cultural exchanges between Poland and the FRG.[32] In March, he told Bierut that although the GDR supported a trade agreement between Warsaw and Bonn, related questions needed to be resolved beforehand. Bolz acknowledged that he did not want the Poles to compromise East German interests in the negotiations with West Germany.[33]

The East German Foreign Ministry told its diplomats that "in the future it will be especially important to watch all appearances of efforts by the Polish authorities to normalize relations with West Germany."[34] Because most Poles still made no distinction between the GDR and the FRG, Heymann requested more propaganda to inform Polish officials about the "progressive Germans" in the GDR. Heymann agreed with his superiors that East Berlin should participate in talks between Warsaw and Bonn on trade and cultural exchanges so that they would not have a "purely West German character."[35]

East German diplomats repeatedly pressed Polish officials for specific information regarding the ongoing trade negotiations with Bonn.[36] The East Germans also dictated the terms of Poland's trade with West Berlin, fearful that this trade would undermine the GDR's efforts to claim that part of the city. Bolz banned direct contacts between East German officials and the Polish Military Mission, still located in West Berlin. When the Polish government protested, Bolz suggested that the mission coordinate its diplomatic efforts with the Polish Embassy in East Berlin. Skrzeszewski asked the East Germans to expedite the transit of Polish goods to West Berlin, but Bolz flatly refused on the grounds that his government would not allow direct trade connections between West Berlin and Poland.[37] He pointed out that West Berlin was a special case: "Here our efforts are intended to make West Berlin as costly as possible for the American and German imperialists. In our opinion this principle must also be considered in the decision to develop economic relations between the PRP and West Berlin."

Bolz said he would weigh the economic benefits of each trade agreement against the political costs. On this point Skrzeszewski agreed, and Cyrankiewicz assured Bolz that trade with West Berlin would only be included in trade agreements with the FRG. He added that "selling [coal] directly to West Berlin was out of the question." The issue was settled for the time being, but resurfaced after Gomułka's return to power in October 1956.[38]

Unable to stop West German rearmament, the Soviet bloc countries formed the Warsaw Pact on May 14. The Soviets signed the Austrian treaty a day later. After the Geneva Conference in July 1955, Khrushchev stopped in East Berlin to assure the East Germans that no agreement on German unification would be made at the expense of the GDR. Khrushchev met Ulbricht again immediately after the Soviets established diplomatic relations with Bonn in September.[39]

The rapidly changing developments in Central Europe in 1955 unnerved Ulbricht and Bierut. [40] Bierut was alarmed by the Adenauer government's increasingly nationalist foreign policy, and rumors that West Germany might produce nuclear weapons.[41] On an official visit to East Berlin that summer, he pledged Poland's support of Soviet and East German diplomacy regarding German unification.[42] According to one East German diplomat, however, Ulbricht's constant lecturing eventually got on Bierut's nerves.[43] Bonn interpreted the visit as an attempt to prop up the East German government and to "strengthen the status quo in the German problem."[44]

The promise of diplomatic relations between Bonn and Warsaw proved to be an illusion. In 1955, the Adenauer government announced the Hallstein Doctrine, which withheld full diplomatic ties from any country that had formal diplomatic relations with the GDR. From the

Poles' point of view, West Germany's refusal to recognize the Oder-Neisse border and entry into NATO precluded any serious consideration of formal diplomatic recognition anyway.

Poland and the East German Peoples' Army

When West Germany joined NATO in 1955, Moscow went ahead with plans for an East German army, as controversial a subject in the Soviet Union as it was in Poland; as Molotov argued, "Why should we fight the West over the GDR?"[45] The Polish government feared that an eventual withdrawal of Soviet troops from East Germany would leave Poland as the Red Army's main western outpost, in which case Poland would be forced to increase military spending and garrison more Soviet troops.[46]

Poles had fresh memories of the German onslaught in World War II, and were vehemently opposed to an East German army.[47] Foreign Minister Bolz assured Warsaw that the East German people would fight along side the Poles to defend the Oder-Neisse border,[48] but few Poles trusted an East German army whose existence depended on the Soviet Union. The Polish government was so concerned about people's reaction to East German rearmament that during one special simultaneous radio broadcast from factories in Warsaw, Prague, and East Berlin in 1955, Polish officials asked the East Germans not to play any marching or martial-sounding music.[49] Heymann speculated that Polish officials had canceled a tour of East German musicians to Poland that summer for fear that their concerts would be disrupted by demonstrations against the creation of an East German army. The Poles also denied an East German request for a performance of a Quartered People's Police (KVP) band at the fifth anniversary celebration of the Oder-Neisse agreement on July 6, 1955.[50] Heymann told his superiors that if more Polish delegations could review East German police and militia units, they could see that these forces had a "class character."[51]

The West German newspaper *Die Welt* cited SED sources who conceded that the Poles and the Czechoslovaks had serious misgivings about an East German army. The newspaper wrote,

> The Czechs objected that there were too many former Wehrmacht officers employed in the Quartered People's Police who have thoughts of revenge. The Poles agreed with the Czechoslovaks' objection. A news conference that is planned for the beginning of February in Warsaw is supposed to arrange the military cooperation between the three countries in such a way that Prague and Warsaw maintain the right of veto and control over Pankow [the GDR government quarter in Berlin].[52]

According to the West German Foreign Ministry, Bolz's discussions with Polish officials in the spring of 1955 did not produce concrete agreements on the role of an East German army in the defense of Eastern Europe. The Poles rejected a unified high command with East German army officers; they surprised the East Germans with a plan for a joint Polish-Czech command of an army group "north."[53]

The Polish and Czechoslovak governments had no way to prevent an East German army,[54] but they insisted that it be limited to 170,000 men.[55] On January 19, 1956, *Trybuna Ludu* welcomed the remilitarization of the GDR with this headline: "The National Peoples' Army—the Defense Arm of the GDR—This Army—Ally of the Polish Nation."[56] The newspaper wrote that this was "not just a German army, but an army of peace and socialism."[57] The East German Embassy in Warsaw encouraged its Foreign Ministry to send articles on German soldiers who had sided with the Republicans in the Spanish Civil War, German resistance fighters who had fought with Poles in the World War II, Germans who had been incarcerated with Poles in Nazi concentration camps, and biographies on Defense Minister Willi Stoph and East German army officers.[58] To further cooperation and information sharing, the Polish and East German governments agreed to exchange military attachés.[59]

The Polish government knew that if war broke out with NATO, however, asking Polish soldiers to sacrifice their lives in defense of the GDR would be virtually impossible. One PZPR functionary told Heymann that many party members recognized that this was a different East German army, but they had real fears that it was no match for NATO forces.[60]

The SED Restricts Cultural Contacts

The PZPR began a process of self-criticism in late 1954. Bierut acknowledged at the Third Plenum that the security apparatus constituted a "state within a state," and he fired the hated security chief, Stanisław Radkiewicz. Other Stalinists were also purged from the party, and Gomułka was set free in December.[61]

Ulbricht had effectively eliminated most of his opposition after the uprising in June 1953; he was not about to risk destabilizing his government by sanctioning the PZPR's liberalization program. The SED's tight restrictions on East Germans' contacts with foreigners continued. The SED leaders were especially wary of exchanges outside the scientific or technological realm; freer discussions of political and cultural matters threatened to undermine the party's Stalinist propaganda and reeducation efforts.[62]

Cultural relations with Poland remained tied with red tape, just the way Ulbricht wanted it.[63] The GDR Foreign Ministry was given more responsibility for fulfilling cultural agreements in 1954,[64] but the ministry soon complained to the central party organs that it took far too long for a Pole to get a three-month visa to visit the GDR; the ministry further argued that only 7 to 10 percent of East German applicants received visas to Poland. The ministry proposed opening more border crossings and allowing border communities more freedom to develop exchanges, but the SED Politburo stymied these proposals as well.[65] At the end of 1955, the SED dictated that all visa applications for GDR citizens had to pass through the party's Department of Foreign Affairs rather than through the less politically reliable Foreign Ministry.[66]

The Polish exile press commented that "the people in Poland hate the Germans as much today as before, and the Soviets' attempt to develop friendly relations to East Germany has brought no result."[67] East German Ambassador Stefan Heymann agreed: "It is well known that there are greater difficulties in relations between Germans and Poles (of course not in relations between our two states) than in relations between Germans and the workers in the other people's democracies." Heymann and other lower-level East German officials frequently expressed interest in better political and cultural cooperation with Poland. In the summer of 1955, Heymann recommended direct cooperation between the corresponding departments of the SED and PZPR Central Committees and between the Polish and East German Foreign Ministries. He also proposed more exchanges of factory, youth, and press delegations.[68]

That fall, Heymann again complained that the SED leadership was placing too many obstacles in the way of cultural cooperation with Poland.[69] He called the overall state of cultural exchanges "unsatisfactory," especially in the artistic sphere.[70] The SED Politburo ignored Heymann's recommendations and ordered the Foreign Ministry to devote more attention to cultural relations with Czechoslovakia.[71]

In contrast to their East German comrades, local PZPR functionaries could issue visas and plan exchanges. The SED's regional office in Rostock asked to have the same authority; it argued that several visits of small Polish delegations to the GDR had changed some East Germans' opposition to the Oder-Neisse border.[72] The SED's Department of Foreign Affairs emphatically rejected the proposal: "We are astonished that you have already developed such close connections to the PZPR in Szczecin without first informing the Central Committee." The department reminded the Rostock office that all exchanges between delegations in the border regions had to have Central Committee approval.[73]

Heymann and other East German diplomats in Warsaw greatly exaggerated the positive results of the official cultural exchanges that did take place. In early 1954, Heymann reported that various cultural events in Poland to promote German-Polish friendship had been a "great success." He noted that the "Week of Progressive German Culture" had been fruitful in acquainting Poles with issues confronting the GDR, and that "the simple people understand the difference between the GDR and West Germany much better." Heymann was particularly pleased that Poles often asked German visitors whether they were a "Pieck-German" or an

"Adenauer-German."[74] At the end of the year, the embassy declared that Polish workers were even beginning to understand the importance of the GDR in the question of German unification. The embassy was also satisfied with the increase in Polish propaganda against Adenauer and the remilitarization of West Germany.[75]

The PZPR leadership doubted that its own propaganda had convinced party members, let alone Poles in general, that the East Germans could be trusted. Helena Jakubowska observed that "a number of our comrades have still not managed to overcome their dislike of Germans, whom they view uniformly, not distinguishing any significant differences between fascist and progressive Germans."[76]

East German propaganda found relatively little echo in Poland because of its strict adherence to Stalinist ideology. Poles thought East German art and literature were devoid of artistic merit; even East German diplomats conceded this point.[77] One Polish journalist reported that the visit of a Polish delegation to the celebration of the fifth anniversary of the founding of the GDR in October 1954 had confirmed Polish suspicions that the GDR was merely an obsequious Soviet puppet state: "Polish Premier Cyrankiewicz received a very cool welcome there. The German communists openly demonstrated their special friendship with the Soviet delegation and paid little attention to the delegations from the satellite states, which hurt the express sensitivity of the Poles. Cyrankiewicz left Berlin two days earlier than planned."[78]

The Polish Embassy in Berlin reported a significant drop in lectures, discussions, and other party propaganda about Poland in 1954. The embassy blamed this in part on the closing of the German-Polish Friendship Society.[79] The Soviet High Commission in Germany was surprised to find that the society had been dissolved, and told Polish diplomats that there was still much work to do to improve understanding between East Germans and Poles.[80]

The SED's own Department of Foreign Affairs knew that too many East Germans, party members among them, rejected the Oder-Neisse border, saw no reason for friendly relations with Poland, and suffered from a general lack of education about the country.[81] Party members confided in Polish diplomats that "if an [East German] mayor is commissioned to carry out a Polish and a Czech performance, he would rather organize the Czech, and it is likewise easier for him to mobilize the public to these performances." According to the Poles, the SED was also having difficulties overcoming the prejudices of the "kulaks and fascists" among the German refugees from Poland.[82] The Polish Embassy reported that "rather often in rural areas [of the GDR] it is possible to encounter statements praising 'the good times' that Hitler created."[83]

In 1955, the SED stepped up its propaganda campaign for better relations with Poland, but all exchanges were still kept under tight party control. On the tenth anniversary of the end of the war in May, *Neues Deutschland* editor Hermann Axen wrote an article praising cooperation between the GDR, Poland, and Czechoslovakia. He stressed that "through the border of peace on the Oder and Neisse Poland has for the first time in its history a reliable, peace-loving neighbor and friend on its western border."[84] The East Germans were encouraged by the Poles' treatment of Grotewohl and Bolz for the fifth anniversary celebration of the Zgorzelec border agreement in July.[85] Even the West German government recognized that the visit had stimulated new diplomatic activity between the two countries.[86] The East German Embassy called the warm Polish reception for the delegation a "breakthrough" in Polish-East German relations. The embassy praised the work of the Polish press in changing the Polish prejudices against Germans, and criticized its own press for "contributing far too little in the fight against misconceptions among our people." The embassy noted, however, that too many Poles questioned the East German delegation about developments in West Germany, and that the FRG still received more coverage in the Polish press than the GDR.[87]

Cultural exchanges were still fraught with problems. Polish officials filed numerous reports about cultural and economic exchanges that went awry. In many cases, cultural events simply verified existing prejudices; Polish officials complained, for instance, that their booth at the Leipzig Trade Fair in 1954 was far too small—much smaller than the Czechoslovak stand.[88] Heymann pointed out that Poland's space at Leipzig was about the same size as Hungary's or Romania's.[89] But as one of the GDR's most important trading partners, the Poles felt slighted. Poland did not send an exhibit to the Leipzig fair in 1955. The East German Embassy interpreted the absence as a sign that the Poles underestimated the importance of the fair,[90] and as usual, saw sinister Western influence behind the Poles' decision. The East German Foreign Ministry speculated that the Western press was stirring up competition between the two trade fairs as part of an overall strategy to divide the Warsaw Pact countries.[91]

East Germans also showed little enthusiasm for the "Week of German-Polish Friendship" that was held in the GDR in 1955.[92] Polish diplomats complained to the East German authorities that a similar Czechoslovak-German friendship week had been much better organized,[93] and the SED's Department of Foreign Affairs acknowledged that local SED organs had shown little enthusiasm for the German-Polish festival.[94]

In many cases, East German visitors to Poland, even party members, left a bad impression. Attendance was so poor at one East German economic historian's lectures that he regretted not leaving Poland earlier than planned.[95] An East German botanist on tour in Poland eagerly photographed Polish art galleries and other cultural exhibitions, but he was indifferent about seeing evidence of the German occupation of Poland in

World War II. The Polish Foreign Ministry reported that "during his stay in Auschwitz he showed minimal interest and did not take one photo. Afterwards he said that the visit to the museum [at Auschwitz] was undoubtedly useful, but that it had taken a considerable part of the day, which could have been better utilized for scientific endeavors."[96]

Polish officials summed up the visit of a mathematics professor from the Polytechnical School in Dresden this way:

> Polish culture did not interest him in the least. . . . It is worth emphasizing, that at festivities in Poznań, Professor Landsberg did not respond with one word to the rector's special greeting and farewell. The same [thing] repeated itself at the conference of the Polish Mathematics Society, where Professor Borsuk said a few words about the friendly relations between Poland and the GDR. Professor Landsberg responded to those words with complete silence.[97]

When the Director of the Romanistic Institute at the Humboldt University in Berlin, Rita Schober, refused to take a third-class sleeper on a Polish train to Warsaw, the Polish Ministry of Culture commented that "Professor Schober still holds a certain chauvinism and revisionist tendency, and she is not even free from anti-Semitism."[98]

Ambassador Heymann recognized that such meetings were counterproductive. He cited another case of two visiting East German musicians who "often expressed themselves very condescendingly over the condition of the orchestras in Poland, and they also held the view that one cannot describe the PRP as progressive."[99] Heymann warned that this kind of behavior, especially by SED functionaries, was compromising other efforts to foster better understanding between the two peoples.[100]

East German officials were equally critical of the actions of their Polish guests. Polish students studying in the GDR complained that they were treated poorly by East German professors, and that their subsidy from the GDR was too small. The East German Ministry of Education had no sympathy for these grievances, responding that "students often forget that they are students, that they are learning, not working." At a convention for all the foreign students in the GDR, Florin awarded diplomas, book prizes, and small grants to twelve of the best students. Polish officials were angered that none of the Polish students was so honored.[101]

The East German diplomats in Warsaw strongly berated the Poles for their interest in making connections to Westerners, especially to West Germans. A veteran East German reporter in Poland told Heymann that "many Poles still do not distinguish between the two parts of Germany. Even progressive Poles often fail to distinguish between the GDR and the Federal Republic."[102] Heymann related what happened when a storm forced six fishing boats from Western countries, among them West Germany, to seek refuge in the Polish harbor of Władisławowo. The owner of a Danish fishing boat was effusive in his gratitude to the Poles: "We have visited numerous harbors, but nowhere have we been so cordially received as by you." Heymann said that the West Germans were also overly complimentary. He noted that East German fishermen were never afforded such hospitality.[103]

The SED's vigilance over these "un-Marxist" elements in Poland extended into such mundane matters as the employment of translators in the East German Embassy in Warsaw. When Heymann expressed his concern that the Polish translators were not members of the PZPR, the Polish Foreign Ministry promised to find at least one party member to translate confidential documents.[104] A year later, the East Germans were still complaining about the problem.[105]

Nonetheless, Heymann was generally optimistic about the state of relations with Poland in 1955. He reported that the people's trust in the GDR had grown "extraordinarily," adding that relations between the two states was now "significantly closer and better in all areas." He cited the increase in delegation visits, cultural relations, and economic ties, and even commented on the "progressive tendencies" of Polish Catholics.[106] Heymann wrote that there was a "growing awareness among the Polish people that the GDR is a worker and peasant state, and that Poland does not have to fear any more attacks from the west. The feeling of security on the western border is the deciding factor in the consolidation of relations."[107] Heymann often blamed East Germans for poisoning the atmosphere, and cited their continued agitation against the Oder-Neisse border; he also complained to the Foreign Ministry about unfulfilled trade agreements. [108]

Heymann's superiors did not share his views. He was replaced in 1957 in part because he was too optimistic about Poland's socialist development. A decade after the end of World War II, relations between the Polish and East German people had not improved much at all. Although most Poles now knew the difference between an "Adenauer-German" and a "Pieck-German," there was no telling which they preferred. After Khrushchev's secret speech to the CPSU in February 1956 and Bierut's death in March, the PZPR began to acknowledge past policy errors, and also reevaluated relations with the SED. The mask of socialist solidarity was removed, and the latent hostilities between the two parties soon came into full view.

Notes

1. Heymann to the Foreign Ministry, June 21, 1955, SED ZK, microfilm FBS 339/13494.

2. See Marc Trachtenberg, *A Constructed Peace: The Making of the European Settlement 1945–1963* (Princeton: Princeton University Press), 1999, p. 139. He argues that by this time the Soviets had abandoned all serious thoughts about German reunification.

3. Izydorczyk speech to the Polish Parliament, April 1954, PZPR KC, group Izydorczyk, 473/6.

4. Izydorczyk to Skrzeszewski, March 29, 1954, MSZ, 10/329/37; see also Peter Bender, *East Europe in Search of Security* (London: Chatto and Windus, 1972), p. 13.

5. Naszkowski notes of meeting with Heymann, February 22, 1956, MSZ, 10/361/39.

6. Skrzeszewski notes of meeting with Heymann, April 23, 1954, PZPR KC, 237/V–146; and Heymann to Fritz Grosse, April 24, 1954, DDR MfAA, Warsaw Embassy, A3579.

7. Izydorczyk to Naszkowski, June 24, 1954, PZPR KC, Bierut Archive, 254/IV–30.

8. See Skrzeszewski notes of meeting with Heymann, April 23, 1954, PZPR KC, 237/V–146.

9. GDR Foreign Ministry analysis of relations with Poland, undated, unsigned, ca. December 1954, DDR MfAA, Minister's Office, A15156.

10. Heymann to Grosse on a meeting with Skrzeszewski, April 24, 1954, DDR MfAA, Warsaw Embassy, A3579.

11. Stude to the GDR Embassy in Warsaw, November 15, 1954, DDR MfAA, Warsaw Embassy, A3616.

12. Knapik to the Polish Foreign Ministry, September 20, 1954, MSZ, 10/367/41.

13. Heymann notes on Polish activities at the United Nations, October 19, 1954, SED ZK, microfilm FBS 339/13492.

14. Heymann to Grosse on a meeting with Skrzeszewski, April 24, 1954, DDR MfAA, Warsaw Embassy, A3579.

15. Quoted in Neil Fodor, *The Warsaw Treaty Organization: A Political and Organizational Analysis* (New York: St. Martin's Press, 1990), p. 17.

16. See the documents on this conference in MSZ, 10/466/48.

17. Florin to Ambassador Koenen in Prague, January 5, 1955, DDR MfAA, Warsaw Embassy, A3670; see also Werner Hänisch, *Aussenpolitik und internationale Beziehungen der DDR, 1949–1955* (The foreign policy and international relations of the GDR, 1949–1955) (Berlin: Staatsverlag der DDR, 1972), p. 248. As usual, East German historians such as Werner Hänisch said that the conference proceeded without acrimony: "Characteristic for this closer cooperation was the fraternal solidarity of the governments, the parliaments, and the people of Poland and Czechoslovakia with the GDR."

18. Heymann to Handke, January 24, 1955, DDR MfAA, Warsaw Embassy, A3670; and Handke to Heymann, February 3, 1955, DDR MfAA, Warsaw Embassy, A3670.

19. Heymann to Florin, February 1, 1955, DDR MfAA, Warsaw Embassy, A3670; and Heymann to the GDR Foreign Ministry, February 7, 1955, DDR MfAA, Warsaw Embassy, A3670; see also Heymann notes on the meetings in Warsaw between Polish representatives and an East German government delega-

tion (led by Bolz), March 7, 1955, DDR MfAA, Warsaw Embassy, A3579. Bolz told Bierut and Cyrankiewicz that his government was also "very interested" in closer ties with Paris.

20. Heymann to Florin, February 1, 1955, DDR MfAA, Warsaw Embassy, A3670.

21. Grunert to the GDR Embassy in Warsaw, February 4, 1955, DDR MfAA, Warsaw Embassy, A3670.

22. Heymann to Florin, February 1, 1955, DDR MfAA, Warsaw Embassy, A3670.

23. Heymann to Florin, January 10, 1955, DDR MfAA, HA/I Secretariat, A37.

24. Heymann to Florin, February 1, 1955, DDR MfAA, Warsaw Embassy, A3670.

25. *Trybuna Ludu*, January 21, 1955, p. 3.

26. Heymann to the GDR Foreign Ministry, January 28, 1955, DDR MfAA, Warsaw Embassy, A3670.

27. Heymann to the GDR Foreign Ministry, November 29, 1955, DDR MfAA, Warsaw Embassy, A3616.

28. GDR Embassy in Warsaw report, December 9, 1955, SED ZK, microfilm FBS 339/13488.

29. Góralski notes of a meeting with Czechoslovak and East German representatives (Hager, Florin, et al.), January 5, 1955, PZPR KC, 237/XXII–821.

30. Michael J. Sodaro, *Moscow, Germany, and the West from Khrushchev to Gorbachev* (Ithaca: Cornell University Press, 1990), p. 56.

31. Heymann to the GDR Foreign Ministry, June 22, 1955, DDR MfAA, Warsaw Embassy, A3670; and report on the relationship between Germany [sic] and Poland in 1955, undated, SED ZK, microfilm FBS 339/13492.

32. Heymann notes on meetings in Warsaw between the GDR government delegation and Cyrankiewicz and Bierut, et al., March 7, 1955, DDR MfAA, Warsaw Embassy, A3579.

33. Bolz to Grotewohl, March 16, 1955, SED ZK, Otto Grotewohl Papers, NL 90/483.

34. Grunert to the GDR Embassy in Warsaw, March 26, 1955, DDR MfAA, Warsaw Embassy, A3616.

35. Heymann to Grosse, April 9, 1955, SED ZK, microfilm FBS 339/13492; see also Grosse to Heymann, June 25, 1955, DDR MfAA, Warsaw Embassy, A3670.

36. Memorandum on a meeting between Skrzeszewski and Heymann, November 24, 1955, MSZ, 10/361/39.

37. Heymann notes on meetings between the GDR government delegation and Cyrankiewicz and Bierut, et al., March 7, 1955, DDR MfAA, Warsaw Embassy, A3579.

38. Bolz to Grotewohl, March 16, 1955, SED ZK, Otto Grotewohl Papers, NL 90/483; see also Heymann to Grosse, May 3, 1955, DDR MfAA, Warsaw Embassy, A3670.

39. See Ann L. Phillips, *Soviet Policy Toward East Germany Reconsidered: The Postwar Decade* (New York: Greenwood Press, 1986), pp. 131–180.

40. See Jerzy Holzer, "Osteuropa und die neue deutsche Staatenordnung" (East Europe and the new German State arrangement), in Werner Weidenfeld and

Hartmut Zimmerman, eds., *Deutschland–Handbuch: Eine doppelte Bilanz 1949–1989* (German handbook: A double balance, 1949–1989) (Munich: Carl Hanser Verlag, 1989), pp. 685–697. Holzer claims that all three states, Poland, Czechoslovakia, and the GDR were apprehensive about Khrushchev's German policy.

41. Trachtenberg, *A Constructed Peace*, pp. 231–233.

42. Bierut speech, undated, ca. July 1955, PZPR KC, Bierut Archive, 254/I–5.

43. Horst Grunert, *Für Honecker auf glattem Parkett: Erinnerungen eines DDR-Diplomaten* (For Honecker on the smooth parquet: Memoirs of a GDR diplomat) (Berlin: Edition Ost, 1995), p. 103.

44. "Problem of the Federal Republic in the Polish View," by the Office of Expellees, September 26, 1955, BRD BfGDF, B137/1282.

45. Quoted in Nikita Khrushchev, *Khrushchev Remembers: The Glasnost Tapes* (Boston: Little, Brown, 1990), p. 70.

46. Von Mende notes on information from Polish journalists, November 12, 1954, BRD BKA, B136/6483; see also Mary Fulbrook, *Anatomy of a Dictatorship: Inside the GDR, 1945–1989* (Oxford: Oxford University Press, 1995), p. 135. Fulbrook maintains that there was considerable opposition to an East German army in the GDR itself: "Fears of loss of family members were combined with a dislike of the notion of Germans shooting on Germans."

47. See Peter Merkl, *German Foreign Policies, West and East: On the Threshold of a New European Era* (Santa Barbara, Calif: ABC-Clio, 1974), p. 99.

48. Izydorczyk to Warsaw, December 31, 1953, PZPR KC, 237/XXII–518.

49. Heymann to Grosse, April 9, 1955, SED ZK, microfilm FBS 339/13492; and Grosse to Heymann, June 25, 1955, DDR MfAA, Warsaw Embassy, A3670.

50. Heymann to the GDR Foreign Ministry, July 2, 1955, DDR MfAA, Warsaw Embassy, A3670.

51. Heymann to the East German Foreign Ministry, November 17, 1955, DDR MfAA, Warsaw Embassy, A3670; and Heymann to the GDR Foreign Ministry, December 30, 1955, DDR MfAA, Warsaw Embassy, A3616.

52. *Die Welt* (The World), January 11, 1955, in BRD BfGDF, B137/427.

53. Berlin Office of the BRD Foreign Ministry to Bonn, March 21, 1955, BRD AA, Department 7, vol. 84.

54. See Fechter notes, March 25, 1955, BRD AA, Department 7, vol. 84.

55. Kopa memo, March 23, 1956, MSZ, 10/380/42; see also Vojtech Mastny, "'We Are in a Bind': Polish and Czechoslovak Attempts at Reforming the Warsaw Pact, 1956–1959," *Bulletin: Cold War International History Project*, no. 11 (winter 1998), pp. 230–250. New archival evidence points to the serious conflicts within the Warsaw Pact in the latter half of the 1950s.

56. *Trybuna Ludu*, January 19, 1956, pp. 1–2.

57. *Trybuna Ludu*, January 20, 1956, p. 2.

58. Bringmann to Wahner, February 14, 1956, SED ZK, microfilm FBS 339/13494.

59. Handke to Grotewohl, June 15, 1956, DDR MfAA, HA/I Secretariat, A37.

60. Heymann to Florin, April 20, 1956, SED ZK, Walter Ulbricht Papers, NL 182/1247.

61. M. K. Dziewanowski, *The Communist Party of Poland: An Outline of History* (Cambridge: Harvard University Press, 1976), p. 256.

62. Helena Jakubowska notes of meeting with Schlage, November 6, 1953, MSZ, 10/475/49.

63. SED report on relations between Germany [sic] and the PRP in 1955, undated, SED ZK, microfilm FBS 339/13492.

64. Izydorczyk to the Polish Foreign Ministry, April 15, 1954, MSZ, 10/367/41.

65. GDR Foreign Ministry analysis of the current foreign relations, undated, unsigned, ca. December 1954, DDR MfAA, Minister's Office, A15156.

66. SED Regional Office in Rostock to Schirdewan, December 24, 1955, SED ZK, microfilm FBS 339/13422.

67. From *Dziennik Polski* (Polish Daily), December 1, 1953, in BRD BKA, B136/6483.

68. Heymann to the GDR Foreign Ministry, June 21, 1955, SED ZK, microfilm FBS 339/13494.

69. Heymann to the GDR Foreign Ministry, October 5, 1955, DDR MfAA, Warsaw Embassy, A3616.

70. Heymann to the GDR Foreign Ministry, November 17, 1955, DDR MfAA, Warsaw Embassy, A3670.

71. Stude notes of meeting between Grunert and East German representatives of the Society for Cultural Relations with Foreign Countries, October 3, 1955, DDR MfAA, HA/I Secretariat, A37.

72. SED Regional Office in Rostock to Schirdewan, December 24, 1955, SED ZK, microfilm FBS 339/13422.

73. SED Central Committee Department of Foreign Affairs to the SED Regional Office in Rostock, February 17, 1956, SED ZK, microfilm FBS 339/13422.

74. Heymann to the GDR Foreign Ministry, January 21, 1954, DDR MfAA, Warsaw Embassy, A3616.

75. Heymann to the GDR Foreign Ministry, January 28, 1955, DDR MfAA, Warsaw Embassy, A3616.

76. Helena Jakubowska notes of a meeting of the PZPR Basic Party Organization (POP), October 29, 1954, PZPR KC, 237/XXII–732.

77. Manfred Schmidt report on cultural events in Poland in the second quarter of 1955, August 9, 1955, SED ZK, microfilm FBS 339/13494.

78. Von Mende notes on information from Polish journalists, November 12, 1954, BRD BKA, B136/6483.

79. Izydorczyk to the Polish Foreign Ministry, April 15, 1954, MSZ, 10/367/41.

80. Pieck answer to a *Trybuna Ludu* reporter, March 7, 1954, SED ZK, Wilhelm Pieck Papers, NL 36/464.

81. Report on relations between the GDR and Poland in 1955, undated, unsigned, SED ZK, microfilm FBS 339/13492.

82. Wierna to Drozdowicz on a meeting with Wende, November 9, 1955, KC PZPR, Bierut Archive, 254/IV–27.

83. Stanisław Albrecht to the Polish Foreign Ministry, December 30, 1955, MSZ, 10/370/41.

84. Article by Hermann Axen, undated, in SED ZK, Hermann Axen Office, IV 2/2.035/159.

85. Heymann notes on the delegation exchange for the five-year anniversary of the Zgorzelec agreement, undated, ca. July, 1955, SED ZK, microfilm FBS 339/13494.

86. Von Mende to Bachmann, July 14, 1955, BRD BKA, B136/6484.

87. GDR Embassy in Warsaw report, December 9, 1955, SED ZK, microfilm FBS 339/13488.

88. Knapik to the Polish Foreign Ministry, September 20, 1954, MSZ, 10/367/41.

89. Heymann to Handke, September 18, 1954, DDR MfAA, Warsaw Embassy, A3579; see also Florin to Ulbricht, October 12, 1954, SED ZK, Walter Ulbricht Papers, NL 182/1247.

90. GDR Embassy in Warsaw report, December 9, 1955, SED ZK, microfilm FBS 339/13488.

91. Stude notes on Warsaw Embassy report for the second quarter of 1955, September 27, 1955, DDR MfAA, Warsaw Embassy, A3616.

92. Stanisław Albrecht to the Polish Foreign Ministry, May 31, 1955, MSZ, 10/369/41.

93. Heymann to the East German Foreign Ministry, July 2, 1955, DDR MfAA, Warsaw Embassy, A3670.

94. Report on relations between the GDR and Poland in 1955, undated, unsigned, SED ZK, microfilm FBS 339/13492.

95. Emil Skaut notes on Hans Mottek's visit, May 3, 1955, KWKzZ, file 152.

96. Stanisław Smiarowski notes on Ernst Reinmuth's visit, May 6, 1955, KWKzZ, file 152.

97. Skaut notes on Hans Landsberg's visit, July 27, 1955, KWKzZ, file 152.

98. Joanna Olkiewicz notes on Rita Schober's visit, December 16, 1955, KWKzZ, file 152.

99. Report on the Week of GDR-Polish Friendship from November 17 to November 22, January 20, 1956, SED ZK, microfilm FBS 339/13494.

100. Heymann to Grosse, April 9, 1955, SED ZK, microfilm FBS 339/13492; see also Grosse to Heymann, June 25, 1955, DDR MfAA Warsaw Embassy, A3670.

101. Notes on a convention of foreign students in the GDR, unsigned, January 25, 1956, PZPR KC, 237/XX-II–732.

102. Internal memo, unsigned, January 19, 1956, SED ZK, microfilm FBS 339/13494.

103. Heymann to the GDR Foreign Ministry, January 28, 1955, DDR MfAA, Warsaw Embassy, A3670.

104. Heymann notes of meeting with Morawski, December 13, 1955, DDR MfAA, Poland Section, A1811.

105. Łobodycz to Bartel, August 22, 1956, MSZ, 10/361/39.

106. Heymann report on Poland's foreign policy in the second quarter of 1955, August 9, 1955, SED ZK, microfilm FBS 339/13494.

107. Heymann to the GDR Foreign Ministry, November 17, 1955, DDR MfAA, Warsaw Embassy, A3670.

108. Heymann to the East German Foreign Ministry, November 17, 1955, DDR MfAA, Warsaw Embassy, A3670; and Heymann to the GDR Foreign Ministry, December 30, 1955, DDR MfAA, Warsaw Embassy, A3616.

6

Khrushchev's De-Stalinization Speech and Gomułka's Return to Power, January–October, 1956.

In the countries that have de-Stalinized the most, Hungary and Poland, ill will toward the 'GDR' has begun to spread because of its maintenance of the Stalinist Ulbricht course.

—*West German diplomat, October 19, 1956.*[1]

Nikita Khrushchev's visit to Belgrade to see Tito in the spring of 1955 was the first clear signal to the Soviet bloc parties that the new Soviet leadership intended to chart a new foreign policy course. The Polish press began to devote extensive coverage to relations with Yugoslavia, as though calling for a Polish Tito and a Polish national road to socialism. The clamor for a thorough reform of the PZPR and a reevaluation of its relations with the other communist parties quickly escalated after Khrushchev's denunciation of Stalin in his secret speech to the Twentieth Party Congress of the CPSU in February 1956.

First Secretary Bolesław Bierut never made it back from the congress. He died in Moscow on March 11, and was succeeded by Edward Ochab. Ochab, like Bierut, had spent the war years in the Soviet Union, but he was no Stalinist. Ochab allowed party reformers to conduct an honest analysis of past policies, including relations with the Soviet Union and the GDR. Reformers set the record straight about what happened to the KPP during the Stalinist purges of the late 1930s, and exposed the crimes Stalin committed against Poland during the war. In February 1956, the Soviet, Polish, Italian, Bulgarian, and Finnish Central Committees declared that the dissolution of the KPP in 1938 had been mistake.[2] Ochab later acknowledged to an East German official that "when we learned 'the bitter truth about the KPP' [in 1956], it was very difficult for the party leadership to fight on against the trends of middle-class ideology."[3] Party reformers began to agitate for the return of Władysław Gomułka, who had been expelled from the party seven years earlier.

Khrushchev's speech sent tremors throughout the SED. As leader of a party that had been formed at Stalin's behest, Ulbricht refused to denounce Stalin's contribution to communism. He grimly defended his Stalinist policies and quashed dissident voices in the SED who sympathized with the Polish reformers. As far as Ulbricht was concerned, the KPD and SED had set the right course for Germany. In March, one SED member confided in a Polish diplomat that "the appropriate climate has not been created in the GDR to discuss the material of the Twentieth Party Congress of the CPSU, as there is in Poland, so that a whole group of publicists and activists in the GDR are waiting for what the 'Zetka' [the SED Central Committee] will decide." Another East German official acknowledged to Polish diplomats that it was not possible in the GDR to have the kind of honest debates that Polish artists and writers were having.[4]

Off the record, officials in the East German Foreign Ministry told Polish diplomat Stanisław Kopa that the SED leadership was having difficulty justifying Stalin's cult of personality to the party faithful, because Ulbricht had developed one himself. One official said that if Ulbricht allowed criticism of the SED's past policies, the leadership would lose members' loyalty and the SED's credibility with the other parties in the National Front, not to mention the trust of "a broad strata of German society."[5]

As more and more SED members complained about the lack of honest debate within the Central Committee, Kopa wrote that "one would think . . . that the CC of the SED has not committed any mistakes, but of course that is not so."[6] In May, Kopa reported that party members still had not been informed of the exact contents of Khrushchev's speech. Although the SED leadership spoke in theoretical terms about "democratizing party life," in practice power remained firmly in Ulbricht's hands.[7]

Although the SED leaders tried to ignore the secret speech, they were powerless to prevent word of it from leaking to the people.[8] The most serious breaches of confidentiality were coming from Poland. The PZPR was the only Soviet bloc party to circulate the secret speech for its membership. In May, a delegation of East German historians to Poland reported that Khrushchev's speech was being sold on the black market, and that serious manifestations of anti-Sovietism were resulting from the public discussions of Stalin's crimes.[9] In April, Ambassador Heymann reported that the situation in the PZPR was "especially difficult" because party members were openly discussing Stalin's dissolution of the KPP before World War II, the Soviet massacre of Polish officers at the Katyn

Forest in 1940, and the failure of the Soviet Red Army to support the War-saw Uprising against the Germans in 1944. Heymann admonished the Poles for resurrecting what he called these "old lies";[10] he noted, too, that the PZPR's May Day celebration was lackluster, and that Edward Ochab's speech that day was barely interrupted by the usual applause. He warned that "the workers' demonstrations carried a marked *national* character."[11] Heymann also reported that many Poles thought that Stalin had moved the Polish border to the Oder-Neisse to create perpetual ani-mosity between Poland and Germany.[12]

Heymann maintained his optimistic outlook on the general state of re-lations with Poland, however, and portrayed the Poles as much more dis-posed to East Germany than they actually were; he predicted that "the last manifestations of animosity toward Germans will soon disappear."[13] He thought that Ochab was consolidating his control over the PZPR, and that the party would not undergo major changes. He even declared that most party members favorably viewed the GDR as the "island of calm," and that their understanding for the GDR's special situation in relation to West Germany had grown.[14] In an interview with the West German newspaper *Frankfurter Allgemeine Nachrichten*, Heymann was typically upbeat about Poland's political development: "The vast majority of the Polish people stand by the Soviet Union and also support a strong friend-ship with the GDR. Of course there are still several circles, above all intel-lectuals, in which anti-Soviet and anti-German attitudes are present. But these circles are insignificant and have no influence on the political de-velopment of the PRP."[15]

The political reality in Poland suggested otherwise, and the de-Stalin-ization process proceeded apace that spring. Former security chief Sta-nisław Radkiewicz was dropped from the government; the Stalinist Jakob Berman, the eminence grise of the Bierut government, resigned from the Politburo in May. Thousands of political prisoners were freed and many others amnestied and rehabilitated. The political balance was shifting away from the old guard in the PZPR, and toward Gomułka.

Ochab was a pragmatist, always following the Kremlin's lead rather than forging his own policies. Although Ochab believed that Gomułka's incarceration had been a mistake, he made pointed references to the dan-gers of Gomułka's nationalist and revisionist positions. Ochab was markedly critical of Gomułka's agricultural policies after the war, which he alleged had allowed the return of "kulaks." As popular support for Gomułka swelled that summer, Ochab contemplated a way to coopt him without granting him real power. Gomułka would have none of it. He wanted a chance to appear before the party membership to clear his record and his name.[16]

Heymann informed his superiors that some PZPR Politburo members were contemplating the return of Gomułka to power and that "reactionary" student and intellectual groups were forming to support him; nonetheless, Heymann thought the Ochab group was in control of the political situation.[17] Heymann's misreading of the situation in Poland would eventually lead to his recall in 1957. To maintain the public facade of good relations between East Germany and Poland was one thing, but the higher-ups in East Berlin expected more honest reporting from their diplomats in the field.

The Poznań Revolt

The workers' rebellion in Poznań on June 28, 1956, resulted in the deaths of fifty-three demonstrators. The revolt was hard evidence that the PZPR was facing more serious political and economic problems than Heymann was letting on. Divisions within the PZPR widened as reformers in the party demanded leadership that would renounce such brutal Stalinist tactics and champion Poland's national interests. Gomułka was just that man.

The Polish press cautiously alluded to the legitimate grievances of the Poznań workers. Even the PZPR organ *Trybuna Ludu* suggested that economic problems were partly to blame for the unrest.[18] In private, the East German Foreign Ministry agreed, and recommended that every effort be made to send promised exports to Poland—above all, more consumer goods. On the political front, the ministry urged that East German workers' delegations be sent to Poland from those factories that had "fought successfully against the fascist coup in the GDR on June 17, 1953."[19]

The Poznań incident abruptly stopped the de-Stalinization campaign in the Soviet press, which portrayed the revolt as an imperialist plot. At first, Ochab condemned the strikers as well, but on the first day of plenary session of the PZPR Central Committee on July 18, he backtracked, acknowledging that the workers were reacting to a real drop in their standard of living. Ochab promoted a limited "democratization" of the party, which met with disapproval from hard-liners in the Kremlin. Speaking to the plenum on July 21, Soviet Premier Nicholai Bulganin alleged that the Poznań rioters had been inspired by Western imperialists; he urged the party to be on the watch for "hostile and opportunist elements."[20]

As usual, the SED followed the Soviet line, blaming the unrest on fascists, imperialists, reactionaries, and Western spies. The East German Embassy concluded that "the methods of the opposition in the preparation and staging of the provocations in Poznań are the same ones that were used on June 17, 1953, in Berlin."[21] *Neues Deutschland* wrote that "it is no coincidence that the enemy chose Poznań as a showplace for the provocation because at that time the international [trade] fair was taking place. It involved besmirching the good name of People's Poland and disrupting its growing peaceful international relations."[22]

Heymann warned that the Western agents had hoped to instigate a similar violent outbreak in East Germany. He cited as proof the discovery of inflammatory pamphlets in German in one of the Polish "resistance nests." Heymann reported that many young priests had sided with the demonstrators, although the Catholic Church had not taken an active role in the events in Poznań. Nonetheless, Heymann interpreted the quick suppression of the alleged putsch as a sign of the political consciousness and reliability of the PZPR and Polish workers.[23]

Throughout the summer of 1956, the SED and its partner parties suppressed all honest discussion of the Poznań demonstrations. Berthold Rose, the head of the East German DBD, told Polish diplomats that

> the enemy [in Poland] is exploiting the [loosened] atmosphere. . . . They brought about provocations in Poznań. We had similar provocations in 1953. Therefore, in order to avoid new ones, we cannot allow ourselves such open discussions like they had and are having in the other people's democracies after the Twentieth Party Congress.[24]

East German Interior Ministry Vice Minister Herbert Grünstein told Kopa that the Polish government's swift suppression of the Poznań demonstrators was right and necessary because the unrest could have spread to the GDR.[25]

The East German press gave few direct indications that there was any tension in relations with Poland, or that Ochab was in trouble. Throughout the summer and into the fall, *Neues Deutschland* carried frequent and mostly positive articles on Poland. East German journalists issued glowing reports of the visit of Polish delegations to the celebration of the sixth anniversary of the Oder-Neisse agreement on July 6, and to the "Week of Polish-German Friendship" in Rostock. One wrote that "the cordiality with which our Polish friends were greeted everywhere in the cities and towns of our republic, bears witness that the German-Polish friendship has become a matter of the heart for a broad section of our population." *Neues Deutschland* pointed out that Poland was East Germany's second most important trading partner in the Soviet bloc, asking rhetorically, "What would our metallurgical factories be—just to name one example—without Polish coke?"[26] An East German parliamentary delegation to Poland stressed the Poles' warm reception, which the East Germans attributed to "the consistent peace policy [conducted] by both governments."[27]

Heymann's report on the twelfth anniversary celebration of the formation of the Lublin provisional government on July 22 was also positive: "[After] the events in Poznań . . . the masses, to a greater extent than before, recognize the machinations of the enemy and therefore are rallying around their government." Heymann again exaggerated the friendly state of relations between the GDR and Poland; supposedly the East German delegation to the celebration had made a good impression and had contributed to "the close bonds between our two peoples."[28] The congratulatory message that Grotewohl and Ulbricht sent on the anniversary also gave the impression that relations were on track: "The fraternal solidarity between our two peoples is expressed in the heartfelt connections to each other."[29]

Many people-to-people meetings contradicted this propaganda. Time and again East German visitors to Poland were confronted with questions about Khrushchev's speech and the crimes committed by the communists parties during Stalin's rule.[30] An official in the Polish Ministry of Culture chastised one visiting East German Slavic expert, Eugen Häusler, for his ignorance of the Nazi occupation of Poland, the Warsaw Uprising in 1944, and his unwillingness to visit Auschwitz.[31]

Cultural exchanges were more dangerous to the SED now. Much to the dismay of the SED leadership, many East German writers and artists were favorably impressed by the new intellectual freedom in Poland and the political engagement of the Polish people.[32] One East German art historian said that his visit to Poland was much more pleasant than a recent trip to the Soviet Union. He confided in one Polish official that the SED placed many more obstacles in the way of artistic freedom than the PZPR.[33] An East German theater delegation praised the Poles for reconstructing monuments to Polish monarchs,[34] and another group of East German journalists was surprised to learn that the Poles operated a central press censorship office. The East Germans said that if an editor in the GDR did not censor his own publication, he immediately lost his job.[35]

The Polish diplomats in East Berlin generally took a less sanguine view of relations that summer. The embassy complained that cultural ties between the two countries had suffered greatly in the last few years. Few East German personnel were devoted to cultural cooperation, and the East Germans would not agree to more unofficial and spontaneous cultural exchanges. The embassy was generally satisfied with the SED's press coverage of Polish affairs, but it characterized the provincial press as "a lot worse."[36]

Although the East German news reports failed to mention problems related to the Friendship Week in Rostock in June, the Polish Embassy in Berlin complained about a number of unsettling incidents. In Rostock, East Germans had smashed shop windows displaying Polish symbols and slogans; and Polish theater and music performances were beset with technical difficulties, lack of publicity, and poor attendance. East German Foreign Ministry officials told the Poles that because Rostock was a port city, foreigners, most likely West Germans, had probably broken the win-

dows, and asserted that the problems connected with the Polish performances were "in no way connected to any hostile gesture toward
Poland."[37]

The Polish diplomatic corps in the GDR was skeptical about whether
the East Germans really wanted better relations with Poland; at the same
time, East German officials blamed their Polish counterparts for a basic
lack of trust in the GDR. Gottfried Grünberg, the head of the Central Political Office in the NVA (National People's Army), told Kopa that "up to
now cooperation between Poland and the GDR has still been superficial
and often too official. Above all there has been too few meetings between
simple people, workers and peasants." He said that what limited cooperation there was between the GDR and Polish defense ministries was still
too formal.[38]

East German officials were not doing much to engender that trust,
however. To prevent Poland's political instability from affecting the
GDR, the party carefully controlled travel to and from Poland and increased surveillance over all Polish visitors; for example, the East German Ministry of Higher Education sent the PZPR a report of the problems it was having with twelve Polish students studying in Leipzig. The
ministry accused the Polish students of being unprepared, undisciplined,
and of handing in other students' work as their own. The ministry also
said that the Polish students isolated themselves from the other international students and lacked interest in cultural and propaganda activities.
In general, the Polish students were making a bad impression, and the
ministry asked the Poles to rectify the situation.[39] The East German authorities also complained about two Polish students who had abandoned
their studies at the Humboldt University in Berlin to defect to the West.
The East Germans saw this as a dangerous precedent.[40]

Ulbricht upbraided Polish Ambassador Stanisław Albrecht for allowing Poles traveling in the GDR to criticize the lack of freedom in the GDR,
the SED's unwillingness to allow any debate of its policies, and the alleged "huge differences in the standards of living in our countries." Ulbricht asked Albrecht to understand that the GDR needed to have an
economy that matched, if not surpassed, that of the FRG. The East German leader said that the GDR could not afford to have the Poles criticizing his country's relative economic prosperity now. Ulbricht allowed that
if the present economic situation continued, every dissatisfied [GDR] citizen would go to the FRG.[41]

The Border Controversy Resurfaces

After ten years as the main political party in the Soviet zone, the SED had
made little headway in convincing East Germans to accept the Oder-

Neisse border. Grünberg informed Kopa that East Germans often expressed their dissatisfaction with Poland's occupation of German territories. They doubted whether Poland could make efficient use of the territories as Germany had before the war.[42] East German officials acknowledged that many of their compatriots characterized the Poles' alleged lack of initiative and hard work as typical of the "Polish economy," an old slur that had offended Poles for years.[43] Kopa urged the Polish government to put more resources into the area, because the bombed-out ruins of houses on the Polish side of the border only confirmed the impression of laziness.[44]

With millions of immigrants from the former German territories now living in the GDR, the SED could not afford to alienate them by accepting Polish historical arguments for the new border. East German officials adhered to the line that Pieck and Ulbricht had set and recognized the border solely as compensation for Hitler's destruction of Poland. Because reparations can be paid off, the East Germans implied that the area could revert back to Germany. The head of the LDP in East Germany, Rudolf Agsten, told Polish diplomat Józef Czechoń that his party would not refer to a Polish historical presence in the Western Territories "because the German community rejects these arguments, saying, for example, that Silesia was always German, and not Polish. The historical argument is not accepted by the GDR population at all."[45] Agsten confirmed that many of his party members still held negative opinions of Poles and vehemently rejected the Oder-Neisse border. They thought that, in Agsten's words, "it is not possible to speak about friendship with Poland until the Germans get back [Poland's] Western Territories." Agsten told Kopa that the Poles did not realize how difficult it was to convince Germans about the need for friendship with Poland.[46]

For years, Polish diplomats in the GDR had criticized the SED for rejecting Poland's historical claim to the Oder-Neisse region. One wrote that "[it is] seldom when one makes use of the argument about our historical right to the Western Territories. . . . it is important to note that we will still have to contend with the symptoms of aggressive revisionism."[47] In one case, the Poles complained that the SED did not censure a professor at the University of Jena for arguing that Poland's Western Territories were historically German, and had been "unjustly awarded to Poland."[48]

Such overt revisionism was obviously unsettling to the Polish population in the territories. The head of an East German teachers' delegation to Poland reported that Poles were still not convinced that the area would remain part of Poland; he observed that many Poles living there worked only for short-term gain. He said that some Poles thought the situation would improve if Poland recovered the eastern territories lost to the Soviet Union.[49]

Gomułka's Election as First Secretary

Władysław Gomułka's election to the PZPR Central Committee on October 20, 1956, and his promotion to first secretary a day later surprised both Khrushchev and Ulbricht. The Soviets had approved of Gomułka's return to the leadership circle of the PZPR, but as the Soviet ambassador to Poland told Heymann, "one never thought that Gomułka would immediately become first secretary."[50]

Khrushchev flew to Warsaw on October 19; Soviet troops moved ominously around Warsaw and the Soviet Baltic fleet made a show of force off Gdańsk. Gomułka refused to be intimidated by his uninvited guest:

> If you talk with a revolver on the table you don't have an even-handed discussion. I cannot continue the discussion under these conditions. I am ill and I cannot fill such a function in my condition. We can listen to the complaints of the Soviet comrades, but if decisions are to be made under the threat of physical force I am not up to it.[51]

The PZPR Central Committee would not allow Khrushchev into their plenary sessions, and Khrushchev eventually accepted the party's decision because Gomułka promised to keep Poland in the Warsaw Pact. Gomułka alluded to the Oder-Neisse border in assuring Khrushchev that

> Poland needs friendship with the Soviet Union more than the Soviet Union needs friendship with Poland. . . . Without the Soviet Union we cannot maintain our borders with the West. We are dealing with our internal problems, but our relations with the Soviet Union will remain unchanged. We will still be friends and allies. . . . The Germans will become a threat to the Poles if our friendly relations with the Soviet Union are ruined.

Although Gomułka did not ask for a removal of Soviet troops from Poland, he did demand the recall of Polish Minister of Defense, Konstantin Rokossovsky, who was a Soviet citizen.[52]

Gomułka not only posed a challenge to Soviet influence in Poland but jeopardized Poland's relations with the GDR through his return. Gomułka's promise to promote Polish interests was bound to weaken the political, economic, and military cooperation among the socialist states. The GDR's diplomatic isolation from the West made it the most politically and economically dependent member of the Warsaw Pact. As Ambassador Heymann put it, the new PZPR leadership would make Soviet bloc foreign policy "significantly more complicated."[53]

Gomułka's election set a dangerous precedent for the Stalinists in the other communist parties, and Ulbricht was one of them. Gomułka's national brand of socialism was a direct challenge to the SED's orthodox Stalinist policies. When the PZPR purged Gomułka in 1949, the SED had obediently echoed the Kremlin by condemning Gomułka's mistakes. Ulbricht had often lumped Tito and Gomułka together and castigated them for various "criminal activities."[54] An East German Foreign Ministry official told Polish diplomat Jan Pierzchała that "the imprisonment and earlier removal from the party permanently compromises comrade Gomułka, and his present election to first secretary reflects badly on our [PZPR] CC."[55]

The succession crisis in the PZPR prompted the Soviet and East German authorities to act quickly to prevent the events in Poland from destabilizing the political situation in the GDR. On October 18, the Polish Embassy in Berlin reported that the Soviet army in East Germany was mobilizing, and that the SED workers' "Fighting Groups" and armed members of the militia-like Society for Sport and Technology were defending government buildings.[56] The government banned demonstrations in support of Gomułka or Imre Nagy, who became the Hungarian minister president on October 23. When a group of students from Humboldt University in East Berlin planned a show of solidarity for the Polish and Hungarian reformers, one SED functionary threatened the students with "workers' fists." Before they could march from the university to Marx-Engels Platz, the leaders were arrested and held for two days.[57] Students at the Academy for Applied Arts had planned a march to meet the Humboldt students, but local SED officials sent two trucks of militiamen to stop them.[58]

The SED suppressed all news reports coming out of Poland. *Trybuna Ludu* alluded to Gomułka's expulsion from the party and arrest in 1949, but the East German press made no mention of Gomułka's past, or of the frank public discussions going on in Poland about the party's errors.[59] East German Ministry of Security official Richard Schmöing told Czechoń that the Polish press's criticism of Bierut's cult of personality and the PZPR's economic policies was the result of a lack of party unity and reflective of the party's unwillingness to suppress "extreme views." Schmöing commented that "things are not going well in Poland if everyone can say what they please, because that does not strengthen the power of the state authorities."[60]

The East Germans cautiously waited for cues from Moscow before making public comments on the Gomułka régime.[61] As usual, Soviet journalists blamed the West for the political unrest in Poland and Hungary, and the East German press immediately followed suit. *Neues Deutschland* criticized U.S. Secretary of State John Foster Dulles and West German Chancellor Konrad Adenauer for encouraging Poland to break away from the Warsaw Pact; the newspaper called such abetting "an imperialist offensive against the socialist world."[62]

On October 21, *Neues Deutschland* reprinted an article from *Prawda* titled "Anti-Socialist Statements in the Polish Press." Among the flurry of attacks on Poland was a criticism of Polish journalist Zbigniew Florczak for urging an end to Marxist "jargon." According to Florczak, "the exploited proletarian is an outmoded expression; today one must think about the exploited people." Florczak had also called on the Polish government to engage the West. The *Prawda* article decried the expressions of anti-Sovietism that were surfacing in Poland, and expressed alarm that some members of the Polish Writers' Congress were calling for a restoration of capitalism. The Soviet newspaper chastised *Życie Warszawy* reporter Jerzy Putrament for claiming that economic relationships with the Soviet bloc countries did not benefit Poland, and that the communist system in Poland worked only with censorship and police terror.[63] *Trybuna Ludu* issued a sharp rebuttal of the *Prawda* article in a commentary that called for "true friendship," not the sham partnerships that thinly masked Soviet hegemony in the socialist camp.[64]

East Germans were so eager for news from Poland that Polish newspapers in Berlin quickly sold out.[65] The Polish Embassy observed that many East German reporters wanted to print more news from Poland: "[East German] journalists deplore the attitude of the SED CC toward the matter of the Polish press [but] leave that subject alone, creating an atmosphere of expectation and reservation."[66] In a meeting with Polish diplomat Jan Jakubowski, SED functionary Paul Wandel candidly expressed his disappointment in the East German press for its lack of independence and its inability to comprehend what was really happening in Poland. He said that the SED was hesitant to support Gomułka because they were not sure about his political future; but he faulted Polish delegations to East Germany for trying to convince SED members of the superiority of the PZPR's "evolutionary path."[67]

East German Charge d'affaires Günter Seyfert told Polish Foreign Ministry official Mieczysław Łobodycz that his embassy had "a guilty conscience" because the East German press coverage of Polish developments was so deficient. Seyfert said that East German journalists in Poland were embarrassed by their lack of objectivity: "Polish colleagues show them literature coming from the GDR and ask why it contains such meager and one-sided information. This is particularly the case with translations of *Prawda* articles about the Polish press."[68]

A few brave East Berlin journalists openly criticized the SED's censorship of news reports from Poland. The editors of the *Wochenpost* (Weekly Post), a SED affiliate, complained that

> the interpretation that a party leadership may choose what the masses may or may not hear about this development in the socialist camp, is in our opinion contradictory to the Leninist standards of party and public life, against

the Leninist principle that the masses must know everything. Above all the notion is mistaken that we can at all prevent the masses from knowing these things.

The editors said that the people were forced to get their news from "enemy" broadcasts, such as RIAS radio from West Berlin. They went on to criticize the party leadership for its unwillingness to admit wrong-doing and warned that the SED was losing the people's trust. The editors suggested that the only way to avoid some of the PZPR's mistakes was to have an honest and open discussion of the recent developments in Poland.[69]

Heymann also recommended that East German officials stay abreast of developments in Poland by engaging in frank discussions with Poles; he even proposed lifting all travel restrictions between the GDR and Poland. Heymann warned of the strong likelihood that Bonn would soon establish an official representation in Warsaw, in which case East German interests would suffer.[70]

The SED leadership stonewalled these recommendations. Instead, the Politburo enacted even stiffer regulations on contacts with Poles, and increased surveillance over alleged U.S. and West German agents working in the GDR.[71] In October, when two East Germans were accused of spying for the United States, the SED called for public meetings in factories and towns, mostly in the border areas with Poland and Czechoslovakia, to publicize these espionage activities.[72]

In the two weeks between Gomułka's election on October 20 and the Soviet suppression of the Hungarian revolt, the SED leadership was on the ideological defensive. One SED official confided in a Polish diplomat that he supported some of Gomułka's reforms, but "for the time being we cannot allow ourselves such a program."[73] The SED's propaganda apparatus geared up for a new defense of the party's policies. Condemnation of the "counterrevolution" in Hungary dominated the pages of *Neues Deutschland* at the end of October. The SED Politburo boasted that it taken steps to avoid the upheavals taking place in Poland and Hungary:

> in contrast to the development in several other peoples' democratic countries (Poland and Hungary), the damaging results of the personality cult were not as extensive [in the GDR], because from the moment of our party's birth to the present we made allowance for the peculiarities of our development. It is a triumph of the German working class that our unified party of the working class developed into a Marxist-Leninist party.[74]

The SED leadership told its members that in light of the West's instigation of the events in Poland and Hungary, the party had to work even harder to win the East German people over to socialism.[75]

The Politburo tried to keep the party rank and file ignorant of developments in Poland and Hungary. Even Central Committee members were not informed. Alfred Neumann, the head of the SED in Berlin, pointedly told East German journalists not to ask the party about Gomułka.[76] East German authorities confiscated the October 21 editions of the SED's *BZ am Abend* (Evening Berliner Zeitung) and *Wochenpost* because they included excerpts from Gomułka's speech to the Eighth Plenum on October 20.[77] On October 25, *Neues Deutschland* at last reported the news of Gomułka's election as first secretary.[78] Simultaneously, the Politburo issued a directive to the Central Committee and the district secretaries that Gomułka's speech was "top secret"—only for their personal consumption.[79] The East German Foreign Ministry was still so uninformed about what was happening in Poland that it had to ask the Polish Embassy for Polish newspapers.[80]

The text of Gomułka's speech did not appear in *Neues Deutschland* until October 28, but even then parts of it were missing. At the end of the month, the Politburo notified the Central Committee that it had restricted access to news from Poland because of the uncertain situation within the PZPR. The Politburo cautioned that the Polish communists were making statements with too many "false formulations."[81] On November 2, the Politburo gave the Central Committee the full text of Gomułka's speech, but with the caveat that Poland had "other conditions."[82]

The Ulbricht régime had good reason to censor these reports. Ulbricht knew that there was widespread support among the East German population and in the SED for Polish-style reforms. Many party members wanted the GDR to embark on its own national road to socialism. Anton Ackermann told Pierzchała confidentially that some party members had removed all signs connecting them with the SED for fear of reprisals from the German people should the party fall from power.[83] According to Pierzchała, East German security officials were monitoring a rise in anti-Soviet attitudes in East Germany. He reported that "almost everyone is making comparisons between June 17 [1953] in Berlin and the present events in Poland. . . . Everyone has much sympathy for Poland. The general attitude [is] against Ulbricht."[84] Robert Mentzel, the vice minister of political affairs in the East German Ministry of Communications, told one Polish diplomat that there were many people in the GDR who sympathized with Poland and felt "solidarity with the direction represented by Nagy in Hungary."[85] Bruno Baum, who headed the SED district office in Potsdam, told a West German journalist that the East German people were whispering, "We need a German Gomułka, a German Nagy." Another East German official confirmed that party members had a "lively sympathy" for the Polish reforms. He said that members often complained about the stagnation of the SED's policies; they envied the dynamic changes taking place in the PZPR and considered them true to socialism. He acknowledged that the top SED leaders were opposed to reforms.[86]

On October 25, the editor of *Neues Deutschland*, Hermann Axen, and the editor of *Trybuna Ludu*, Artur Kowalski, met in East Berlin. Their heated exchange reflected how deep the ideological divide between the SED and the PZPR had become. Axen knew Kowalski from the Spanish Civil War, and the two had been imprisoned together in the concentration camp at Vernet, France, during World War II. Axen considered Kowalski an experienced and loyal Marxist, but Axen expressed his disappointment in Kowalski's "nationalist and anti-Soviet conceptions." Axen said that "this is even more troubling when one considers that comrade Kowalski sincerely loves the Soviet people and the CPSU." Axen was also critical of Kowalski and his comrades for blaming Poland's economic difficulties on Soviet economic advisors. He argued that the GDR had experienced successful economic growth by following the Soviet economic model, and that the mistakes in Poland's industrialization program were the result of nationalistic policies, not bad Soviet advice. Axen was shocked that Kowalski accused Khrushchev of meddling in Polish affairs by flying to Warsaw on October 19. When Kowalski charged the CPSU with anti-Semitism, Axen told him that more likely the PZPR was nationalist and anti-Semitic. Axen concluded, "We think it is very dangerous that comrades with such—gently put—ambiguous and anti-Soviet ideas travel around here. He got from us a cup of coffee and just ideological fireworks otherwise."[87]

Gomułka's attempt to make the PZPR more reflective of workers' interests also challenged the SED's Leninist view of the party's leading role in building socialism. Gomułka rejected the notion that all workers' protests in a people's democracy were inherently anti-socialist, including the Poznań demonstrations that summer. Gomułka declared in his speech to the Eighth Plenum that

> the workers in Poznań, when they went out on the streets of the city, were not protesting against People's Poland, [or] against socialism. They were protesting against the ills which had vastly multiplied in our social system, which had also painfully affected them, [and] against the warped fundamental principles of socialism.[88]

East German officials, the director of the SED's party schools, Hanna Wolf, for instance, termed Poznań "a failed fascist putsch."[89]

The Suppression of the Hungarian Revolt

Unlike the East German press, Polish journalists did not blame either the Poznań or the Hungarian uprisings on foreign agents and bourgeois reactionaries. *Trybuna Ludu* characterized the Hungarian affair as a tragedy, and on October 29, the newspaper reported that three Polish transports of medicine were on their way to Budapest. The next day, another article expressed Poland's sympathy and declared solidarity with the Hungarian people.[90] On November 1, the PZPR denounced the use of Soviet troops in Hungary,[91] and the Politburo issued a statement that the Hungarians should be allowed to resolve their own problems.[92] The PZPR rejected the SED's characterization of Nagy as a counterrevolutionary and Western agent. Many Polish communists viewed him as the "Hungarian Gomułka"—the legitimate leader of another national communist movement; however, Ulbricht warned that "Hungary teaches that whoever gives even his little finger to reaction will end by losing his life."[93]

Ulbricht was prophetic. On November 4, the Soviet army deposed Nagy and declared martial law. Evidently Khrushchev thought that Hungary might go the way of Tito in 1948, and even Tito saw the danger of the Hungarian "counterrevolution."[94] Over 2,000 Hungarians died in the fighting. Gomułka could not publicly support the Soviet action in Hungary without losing some of his popular support; but at the same time he did not want to jeopardize his compromise with Khrushchev. In a symbolic gesture, the Polish delegation in the U.N. General Assembly abstained on the resolution condemning the Soviet Union's intervention.[95]

Imre Nagy took refuge in the Yugoslav Embassy in Budapest. In the summer of 1958, he was kidnapped by Soviet agents; on June 16, 1958, after a short trial, he was executed. The Polish government was shocked by Nagy's death. Gomułka sent a personal letter to Khrushchev expressing his remorse, and Rapacki spoke out publicly against the execution. The official Polish press was silent, but Polish intellectual and church groups held numerous protests. Students at the Catholic University in Lublin wore black adorned with the green-white-red colors of the Hungarian flag; graves in Poznań were decorated with green-white-red streamers. The PZPR did not stop these protests.[96] According to East German diplomats in Moscow, Rapacki eventually had to stifle his opposition and support Moscow's foreign policy, but the East Germans doubted his sincerity.[97]

During a visit to Poland in early November, 1956, East German President Friedrich Ebert declared that "we will never let the fraternal relations between the German and Polish nations become troubled or ruined. We wish the Polish people further successes in building socialism as well as in the struggle to raise the standard of living for the working masses."[98] At the same time, Pierzchała reported that some of the younger officials in the East German Foreign Ministry who had previously judged Gomułka as unfit to lead the PZPR were now having a change of heart. One top Foreign Ministry official told Pierzchała that the SED's position toward Poland immediately after Gomułka's election was "essentially false," and that "it even brought much harm."[99]

The SED and the PZPR were headed in different ideological directions, however. The Ulbricht régime had teetered on the brink in 1953, only to be saved by the Soviet suppression of the June uprising. Gomułka's return to power had threatened Ulbricht's régime again, but the violent end to the Hungarian crisis solidified Ulbricht's position. The Hungarian revolt put a brake on de-Stalinization; the Kremlin now favored policies that were closer to Ulbricht's Stalinist course.

By quick suppression of opposition in the GDR, the Ulbricht régime managed to avoid the political turmoil experienced by Poland and Hungary in the fall of 1956. But the SED's sharp condemnation of Gomułka's allegedly un-Marxist and nationalist policies and the Polish communists' equally vituperative criticisms of Ulbricht's unrepentant Stalinism soon erased what little good will the two parties had developed over the past decade.

Notes

1. Maltzan (West German Embassy in Paris) to the FRG Foreign Ministry, October 19, 1956, BRD AA, Department 7, vol. 77.

2. *Trybuna Ludu*, February 19, 1956, p. 1.

3. Memorandum on East German Minister of Culture Alexander Abusch's visit to Poland, unsigned, January 31, 1961, DDR MR, DC–20, file 700.

4. Jan Mostowik notes of meeting with Dr. Hermann, April 19, 1956, MSZ, 10/377/42.

5. Kopa notes of meeting with Nossti, April 27, 1956, MSZ, 10/377/42.

6. Kopa notes of meeting with Siegewasser, April 27, 1956, MSZ, 10/377/42.

7. Kopa notes of meetings with SED members, May 11, 1956, MSZ, 10/377/42.

8. See M. K. Dziewanowski, *The Communist Party of Poland: An Outline of History* (Cambridge: Harvard University Press, 1976), p. 176.

9. Dlubek report on East German historians' trip to Poland from May 7 to May 12, May 12, 1956, SED ZK, Walter Ulbricht Papers, NL 182/1247.

10. Heymann to Florin, April 20, 1956, SED ZK, Walter Ulbricht Papers, NL 182/1247.

11. Heymann to the GDR Foreign Ministry, May 2, 1956, SED ZK, microfilm FBS 339/13494.

12. Heymann to the GDR Foreign Ministry, May 28, 1956, SED ZK, Walter Ulbricht Papers, NL 182/1247.

13. Ibid.

14. Heymann to the GDR Foreign Ministry, June 11, 1956, SED ZK, Walter Ulbricht Papers, NL 182/1247.

15. Heymann to the GDR Foreign Ministry, May 30, 1956, SED ZK, microfilm FBS 339/13494.

16. Nicholas Bethell, *Gomułka, His Poland and His Communism* (London: Longmans, Green and Co., 1969), pp. 203, 206–207.

17. Heymann to the GDR Foreign Ministry, June 11, 1956, SED ZK, Walter Ulbricht Papers, NL 182/1247.

18. See *Trybuna Ludu*, June 29–30, 1956.

19. Bringmann to Kundermann, June 29, 1956, DDR MfAA, HA/I Secretariat, A37.

20. R. F. Leslie, et al., *The History of Poland Since 1863* (Cambridge: Cambridge University Press, 1980), p. 351; and Bethell, *Gomułka, His Poland and His Communism*, pp. 208–209.

21. Seyfert to Handke, June 29, 1956, SED ZK, microfilm FBS 339/13488.

22. *Neues Deutschland*, June 29, 1956, p. 5; September 25, 1956, p. 5; and September 27, p. 5.

23. Heymann notes of meeting with Stasiak (First Secretary of the PZPR in Poznań), July 19, 1956, SED ZK, Walter Ulbricht Papers, NL 182/1247.

24. Jakubowski notes of a meeting with Rose, July 24, 1956, MSZ, 10/378/42.

25. Kopa notes of a meeting with Grünstein, August 1, 1956, MSZ, 10/378/42.

26. *Neues Deutschland*, July 5, 1956, p. 5. The GDR did the most trade with the Soviet Union.

27. Report of an East German parliamentary delegation to Poland, October 8, 1956, SED ZK, microfilm FBS 339/13492.

28. Heymann to the GDR Foreign Ministry, July 25, 1956, SED ZK, microfilm FBS 339/13494.

29. Dieckmann, Grotewohl, and Ulbricht to Zawadski and Cyrankiewicz, July 22, 1956, SED ZK, microfilm FBS 339/13492.

30. See S. Liszewska report of Humboldt University Professor of History Heinz Lemke's visit to Poland, April 6, 1956, KWKzZ, file 153.

31. S. Liszewska report of Eugen Häusler's visit to Poland from April 19 to May 3, May 15, 1956, KWKzZ, file 153.

32. See H. Skolik notes of a visit to Poland by University of Leipzig Professor Hans Baeyer and Humboldt University Professor Manfred Nussbaum from April 26 to May 17, May 17, 1956, KWKzZ, file 153; see also Zbigniew Brzezinski, *The Soviet Bloc: Unity and Conflict* (Cambridge: Harvard University Press, 1967), p. 98. The SED prided itself on the rapid development of socialism in East Germany and the engagement of the populace in the political process. In 1954, the PZPR had 1,297,000 members, from a total population in Poland of 27.5 million. The SED had 1,272,987 members, from a total population of just over 18 million.

33. Emil Skaut report of art historian Kurt Schifner's visit to Poland from July 26 to August 9, 1956, KWKzZ, file 153.

34. Report on an East German theater delegation to Poland from May 15 to May 18, signature unintelligible, May 18, 1956, KWKzZ, file 153.

35. S. Liszewska report of visit to Poland of East German writers and journalists from April 12 to May 30, June 12, 1956, KWKzZ, file 153.

36. Polish Embassy in Berlin report from January 1 to March 15, 1956, MSZ, 10/370/41.

37. Bringmann to Wahner, June 9, 1956, SED ZK, microfilm FBS 339/13494; and Pierzchała notes of a meeting with Wenck and Kinigkeit, July 10, 1956, MSZ, 10/378/42.

38. Kopa notes of a meeting with Grünberg, September 28, 1956, MSZ, 10/378/42.

39. Ministry of Higher Education memo on Halina Zalewska's visit to the GDR, August 24, 1956, PZPR KC, 237/XXII–732.

40. Pierzchała notes of meeting with Kinigkeit, September 6, 1956, KC PZPR, 237/XXII–732.

41. Łobodycz to Góralski on Ambassador Albrecht's meeting with Ulbricht, July 13, 1956, PZPR KC, 237/XXII–822.

42. Kopa notes of a meeting with Grünberg, September 28, MSZ, 10/378/42.

43. Report on obtaining visas to Poland, unsigned, September 28, 1956, SED ZK, microfilm FBS 339/13488.

44. Kopa notes of a meeting with an East German border guard in Frankfurt/Oder, April 5, 1956, MSZ, 10/377/42.

45. Czechoń notes of meeting with Agsten, July 20, 1956, MSZ, 10/378/42.

46. Kopa notes of a meeting with Agsten, June 22, 1956, MSZ, 10/377/42; see also Fulbrook, *Anatomy of a Dictatorship*, p. 189.

47. Polish Embassy in Berlin report from January 1 to March 15, 1956, MSZ, 10/370/41.

48. Kopa notes of a meeting with Namiot (Polish student studying in Leipzig), October 8, 1956, MSZ, 10/378/42.

49. Fritz Baats report of an East German teachers' delegation to Poland, October 10, 1956, SED ZK, Walter Ulbricht Papers, NL 182/1247; see also Nikita Khrushchev, *Khrushchev Remembers: The Last Testament* (Boston: Little, Brown, 1974), p. 207.

50. Heymann to the GDR Foreign Ministry, January 20, 1957, SED ZK, Walter Ulbricht Papers, NL 182/1249.

51. Quoted in Gaddis, *We Now Know*, p. 211.

52. Khrushchev, *Khrushchev Remembers: The Glasnost Tapes* (Boston: Little, Brown, 1990), pp. 115, 118–120. Rokossovsky, a native Pole, had commanded the Soviet Army on the East bank of the Vistula River in Warsaw during the uprising against the Germans in 1944. Many Poles blamed Stalin and Rokossovsky for allowing the Germans to destroy the Polish Home Army, thus eliminating the military wing of the Polish government in London. Gomułka's old ally, Marian Spychalski, replaced Rokossovsky as commander-in-chief of the Polish armed forces.

53. Heymann to the GDR Foreign Ministry, October 20, 1956, DDR MfAA, Warsaw Embassy, A3579.

54. Dietrich Staritz, *Geschichte der DDR, 1949–1985* [History of the GDR, 1949–1985] (Frankfurt/Main: Suhrkamp Verlag, 1985), p. 24.

55. Pierzchała to the Polish Foreign Ministry, October 26, 1956, PZPR KC, 237/XXII–822.

56. Pierzchała to the Polish Foreign Ministry, October 26, 1956, PZPR KC, 237/XXII–822; see also Joachim Görlich, "Kommunistische Freundschaft an der Oder und Neisse" (Communist friendship on the Oder and Neisse) *Osteuropa* (East Europe), no. 10 (1964), p. 726. According to Görlich, a "wasserpolnisch" autochthon who left Poland in 1959, a Catholic publication from Poznań condemned the East German army's actions in October 1956.

57. Fritz Schenk, *Im Vorzimmer der Diktatur; 12 Jahre Pankow* (In the antechamber of the dictatorship: Twelve years Pankow) (Cologne: Kiepenheuer and Witsch, 1962), p. 180; see also Staritz, *Geschichte der DDR, 1949–1985*, p. 116.

58. Jakubowski notes of a meeting with Wandel, October 26, 1956, MSZ, 10/378/42.

59. *Trybuna Ludu*, October 20, 1956, p. 1.

60. Czechoń notes of a meeting with Richard Schmöing, October 20, 1956, MSZ, 10/378/42.

61. Pierzchała to the Polish Foreign Ministry, October 26, 1956, PZPR KC, 237/XXII–822.

62. *Neues Deutschland*, October 23, 1956, p. 1.

63. *Neues Deutschland*, October 21, 1956, p. 5.

64. *Trybuna Ludu*, October 21, 1956, p. 2.

65. *Trybuna Ludu*, October 24, 1956, p. 1.

66. Pierzchała to the Polish Foreign Ministry, October 26, 1956, PZPR KC, 237/XXII–822.

67. Jakubowski notes of a meeting with Wandel, October 26, 1956, MSZ, 10/378/42.

68. Łobodycz notes of a meeting with Seyfert, October 26, 1956, MSZ, 10/361/39.

69. Letter from the chief editors of the *Wochenpost* to Rudi Wetzel, et al., October 27, 1956, in SED ZK, Politburo Draft Protocol No. 54, October 30, 1956, J IV 2/2A/528.

70. Heymann to the GDR Foreign Ministry, October 20, 1956, DDR MfAA, Warsaw Embassy, A3579.

71. Briefing on the court proceedings against U.S. secret service agents, October 26, 1956, in SED ZK, Politburo Draft Protocol No. 54, October 30, 1956, J IV 2/2A/528.

72. Propaganda Department plan for public agitation after the trials of Sticker and Schulze, et al., October 26, 1956, SED ZK, Politburo Draft Protocol No. 54, October 30, 1956, J IV 2/2A/528.

73. Jakubowski notes of a meeting with Wenk, October 26, 1956, MSZ, 10/361/39.

74. "Nothing Can Stop the Progressive Development," in SED ZK, Politburo Draft Protocol No. 54, October 30, 1956, J IV 2/2A/528.

75. Politburo letter to the members and candidate members of the Central Committee, SED ZK, Politburo Draft Protocol No. 54, October 30, 1956, J IV 2/2A/528.

76. Kopa notes of meeting of the PZPR POP [Basic Party Organization] on October 24, October 25, 1956, MSZ, 10/378/42.

77. Łobodycz notes of a meeting with Seyfert, October 26, 1956, MSZ, 10/361/39.

78. *Neues Deutschland*, October 25, 1956, p. 5.

79. SED Politburo decree, October 25, 1956, SED ZK, Politburo Protocol No. 53, J IV 2/2/507.

80. Jakubowski notes of a meeting with Wenk, October 26, 1956, MSZ, 10/361/39.

81. SED Politburo letter to the members and candidate members of the Central Committee, SED ZK, Politburo Draft Protocol No. 54, October 30, 1956, J IV 2/2A/528.

82. SED Politburo memorandum, SED ZK, Politburo Protocol No. 55, November 2, 1956, J IV/2/2/509.

83. Pierzchała notes, cited in Kopa to the Polish Foreign Ministry, November 9, 1956, MSZ, 10/378/42.

84. Pierzchała to the Polish Foreign Ministry, October 26, 1956, PZPR KC, 237/XXII–822.

85. Janusz Rachocki notes of a meeting with Robert Mentzel on November 16, November 22, 1956, MSZ, 10/378/42.

86. Nasielski notes, cited in C. Urbaniak (Polish Military Mission) to Łobodycz, October 26, 1956, MSZ, 10/378/42.

87. Notes of a meeting between Hermann Axen, Georg Hansen and Artur Kowalski on October 25, October 29, 1956, SED ZK, Hermann Axen Office, IV 2/2.035/43; see also Pierzchała notes, cited in Kopa to the Polish Foreign Ministry, November 9, 1956, MSZ, 10/378/42. The SED had the same problems in overcoming anti-Soviet attitudes in the GDR. Pierzchała noted a definite distaste among East German students for studying Russian.

88. *Trybuna Ludu*, October 21, 1956, p. 3.

89. See "Notes on Current Events and Relations between Poland and the GDR," unsigned, December 8, 1956, MSZ, 10/378/42.

90. *Trybuna Ludu*, October 29, 1956, p. 1; and October 30, 1956, p. 2.

91. Csaba Bekes, "New Findings on the 1956 Hungarian Revolution," *Bulletin: Cold War International History Project*, no. 2 (fall 1992), p. 3. The PZPR changed its position after the Soviet suppression of the Hungarian revolution on November 4.

92. *Trybuna Ludu*, November 2, 1956, p. 1.

93. Quoted in Carola Stern, *Ulbricht: A Political Biography* (New York: Frederick Praeger, 1965), p. 161.

94. Khrushchev, *Khrushchev Remembers: The Glasnost Tapes*, p. 127.

95. See Norman Davies, *God's Playground: A History of Poland, Volume II: 1795 to the Present* (New York: Columbia University Press), 1982, p. 587.

96. Linder (GDR Foreign Ministry) to Florin, July 28, 1958, SED ZK, Walter Ulbricht Papers, NL 182/1250.

97. Rossmeisl (GDR Embassy in Moscow) notes of meeting with Krekotin (Soviet Foreign Ministry), July 23, 1958, SED ZK, Walter Ulbricht Papers, NL 182/1250.

98. *Trybuna Ludu*, November 3, 1956, p. 2.

99. Pierzchała notes cited in Kopa to the Polish Foreign Ministry, November 9, 1956, MSZ, 10/378/42; see also Franz Sikora, *Sozialistische Solidarität und nationale Interessen* (Socialist solidarity and national interests) (Cologne: Verlag Wissenschaft und Politik, 1977), p. 142.

7

The Cold Winter of
Polish–East German Relations,
1956–1957

Well, when are you [the SED] going to oust the Stalinists?

—PZPR member to East German journalist Suzanne Drechsler[1]

Ominous portent attended Gomułka's trip to Moscow ten days after the Soviet Union ended the Hungarian revolt on November 4, 1956. No one in Poland was confident that Khrushchev would allow Gomułka to remain in power, and many feared that he would never come back from the Soviet Union. When Gomułka returned after four days of productive talks, his position was no longer in doubt. He even obliged Khrushchev to acknowledge that the Soviet Union had underpaid for Polish coal from 1945 to 1953, and had not adequately compensated Poland for the stationing of Soviet troops. Khrushchev agreed to cancel all Poland's debts.

That November, the Kremlin informed a GDR delegation of its support for Gomułka. Ulbricht now knew that he would have to reconcile himself with his old rival, but he would not make any compromises with Gomułkaism. Ulbricht stayed on his immutable Stalinist course. By this time, he had firmly aligned most of the SED membership behind him.

Ulbricht worried, nonetheless, that Khrushchev's criticism of Stalin's cult of personality had already gone too far, for it threatened to expose his own. An SED Politburo report on the Polish and Hungarian crises insisted that "the clear ideological front between Marxist-Leninist and bourgeois ideology must last, and this has to continue despite opportunistic views, liberal degeneracies, [and] the renunciation of Leninist standards of party life." The SED leadership boasted that "some People's Republics are surprised by our calm development," but advised party members to avoid contacts with Poles if the PZPR went down a different road to socialism.[2]

East German journalists told Polish diplomat Janusz Rachocki that differences between the two parties should remain on a theoretical rather than a personal level, and maintained that "it is necessary to respect that Stalin's name was dear to all communists as a symbol of socialism."[3] Most Poles thought differently about Stalin, and an intense debate ensued that fall between reformers in the PZPR and hard-liners in the SED. Polish and East German officials made unprecedented public denunciations of each other: The Poles chided the East German communists for their blind devotion to Stalinist political, social, and economic policies, and the East Germans lectured the PZPR for deviating from orthodox Marxist-Leninist principles.

The Polish Embassy in Berlin reported that the SED was convinced that Gomułka was carrying out his old nationalist program, and that Gomułka and Tito understood each other on this score. Ulbricht warned the East German press that Polish journalists were coming to Berlin only to make contacts in West Berlin and West Germany. The SED stopped sending journalists to Poland and strictly prohibited the publication of Polish newspaper and journal articles. Polish diplomats speculated that Ulbricht still thought that counterrevolutionaries might seize power in Poland.[4]

At the end of November, the Polish newspaper *Expres Wieczorny* (Evening Express) reported Ulbricht's assertion that Stalinism had never existed in the GDR. Alluding to the developments in Poland since October, Ulbricht argued that "liberalization really [means] the reestablishment of capitalist conditions." The East German ambassador, Stefan Heymann, told the newspaper's editor that Ulbricht had said only that there had never been one-man leadership in the SED, but nothing about Stalinism or "liberalization."[5]

The East German leadership maintained that Gomułka's reforms had no relevance for the development of socialism in the GDR, and they made it clear to the Poles that the SED would not make abrupt policy changes.[6] Robert Mentzel told one Polish diplomat that he and his comrades thought the Polish reforms were dangerous deviations from good socialist practices. The SED was particularly critical of the PZPR's personnel changes and decentralized economic plan.[7] During a visit to Poland that fall, SED functionary Conrad Neumann chided Polish officials for exaggerating Poland's socialist political development in recent months. Neumann reported that he often encountered this argument in Poland, notably among workers: "The GDR is twenty years ahead of us in technology—but Poland is twenty years ahead of the GDR in democratization." Neumann also criticized the Poles for declaring that East

German journalists "merely recapitulated what TASS chewed first."[8] He accused the PZPR of making numerous ideological mistakes that deviated from "Leninist directives." He concluded that Poland was a "complete mess."[9]

The SED kept its state security forces on full alert to prevent that "mess" from spilling over into the GDR, and sent party members into the factories to spread more propaganda among the workers. The East German communists were most concerned that the unfettered Polish press would undermine the SED's strict control over political thought in the GDR. Heymann complained that the Polish press was doing too little to counteract anti-Soviet and anti-Semitic displays in Poland,[10] and the East German Ambassador to Czechoslovakia, Bernard Koenen, told a Polish diplomat that the economic problems in Poland were the direct result of the PZPR's lack of press censorship.[11] The SED restricted the circulation of the Polish press in the GDR, and East German journals ignored the PZPR's public statements and communiqués resulting from the PZPR's talks with the Soviet, French, Italian, and Chinese communist parties.[12]

Numerous SED intelligence reports alluded to the danger of the free Polish press, which was openly reporting on previously taboo subjects; for instance, Poles told East German officials that the thousands of Polish officers found buried in the Katyn Forest near Smolensk had been shot by the Soviets in 1940, not by the Germans after Hitler attacked the Soviet Union in 1941. One East German official was incredulous: "How can one speak of an ally here when they make such anti-Soviet statements?"[13] The head of the SED in Leipzig thought that the Polish press was guilty of printing falsehoods about socialism and the other socialist parties. As he told one visiting Polish professor, "our sources of information are Moscow and *Neues Deutschland*, and not Warsaw, RIAS, or the BBC [British Broadcasting Corporation]. We do not depend on Poland for anything, and we absolutely disagree with the politics of that party [the PZPR]."[14]

Polish officials, however, were disdainful of the East German press for its incomplete and biased reporting on the Polish October.[15] The Polish Foreign Ministry criticized the SED for cutting the populace off from "honest and objective information about Poland," and for engaging in "one-sided commentary" about Polish political developments. The ministry also carped at East German officials for questioning Gomułka's personnel changes.[16]

In October 1956, the Polish student political journal *Po Prostu* (Straight Talk) published an article deploring the Stalinists' practice of glorifying all things Russian.[17] In the November issue of the Polish Ministry of Culture and Art organ *Przegląd Kulturalny* (Cultural Review), Edda Werfel also called for the elimination of the "yes men" from the Soviet bloc communist parties.[18] Western radio and press also picked up the article.

This toady behavior was markedly true of the Ulbricht régime. Polish diplomat Józef Czechoń reported that Ulbricht was incensed by these articles. East German officials were notably disparaging of Werfel's piece, which they decried as interference in another party's domestic affairs.[19] In one of the sharpest polemics against Werfel, *Neues Deutschland* editor Hermann Axen rejected her contention that the Polish October was the real revolution for workers. Instead, Axen credited the Soviet army's victory in 1945 for the creation of the workers' republics. In an indirect reference to Ulbricht, Axen defended those who had loyally served the communist parties under Stalin's leadership. He assailed Werfel's call for a new "humane socialism," which he equated with the false conceptions of the nineteenth-century Utopian Socialists and Kurt Schumacher's Social Democrats. As Axen put it, "the most humane socialism was and is the socialism of the Soviet Union."[20]

Axen was most offended by Werfel's assertion that whoever was against the 1956 Polish revolution was for "counterrevolution." He lumped Werfel together with such other "renegades" as author Arthur Koestler, and the Hungarian intellectuals in the Petöfi Club, and RIAS. He criticized Werfel for interfering in East German affairs, and pointed out that Western propaganda agencies were using her article to attack the GDR. Axen concluded that "we [Poles and East Germans] are fraternal people and fraternal parties. Enemies should never and will never separate us, not even such scribes as Edda Werfel."[21]

Polish officials vigorously censured Axen's attack. The foreign policy editor of *Nowe Drogi* acknowledged that Werfel had made several ideological mistakes, but told Heymann that he thought it was wrong for Axen to respond with such "crude attacks" in the SED's main newspaper rather than in a cultural journal on the same level as *Przegląd Kulturalny*. He added that Axen's venomous tone was precluding sober debate of the issues.[22] An editor from *Trybuna Ludu* called Axen's article an "outrage"; he accused Axen of sticking his nose in another party's affairs. He said that if Axen got his news anywhere else but from *Neues Deutschland*, he would not have arrived at such "false generalizations." *Życie Warszawy* (Warsaw Life) characterized Axen's diatribe as hitting Werfel with a "sledge hammer."[23]

Later in the year, Hanna Wolf denounced *Po Prostu* for saying that the Stalinist era had ended with Khrushchev's secret speech. Wolf wrote in *Neues Deutschland* that she was saddened by *Po Prostu*'s assertion that the Polish working class had lost its leading role and that the PZPR had "degenerated." Wolf added that "it fills me with pain that the comrades talk about their own class and their own party in such a way." She asserted that the Leninist principle of the party's central control was necessary to prevent another Hungarian-style uprising. Wolf also criticized the PZPR's removal of the former ambassador to the GDR, Jan Izydorczyk, from his post as first secretary of the PZPR in Poznań; she said that Izy-dorczyk had proven his loyalty to the communist movement through his imprisonment in a Nazi concentration camp. In what was to become a common postscript to these attacks on a partner party, Wolf defended her right to criticize the PZPR by contending that what happened in Poland affected the entire socialist camp.[24]

The SED Limits Cultural Exchanges

For years, the SED had tried to regulate all official and unofficial contacts between Poles and East Germans. With some East Germans calling for their own "Polish October," Ulbricht took stronger measures to stamp out revisionism.[25] For example, East German professors at the Karl Marx University in Leipzig told visiting University of Warsaw Professor Tadeusz Kupis that the old Stalinists in the SED were promoting their policies as suitable for the East German national condition. Some East German professors complained that the SED wanted to quarantine East German citizens from the unreliable Poles; Kupis reported that the SED had ordered party members to avoid contact with the Polish professors at the university.[26]

The hard-liners in the SED were notably angered by Poles in East Germany who criticized the Ulbricht régime and urged liberal reform.[27] In early November, when Polish students studying at Leipzig proposed a meeting with East German students to discuss the political develop-ments in Poland, the district SED office would not allow it.[28] The East German students at Leipzig, indoctrinated by the SED, accused Gomułka of leaving the Soviet camp and allowing the bourgeoisie to dictate politi-cal and economic policy.[29] That fall, East German officials refused to per-mit its youth delegation to go to Warsaw for the Polish Writers' Union Congress.[30] Only a few East German writers were permitted to attend, on the grounds that the Poles had invited too many Westerners.[31]

At a meeting of Polish and East German historians in Berlin that No-vember, some of the Poles predicted that the SED also would eventually have to undergo a democratization process. One Polish historian thought that the recently rehabilitated Franz Dahlem was a good candidate to be the "East German Gomułka"; the historian noted that Dahlem had re-cently complimented Poland for going through "a stormy, [but] fortunate development." Another historian all but demanded that Dahlem replace Ulbricht, and another told Otto Winzer that Dahlem was no answer be-cause "Dahlem is of course as big an apparatchik as Ulbricht."[32]

Word of this exchange got back to Ulbricht. Ulbricht had never trusted Dahlem or any other German communist who had spent the war years in Germany. Dahlem, like Gomułka, had been purged from the party and then rehabilitated.[33] Ulbricht now suspected Dahlem because he had been in Poland during the October days, and had praised the Eighth Plenum for showing the SED that a national road to socialism was possible. In a fit of anger, Ulbricht canceled a banquet for the historians and ordered them to leave the country immediately. He told Winzer to inform the Polish Embassy about the incident, and to tell the Polish government that its delegations should not meddle in East Germany's internal affairs.[34] Stanisław Kopa apologized to Winzer for the affair,[35] but Kopa's colleague Jan Pierzchała characterized the historians' visit as an overall success, even though some SED functionaries had behaved coldly toward them.[36] As a direct result of this incident, the SED postponed the visit of another ten Polish professors and suspended other scheduled visits of East German scholars, students, and youth delegations to Poland.[37]

In October, the PZPR relaxed controls on tourist visas for foreigners and Poles. The SED Politburo responded by tightening regulations on travel to and from Poland and Hungary. In a move to shield its populace from politically unreliable elements, the Politburo alerted its security agencies to run checks on the passports of all travelers between the GDR, Poland, and Hungary.[38] The SED also decreed that visitors from these countries were to be kept to a minimum, and restricted to "politically qualified persons." In any case, all foreigners were to be given "political escorts."[39] The GDR Foreign Ministry was given authority to monitor all student and trade delegations to Poland; social organizations that wanted to visit Poland had to get Central Committee approval.[40]

East German diplomats had difficulty justifying a policy meant to limit exchanges. When the SED suddenly postponed the scheduled visits of several Polish delegations that fall, East German attaché Günter Seyfert told Polish Foreign Ministry official Mieczysław Łobodycz that groups from the other peoples' republics had been scheduled to come at the same time. Łobodycz observed that Seyfert was visibly embarrassed about having to lie about the cancellations. Łobodycz wrote Polish Foreign Minister Adam Rapacki that he knew the East German government did not want Polish delegations discussing the PZPR's recent reforms with East Germans.[41]

By requiring visas for travelers from every country, East German officials tried to allay suspicions that the Poles and Hungarians were the sole targets of the new measures.[42] In December, however, the SED took the unprecedented step of adding visa requirements for all diplomats and travelers passing through the GDR to and from Poland. Kopa told Winzer that his government would have a difficult time accepting the rationale behind these measures. He said that Poles would draw the logical conclusion that the GDR was trying to isolate Poland.[43]

In the fall, the Ulbricht régime tried to preempt unrest in the GDR by improving working conditions and raising the standard of living. The

SED lowered work norms for workers and increased the supply of consumer goods. The Polish diplomats in Berlin ridiculed the notion that these measures were necessary because of a "specific German situation," and interpreted them as a sign that the East German authorities feared their own people. The embassy concluded that the SED was continuing down its old Stalinist political and economic path.[44]

Ulbricht sent Matern, Ebert, and Rau to Warsaw in December to meet with Gomułka, Stefan Jędrychowski, and Rapacki. Outwardly, the two sides maintained decorum and showed no signs of the serious differences that had surfaced that winter. *Trybuna Ludu* characterized the meetings as "sincere, friendly and fruitful," but devoted more coverage to a Yugoslav delegation that was in Warsaw at the same time.[45] The director of the SED Central Committee's Department of Propaganda, Karl Wloch, reported that Gomułka was miffed that Ulbricht had not come. According to Wloch, Gomułka and the PZPR leadership interpreted this slight as a sign that Ulbricht was adamantly opposed to the party's new course. Gomułka's suspicion that Ulbricht did not want to meet him face-to-face was accurate. At this point, Ulbricht was not ready to sanction Gomułka and his reforms by going to Warsaw. Ulbricht still compared the Polish October to the uprising in East Germany three years earlier, and he blamed enemy agents for both. He feared those agents now wanted to export the "counterrevolution" to the GDR.[46] Dr. Roman Karst, a Polish professor of German at Warsaw University, confided in an East German diplomat that the meetings had "more likely worsened than improved the relationship."[47]

That winter, the mainstream Polish press tried to foster the impression that relations with the GDR had returned to normal. In late December, *Trybuna Ludu* printed an article by East German journalist Hans Mueller in which he predicted that within a year the PZPR would achieve the aims it had set out in October.[48] The newspaper also cast Grotewohl's recent visit to Moscow in a positive light; it quoted him as saying that "all the efforts of the imperialist circles to poison the atmosphere between Poland and the GDR are bound to fail." Rapacki highlighted Poland's growing international importance, but emphatically reassured the other Warsaw Pact countries that Poland was not leaving the socialist camp.[49]

The East German leadership hoped that the new Polish ambassador, Roman Piotrowski, would usher in a new spirit of cooperation in 1957, but the East Germans themselves made that virtually impossible.[50] On January 11, 1957, Ulbricht informed Piotrowski that the SED intended to tighten controls on contacts between East Germans and Polish diplomats, officials, journalists, and visitors. The Polish Embassy complained that this practice had already subverted its work and had undermined cultural programs that called for direct connections between Polish and East

German institutions. The Polish Foreign Ministry was annoyed by Ulbricht's statement that the Polish diplomats in Berlin were involving themselves in affairs in which they had no business. Łobodycz hinted that relations were reaching an impasse: "If the isolation of our embassy by the GDR authorities intensifies and persists for a longer time, it will be necessary to limit the size of the diplomatic, press and cultural apparatus." He advised his diplomats to cultivate the informal contacts they already had with East Germans, but to avoid certain sensitive subjects. He also asked them to report their treatment if it was different from that of the other diplomatic representatives in the GDR.[51]

In February, Ambassador Piotrowski complained to Florin that the SED's strict enforcement of the restrictions on direct contacts with foreigners was an obvious attempt to control information coming from Poland. Florin said that the SED had no reservations about the activities of the Polish Cultural Center in Berlin, but two East German workers in the center told Polish diplomats that East German security agents had it under surveillance.[52]

For years, Polish officials had raised the question of whether these limits on face-to-face meetings, in Łobodycz's words, "served the development of relations between Poland and the GDR."[53] They obviously did not.

Ulbricht Rejects Gomułka's National Road to Communism

The controversy over the Polish October sharpened policy debates between the PZPR and the SED that had lain dormant since the late 1940s. Most of their differences were related to Tito's national communism and his expulsion from Cominform almost a decade earlier. When one East German Foreign Ministry official told Polish diplomat Jan Pierzchała that he was concerned about the numerous articles in the Polish press alluding to Poland's national road to socialism, Pierzchała replied that "it is necessary to take into consideration the existence of national characteristics, peculiarities, and idiosyncracies."[54] An article in the January issue of *Nowe Drogi* stressed that "Poland's path does not mean a national socialism or a national communism in the nationalist sense, as some would like to view it. Socialism is socialism, and we are simply building a model of socialism that specifically suits our country and our people." As for Poland's foreign policy challenges, the journal pointed to the German problem, but without reference to its Warsaw Pact ally to the west.[55]

Ulbricht vehemently rejected all national roads to communism. Stalin was Ulbricht's model, not Tito. Although Gomułka's legitimacy was based on Khrushchev's de-Stalinization program, Ulbricht owed his job to the former Soviet dictator. The Hungarian ambassador to the GDR told

Kopa that the SED leadership thought Gomułka's nationalistic policies were a "dangerous game," and worried that Poland would leave the socialist camp.[56] Ulbricht told *Neues Deutschland* that "the most important lesson learned from the events in Hungary is: *there is no third way.*"[57]

During meetings with Chinese communist leaders in Warsaw in January, Gomułka candidly informed Tschou En-Lai that it was impossible to talk about Stalin's "great contribution" to socialism because so many of Stalin's policies had been disastrous for Poland. Gomułka said that most Poles hated Stalin.[58] The Poles rejected a Chinese proposal for a joint declaration on the Soviet Union's leading role in the socialist camp on the grounds that it would complicate the domestic situation in Poland. Gomułka also refused to back a statement in support of the Soviet suppression of the Hungarian reformers; he countered with a declaration that the PZPR was putting Marxism-Leninism on an entirely new foundation, but the Chinese refused to go along with this formulation.[59]

Ulbricht attributed Poland's economic problems and East Germany's relative prosperity to the PZPR's deviation from the Soviet model. He said that East Germany did not want or need Poland's economic reforms: "The development of the GDR economy is absolutely correct, while in Poland mistakes were made in the process of socializing economic life, and hence the standard of living of the working people in Poland is significantly lower than in the GDR."[60] The Poles, however, thought Ulbricht hypocritical for criticizing Poland's national road to socialism while pleading for special Soviet bloc political and economic support on the basis of the GDR's extraordinary circumstances as the only socialist German state.

The SED received thorough reports on developments in Poland in 1957 from one of its correspondents in Warsaw, Suzanne Drechsler. Drechsler was no friend of the Gomułka régime. She decried the PZPR's appeal to Polish nationalism and the unbridled policy debates going on within the party. As she put it, "the attempt, to settle everything 'democratically' and in public often gives the demagogic elements in the party the chance to cook their dirty soup to the applause of those outside of the party." Drechsler contrasted the ideological and organizational confusion in the PZPR with the SED's steady course: "The PZPR [is] in no way as rigidly organized as our party (Democratic Centralism). One does not interpret party discipline the same here." Drechsler said that Polish workers were in full support of the new PZPR leadership, and that before Gomułka had gone to Moscow [in November 1956] he had received thousands of letters warning him that he would be killed there. She alleged that many had even suggested that he bring his own cook. She held Gomułka personally responsible for the proliferation of these anti-Soviet attitudes.[61]

Drechsler took heart that many of her right-wing friends in the PZPR greatly regretted the rift with the SED and the witch hunt of "Stalinists" in Poland. She added, however, that "the wild '*Revoluzza'*" were asking her point blank when the SED was going to purge its Stalinists.[62] In March, Drechsler reported that the PZPR's attacks on alleged Stalinists had ebbed somewhat, but that many party members still equated Stalinism with the East German régime:

> If one argues that the prerequisite for eliminating the difficulties in the political and economic sphere [in Poland] is the restoration of the leading role of the party and its unity on the basis of Marxism-Leninism, one is then often categorized as a dogmatic or a 'Stalinist' who cannot see things any other way, because the situation in the GDR is different and there the 'Stalinists' are still at the helm.[63]

The SED predicted that the Polish parliamentary elections scheduled for January 20 would turn out badly for the PZPR[64] and recommended postponing them until the political and economic situation had stabilized.[65] Shortly before the elections, a high-level East German delegation to Poland reported that the PZPR was in ideological confusion, and that many party candidates held anti-Soviet, anti-Semitic, and demagogic views: "All of the party candidates that we heard talk a lot about sovereignty . . . it appears as if one has to defend the sovereignty [of Poland] against the Soviet Union and other socialist countries. We did not hear scarcely one word against the threat of imperialism and especially of German militarism." One Polish official acknowledged to the East Germans that Gomułka's popularity was based in part on his rejection of Soviet hegemony. The delegation predicted that Gomułka and the party leadership would eventually have to come out "against nationalism and the [West's] imperialist aggression policy if they themselves did not want to get run over."[66]

In the midst of the election campaign, *Neues Deutschland* attacked Gomułka for condemning the PZPR's past political and economic policies: "Gomułka said that it was a mistake for Poland to base its construction of socialism on the main principles of the socialist system that were developed by the Soviet Union and by the other countries now building socialism."[67]

Gomułka was a convinced Leninist and hard-nosed realist, however; he knew the limits of his national reform movement. He warned Poles not to cross the PZPR candidates off the election ballot because the Soviets might intervene in Poland as they had in Hungary: "The appeal to cross PZPR candidates off the ballot paper is tantamount not only to the appeal to cross out socialism. Crossing off our Party's candidates means crossing out the independence of our country, crossing Poland off the map of European states."[68]

The elections were held on time, and the PZPR and the other parties in the National Unity Front claimed 90 percent of the vote. One PZPR candidate was not elected because his name had been crossed off the ballot.[69] *Neues Deutschland* reported that the efforts of "reactionaries and imperialists" to undermine socialism in Poland had failed. But the SED still had no confidence in the PZPR to manage the political and economic crisis. Ulbricht's advisor, Erich Glückauf, told him that the elections had not settled anything, and might even have strengthened the forces threatening the socialist state.[70]

Meanwhile, the SED was pressuring the PZPR to revert back to Bierut's political and economic policies. Heymann reported that the PZPR and the Polish press were not engaging in meaningful ideological dialogue; he said that the other socialist countries were also taking issue with the PZPR's "false interpretations" of socialism, especially the party's attacks on Stalinists.[71] East German officials lectured the Poles that compromises to private business, private farming, and foreign capitalist investment were incompatible with any form of socialism.[72] When one East German official told Kopa that he was skeptical about whether Poland was developing a true dictatorship of the proletariat, Kopa caustically replied that it was impossible to build socialism, as Poland was doing, without basing it on working-class rule. Kopa said that the ideological debate should focus instead on the various national forms of the proletarian dictatorship.[73]

The Debate over Collectivization

The problems of socialist agriculture had confounded Soviet policymakers since the early days of the Bolshevik régime. Stalin's draconian collectivization program had not proved any more efficient than Lenin's New Economic Policy (NEP), and after initial successes, Khrushchev's "virgin lands" program became an economic disaster. There were chronic shortages of investment in agricultural equipment, storage facilities, and transport. Contrary to socialist propaganda championing the efficiency of collective agriculture, the peasantry always produced more on their private plots.

The PZPR never fully adopted Stalinist agricultural policies. Its modest collectivization program was a failure; from 1950 to 1952, agricultural production in Poland dropped 0.9 percent.[74] Ulbricht followed the Soviet economic model, embarking on a rapid nationalization of agriculture in the early 1950s. By 1956, East Germany had collectivized 33 percent of its arable land, but Poland only 24 percent, the lowest percentage in the Soviet bloc. Seven percent more of East Germany's arable land was collectivized by 1957, and collectives in Poland accounted for 10 percent less.[75] According to one SED report in late 1956, in some regions of Poland only 20 percent of the collectives remained.[76]

Although Poland's collectives were obviously not as productive as private farms, the SED took its cues from *Prawda's* sharp attacks on Gomułka's retreat from collectivization.[77] Paul Wandel told a Polish diplomat that he and his government were in total disagreement with Gomułka's agricultural policy, and took no lessons from it.[78] Alfred Neumann, the head of the SED in Berlin, told an SED gathering, "I ask myself, are our productive cooperatives bad, do our collectives work poorly? If farming in Poland is managed poorly, does that lead us to the conclusion that there is bad farming in the GDR?"[79] The SED maintained that the continuation of small peasant farming in Poland constituted a deviation from socialist principles—a dangerous compromise with bourgeois elements in Polish society. In addition, the East German communists thought that the Polish Catholic Church had far too much influence in the countryside.[80]

In early 1957, one East German diplomat called the situation in the Polish collectives "chaotic" because Polish farmers were now free to leave them.[81] Drechsler agreed that the PZPR had lost control of the rural areas, and that the church was rapidly gaining strength there. She wrote that the streets, buildings, and houses were in terrible shape, and that ruins from the war were still evident everywhere. Drechsler was nonetheless surprised by the Poles' lack of animosity toward her personally: "As a German one has a damned unpleasant feeling. Sometimes one wonders why there is no hatred of Germans. One seldom comes across it."[82]

The SED feared that its partner party, the DBD (German Democratic Peasant Party), might sympathize with the Polish agricultural reforms and expand ties to its Polish counterpart, the Polish Peasant Party (ZSL).[83] But the DBD leadership did not challenge the SED's agricultural policy; party head Berthold Rose told Polish diplomat Józef Czechoń that he disagreed with the Polish government's concessions to the ZSL as a "retreat to the past."[84] The DBD leadership also attributed the crisis in Poland's agricultural sector to the PZPR's inconsistent collectivization policy, which the DBD called a "huge step backward."[85] Rose told Kopa and Jakubowski that the ZSL was attempting to gain complete political and economic control of the countryside, and expressed his concern about private land speculation.[86] In April 1957, Polish officials tried to assure the new East German ambassador, Josef Hegen, that the ZSL was fully cooperating with the PZPR, and that neither the ZSL nor its rural constituents posed any real danger to the régime.[87] Hegen was not so sure, and warned his superiors that the ZSL was still gaining strength in the villages.[88]

The SED drew a direct connection between the PZPR's agricultural policy and the resurgence of the Polish Catholic Church.[89] The members of an East German delegation to Poland in January had the impression that the Catholic Church had more influence in deciding the future of the collectives than the farmers or the PZPR.⁹⁰ After a visit to the Wrocław area in May, one East German diplomat reported that collectives in the region had been reduced from 1,700 before October 1956 to only 96 now. He said that the Catholic Church was gaining influence in rural Poland, that private farmers were growing rich, and that Poles were defaming alleged Stalinists. Class conflict had returned.⁹¹ After the Ninth Plenary Session of the PZPR that same month, Hegen termed Gomułka's agricultural policy "anti-Marxist, anti-Leninist," and saw it as an invitation for more private farming.⁹²

Socialist Unity Party (SED) functionaries pointed to their own collectivization program as a model for Poland, even though agricultural production in the GDR had gone down in recent years. The East Germans were smug about the supposed success of their propaganda campaigns among farmers and workers and frequently scolded Polish officials for not taking the reeducation of Polish workers more seriously. East German delegations visiting Polish enterprises often commented that the Poles were not interested in political discussions, only in meetings with East German technicians and economic specialists. Polish workers asked one surprised delegation leader such embarrassing questions as, "Why haven't you radically changed anything in the GDR?" "Didn't you hear anything about the Twentieth Party Congress of the CPSU?" In May, Polish workers from Zielona Góra told an SED delegation that they were satisfied with their newfound freedom and the reforms of the Gomułka government; the PZPR ran politics and the workers' councils ran the economy. The delegation concluded that the PZPR was losing control of the factory floor and that the workers had no ideological direction. One East German official wrote that "the representatives of the workers' councils talk about their own road to socialism in Poland, but none of them could tell us what this road actually looks like."⁹³

Poland's Western Territories

The open and acrimonious debates between the two parties after the Polish October touched on the most sensitive and volatile issue in Polish-German relations, the Oder-Neisse border. The Polish government scored a minor victory in the border controversy in late 1956 when the Vatican decided to name Poles as bishops in the former German areas of western Poland. *Neues Deutschland* had to acknowledge that this development further confirmed the Polish character of the Western Territories.⁹⁴

The relative lack of Polish investment and development in the towns along the Oder-Neisse border gave the East Germans the impression that the Polish government either did not care about the Western Territories or did not have the resources to develop them. One East German university official from Greifswald told Rachocki that there was a marked difference between the Polish and East German sides of Guben, Pieck's birthplace. He said that East Germans wondered why Poles had taken the land in the first place if they were incapable of farming it. He added that "among the German people the conviction is propagated that Poland is not putting any emphasis on reconstructing the territories on the border because it is not sure if they will remain Polish."[95]

East German officials were genuinely surprised by some Poles' lukewarm interest in keeping the Western Territories; for instance, one East German delegation to Silesia found that many Polish immigrants from the lands lost to the Soviet Union were willing to leave western Poland if they could return to their old homes. Wandel said that these sentiments put the East German delegation in an "awkward situation" as the sole defenders of the current border. Jan Jakubowski allowed that many Poles from the eastern territories were sentimentally attached to the old homeland, but he flatly refused to enter into discussion about changing the Oder-Neisse border.[96]

In late 1956, some East German officials exploited the political instability in Poland to insinuate that the border could be revised. Politburo member Karl Schirdewan issued a warning to Polish communists who had raised the possibility of regaining Poland's lost eastern territories: "Poles alluding to the problem of their eastern border—ought not to forget about the western [border] as well.[97] Schirdewan's statement elicited a storm of protest from the PZPR, as did his attribution of the Polish and Hungarian revolutions to "bourgeois ideologues and their collaborators." Schirdewan vehemently rejected suggestions from some PZPR members that the SED adopt similar reforms.[98] When Berthold Rose also told Polish diplomats that Poland should return to its 1937 borders, Rose said that they reacted "as though hit with cold water."[99]

On January 29, the *New York Times* broke the story that during the succession crisis in Poland in October 1956, the East Germans had informed the PZPR that Poland's political development could influence their position regarding the border. Although Schirdewan had suggested exactly that, *Neues Deutschland* issued an angry reply: "This report of the American newspaper the *New York Times* is invented and false from A to Z."[100] The PZPR also publicly denounced the article. *Trybuna Ludu* ran a series of front-page articles supporting the SED, and blamed U.S. journalists and West German Foreign Minister Heinrich von Brentano, for trying to drive a wedge between Poland and the GDR.[101]

Nonetheless, Gomułka was concerned with the *New York Times'* report. He had not forgotten that Ulbricht and the rest of the SED had officially rejected the border in 1946. Repeating propaganda that the PPR had used right after the war, the PZPR stressed its partnership with the other Slavic communist parties as the main guarantee of the Oder-Neisse border. The Polish press even lauded China as an important contributor to the security of the border, while down playing the role of the GDR.[102]

Heymann's Recall

The East German ambassador, Stefan Heymann, left Poland in February 1957. Polish officials had a good working relationship with Heymann, but that may have contributed to his recall. The SED leadership thought that Heymann was not taking the threat of the PZPR's liberalization seriously enough, and that his reports on Poland were generally too optimistic; for instance, Heymann had predicted that because Edward Ochab had long been a supporter of collectivization, his naming as Minister of Agriculture in January was a positive sign for the restoration of socialism in the countryside.. The number of collectives continued to decline, however.[103]

After a meeting with Jan Izydorczyk in early February, Heymann was confident that there had been a significant change in the PZPR's acceptance of the conservatives in the party, and that Gomułka now regarded the revisionists as his biggest threat.[104] Heymann's superiors, however, remained unconvinced of Gomułka's political reliability. An East German government official told Kopa that most SED party members had reservations about the Polish situation and whether the GDR could depend on Poland. He said that some East German diplomats evaluated Polish affairs "too rosily."[105]

Florin wrote Ulbricht that "Comrade Heymann's reporting and his political stance show that he is not equal to the demands of the present situation in Poland." Florin recommended State Secretary and Deputy Foreign Minister Georg Handke for the post, but Ulbricht chose Ministry of Interior official Josef Hegen. Hegen's credentials with the Ministry of Interior were probably the deciding factor in his nomination. Ulbricht saw enemy agents behind any reform movement, including Gomułka's, and he was confident that Hegen would keep him abreast of connections between Polish and East German "counterrevolutionaries."[106]

Ulbricht had reason to worry, for Hegen began sending reports that painted a much bleaker picture of the situation in Poland than his predecessor had. Hegen blamed the PZPR leadership for not adopting a clear, consistent, and rational Marxist-Leninist political and economic program. He cited as evidence twenty-five workers' strikes in Poland in March and April, sporadic demonstrations against higher prices, and the increased activism of the Polish Catholic Church. Hegen maintained that anti-Sovietism was gaining strength in Poland, and that the PZPR was tolerating too many anti-Marxist, bourgeois elements. He and other East German officials bluntly informed Gomułka that it would be wise to follow the path laid down by the SED.[107]

Ulbricht was also receiving numerous intelligence reports about the dangers of allowing personal contacts between East Germans and Poles; in early 1957, for instance, Ulbricht gave Florin instructions to inform the Polish government about the questionable behavior of several Polish athletes at an international swim meet in Magdeburg. At a reception for the swimmers, one of the Poles had allegedly expressed regret that the Hungarian athletes could not participate, and then shouted, "Freedom in Hungary lives. . . . Hopefully we will also succeed in driving the Russians from our countries." The Poles also wanted to visit West Berlin, but Ulbricht had already decreed that Polish delegations to the GDR would not be allowed to go to West Berlin or West Germany.[108]

The Harich Affair

A far more serious case of alleged Polish meddling in East German affairs was the arrest of East German writer Wolfgang Harich, who was accused of plotting to overthrow Ulbricht and the entire socialist system. In early November, Ulbricht met with Harich and asked him to name others who had similar ideas of "democratizing" the SED. Three weeks later, Harich and his friends were behind bars.[109] *Trybuna Ludu* ignored the Harich affair, but *Neues Deutschland* reported the arrests and Harich's alleged connections with the Hungarian writers' "counterrevolutionary" Petöfi Club.[110]

When Harich had discussed the ongoing reforms in Poland with Polish intellectuals, he had raised the possibility of a similar liberalization in East Germany. In December, twenty-six members of the Department of Philosophy and Sociology of Warsaw University, all PZPR members, wrote a letter to the SED in Harich's defense. The Poles vehemently rejected the charges that Harich had contacted foreign agents in Poland, or that he was trying to reinstitute capitalism in the GDR. They called for an open and honest trial, and added that they would never believe that Harich was guilty of anything. The SED accused the Poles of casting doubt on the East German legal system.[111]

The SED used the letter as evidence that Harich's group had conspired with Polish intellectuals. In January, an SED Central Committee report accused Polish writers Adam Schaff, Leszek Kołokowski, Roman Karst, and Anatoli Ranitzki of trying to influence Harich's band of "counterrevolutionaries."[112] The indictment against Harich included his meeting with Karst and Ranitzki during the Heinrich Heine Conference in Weimar in

October 1956. The Poles allegedly had told Harich that the SED should undertake the same struggle against "Stalinist forces" as the PZPR. According to the indictment, the Poles had given Harich arguments that he used "in his traitorous conceptions for the liquidation of socialist conditions in the German Democratic Republic." Harich was also accused of planning a trip to Poland to meet with sympathetic Poles and to propagate his ideas so that the Western press could publicize them.[113]

In early March, Harich was found guilty and sentenced to ten years in prison. Polish diplomat Stanisław Kopa protested that Harich was merely proposing the same kind of changes that Gomułka had inaugurated in the PZPR: "Harich did not agree with continuing the rigid domestic policies of the party and the government, and therefore the leadership of the party realized that it was necessary to isolate him. The accusations against Harich are definitely unfounded and biased interpretations of his views." Kopa concluded that there was no basis to the charge that Polish intellectuals were responsible for Harich's actions.[114]

Other Polish officials reacted angrily to *Neues Deutschland*'s allegation that Harich's group was planning to use Poland as a springboard for counterrevolution in the GDR. On March 13, Foreign Minister Adam Rapacki issued a formal protest to Ambassador Hegen:

> The way in which these questions were treated by the federal prosecutor, and the publications about them, gives rise to the thinking that the events surrounding Harich were inspired by the PRP. The state prosecutor did not make any distinction between the efforts of the accused and the PRP. . . . In the publications things were portrayed as if Harich had been directly inspired to his actions from hearing news about the October events in Poland.[115]

On March 14, *Trybuna Ludu* denounced the accusation that Harich's group was going launch its revolution from Poland, and chastised *Neues Deutschland* for "improper and regrettable reports." The paper denied that Poland was in any way responsible for attacks on the East German state.[116]

In an aide-memoire to the Polish Foreign Ministry on March 20, the East German Foreign Ministry pointed to Harich's admission that he had learned about the PZPR's Eighth Plenary Session through Western broadcasts. The East Germans said that Harich had distorted the PZPR reforms, and had entertained ideas about beginning his propaganda movement in Poland. They asserted that Harich had support from "reactionary circles" in West Germany and Poland.[117]

That spring, Florin upbraided Polish journalist Stanisław Brodzki for telling East German officials that the SED's censored press was not giving them the truth about Poland. Brodzki had charged that writer Wolfgang Harich was in prison simply because he wanted to bring Polish-style reforms to East Germany.[118] Drechsler reported that the Harich affair was a hot topic of conversation in Polish universities. Polish students frequently confronted her with the question, "What did you do with Harich? This really cannot be true." She was shocked when the rector at Gdańsk University and a professor (and party member) at Warsaw University made similar inquiries. Drechsler recommended the recall of East German students studying in Poland as soon as the semester was over: "What they can learn in Polish universities at this time can only hurt them and us."[119]

Lasota and the Closing of *Po Prostu*

Another controversy broke out in early 1957 over an appearance on West German television by the editor of *Po Prostu*, Eligiusz Lasota. During a panel discussion on German unification, Lasota called on East Germany to conduct a more "elastic" policy toward West Germany. He also said that Harich's imprisonment was proof that Stalinists still ruled the GDR. Lasota defended some of his journal's critiques of Marxism as an attempt to provide Poles with less dogmatic and more factual reporting.[120]

Lasota said that his invitation to West Germany "showed that things had changed between Poland and Germany," meaning, of course, West Germany. When the West German commentator differentiated the "national Bolshevist" Lasota from the strict Bolshevists of the GDR, Lasota did not protest. The East Germans were markedly angered when Lasota completely ignored the GDR in his response to the suggestion that Warsaw could mediate German reunification.[121]

The SED sent a strongly worded letter to the PZPR protesting Lasota's behavior. The East German press also went after Lasota and *Po Prostu* with a vengeance. In *Neues Deutschland*, Harri Czepuck denounced the West German newspaper *Die Welt* for declaring that the Gomułka government had rid itself of the Stalinists' "fetish" with the danger of West German imperialism and militarism. Czepuck compared the *Die Welt* article to Lasota's unwillingness to defend the GDR: "[Lasota] put up with an unbridled attack against the GDR and our party leaders." Czepuck censured another Polish journalist who had appeared in *Die Welt*, Tadeusz Szafar, for writing that Poland did not consider the GDR a "front line bastion that separates us [Poland] from an eventual aggressor." Szafar had argued that a democratic (West) Germany was a "hundred times better guarantor of peace and the integrity of Poland's borders," and had said that it was utopian to think the East German economic and political system was a model for all Germany. Czepuck concluded that Lasota and

Szafar probably did not have much experience with the dangers of German militarism and fascism.[122]

Ambassador Piotrowski told Bolz that Lasota's and Szafar's remarks did not represent his government's position. He said that he was in complete agreement with Czepuck's denunciation of them. He added that as far as his government was concerned, the Harich affair was closed.[123] The Foreign Affairs Committee of the PZPR also sent a letter to the SED in April acknowledging that Lasota's participation in the discussion on West German television had been a mistake, and that he had been admonished.[124]

The Polish government nonetheless allowed a letter from Lasota to the editors of *Neues Deutschland* to appear in the April 24 issue of *Po Prostu*. Lasota called the attacks on him "slanderous." He concluded that it was in the interest of both countries to sustain good relations, "but Harri Czepuck's article, relying on unsubstantiated facts, certainly serves this end badly."[125] *Neues Deutschland* did not publish Lasota's letter.

Lasota was removed as editor of *Po Prostu* later that spring. Both Khrushchev and Ulbricht had had enough of *Po Prostu*'s allegedly anti-Soviet and anti-Marxist articles, and told Gomułka to stop publishing it. The journal was shut down in October. Gomułka had little choice in the matter: Khrushchev repeatedly reminded him that the Oder-Neisse border and Poland's independence depended on Soviet support.[126]

The Harich and Lasota affairs convinced the Ulbricht régime that it could not allow Polish intellectuals to voice their opinions openly in the GDR. The Polish Embassy confirmed that the SED wanted to prevent East German visitors to Poland from hearing the Polish version of Harich's activities; the embassy also reported that the SED had replaced some politically unreliable professors. The embassy lamented this poor state of relations with the GDR:

> Today the [cultural] contacts lie in ruin, people looking for inspiration in Poland are isolated now. . . . It has gone so far in relation to Poland that in speeches for the observations of the anniversary of the murder of R. Luxemburg and K. Liebknecht—the activity of Rosa in the SDKPiL [Social Democratic Communist Party of Poland and Lithuania] was passed over in silence. . . . In the heart of the matter the GDR leadership has a distrusting and suspicious attitude in relation to the changes taking place in Poland.[127]

The fallout from the Polish October was also evident in economic affairs. Gomułka was determined to base Poland's trade on profit, not on politics. Trade with East Germany suffered when Poland began to shift some of its exports to Western capitalist countries. Warsaw's attempts to reach political and economic agreements with Bonn also put the issue of German repatriation back on the agenda. The East Germans tried to counteract West German influence among the Germans in Poland by registering potential emigrants at the East German Embassy in Warsaw. The East Germans nonetheless thought that the Gomułka régime more often deferred to West German interests in this matter. Gomułka's trade and repatriation policies, the subjects of the next chapter, added to the animosity between Poland and the GDR.

Notes

1. Suzanne Drechsler report, January 9, 1957, SED ZK, Walter Ulbricht Papers, NL 182/1249.
2. Politburo report on relations with the other People's Republics, SED ZK, Politburo Draft Protocol No. 58, November 10, 1956, J IV 2/2A/532.
3. Rachocki notes of a meeting with Schroeder and Mentzel December 5, 1956, PZPR KC, 237/XXII–822.
4. Foreign Ministry memo on current events and relations between Poland and the GDR, December 8, 1956, MSZ, 10/378/42.
5. Heymann to the GDR Foreign Ministry, November 26, 1956, SED ZK, microfilm FBS 339/13494.
6. Kopa notes of meeting with Heide, November 29, 1956, MSZ, 10/378/42.
7. Rachocki notes of a meeting with Mentzel, November 22, 1956, MSZ, 10/378/42. The SED sharply criticized the removal of the Soviet Polish Minister of Defense, Konstantin Rokossowski.
8. Conrad Neumann notes of his visit to Poland, November 12, 1956, SED ZK, Walter Ulbricht Papers, NL 182/1247.
9. Karkut notes of a meeting with Lungewitz, November 29, 1956, PZPR KC, 237/XXII–822.
10. Heymann to the GDR Foreign Ministry, November 26, 1956, SED ZK, microfilm FBS 339/13494.
11. Foreign Ministry memo on current events and relations between Poland and the GDR, December 8, 1956, MSZ, 10/378/42.
12. The SED ideological journal *Einheit* did not publish any articles about Poland in the last two months of 1956.
13. Heinz Wolff report on a fishing trip to Gdynia, November 30, 1956, SED ZK, Walter Ulbricht Papers, NL 182/1247.
14. Tadeusz Kupis notes of his visit to Karl Marx University from October 13 to November 12, November 16, 1956, PZPR KC, 237/XXII–822.
15. Winzer report on the second meeting of the German-Polish Historians Commission in Berlin, November 22, 1956, SED ZK, Walter Ulbricht Papers, NL 182/1247.
16. Polish Foreign Ministry report, unsigned, November 30, 1956, MSZ, 10/378/42.
17. *Po Prostu*, October 28, 1956, p. 2. Historians differ on their translation for "po prostu," among them are "quite simply" or "straight away."
18. Franz Sikora, *Sozialistische Solidarität und nationale Interessen* (Socialist solidarity and national interests) (Cologne: Verlag Wissenschaft und Politik, 1977), p. 144.

19. Czechoń notes, November 16, 1956, MSZ, 10/378/42.

20. *Neues Deutschland*, November 27, 1956, p. 3.

21. Ibid.

22. Heymann notes of meeting with Menzel (Foreign Editor of *Nowe Drogi*), November 30, 1956, SED ZK, microfilm FBS 339/13494.

23. Seyfert to the GDR Foreign Ministry, November 29, 1956, SED ZK, microfilm FBS 339/13488.

24. *Neues Deutschland*, December 2, 1956, p. 5; see also "Notes on Current Events and Relations between Poland and the GDR," December 8, 1956, MSZ, 10/378/42.

25. Kopa to the Polish Foreign Ministry, undated, ca. December 1956, MSZ, 10/378/42.

26. Tadeusz Kupis notes of his visit to Karl Marx University from October 13 to November 12, November 16, 1956, PZPR KC, 237/XXII–822.

27. SED Politburo proposal to send a letter to the PZPR, October 29, 1956, in SED ZK, Politburo Draft Protocol No. 54, October 30, 1956, J IV 2/2A/528.

28. Stanisław Karkut to the Polish Foreign Ministry, November 2, 1956, PZPR KC, 237/XXII–732.

29. Karkut notes of meeting with Lungewitz, November 29, 1956, PZPR KC, 237/XXII–822.

30. Pierzchała to the Polish Foreign Ministry, October 26, 1956, PZPR KC, 237/XXII–822.

31. Pierzchała notes cited in Kopa to the Polish Foreign Ministry, November 9, 1956, MSZ, 10/378/42; see Trepte, "Polish Literature and Culture in East Germany: A Window to the West?" pp. 67–68, for a discussion of the SED's quarantine of Polish literature after October 1956.

32. Änne Kundermann notes of a meeting with Winzer and Kopa, November 24, 1956, DDR MR, DC–20, file 619; Winzer report on the second meeting of the German-Polish Historians Commission in Berlin, November 22, 1956, SED ZK, Walter Ulbricht Papers, NL 182/1247; and Pierzchała notes of a visit of Polish historians to East Germany, November 29, 1956, PZPR KC, 237/XXII–822.

33. See Peter Grieder, *The East German Leadership, 1946–1973* (Manchester: Manchester University Press, 1999), pp. 33–36.

34. Ulbricht to Winzer, November 23, 1956, SED ZK, Walter Ulbricht Papers, NL 182/1247.

35. Änne Kundermann notes of a meeting with Winzer and Kopa, November 24, 1956, DDR MR, DC–20, file 619.

36. Pierzchała notes of a visit of Polish historians to East Germany, November 29, 1956, PZPR KC, 237/XXII–822.

37. SED Department of Science and Propaganda to Ulbricht, signature unintelligible, November 23, 1956, Walter Ulbricht Papers, NL 182/1247.

38. Politburo Draft Protocol No. 54 for the Politburo meeting of October 30, 1956, SED ZK, J IV 2/2A/528.

39. Kundermann notes of a meeting with Rentmeister (Polish Ministry of Culture) and Wiese (Society for Cultural Relations), SED ZK, Politburo Protocol No. 54, October 30, 1956, J IV/2/2/508.

40. SED Politburo proposal to send a letter to the PZPR, October 29, 1956, in SED ZK, Politburo Draft Protocol No. 54, October 30, 1956, J IV 2/2A/528.

41. Łobodycz to Rapacki on his meeting with Seyfert, November 5, 1956, MSZ, 10/361/39.

42. Florin to Ulbricht, November 27, 1956, in SED ZK, Politburo Draft Protocol No. 62, November 27, 1956, J IV 2/2A/536.

43. Kundermann notes of a meeting between Kopa and Winzer, December 1, 1956, DDR MfAA, HA/I Secretariat, A37; and Kopa to Rapacki, December 1, 1956, KWKzZ, file 153.

44. Czyrek notes of a meeting of the SED party organization meeting in Berlin, December 19, 1956, PZPR KC, 237/XXII–732; and Polish Embassy report from October 1, 1956, to March 15, 1957, MSZ, 10/371/41.

45. *Trybuna Ludu*, December 13, 1956, p. 1.

46. Rachocki notes of a meeting with Wentzel (editor of *Sonntag*), December 21, 1956, MSZ, 10/378/42.

47. Memo on the situation in the PZPR, unsigned, undated, ca. December 1958, SED ZK, microfilm FBS 339/13424.

48. *Trybuna Ludu*, December 26, 1956, p. 5.

49. *Trybuna Ludu*, January 9, 1957, pp. 2, 4.

50. Pierzchała notes of meeting with Bringmann, January 18, 1957, MSZ, 10/379/42.

51. Łobodycz memorandum, January 18, 1957, MSZ, 10/379/42.

52. Piotrowski notes of meeting with Florin on February 4, February 8, 1957, MSZ, 10/379/42.

53. Łobodycz to Naszkowski, March 2, 1957, MSZ, 10/379/42.

54. Pierzchała notes of a meeting with Bringmann (East German Foreign Ministry), January 18, 1957, MSZ, 10/379/42.

55. "W oczach zagranicy," (In view of the border), *Nowe Drogi* 11, no. 1 (January-February 1957), pp. 44–45.

56. Kopa notes of a meeting with Beck (Hungarian ambassador to the GDR), January 31, 1957, MSZ, 10/379/42.

57. *Neues Deutschland*, December 30, 1956, p. 1.

58. Heymann to Winzer, January 29, 1957, SED ZK, Otto Grotewohl Papers, NL 90/485.

59. Schwab to Ulbricht, April 15, 1957, SED ZK, Walter Ulbricht Papers, NL 182/1249.

60. Polish Embassy report from October 1, 1956 to March 15, 1957, MSZ, 10/371/41.

61. Drechsler report, January 9, 1957, SED ZK, Walter Ulbricht Papers, NL 182/1249.

62. Ibid.

63. Drechsler report, March 14, 1957, SED ZK, Walter Ulbricht Papers, NL 182/1249.

64. Kopa notes of meeting with Nowotny, (SED member and head of the "Sorbian Institute") on January 15, January 17, 1957, MSZ, 10/379/42.

65. Czechoń notes of meeting with Schwotzer (Director of the Foreign Affairs Department of the SED Central Committee) on January 14, January 18, 1957, MSZ, 10/379/42.

66. Erich Glückauf to Ulbricht, January 20, 1957, SED ZK, Walter Ulbricht Papers, NL 182/1249.

67. *Neues Deutschland,* January 11, 1957, p. 1.

68. Quoted in R. F. Leslie, et al., *The History of Poland Since 1863* (Cambridge: Cambridge University Press, 1980), p. 365.

69. *Neues Deutschland,* January 22, 1957, p. 1; and Leslie, p. 365.

70. Glückauf to Ulbricht, February 1, 1957, SED ZK, Walter Ulbricht Papers, NL 182/1249.

71. Heymann notes of meeting with Soviet diplomat Karpow and the Romanian, Czechoslovak, and Albanian ambassadors, January 29, 1957, SED ZK, Walter Ulbricht Papers, NL 182/1249.

72. See Jakubowski notes of meeting with Wenk on February 19, February 20, 1957, MSZ, 10/379/42.

73. Kopa notes of meeting with Kundermann on February 9, February 14, 1957, MSZ, 10/379/42.

74. M. K. Dziewanowski, *The Communist Party of Poland: An Outline of History* (Cambridge: Harvard University Press, 1976), p. 234.

75. Zbigniew Brzezinski, *The Soviet Bloc: Unity and Conflict* (Cambridge: Harvard University Press, 1967), p. 100.

76. Conrad Neumann report of his visit to Poland, November 12, 1956, SED ZK, Walter Ulbricht Papers, NL 182/1247.

77. See Wlodzimierz Brus, "Economic Reforms as an Issue in Soviet-East European Relations," in Karen Dawisha and Philip Hanson, eds., *Soviet-East European Dilemmas: Coercion, Competition, and Consent* (London: Heinemann Educational Books, 1981), p. 85. Brus writes, "In 1955, at an East Berlin conference of economists from socialist countries, a Polish paper with a number of reform ideas received a great deal of sympathetic attention, particularly from the hosts; in the course of the subsequent year and a half relations between East German and Polish economists developed extremely well, and several quite radical reformist articles were published in leading GDR journals"; see also Nicholas Bethell, *Gomułka, His Poland and His Communism* (London: Longmans, Green and Co., 1969), p. 240.

78. Jakubowski notes of meeting with Wandel, October 26, 1956, MSZ, 10/378/42.

79. Kopa notes of meeting of the SED party organization in Berlin on October 24, October 25, 1956, MSZ, 10/378/42.

80. Helmer report, undated, ca. July 1955, SED ZK, microfilm FBS 339/13494.

81. Lugenheim report on the agricultural situation in Poland, January 14, 1957, SED ZK, microfilm FBS/13489.

82. Drechsler report, January 9, 1957, SED ZK, Walter Ulbricht Papers, NL 182/1249.

83. Czechoń notes of conversation with Rose and Stude on November 7, November 9, 1956, MSZ, 10/378/42.

84. Czechoń notes of meeting with Rose, Hlusziczka (Second Secretary of the Czechoslovak Embassy), and Sung Chih Kuang (First Secretary of the Republic of China Embassy) on November 29, November 30, 1956, MSZ, 10/378/42.

85. Kopa notes of a meeting with Goldenbaum (DBD) on April 27, May 2, 1957, MSZ, 10/379/42.

86. Kopa notes of a meeting with Rose on June 13, June 14, 1957, MSZ, 10/379/42.

87. Hegen notes of a meeting with Czesak, April 1, 1957, SED ZK, Walter Ulbricht Papers, NL 182/1249.

88. Hegen to the GDR Foreign Ministry, April 17, 1957, SED ZK, Otto Grotewohl Papers, NL 90/485.

89. See *Neues Deutschland*, December 9, 1956, p. 5; see also Leslie, *The History of Poland Since 1863*, p. 362. Gomułka had freed Cardinal Wyszinski in October, and in December the government rescinded the 1953 decree barring the church from making ecclesiastical appointments. The government also renewed a 1950 agreement allowing freedom of worship, the formation of catholic associations, and religious instruction in state schools.

90. Glückauf to Ulbricht, January 20, 1957, SED ZK, Walter Ulbricht Papers, NL 182/1249.

91. Fritzsche to the GDR Foreign Ministry, April 16, 1957, DDR MfAA, HA/I Secretariat, A38.

92. Hegen to the GDR Foreign Ministry, May 29, 1957, DDR MfAA, HA/I Secretariat, A38.

93. Blankenhagen report on a delegation visit to Zielona-Góra, May 6, 1957, SED ZK, Walter Ulbricht Papers, NL 182/1249.

94. *Neues Deutschland*, December 9, 1956, p. 5.

95. Rachocki notes of a meeting with Nichtweiss (Prorektor of the University of Greifswald), December 5, 1956, PZPR KC, 237/XXII–822.

96. Jakubowski notes of a meeting with Wandel, October 26, 1956, MSZ, 10/378/42.

97. Kupis notes of his visit to Karl Marx University from October 13 to November 12, November 16, 1956, PZPR KC, 237/XXII–822.

98. Polish Foreign Ministry report, unsigned, November 30, 1956, MSZ, 10/378/42.

99. Czechoń notes of a meeting with Rose, Hluszczka (Second Secretary of the Czechoslovak Embassy), and Sung Chih Kuang (First Secretary of the Republic of China Embassy), November 30, 1956, MSZ, 10/378/42; see also Czechoń notes of a meeting with Rose, December 7, 1956, PZPR KC, 237/XXII–822.

100. *Neues Deutschland*, February 6, 1957, p. 1.

101. *Trybuna Ludu*, February 6, 1957, p. 1; and February 9, 1957, p. 1.

102. See Sikora, *Sozialistische Solidarität und nationale Interessen*, p. 147.

103. Heymann report of a meeting with Tschou En-lai at the Warsaw airport, January 11, 1957, SED ZK, Otto Grotewohl Papers, NL 90/485.

104. Heymann to Winzer, February 6, 1957, SED ZK, Walter Ulbricht Papers, NL 182/1249.

105. Kopa notes of a meeting with Bitterlich on January 26, January 31, 1957, MSZ, 10/379/42.

106. Florin to Ulbricht, November 30, 1956, SED ZK, Otto Grotewohl Papers, NL 90/484.

107. Hegen to the GDR Foreign Ministry, April 17, 1957, SED ZK, Otto Grotewohl Papers, NL 90/485.

108. Ulbricht to Florin, January 18, 1957, SED ZK, Walter Ulbricht Papers, NL 182/1249.

109. Staritz, *Geschichte der DDR, 1949–1985*, p. 113. In March 1957, Harich was sentenced to ten years in prison, and Walter Janke was given five years. In an in-

terview in the *Berliner Zeitung* in 1991, Janke accused Harich of having worked
for the KGB and of planning Ulbricht's overthrow. Janke also accused Harich of
implicating him; for a full account of the Harich case, see Grieder, *The East German Leadership, 1946–73*, pp. 110f.

110. *Neues Deutschland*, December 1, 1956, p. 1.

111. Enclosed in a letter from the Secretary of the Foreign Policy Commission
of the SED Central Committee to the PZPR Central Committee, March 22, 1957,
PZPR KC, 237/XXII–823.

112. Report on the "counterrevolutionary group Harich and others", unsigned,
January 26, 1957, SED ZK, Walter Ulbricht Office, J IV 2/202/7.

113. Enclosed in a letter from the Secretary of the Foreign Policy Commission
of the SED Central Committee to the PZPR Central Committee, March 22, 1957,
PZPR KC, 237/XXII–823.

114. Kopa to the Polish Foreign Ministry, March 14, 1957, PZPR KC,
237/XXII–823.

115. Hegen notes of a meeting with Rapacki on March 13, March 14, 1957, SED
ZK, Otto Grotewohl Papers, NL 90/485.

116. Translation of a *Trybuna Ludu* article on Harich, March 14, 1957, in SED
ZK, Otto Grotewohl Papers, NL 90/485.

117. GDR Foreign Ministry aide-memoire to the Polish Foreign Ministry,
March 20, 1957, DDR MfAA, Minister's Office, A15156.

118. Schwanz to the SED Central Committee, March 20, 1957, SED ZK, micro-
film FBS 339/13489; Wollweber to Honecker, March 30, 1957, SED ZK, microfilm
FBS 339/13489; and Florin to the PZPR Central Committee, April 15, 1957, SED
ZK, microfilm FBS 339/13489.

119. Drechsler report, March 14, 1957, SED ZK, Walter Ulbricht Papers, NL
182/1249.

120. Kurt Turba report on Lasota's press conference on January 18, 1957, January 21, 1957, SED ZK, microfilm FBS 339/13489.

121. Enclosed in a letter from the Secretary of the SED Central Committee Foreign Affairs Commission to the PZPR Central Committee, March 22, 1957, PZPR
KC, 237/XXII–823.

122. *Neues Deutschland*, March 27, 1957, p. 2.

123. Kundermann notes of meeting between Bolz and Piotrowski, March 28,
1957, DDR MfAA, HA/I Secretariat, A38.

124. Czesak to the SED Central Committee, April 24, 1957, SED ZK, microfilm
FBS 339/13489.

125. *Po prostu*, April 24, 1957, p. 3.

126. Peter Raina, *Gomułka: Politische Biographie* (Gomułka: Political biography)
(Cologne: Verlag Wissenschaft und Politik, 1970), p. 120; and Douglas Selvage,
"Khrushchev's November 1958 Berlin Ultimatum: New Evidence from the Polish
Archives," *Bulletin: Cold War International History Project*, no. 1 (winter 1998), p.
200–201.

127. Polish Embassy report for October 1, 1956, to March 15, 1957, MSZ,
10/371/41.

8

Gomułka's Trade Policies and the Recurring Problem of German Repatriation, 1953–1957

Today the FRG takes one of the leading positions among our capitalistic trading partners. Of course not from an ideological perspective, but because it is mutually beneficial for the FRG and for Poland.

—**Trybuna Ludu**, *December 9, 1956.*[1]

Stalin's political repression and autarkic economic policies, and the West's controls on exports to the Soviet bloc forced Poland and East Germany into a closer economic partnership in the early 1950s. But neither side thought their trade was built on the principle of mutual advantage (see Chapter 3). After Stalin's death, the East Germans and Poles began to pursue their own national economic interests with more vigor. It soon became apparent that those interests were contradictory. Although the volume of Polish-East German trade actually increased from 1953 to 1956, it was largely the result of the growth of their economies rather than an increase in trade share. Poland's trade with East Germany become relatively less important after 1954, amounting to slightly over 14 percent of all Polish trade in that year, dropping to 13.4 percent in 1955 and 12.2 percent in 1956.[2]

Both sides openly accused the other of reneging on promised exports; the Polish government, for instance, repeatedly asked for more chemicals than the East Germans were willing to, or could, supply.[3] In the spring of 1954, a shortage of East German chlorine exports to Poland caused four Polish factories to shut down, and created other bottlenecks in the textile, chemical, and paper industries.[4] When the situation had not improved by the end of the year, the East German Foreign Ministry began to worry

about detrimental political ramifications. The Foreign Ministry acknowledged that although the Poles had fulfilled about two-thirds of a supple-
mentary trade agreement for 1954, "almost nothing was delivered from
our side." As a result, the Poles delayed talks on a new trade agreement.[5]

The East Germans complained bitterly, however, about Polish exports
that were being diverted from the GDR to the capitalist countries. The
SED saw this as a betrayal of a fellow socialist country and a direct attack
on the unity of the socialist bloc.[6] The East Germans were mainly angered over the drop in Polish coal deliveries. Many East German industries had been built to make use of Polish coal and coke; when Polish exports of coal to East Germany fell from over 4 million tons in 1954 to 3.8
million tons in 1955, the entire East German economic plan was jeopardized.[7]

Polish trade officials appeared to be more interested in trade with West
Germany. The East Germans repeatedly reminded them of the importance of socialist political and economic solidarity on this front.[8] Ambassador Heymann recommended that, to minimize its trade with capitalist
countries, his government pursue "maximal cooperation" with Poland;[9]
but when Poland's trade with the West continued to rise in 1955, he
blamed Poland for doing "great damage" to the East German economy.[10]

The East Germans overlooked their own brisk trade with the FRG,
which they considered to be a domestic German matter. By 1955, West
Germany, which now represented approximately 11 percent of East Germany's total trade, had replaced Poland as East Germany's second most
important trading partner.[11] East Germany's trade with capitalist countries as a whole rose 16 percent in the first half of 1955, and East German
exports to the other Soviet bloc countries decreased, with the exception
of exports to Czechoslovakia. East German exports to Poland in the first
half of 1955 decreased 16 percent in comparison with the first half of
1954. Hurt by the West's export controls on certain strategic goods, Polish
officials asked the East Germans for more imports of essential machinery,
but to no avail. The Poles accused East Germany of demanding higher
prices for their machines than other countries charged, and pointed out
that East Germany paid less for coal and coke than the capitalist countries. Even Czechoslovakia charged more than Poland. Much to the
Poles' irritation, the East Germans pressed for more Polish coal at even
lower prices.[12]

At the end of 1955, Heymann reported that trade negotiations with
Poland were encountering "extraordinary difficulties."[13] The East German Foreign Ministry criticized Warsaw for not recognizing that the
West had some purely political motives in buying Polish coal: "In our
opinion the orders from the capitalist countries are part of deliberate
measures to damage the economy of the GDR because Polish coal is still
more expensive than English coal."[14]

When the East Germans asked the other socialist countries for economic concessions, they never mentioned the GDR's own trade with West Germany.[15] The Poles accused the SED of hypocrisy for attacking Polish trade policy.[16] The Poles had no compunction about reducing coal exports to East Germany, in part because the East Germany economy was outperforming Poland's. The East Germans' rising standard of living in the mid-1950s created especially hard feelings among Poles. Heymann reported that "one can often hear the opinion, not only among functionaries in the lower and middle ranks [of the PZPR], but *also shared in leading government circles*, that people in the GDR live significantly better than Polish workers." One Polish official claimed that the GDR had "everything in surplus," and another commented that "sometimes one has the impression that World War II was won by the Germans and not by the Poles."[17] The issue was so sensitive that the East German Foreign Ministry downsized the GDR's exhibition at the Poznań fair in 1955 so that it would not give the impression that East Germans had a higher standard of living.[18]

Poland's Trade with the West in 1956

Khrushchev's determination to put Soviet bloc relations on a more equal footing in 1956 allowed the Polish government to develop new economic and political connections to Western Europe, particularly to West Germany. Trade with the West was seen as a way to meet the government's new ambitious economic goals. The government had fulfilled the Six-Year Plan for industrial production, but had fallen short in investments, agricultural production, and consumer goods.[19]

At the meeting of Comecon that May, Ulbricht expressly blamed Polish steel exports to capitalist countries for steel shortages in East Germany and the Soviet bloc as a whole. He claimed that the lack of steel, coal, coke, and other imports from Poland had prevented the GDR from fulfilling its economic plan for the first quarter of 1956. Ulbricht once again appealed to Poland and the other Soviet bloc countries for special trade concessions; he argued that a strong East German economy was the only way to win over German working classes: "In contrast to the other people's democracies we have open borders with West Germany and stand in open competition with the strong economic forces of West German monopoly capital." Ulbricht pointed out that the FRG had a higher per capita consumption and that it was urgent for the GDR to catch up. The SED had recently promised an end to rationing and a reduction in working hours to match the 45-hour work week that West German unions had negotiated. Ulbricht called a Polish proposal to further reduce coal shipments "unacceptable" because the GDR could not possibly fulfill its economic plans without Polish coal; he promised assistance to develop the

Polish coal industry, and the Soviets agreed to send coal industry experts.[20] The East Germans were aware that if Comecon did not furnish investment funds and mining equipment, Poland would not be able to increase its coal production.[21] The East Germans also suggested that Poland use East German brown coal in industries that did not need high-quality coal, and offered help to increase brown coal production.[22]

The East German exhortations fell on deaf ears. Faced with serious economic and political problems of its own, the Polish government could not afford to make economic sacrifices for the GDR. The Poles were acutely aware of the widening disparity in living standards between the two countries; Poles and East Germans could easily see the differences. Józef Winiewicz told Heymann that a delegation of Polish Catholics returning from the CDU party congress that fall "had made several comparisons with life in the GDR [that were] unfavorable for Poland."[23] One delegation of East German educators to Poland concluded that the standard of living in Poland was "a lot lower" than in the GDR.[24]

The Polish government was in no position to increase coal exports: Ochab estimated that Poland faced a deficit of 2.5 million tons of coal in 1956. Heymann confirmed that Poland's economy was in trouble, in part because of the shift to military production in 1951.[25] A prisoner amnesty resulted in a shortage of coal miners, and coal production fell 280,000 tons in May. Polish authorities had to use 3,000 soldiers in the mines. The Polish economic plan called for a 30 percent rise in the standard of living of workers and peasants by the late 1950s, but to achieve that the Polish government could not afford to increase coal exports to the Soviet bloc countries at reduced prices.[26]

Selling coal to the West was therefore a logical economic choice for the Polish economic planners. *Trybuna Ludu* reported that East Germany, Czechoslovakia, and Hungary paid $20.5 per ton of coal, and the Soviet Union only $19. Capitalist countries paid between $20 to $25.[27] When Cyrankiewicz appealed to the Western countries that were importing Polish coal to invest in the Polish coal industry, he made it clear that his government would accept economic assistance from any source.[28]

Cyrankiewicz informed Grotewohl in September that Poland would not be able to meet its commitments for coal exports to the GDR in 1956. Cyrankiewicz said that part of the problem was a reduction in the coal miners' work week.[29] Grotewohl replied in a personal letter to the PZPR Politburo that the coal shortages were causing serious problems for the East German economy, and requested immediate high-level discussions.[30] Two weeks later, Grotewohl wrote another letter to Cyrankiewicz expressing his government's deep disappointment in Warsaw's decision to reduce coal exports to the GDR. Grotewohl complained that the energy shortages were causing East German industries to curb production, and that in some areas of the country people had no coal or natural gas to light and heat their homes. In contrast to the reduction of the Polish miners' work week, he pointed out, East German miners were putting in extra hours to make up for the coal shortage; they would have only one more holiday that year—Christmas Day. Grotewohl expected Polish miners to work equally as hard. He informed Cyrankiewicz that he would ask Khrushchev, Soviet Premier Nicholai Bulganin, and the other Comecon leaders for a special Comecon meeting to deal with the energy crisis.[31]

In the letter to A. A. Pawlow, the Soviet secretary of Comecon, Grotewohl wrote that Poland's coal deliveries to the GDR were falling far short of the promises that the Poles had made at the Comecon meeting in Budapest in December 1955. Grotewohl noted that "even at the signing of the [Comecon] agreements it was clear that the People's Republic of Poland was not prepared to keep the Budapest recommendations for the agreed level of exports of metallurgical coke. . . . The missing coal and coke imports are having the most difficult impacts on the GDR economy."[32]

In October, the SED sent Matern and Florin to meet with Gierek and Jędrychowski to ask for more Polish coal. The Poles explained that they had been forced to shorten the miners' hours because of the uncertain political situation following Khrushchev's secret speech and the demonstrations in Poznań (see Chapter 6). They said that the PZPR had to consider Poland's energy needs first. Gierek and Jędrychowski reminded the East Germans that prisoners were no longer being used in the mines. They promised to reduce coal exports to capitalist countries, but not by much; they argued that a collapse of Poland's trade agreements with Western countries would have serious repercussions for the Polish economy.[33]

The Poles were also dissatisfied with the quality of East German manufactured goods. The Polish government complained to East German authorities in April about defective East German electric locomotives that had put the rail lines between Częstochowa and Warsaw out of service. The Poles could not even obtain spare parts to repair them.[34] Heymann warned Grotewohl that the reputation of both governments was being damaged and recommended rectifying their trade differences as soon as possible.[35]

It was already too late; the GDR gradually lost ground as one of Poland's most important trading partners. Polish exports to the GDR amounted to 10.5 percent of all Polish exports in 1949, 13 percent in 1954, 13.1 in 1955, but dropped to only 10.9 percent in 1956. Polish coal exports to the GDR fell from 15.7 percent of all Polish coal exports in 1955 to 12.9 percent in 1956. Forty-six percent of Polish coke exports went to the GDR in 1955, but only 25 percent in 1956.[36] Much to the anger of East German officials, Poland's monthly coal exports to West Germany from January to July 1956 averaged 9 percent more than the year before.[37]

In early June 1956, *Trybuna Ludu* wrote that "next to the development of relations to the GDR we will not preclude friendly cooperation with West

Germany on the basis of mutual benefit."[38] The newspaper also printed an interview with SPD leader Herbert Wehner in which he encouraged an expansion of Polish-West German economic relations.[39] On the seventh anniversary of the founding of the GDR in October, *Trybuna Ludu* reiterated that Poland could have friendly ties with both East and West Germany.[40]

The East Germans' concern grew as Poland began to cultivate economic ties to the FRG in 1956. From the inception of the two German states in 1949, the East Germans had publicly encouraged closer relations between Warsaw and Bonn, and had offered to act as intermediaries in trade talks; the East German communists, however, were worried about being left out of political or economic deals. Now Ulbricht insisted on being informed about new talks even if he was not included in them. In March, Polish Deputy Foreign Minister Marion Naszkowski assured Heymann that his government would keep East Berlin abreast of meetings with West German officials, but that did not happen.[41] A few months later, Heymann had to ask the Polish Foreign Ministry for more information regarding Poland's relations with West Germany, and their possible impact on Poland's agreements with the GDR.[42]

As usual, Heymann hid the real truth about his government's position on Polish-West German relations. He told a group of West German visitors to Poland that understanding between the FRG and Poland would serve to secure the peace and fight the "chauvinist agitation in West Germany." Although the competition from West German trade was certainly a concern to his government, Heymann said that "an expansion of the present trade relationship between the PRP and the Federal Republic would in no way lead to a reduction of the economic ties between the GDR and the PRP."[43]

Ulbricht was in fact very concerned about competition from West German trade. East German officials repeatedly urged the Poles to engage in anti-West German propaganda and support those political elements in West Germany who opposed Bonn's foreign and military policies. But Warsaw was not about to jeopardize relations with Bonn at this time.[44] Later that fall, the SED's Department of Foreign Affairs had to reassure Ulbricht that according to Warsaw Pact bylaws, the Polish government was obligated to consult with the GDR before it made concessions to West Germany, or if Warsaw contemplated establishing diplomatic relations with Bonn.[45]

Gomułka's Foreign Economic Policy

The political and ideological rift in Polish-East German relations following the Polish October had serious repercussions on trade relations. Gomułka was determined to develop trading partners for economic rather than for political reasons. Soon after returning to power, he declared that Poland's economic interests would now take top priority. The East Germans repeatedly evoked political arguments to lobby for more favorable terms of trade, and Ulbricht often accused Gomułka of un-socialist economic practices. He began to regard Poland as an unreliable supplier and an unstable market.

The Gomułka régime stated that it was no longer willing to trade Poland's valuable raw materials for inferior East German goods. Polish officials informed the East Germans that their "difficult political situation" was forcing them to cover their own domestic needs first. That fall, the East Germans complained that coal shortages were causing serious bottlenecks in some East German factories, and repeated warnings that the scarcity of coal would create difficulties for the GDR in fulfilling its trade agreements with Poland.[46]

The shortages put many East German power plants out of service. The frequent electrical outages reminded one East German official of conditions right after the war.[47] The situation became so serious by the end of November that Grotewohl sent a personal telegram to Cyrankiewicz informing him that Heinrich Rau was hurrying to Warsaw to request more coal. Rau's mission was a failure.[48] The West German newspaper *Die Welt am Sonntag* (The World on Sunday) predicted that it would be a "meager Christmas in the [Soviet] zone."[49]

The drop in trade contradicted the SED's propaganda campaign promoting friendly relations with Poland. A factory in Stalinstadt that had adopted the slogan "We Forge with Polish Coal and Soviet Steel" now lay idle.[50] The East German government did not deny that the brownouts and work stoppages were the direct result of delinquent Polish coal deliveries. On October 23, the Polish Military Mission reported that the coal shortages were being openly discussed in factory meetings, where there was a palpable "anti-Polish atmosphere." Polish diplomats accused some SED members of intentionally fostering these attitudes among the workers by criticizing Poland for not keeping its trade agreements.[51]

Many East German workers came to the logical conclusion that their economic problems were caused by the loss of Silesia to Poland. Party members were also grumbling about Poland's acquisition of German coal mines. The East Germans knew that Silesian coal originally planned for export to the GDR was now going to West Germany, although it was the East German state that had recognized the Oder-Neisse border.[52] One East German official accused Poland of sending more coal to West Germany than called for in trade agreements. He criticized the Poles for building fewer ships in Gdańsk and instead making more turbo generators, a specialty of the GDR. He questioned whether these policies were contributing at all to the spirit of socialist economic cooperation.[53]

The East German diplomats in Warsaw were disappointed by Gomułka's willingness to deny the socialist economies essential goods for trade with the West.[54] They were also shocked to find Polish officials openly discussing the Soviet Union's exploitation of the satellite economies.[55] In early November, representatives from the Polish Trade Commission informed the East Germans that trade agreements with the GDR had been detrimental to Poland as well. The Poles said that their government would seek trade with complementary economies, not just socialist economies.[56]

In November 1956, *Trybuna Ludu* proudly declared that Poland was West Germany's most important trading partner in the Soviet bloc (excluding the GDR).[57] The newspaper editorialized that Poland needed to look to the capitalist countries for the best machines and the newest technology,[58] and that ideological considerations were now secondary in economic decisionmaking: "Today the FRG takes one of the leading positions among our capitalistic trading partners. Of course not from an ideological perspective, but because it is mutually beneficial for the FRG and for Poland."[59] East German officials were particularly irritated with this and other press reports extolling Poland's growing trade with West Germany.[60]

As Poland began to increase trade with the West that fall, East Germany turned to the Soviet Union to fill the void.[61] At the end of October, the SED Politburo informed the Central Committee that the political crises in Poland and Hungary had contributed to the GDR's economic problems, and that the Soviets had been asked for help.[62] According to East German trade official Rudi Demel, the Soviets, in contrast to the Poles, responded positively to some of the East German requests for special trade concessions, even though the GDR economy was already the most developed in the Soviet bloc. Demel pointed out that the GDR was on the front line against NATO, and proudly cast East Germany as a model for the socialist movement in Western Europe: "The struggle for the superiority of the socialist world system reflects itself in the German Democratic Republic."[63]

Contrary to Demel's claim, however, Soviet Premier Bulganin informed the East Germans that the Soviet Union was in no position to increase coal shipments to the GDR. The Poles further complicated an expansion in Soviet-East German trade by asking the East Germans to pay transit fees in convertible currency.[64] By the end of 1956, the GDR was in arrears to Poland for these transit costs.[65]

In December, the SED Politburo resolved to address the problem of Polish coal deliveries at the next Comecon meeting, along with the entire system of transport between the GDR, Poland, and the Soviet Union. The East Germans planned to appeal once again for the economic unity of the socialist camp, and to ask Poland to reduce coal exports to the West.[66] Rau declared in *Neues Deutschland* that the GDR's biggest foreign trade problem was the shortage of Polish coal and coke imports. He drew attention to the high cost of transporting Soviet goods through Poland, and concluded that East Germany could only fulfill its trade agreements through Poland's cooperation.[67]

An East German analysis of trade with Poland in 1956 found that the GDR had met all its export obligations to Poland, but claimed that Poland had fulfilled only 94 percent of its promised exports to the GDR. The report faulted the Poles for shortages in essential deliveries of coal, coke, and brown coal. In 1956, Poland sent only a little over one-third of the coke that the GDR had requested.[68] East German economists estimated that the GDR lost 138.7 million rubles worth of projected imports from Poland and 73.8 million rubles in projected exports to Poland. Coal and coke amounted to over half the shortage in imports that year.[69]

The Polish government was unwilling to meet Comecon's recommended increase in Polish coal exports to East Germany. In their export plan for 1957, the Poles reduced coal deliveries to East Germany by 500,000 tons, which made it virtually impossible for the East Germans to fulfill its own export plans. In January, the Polish government gave the East Germans an ultimatum to deliver promised goods to Poland within a week or it would order a halt to all exports to the GDR. The East Germans in turn refused to provide promised investment credits to Poland on the grounds that it was the GDR that needed credits. East German trade officials complained that negotiations with the Poles did not conform to "the typical practices between socialist partners."[70] Florin again told Ambassador Piotrowski that the lack of Polish coal deliveries was creating political problems for the SED because many East Germans equated the energy shortages to the loss of Silesia.[71]

Although they were well aware of Poland's ongoing economic problems, the East Germans found it inconceivable that the Polish government refused to compromise in the interest of the Soviet bloc countries.[72] The head of the DBD, Berthold Rose, upbraided Polish diplomats for Poland's coal exports to capitalist countries because they came at the direct expense of the GDR and its industries.[73] Suzanne Drechsler, the East German journalist in Poland, reported that West German companies tried to buy off Polish importers by including in their shipments cheap watches, fountain pens, and other "bribes" to keep the Poles buying Western products: "This gets around the [Polish] company very fast so that all the workers are for making purchases only in capitalist countries."[74]

Desperate for higher-grade Polish coal and coke, the East Germans persisted in their efforts to help the Poles develop their brown coal industry. The GDR was willing to supply machinery on credit if the Poles would agree to a long-term agreement to export more coal to the GDR.[75]

In the spring of 1957, the East Germans promised Poland a $25-million credit for equipment and technical assistance for the brown coal industry. Although they would not acknowledge it, the East Germans were most interested in investing in the former German territories that might some-day return to Germany.[76]

In March 1957, Polish economic planners said that they could increase coal exports to Comecon members by about 1 million tons if Poland received gold, hard currency, or goods that could be sold in the West for hard currency. The move prompted the East Germans to reevaluate their entire system of trade with Poland.[77]

The Gomułka régime had already done that. The East German Foreign Ministry circulated an article in May directly accusing many PZPR members of declaring that Poland's trade with the socialist countries was not beneficial.[78] There was much truth to this claim; one of the reasons that the Polish government wanted to sell more coal to the West was its dissatisfaction with the quality and quantity of imported East German consumer goods.[79] One East German official told Kopa that he was aware that Poles were more impressed with U.S. and British brand names than with goods from socialist enterprises.[80]

That same month, the head of the Polish parliament, Czesław Wycech, told his East German counterpart Johannes Dieckmann that the only way for Poland to overcome its economic problems was to reach out to the West—particularly to the United States. Wycech said the Polish people were becoming increasingly dissatisfied with their poor standard of living, which was significantly lower than East Germany's. He informed Dieckmann that

> what Poland needs in the first place are the most modern mining machines, which until now the socialist countries have not supplied. Poland can get these machines from the USA without having to pay for them immediately, which Poland presently is in no position to do. The Soviet Union cannot help either because of its great obligations to China.[81]

Dieckmann was sympathetic to Poland's economic predicament, but he was firmly opposed to a socialist country's accepting loans from the United States. Despite Wycech's assurances that there were no political conditions attached to the credits, Dieckmann gave Wycech an indirect warning that the Oder-Neisse border could be jeopardized if Poland traded more with the capitalist countries: "Of course no one in Poland can have any doubt that only the socialist bloc guarantees Poland's border of peace. Taking a credit from America also means, in my opinion, an imperialist attempt at least to make the border a topic of discussion." When Wycech pointed out that the GDR had extensive trade ties to capitalist countries, especially to West Germany, Dieckmann dismissed it as a simple exchange of goods without credit arrangements or political concessions.[82]

Poland's trade with East Germany declined significantly in 1956–1957, forcing the East Germans to make numerous revisions in their new Five-Year Plan. Once again they turned to the Soviet Union for help, but the Soviets could not replace Polish coal because of the prohibitively high costs of transportation. In 1957, the Soviets began to ship some coal and coke to the GDR from the Donetz region, but this was a distance of over 2,000 kilometers; in addition, the difference in railroad gauges between Poland and the Soviet Union meant that the coal had to be loaded and unloaded at the Polish-Soviet border.[83]

The East Germans suspected the Poles of hindering that trade. In the fall, the East Germans were making daily appeals to the Polish government to get trains from the Soviet Union moving through Poland. In desperation, Grotewohl sent a letter to Cyrankiewicz in November informing him that 1,726 loaded railroad cars were standing in Brest on the Polish-Soviet border, all waiting to go to the GDR. Twenty more trains in Frankfurt/Oder waited for Polish locomotives to take them to the Soviet Union.[84] Several days later, the East German Ministry of Commerce informed Grotewohl that the situation had not changed.[85]

Three weeks passed before Cyrankiewicz responded to Grotewohl's letter. Cyrankiewicz pointed out that Poland had already agreed to transport twice as many goods in 1957 as in 1956, but that this trade depended upon the regular arrival of goods from the Soviet Union on Poland's eastern border and on a steady supply of empty railroad cars from the GDR. He said that this was not happening. Cyrankiewicz noted that in spite of these problems, 99.6 percent of the planned transports had moved through Poland in October, and 117.1 percent in November. Cyrankiewicz promised that the Polish railroad authorities were doing all they could to meet their obligations.[86]

In the fall of 1957, the Poles at last agreed to accept the East German offers to help increase brown coal production and Poland's manufacture of heavy machinery, machine tools, ships, railroad cars, automobiles, and electronic goods.[87] But the damage to the East German-Polish trade relationship had already been done. The SED began to synchronize its exports with the needs of the Soviet Union, so that by the end of the 1950s, East Germany was the Soviet Union's most important trading partner.

The Recurring Problem of the Germans in Poland

The repatriation of the Germans in Poland returned to the agenda of Polish-East German relations after Stalin's death (see Chapter 4). In the mid-1950s, Warsaw improved the economic and political situation for the Germans in Poland.[88] Although most had access to German schools and newspapers and were afforded full citizenship rights, many wanted to leave Poland anyway.[89]

Heymann wrote Ulbricht about several alarming instances of German "fascist" demonstrations against Poles in Silesia.[90] After a visit to the German areas in 1955, East German scholar Günter Schmerbach reported that nationalist attitudes were rampant and that Germans were hoping for a strong, united Germany to free them from Polish rule. Schmerbach said that he dined at one restaurant in Opole where Germans were boisterously singing along with a band playing "chauvinistic and fascist German marches and songs."[91] In another case, East Germans officials visiting the Wrocław area were greeted with several provocative demonstrations by German nationalists. The East Germans were also shocked by the level of German poverty there.[92]

These displays of German nationalism were a constant source of embarrassment for the East German government. A Polish official responsible for cultural work with the Germans in the Western Territories told an East German diplomat "that the attitude of the German population up to that point had not exactly made friends of the Peoples' Republic of Poland and the GDR."[93] One Polish official from Wałbrzych told East German diplomats that older German miners complained they did not receive the same pension as the Poles, and that the Polish authorities would not provide medical insurance to cover the cost of treating black lung disease. The miners also protested the Polish government's confiscation of their houses.[94]

In 1954, the Polish authorities decided to expel Germans who held anti-Polish and anti-socialist attitudes.[95] Some of them were allowed to emigrate to the FRG; the Poles thought that this gesture would improve relations with Bonn and result in more trade.[96] Surprised by this development, the East German government initially refused to allow the transport of Germans through the GDR to West Germany.[97]

East German officials were also caught off guard in 1954 by a new agreement between the West German and Polish Red Cross for the reunification of families.[98] In response, Ambassador Heymann recommended that his government reopen high-level talks with the Poles to address East Germany's interests in this matter.[99] In March 1955, Foreign Minister Bolz told Bierut and Cyrankiewicz that the GDR would no longer block the transports to West Germany, but that East Berlin wanted to be a party to new repatriation deals between Bonn and Warsaw. Bolz said that his government also wanted to accept transports. For propaganda purposes, Bolz suggested making the GDR look as though it was the initiator of repatriation agreements with West Germany.[100]

When the Polish government refused to comply with Bolz's requests, the SED's credibility among the millions of Germans from Poland living in the GDR sank even further. The emigrés constantly lobbied the East German government to remember their kinsmen in Poland; this caused some Polish officials to doubt whether the East German authorities could keep the emigrés under control. Heymann admitted that "considering the historical record in a certain sense this mistrust is undoubtedly justified."[101]

In December 1955, the Polish government signed another agreement with the West German Red Cross to reunify an additional 800 to 1,000 Germans with their families in the FRG. East German officials were furious about being left out of the negotiations, and would not allow the East German Red Cross to cooperate in this operation; they even denied warm meals to the passengers passing through the GDR by train. Numerous appeals from Polish officials were ignored.[102]

It was particularly embarrassing for the SED that nearly all the Germans wanted to go to the FRG rather than to the GDR. Heymann wrote Ulbricht that some of the Germans who did not have Polish citizenship looked to the East German Embassy to represent them, but were disappointed by the embassy's lack of interest.[103] A veteran East German correspondent in Poland told Heymann that "the GDR is rather hated by the Germans in the People's Republic of Poland. These people say that the GDR has not stood up for their interests, but instead has allowed them to be declared as Polish citizens." The reporter said that the Germans in Poland thought that West German officials would never behave like this and they hoped that Bonn would open a diplomatic mission in Warsaw to represent them.[104]

East German officials complained to the Poles that it was easier for the Germans in Poland to get exit visas to West Germany than to the GDR.[105] After a visit to Poland that summer, Berthold Rose told Polish diplomat Józef Czechoń that he was concerned about the bad blood between the Germans in Poland and the Polish government, especially in regard to repatriation. He said that if most Germans in Poland wanted to go to West Germany, it would reflect badly on both the Polish and East German governments.[106]

The Polish government ignored East German demands that an equal number of Germans be reunified with families in the FRG and the GDR.[107] As a result, the Germans in Poland thought that the East German Embassy was indifferent to their plight.[108] The FRG received preferential treatment in part because the West Germans paid for the transports of Germans from Poland, but the Polish government had to cover the cost of repatriation to the GDR.[109] In September 1956, the SED informed the PZPR that the present situation was unacceptable: "In principle the question of family reunification and other similar questions in regard to the relations between Germany and the Germans living in the People's Republic of Poland must be handled by the People's Republic more generously for the GDR than for West Germany."[110] The Polish Foreign Ministry responded that the Germans could not be forced to stay in Poland or to go to the GDR.[111]

Heymann thought the situation serious enough to warrant talks at the Politburo level, and recommended that the Germans in Poland be permitted to register with the East German Embassy.[112] Grotewohl intervened directly by writing to the PZPR Politburo on September 29. He warned that the Adenauer government was trying to act as the sole representative of the German people, and complained that it was easier for the Germans in Poland to emigrate to West Germany.[113]

In early October, the Polish government at last agreed to limit the number of Germans going to the FRG and to increase emigration to the GDR.[114] At the end of the year, Poland signed a new protocol with the GDR on family reunification. Nonetheless, Polish officials did not think there would be a significant increase in repatriation to East Germany. According to the Poles, the East Germans demanded 1,000 złoty for every German emigrating to the GDR, but the West Germans were still subsidizing the transports to the FRG. Polish officials suspected that the SED was not really interested in reunifying families in the GDR, but rather in preventing Germans from going to the FRG. After one meeting with East German officials, Polish Ministry of Interior representatives reported that "the [East] German side made efforts to include in the protocol an obligation that the Polish authorities consult with them on every further step taken in the matter of reuniting families in the FRG."[115]

A SED report at the end of 1956 found that the number of transports of Germans going to West Germany was four times the number going to the GDR. The report said that many Germans who had the necessary documents to emigrate to the GDR were not allowed to leave. The SED charged the Poles with putting obstacles in the way of family reunification to the GDR while aiding transports to the FRG. The report concluded that "the behavior of the Polish state is not inclined to strengthen the friendly relationship between the People's Republic of Poland and the GDR."[116]

The Registration of the Germans in Poland

In late 1956, the East Germans warned the Poles that expanding diplomatic relations with West Germany would result in attempts by Bonn to register the Germans in Poland.[117] These Germans already thought that the East German Embassy in Warsaw was ignoring them; few had received visas to visit the GDR.[118] The East German Foreign Ministry observed that "there is no inclination from the Polish side to undertake cooperative measures to repress West German influence on the German-speaking population and to keep these people in the socialist camp."[119] Ambassador Hegen reported that the number of West German publications sent to the Germans in Poland dwarfed the number of East German publications.[120]

In November 1956, Ruth Wenk recommended that the embassy register these Germans, and suggested opening two new consulates to simplify the process.[121] Wenk's colleague Rudolf Fritzche warned his superiors that

> if we do not take immediate fundamental and fast action, the remaining Germans residing here will all go over to the Western camp. The ill will [toward East Germany] that already exists suggests such a development. We are therefore of the opinion that our government must make a decision *immediately* about the registration of the Germans in Poland.[122]

At a meeting with Ambassador Hegen in the spring of 1957, Polish Minister of Interior Władysław Wicha conceded that the Polish government had made some mistakes in its handling of these Germans, but that the policy was now under careful review. Hegen commented that "obviously Minister Wicha wanted to convince me that the Federal Republic had no advantage in the resettlement [of Germans from Poland]."[123] In May, the East German Embassy was allowed to begin registering the German-speaking population, but only those who were not Polish citizens. By the middle of June, 810 people had tried to register, but only 27 East German passports were issued.[124] To step up propaganda with the German community in Poland, the East German Foreign Ministry decided to send more periodicals, hold more lectures in the new East German cultural center in Warsaw, and invite German children from Poland to spend their holidays in the GDR.[125]

That fall, the East German government sent a note to the Polish Embassy in East Berlin complaining that the registration of Germans in Poland was going slowly because West Germany was encouraging them to emigrate to the FRG. The East Germans urged Polish authorities to stop this propaganda,[126] but little was done. Warsaw even encouraged West German tourism to Poland.[127] The East German Embassy protested that "through the [West German] tourist traffic arguments against the GDR and the PRP are best disseminated."[128]

After of several years of delay, in May 1958 the Polish government at last authorized the GDR to open another consulate in Wrocław. East German diplomats hoped the consulate would speed the registration process and aid their propaganda campaign in the Western Territories. But the East Germans were constantly hindered in their work by the Poles' lack of cooperation. Polish security police kept a close watch on the consulate to prevent it from having too much influence on the Germans in Poland. The East Germans reported that when they protested the surveillance of a friendly state's consulate, the Polish police "laughed ironically."[129] The Poles also refused offers for East German teachers and would not allow the German teachers already in the Polish schools to form FDJ or SED student groups.[130] The Polish government authorized the East Germans to circulate a newspaper in the Western Territories in 1958, but ended its run a year later; the Poles said that such a small German minority did not need its own daily.[131]

One of the most sensitive issues for both the Polish and East German governments was the legal status of the autochthons, most of whom lived in and around Opole, Katowice, and Olsztyn. Although most had been given Polish citizenship in 1951, many considered themselves German and complained about discrimination by the Polish authorities.[132] The Polish government regarded them as Poles who had been Germanized under German rule, and therefore doubted their political reliability.[133] In March 1957, East German reporter Suzanne Drechsler wrote that many Germans and autochthons in Poland "have a frightening, deep hate for Poles. . . . This hate is directed not only against the Poles, but plainly against socialism too."[134] Much to the embarrassment of the East Germans, the autochthons flocked to the embassy to register.[135] The Polish authorities refused to allow their registration, which only increased their distrust in both the Polish and East German governments.[136]

When the Polish-East German Commission on the Germans in Poland met in Warsaw in January 1958, West Germany's willingness to accept all the Germans in Poland, including the autochthons, was high on the agenda.[137] Otto Winzer warned the Poles about the threat of West German propaganda among these Germans and their potential as a fifth column.[138] Winzer reported that a group of Germans from Poland attending a recent soccer match in Leipzig had expressed the hope that Adenauer would eventually liberate them.[139] Naszkowski told Winzer that frankly he did not think that the danger from Bonn was that great.[140]

Initially, the Polish government was opposed to East German cultural activity among the autochthons because it would undermine efforts to re-Polonize them. When the East Germans complained that this put them at a disadvantage in relation to West Germany, the Polish government relented. The Polish authorities forbade any attempts to Germanize the autochthons, however, and reserved the right to designate those eligible to register with the GDR Embassy. They also stipulated that registered Germans were not necessarily candidates for repatriation. East Germans officials were dissatisfied with this state of affairs, mainly because the West German government did not have to operate under the same restrictions.[141]

By the beginning of 1958, only 1,000 Germans had registered as East German citizens.[142] East German officials told the Poles that there were still 39,000 German speakers in Poland who did not have Polish citizenship, and 80,000 German speakers with Polish citizenship. The East Germans said that some of the second group had been forced to become Polish citizens; Polish officials said that these figures were inflated.[143] The Poles denied a request from the East German Embassy to examine the approximately 14,000 emigration petitions from Germans in the Katowice and Olsztyn areas. Polish officials did not see any reason for East German diplomats to discuss emigration with Polish citizens, even if German was their first language.[144]

In January 1959, the East German Embassy reported that the registration of Germans without Polish citizenship was almost complete. About half the registrants had left Poland by that time.[145] According to East German sources, 2,532 more Germans emigrated to the GDR in 1959, and 3,300 went to West Germany. In the first eight months of 1960, 754 went to the GDR, and 3,958 to the FRG.[146]

The process did not end there, however. In early 1961, the East German government estimated that there were another 15,000 Germans whose Polish citizenship was in question and who would be eligible to register as citizens of the GDR.[147] The Polish government disagreed with this figure, and by January 1961 only 1,128 more Germans had registered with the East German Embassy.[148] It is obvious from these figures that the Polish government was indifferent to the GDR's interests in the matter of repatriating the Germans from Poland.

The East German government was not really concerned about the Germans' fate anyway; in February 1961, the East German Embassy conceded that the registration process was mainly intended to counter West German influence. The East German communists could not admit that they hoped to gain political support in the area should it ever revert to Germany.[149] When Gomułka declared in a speech to the United Nations in September 1961 that there were no more Germans in Poland eligible to emigrate, the East German government did not protest.

The disputes over trade and repatriation contributed to an overall deterioration in relations in 1957. The Ulbricht régime became increasingly nervous about Poland's cultural freedoms, economic reforms, de-Stalinization, and workers' protests. Gomułka's flirtation with West Germany particularly rankled Ulbricht. Their first face-to-face meeting in June failed to clear the air.

Notes

1. *Trybuna Ludu*, December 9, 1956, p. 6.

2. Franz Sikora, *Sozialistische Solidarität und nationale Interessen* (Socialist solidarity and national interests) (Cologne: Verlag Wissenschaft und Politik, 1977), pp. 137–138. Polish coal shipments to the GDR fell even further, to 1.73 million tons in 1957.

3. Schlage report on political, economic and cultural relations between the GDR and Poland from July 1950 to March 1954, February 19, 1954, DDR MfAA, Warsaw Embassy, A3608.

4. Heymann notes of a meeting with Polish Foreign Trade Minister Dąbrowski, April 22, 1954, DDR MfAA, HA/I Secretariat, A37.

5. GDR Foreign Ministry analysis of the present relations with Poland, undated, ca. December 1954, DDR MfAA, Minister's Office, A15156.

6. See Wolf Oschlies, "Aktionen der DDR-Reaktionen in Osteuropa" (Actions of the GDR-reactions in Eastern Europe), in *Die Rolle der DDR in Osteuropa* (The role of the GDR in Eastern Europe), ed. Gerd Leptin (Berlin: Duneker und Humboldt, 1974), p. 112. Oschlies says that the SED interpreted economic reforms as a return to capitalism.

7. Sikora, *Sozialistische Solidarität und nationale Interessen*, pp. 137–138.

8. GDR Embassy in Warsaw report, December 9, 1955, SED ZK, microfilm FBS 339/13488.

9. Heymann to the GDR Foreign Ministry, June 21, 1955, SED ZK, microfilm FBS 339/13494.

10. Heymann to the GDR Foreign Ministry, November 17, 1955, DDR MfAA, Warsaw Embassy, A3670.

11. Report on the economic relations of the Soviet zone of Germany with the East bloc countries, October 1956, BRD BfGDF, B137/427. East Germany's exports to Poland in 1954 amounted to 10.5 percent of the GDR's total trade. Imports from Poland in 1954 amounted to 10.2 percent. Those figures dropped to 9.7 percent and 9.8 percent in 1955. The figures for East Germany's trade with West Germany, however, went up from 8.2 percent of all exports and 9.5 percent of all imports in 1954 to 10.7 percent and 11.2 percent in 1955.

12. Notes on trade with the GDR, December 16, 1955, PZPR KC, Bierut archive, 254/IV–27; see also Sikora, *Sozialistische Solidarität und nationale Interessen*, p. 171. Trade with the GDR amounted to 13.1 percent of all Polish imports in 1955, and 13.6 percent of all exports.

13. Heymann to the GDR Foreign Ministry, December 30, 1955, DDR MfAA, Warsaw Embassy, A3616; see Alexander Fischer, "Aussenpolitische Aktivität bei ungewisser sowjetischer Deutschland-Politik (bis 1955)" (Foreign policy activity in uncertain Soviet German policy to 1955), in Hans Adolf Jacobsen, Gerd Leptin, Ulrich Scheuner, and Eberhard Schulz, eds., *Drei Jahrzehnte Aussenpolitik der DDR*, 51–84 (Munich: R. Oldenbourg Verlag, 1979), p. 72; and Christoph Royen, "Osteuropaische Staaten" (East European states), in Hans Adolf Jacobsen, Gerd Leptin, Ulrich Scheuner, and Eberhard Schulz, eds., *Drei Jahrzehnte Aussenpolitik der DDR*, 599–619 (Munich: R. Oldenbourg Verlag, 1979), pp. 604–605. From 1954 to 1956 the trade balance favored the GDR, and the East Germans used this profit to cover transportation costs of trade between the GDR and the Soviet Union.

14. GDR Foreign Ministry analysis of relations with Poland, undated, ca. December 1954, DDR MfAA, Minister's Office, A15156. In fact, there was still a huge demand for coal in Western Europe.

15. See Edwina Moreton, *East Germany and the Warsaw Alliance: The Politics of Détente* (Boulder: Westview Press, 1978), pp. 35, 37.

16. Report on the relations between the GDR and Poland in 1955, undated, SED ZK, microfilm FBS 339/13492.

17. Heymann to Handke, September 18, 1954, DDR MfAA, Warsaw Embassy, A3579. Florin relayed this message to Ulbricht on October 12.

18. Stude to GDR Embassy in Warsaw, November 15, 1954, DDR MfAA, Warsaw Embassy, A3616.

19. See R. F. Leslie, et al., *The History of Poland Since 1863* (Cambridge: Cambridge University Press, 1980), p. 339.

20. Ulbricht speech to Comecon, May 19, 1956, SED ZK, Walter Ulbricht Office, J IV 2/202–194; and Khrushchev to Ulbricht, July 2, 1956, SED ZK, Walter Ulbricht Papers, NL 182/1247; and Jakubowski notes of meeting with Wandel, October 26, 1956, MSZ, 10/378/42. Paul Wandel acknowledged to a Polish diplomat that workers' productivity in the East German manufacturing sector was only about 70 percent of that in West Germany.

21. Piotr Jaroschewitsch to the Secretary of Comecon, A. A. Pawlow, in Moscow, October 1, 1956, SED ZK, Walter Ulbricht Office, J IV 2/202–242.

22. Selbmann to Ulbricht, July 14, 1956, SED ZK, Walter Ulbricht Papers, NL 182/1247.

23. Heymann notes of meeting with Winiewicz, undated, SED ZK, microfilm 339/13493.

24. H. Klicka report of East German educators' visit to Poland from September 19 to October 2, October 2, 1956, KWKzZ, file 152.

25. Heymann notes of meeting with Stasiak, July 19, 1956, SED ZK, Walter Ulbricht Papers, NL 182/1247.

26. Heymann report, June 11, 1956, SED ZK, Walter Ulbricht Papers, NL 182/1247.

27. *Trybuna Ludu*, September 30, 1956, pp. 1, 5.

28. Excerpt from an October 9, 1956 report by the Montan Verlag: VWD-Vereinigte Wirtschaftsdienste, Frankurt/Main (Montan Publishing: VWD-United Economic Service), October 9, 1956, DDR MR, DC–20, file 619.

29. Cyrankiewicz to Grotewohl, September 24, 1956, SED ZK, Walter Ulbricht Office, J IV 2/202–196.

30. Grotewohl to the Politburo of the PZPR, September 29, 1956, PZPR KC, 237/XXII–822.

31. Grotewohl to Cyrankiewicz, October 15, 1956, SED ZK, Walter Ulbricht Office, J IV 2/202–196.

32. Grotewohl to Pawlow, October 15, 1956, SED ZK, Walter Ulbricht Office, J IV 2/202–196.

33. Matern and Florin report of a meeting with Gierek and Jędrychowski, October 16, 1956, SED ZK, Politburo Protocol No. 49, J IV/2/2/503.

34. Polish government aide-memoire to the GDR Embassy in Warsaw, April 10, 1956, SED ZK, Otto Grotewohl Papers, NL 90/484.

35. Heymann to Grotewohl, April 26, 1956, SED ZK, Otto Grotewohl Papers, NL 90/484.

36. From the Statistical Yearbooks of the GDR (1953–1956) and Poland (1956) in Sikora, *Sozialistische Solidarität und nationale Interessen*, p. 137–138. Polish exports of coal to East Germany fell from 3.8 million tons in 1955 to only 2.47 million tons in 1956, and 1.73 million tons in 1957.

37. German Economic Institute (Deutsches Wirtschaftsinstitut) report on Poland's coal and coal exports, October 16, 1956, DDR MR, DC–20, file 619.

38. *Trybuna Ludu*, June 7, 1956, p. 1.

39. *Trybuna Ludu*, October 5, 1956, p. 2.

40. *Trybuna Ludu*, October 7, 1956, p. 1.

41. Vice Director of the East German Department of the Polish Foreign Ministry (signature unintelligible) to Poleszczuk (Director of the Department of Press and Information), March 12, 1956, MSZ, 10/361/39.

42. Heymann aide-memoire to the Polish Foreign Ministry, July 28, 1956, MSZ, 10/361/39.

43. Heymann to the GDR Foreign Ministry, May 30, 1956, SED ZK, FBS 339/13494; see also Moreton, *East Germany and the Warsaw Alliance*, p. 180. She argues that for most of its history "the prime concern of GDR foreign policy was to ensure that West Germany gained no political influence in Moscow or Eastern Europe at the expense of the GDR."

44. Naszkowski notes of meeting with Heymann, February 22, 1956, MSZ, 10/361/39.

45. SED Central Committee Department of Foreign Affairs to Handke, September 14, 1956, SED ZK, microfilm FBS 339/13493.

46. SED Politburo report on relations with the other People's Republics, SED ZK, Politburo Draft Protocol No. 58, November 10, 1956, J IV 2/2A/532.

47. Ibid.

48. SED Politburo Draft Protocol No. 62, November 27, 1956, SED ZK, J IV 2/2A/536.

49. Quoted from *Welt am Sonntag* (The World on Sunday), November 8, 1956, BRD BfGDF, B137/427.

50. Karkut notes of meeting with Lungewitz, November 29, 1956, PZPR KC, 237/XXII–822; and Pierzchała notes of a visit of Polish historians to East Germany, November 29, 1956, PZPR KC, 237/XXII–822.

51. Nasielski notes, in Urbaniak to Łobodycz, October 26, 1956, MSZ, 10/378/42.

52. Kopa to the Polish Foreign Ministry, undated, MSZ, 10/378/42.

53. Karkut notes of meeting with Lungewitz, November 29, 1956, PZPR KC, 237/XXII–822; and Pierzchała notes of a visit of Polish historians to East Germany, November 29, 1956, PZPR KC, 237/XXII–822.

54. Kirchner (Warsaw Embassy) to Staimer (GDR Ministry of Foreign Trade and Inner German Trade), November 15, 1956, SED ZK, Walter Ulbricht Papers, NL 182/1247.

55. Heinz Wolff report on a fishing trip to Gdynia, November 30, 1956, SED ZK, Walter Ulbricht Papers, NL 182/1247.

56. Heymann to the GDR Foreign Ministry, November 8, 1956, SED ZK SED, microfilm FBS 339/13488.

57. *Trybuna Ludu*, November 17, 1956, p. 1.

58. *Trybuna Ludu*, November 22, 1956, p. 6.

59. *Trybuna Ludu*, December 9, 1956, p. 6.

60. *Trybuna Ludu*, February 21, 1957, p. 2.

61. State Planning Commission current estimates of the most important problems of economic development in 1957, November 22, 1956, Politburo Draft Protocol No. 62, November 27, 1956, SED ZK, J IV 2/2A/536.

62. Politburo letter to the members and candidate members of the Central Committee, SED ZK, Politburo Draft Protocol No. 54, October 30, 1956, J IV 2/2A/528.

63. Rudi Demel report on Soviet economic assistance for the GDR, October 19, 1956, SED ZK, IV/2/20/32. Originally Demel included military assistance as well, but an unidentified editor struck this from his text.

64. Schenk, *Im Vorzimmer der Diktatur*, p. 181.

65. Łobodycz to the Polish Foreign Ministry, December 18, 1956, MSZ, 10/385/42.

66. SED Politburo Protocol No. 65, December 18–20, 1956, SED ZK, Politburo Protocols, J IV 2/2/519.

67. *Neues Deutschland*, December 30, 1956, p. 5.

68. Analysis of the trade agreement between the GDR and Poland for 1956, January 11, 1957, DDR MfAuIH, DL–2, 2392. The East Germans asked for 715,000 tons of coke; see also Jonathan Steele, *Inside East Germany: The State that Came in from the Cold* (New York: Urizen Books, 1977), p. 120.

69. Report on trade between the GDR and Poland, December 29, 1956, SED ZK, Politburo Protocol No. 66, J IV 2/2/520. There was a shortage of 36 million rubles in East German steel imports, and approximately 20 million rubles in foodstuffs.

70. Information for Ulbricht from the Department of Domestic and Foreign Trade, January 25, 1957, SED ZK, Walter Ulbricht Papers, NL 182/1249.

71. Piotrowski notes of meeting with Florin on February 4, February 8, 1957, MSZ, 10/379/42.

72. *Neues Deutschland*, February 3, 1957, p. 7. In early 1957, *Neues Deutschland* reported that annual coal production in Poland would drop about 2.1 million tons in 1957, and that there would be a 3.5 percent reduction in agricultural production. The newspaper blamed the shortage of food production on the breakup of Poland's collective farms.

73. Kopa notes of meeting with Rose on February 23, February 28, 1957, MSZ, 10/379/42.

74. Drechsler report, March 14, 1957, SED ZK, Walter Ulbricht Papers, NL 182/1249.

75. Report on the GDR's assistance for the Polish coal industry, undated, ca. January 1957, SED ZK, Walter Ulbricht Office, J IV 2/202–242.

76. Information on the Comecon meeting in Warsaw from June 18–22, 1957, June 27, 1957, SED ZK, Walter Ulbricht Office, J IV 2/202/195; Kaser, *Comecon*, pp. 78–79; and Sikora, *Sozialistische Solidarität und nationale Interessen*, p. 150. The loan was for 17 years at 1.5 percent interest.

77. Protocol on the recommendation of the Chairman of the State Planning Commission to the members of the CMEA, March 12–14, 1957, SED ZK, Walter Ulbricht Office, J IV 2/202–242.

78. Translation of an article from the SED Central Committee Department of Foreign Affairs, "From the International Workers' Movement," May 31, 1957, in MSZ, 10/448/47.

79. Hegen notes of a meeting with Polish Foreign Trade Minister Tramczynski on March 28, April 1, 1957, SED ZK, Walter Ulbricht Papers, NL 182/1249.

80. Kopa notes of a meeting with Szczepecki (Vice Minister of the German Railroad) on April 4, 1957, April 5, 1957, MSZ, 10/379/42.

81. Dieckmann notes of meeting with Wycech on May 11, 1957, May 16, 1957, SED ZK, Otto Grotewohl Papers, NL 90/485.

82. Ibid.

83. Report on East German assistance for the Polish coal industry, undated, ca. January 1957, SED ZK, Walter Ulbricht Office, J IV 2/202–242.

84. Grotewohl to Cyrankiewicz, November 1, 1957, SED ZK, Otto Grotewohl Papers, NL 90/485.

85. GDR Ministry of Commerce to Grotewohl on the transit problems in Poland, signature unintelligible, November 4, 1957, SED ZK, Otto Grotewohl Papers, NL 90/485.

86. Cyrankiewicz to Grotewohl, November 25, 1957, SED ZK, Otto Grotewohl Papers, NL 90/485.

87. Report on the political development in the Soviet zone of Germany, November, 1957, BRD BfGDF, B137/1473.

88. Heymann to Florin, January 10, 1955, DDR MfAA, HA/I Secretariat, A37; Heymann to Ulbricht, November 23, 1955, SED ZK, Walter Ulbricht Papers, NL 182/1247; and Heymann to the GDR Foreign Ministry, December 30, 1955, DDR MfAA, Warsaw Embassy, A3616. Heymann rejected his own ministry's estimates that there were still hundreds of thousands of Germans living in Poland. Heymann calculated that there were between 80,000 to 100,000 Germans in the Western Territories without Polish citizenship.

89. Otto Schön to Florin, December 1, 1955, SED ZK, microfilm FBS 339/13492.

90. Heymann to Ulbricht, October 26, 1954, SED ZK, Walter Ulbricht Papers, NL 182/1247.

91. Heymann notes of meeting with Günter Schmerbach, December 3, 1955, DDR MfAA, Poland Section, A1811.

92. Klaus Steiniger and Raoul Gefroi to the SED CC on their visit to Poland, August 13, 1956, SED ZK, Walter Ulbricht Papers, NL 182/1247.

93. Cultural Attaché Manfred Schmidt notes of meeting with Lech (head of the Cultural Department of the Central Council of Polish Unions), April 23, 1956, SED ZK, FBS 339/13494.

94. Seyfert to the SED Central Committee, August 8, 1957, SED ZK, FBS 339/13495.

95. Heymann to Florin, January 10, 1955, DDR MfAA, HA/I Secretariat, A37.

96. Heymann to the GDR Foreign Ministry, January 28, 1955, DDR MfAA, Warsaw Embassy, A3616.

97. Report on relations between East Germany and Poland in 1955, undated, SED ZK, microfilm FBS 339/13492.

98. Heymann to the GDR Foreign Ministry, December 30, 1955, DDR MfAA, Warsaw Embassy, A3616.

99. Heymann to Florin, January 10, 1955, DDR MfAA, HA/I Secretariat, A37.

100. Bolz to Grotewohl, March 16, 1955, SED ZK, Otto Grotewohl Papers, NL 90/483; and Heymann notes of meeting between Bolz, Cyrankiewicz, and Bierut, etal., March 7, 1955, DDR MfAA, Warsaw Embassy, A3579.

101. Heymann to Florin, January 10, 1955, DDR MfAA, HA/I Secretariat, A37; and Polish Embassy in Berlin report from January 1 to March 15, 1956, MSZ, 10/370/41.

102. Łobodycz notes of a meeting with Helmer, December 24, 1955, PZPR KC, Bierut archive, 254/IV–30.

103. Heymann to Ulbricht, November 23, 1955, SED ZK, Walter Ulbricht Papers, NL 182/1247.

104. SED Central Committee Department of Foreign Affairs memo, unsigned, January 19, 1956, SED ZK, microfilm FBS 339/13494.

105. Anheyer to the Headquarters of the German Folk-Policy in Berlin, September 28, 1956, SED ZK, microfilm FBS 339/13488.

106. Józef Czechoń notes of meeting with Rose and Stude, November 9, 1956, MSZ, 10/378/42.

107. Handke notes for the Politburo, September 15, 1956, SED ZK, Politburo Protocol No. 45 from September 18, 1956, J IV 2/2A/519. From January to September 1956, 7,703 Polish Germans went to West Germany, and 2,963 to East Germany.

108. Memo to Grotewohl on a report by Heinrich Goeres on his trip to Poland, unsigned, July 20, 1956, SED ZK, Otto Grotewohl Papers, NL 90/484.

109. Matern and Florin report of meeting with Gierek and Jędrychowski, October 16, 1956, SED ZK, Politburo Protocol No. 49, J IV/2/2/503.

110. Handke notes for the Politburo, September 14, 1956, SED ZK, microfilm FBS 339/13493; and SED Central Committee note to the Politburo of PZPR, September 1956, SED ZK, microfilm FBS 339/13493.

111. Fritzsche notes of a meeting with Zawadski, September 27, 1956, SED ZK, microfilm FBS 339/13493.

112. Heymann to Ulbricht, November 23, 1955, SED ZK, Walter Ulbricht Papers, NL 182/1247.

113. Grotewohl to the Politburo of the PZPR, September 29, 1956, PZPR KC, 237/XXII–822.

114. Heymann notes of a meeting with Winiewicz, October 4, 1956, SED ZK, microfilm FBS 339/13493.

115. Notes of meetings between Polish and GDR Ministry of Interior officials from December 4 to December 7, 1956, unsigned, PZPR KC, 237/XXII–822.

116. SED Central Committee report on the unification of families from Poland to the GDR and FRG, unsigned, undated, ca. December 1956, SED ZK, microfilm FBS 339/13493; and SED Central Committee report on registered German citizens in Poland, unsigned, October 1957, SED ZK, microfilm FBS 339/13493. From July to September 1957, 3,888 Germans of Polish citizenship emigrated from the Wrocław, Koszalin, and Szczecin regions to the GDR. In the same period, between 8,000 and 10,000 Germans from the area went to West Germany.

117. Recommendations for the talks with the Polish government delegation on the question of German citizens in Poland, undated, unsigned, ca. June, 1957,

SED ZK, Otto Grotewohl Papers, NL 90/483. The Polish government estimated that there were approximately 40,000 Germans eligible for registration, mostly in the districts of Wrocław, Koszalin, and Szczecin.

118. Fritzsche notes of a meeting with Germans from Wałbrzych, November 22, 1956, DDR MfAA, Poland Section, A1811.

119. GDR Foreign Ministry report on the first meeting of the German-Polish Commission, unsigned, June 20, 1957, DDR MfAA, M. B. König, A16407.

120. Hegen notes of meeting with Wicha (Polish Ministry of Interior), April 4, 1957, SED ZK, Walter Ulbricht Papers, NL 182/1249.

121. Wenk to Kundermann, November 16, 1956, DDR MfAA, HA/I Secretariat, A37.

122. Fritzsche to Böhm (GDR Foreign Ministry), November 26, 1956, DDR MfAA, Poland Section, A1811.

123. Hegen notes of meeting with Wicha, April 4, 1957, SED ZK, Walter Ulbricht Papers, NL 182/1249.

124. Recommendations for the talks with the Polish government delegation on the question of German citizens in Poland, undated, unsigned, ca. June, 1957, SED ZK, Otto Grotewohl Papers, NL 90/483.

125. GDR Foreign Ministry memo on discussions with the GDR Embassy in Warsaw, unsigned, September 25, 1957, SED ZK, Walter Ulbricht Papers, NL 182/1249.

126. GDR Foreign Ministry to the Polish Embassy in Berlin, unsigned, September 13, 1957, DDR MfAA, HA/I Secretariat, A14759.

127. Report on the impact of tourist traffic between Poland and West Germany, unsigned, undated, ca. fall 1957, DDR MfAA, M. B. König, A17151.

128. Hegen to Winzer, October 25, 1957, DDR MfAA, HA/I Secretariat, A14759.

129. Joachim G. Görlich, "Kommunistische Freundschaft an der Oder und Neisse" (Communist friendship on the Oder and Neisse), *Osteuropa* 14, no. 10 (1964): 724–728, p. 726.

130. Joachim Görlich report on the Germans in Poland, October 1956, BRD BfGDF, B137/1246.

131. Görlich, "Kommunistische Freundschaft an der Oder und Neisse," p. 726.

132. Hegen to Winzer, October 25, 1957, DDR MfAA, HA/I Secretariat, A14759.

133. Joachim Görlich letter in *Po prostu*, January 27, 1957, p. 7.

134. Drechsler report, March 14, 1957, SED ZK, Walter Ulbricht Papers, NL 182/1249.

135. Report on the impact of tourist traffic between Poland and West Germany, unsigned, undated, ca. fall, 1957, DDR MfAA, M. B. König, A17151.

136. Hegen to Winzer, October 25, 1957, DDR MfAA, HA/I Secretariat, A14759.

137. Report on the meeting of the German-Polish Commission on Germans in Poland, January 10, 1958, SED ZK, microfilm FBS 339/13493.

138. Stenographic record of the meeting of the Polish-German Commission on Germans in Poland, January 8–10, 1958, DDR MfAA, Warsaw Embassy, A3755.

139. Protocol from the meeting of the Polish-German Commission on Germans in Poland, January 9, 1958, MSZ, 10/327/37.

140. Stenographic record of the meeting of the Polish-German Commission on Germans in Poland, January 8–10, 1958, DDR MfAA, Warsaw Embassy, A3755.

141. Report on the recommendation of the Polish-German Commission on Germans in Poland, undated, ca. January, 1958, DDR MfAA, Warsaw Embassy, A3755; and protocol from the meeting of the Polish-German Commission on Germans in Poland, January 9, 1958, MSZ, 10/327/37. The Wrocław consulate was closed in 1961, but by the end of 1962, the consulates opened in Katowice and Gdańsk.

142. Kolasa (GDR Foreign Ministry) to Winzer, October 10, 1957, DDR MfAA, HA/I Secretariat, A14759.

143. Briefing for the January 1958 meeting of the Polish-German Commission, undated, ca. December 1957, DDR MfAA, HA/I Secretariat, A14759; see also "Problems of the FRG from the Polish Perspective" by the Bureau for Expellees, undated, in BRD BfGDF, B137/1282. In 1961 the West German government estimated that 132,000 Poles in Germany had German citizenship.

144. Broniatowski to Łobodycz, May 20, 1958, MSZ, 10/327/37.

145. Fritzsche report on the activity of the Consular Department of the GDR Embassy in Warsaw, January 31, 1959, SED ZK, microfilm FBS 339/12495.

146. GDR Embassy in Warsaw briefing for the Council on Repatriation Questions, January, 1961, SED ZK, microfilm FBS 339/13493.

147. Fifth Meeting of the Council on Repatriation Questions, February 1, 1961, DDR MfAA, LS-A406.

148. GDR Embassy in Warsaw briefing for the Council on Repatriation Questions, January, 1961, SED ZK, microfilm FBS 339/13493.

149. GDR Embassy in Warsaw briefing for the Council on Repatriation Questions, January, 1961, SED ZK, microfilm FBS 339/13493; see also Bienert (Embassy attaché) notes of meeting with Cerny (Czechoslovak Embassy in Warsaw) February 12, 1960, DDR MfAA, Warsaw Embassy, A3725.

9

Gomułka's Foreign Policy and the Ulbricht-Gomułka Summit, 1956–1957

The malicious criticisms by the [East] German comrades are not decreasing, especially concerning our economic situation.

—*Polish Embassy report, August 1957*[1]

Gomułka's assertion of Poland's economic interests abroad was part of a strategy to balance Poland's relations between the two blocs and the two Germanies. Ulbricht was adamantly opposed to this "Titoist" foreign policy, especially a rapprochement between Bonn and Warsaw. The SED could not afford the embarrassment of having two socialist states, Yugoslavia and Poland, regarding the GDR as the lesser German state.[2]

On November 8, 1956, West German Chancellor Konrad Adenauer declared that the FRG would seek to resolve all questions with the new "free Poland." A week later, the West German newspaper *Tagesspiegel* (Daily Mirror) hinted that Poland might have set a new course in East-West relations: "De-Stalinization has progressed much farther in Poland than in the Soviet zone of Germany. Normal relations between the Federal Republic and Poland could possibly contribute to the acceleration of the same process in the 'GDR.'" The newspaper predicted that the exchange of trade missions with Poland would be the first step toward full diplomatic relations.[3]

The East Germans suspected that Poland's expanding trade connections to West Germany had long-range diplomatic implications. Ulbricht's confidant, Erich Glückauf, told him that the Polish government would sacrifice its relations with East Germany for diplomatic relations with West Germany. As he put it, "the thesis of the people in the Polish party that there are also different state interests between the socialist countries could become the basis of a policy of understanding between Poland and West Germany at the expense of the GDR."[4] Glückauf suggested that the East German Embassy in Warsaw step up its propaganda campaign in Poland to contrast West Germany's militarism with East Germany's peace initiatives. He also recommended increasing exchanges between the towns on the Oder-Neisse border, and more delegation exchanges in general; the recommendations contradicted Ulbricht's order to curb direct contacts with Poland, however, and were shelved.[5]

Although Gomułka sought to expand political and economic ties to the FRG, diplomatic recognition was still out of the question as long as Bonn refused to recognize the Oder-Neisse border. Furthermore, the only exception that Bonn would make to the Hallstein Doctrine was the Soviet Union (see Chapter 5), in part because it was one of the occupying powers. If the FRG recognized Poland as another occupier, it could make another exception; but Warsaw would not contemplate jeopardizing the legal status of the Western Territories by accepting the status of an occupier. The territories were now an integral part of the Polish state.

The PZPR took steps to alleviate East German fears that a deal for diplomatic relations with the FRG was being discussed. In an editorial in *Trybuna Ludu*, Artur Kowalski expressed optimism about the future of Polish-West German relations, but warned Bonn not to try to weaken Poland's ties to the Warsaw Pact: "There exists in certain circles in the FRG the stubborn tendency to set Poland against the GDR, weakening the fraternal alliance tying us to the German Democratic Republic. This calculation . . . is completely mistaken and does not have the least chance of realization."[6] On December 8, 1956, *Neues Deutschland* reprinted another editorial from *Trybuna Ludu* pledging that Poland would not compromise its relations with the Soviet Union and the GDR for diplomatic recognition from West Germany.[7]

Gomułka's cultivation of West Germany and the United States, however, confirmed Ulbricht's suspicions. That winter, the Polish press softened its criticism of the capitalist countries and stressed Poland's independence.[8] In an article in *Nowe Drogi* about the Hungarian crisis, Jerzy Wiatr declared that "our party stresses the right of every nation to their own decisions about their own destiny." Wiatr noted that the PZPR's reaction to the initial phase of the Hungarian revolution mirrored that of the Chinese, Yugoslav, Italian, Belgian, and American communist parties, which had all rejected the notion that it was a "counterrevolutionary plot." Wiatr acknowledged that the Hungarian revolt had become dangerous, but he reiterated that "above all our party stressed again that it stands unshaken on the principle of the sovereignty of every nation and nonintervention in their internal affairs." Wiatr's argument was a direct contradiction of the SED's outright condemnation of the Hungarian revolution and support of the Soviet intervention.[9]

In the wake of the Suez and Cypress crises in 1956, the East German government speculated that NATO might try to overcome its differences within the Western alliance by acting against the Warsaw Pact. Ambassador Heymann proposed to Józef Winiewicz a trilateral communiqué with Czechoslovakia declaring that an attack on one country was an attack on them all. Winiewicz thought that "Heymann's intervention can be judged like the series of alarmist GDR communications in the past few weeks" and recommended that the Polish government sit on the proposal.[10] In December, *Trybuna Ludu* printed the SED and CzCP communiqué without mentioning that the PZPR had declined to sign it.[11]

When it seemed likely that NATO would station nuclear weapons in West Germany in 1957, the SED again proposed a formal East German-Polish-Czechoslovak protest; once more the Poles opposed the idea. Instead of preventing the nuclearization of the FRG, the Poles argued that a protest would only serve to unify NATO and undermine domestic opposition to the plan in the United States. East German Charge d'affaires Günter Seyfert assured Winiewicz that his government was merely proposing a separate declaration that would complement the Soviet resolution in the United Nations, but Winiewicz repeated that the foreign policies of the two countries should "undermine the coherence of the Atlantic alliance, not result in its consolidation." Seyfert replied that the GDR, unlike Poland, had a significant problem in West Germany and needed to defend itself against Bonn's aggressive foreign policy. But Winiewicz countered that Poland was already doing enough on this front. He reminded Seyfert that Gomułka and Cyrankiewicz had frequently warned of the impending danger of West German chauvinism and militarism.[12]

One East German Foreign Ministry official concluded that the Poles were worried about complicating their relations with the United States. He accused the Poles of underestimating the dangers of "West German imperialism."[13] After visiting Poland that fall, another SED functionary denounced Gomułka for conducting a blatantly anti-Soviet, pro-Western policy. Several local PZPR leaders told the East German that "it would be best if we [East Germans] would create the unification of Germany as fast as possible, whether with or without Adenauer, so that together—Germany and Poland—we can stand up against the Soviet Union."[14]

At the same time that the Polish government was pursuing West German political parties and trade links,[15] the SED was increasing the number and vitriol of its attacks on the Adenauer government, accusing it of harboring militarists, fascists, and former Nazis. The Polish government rejected repeated East German entreaties to join in this campaign. The Polish Embassy criticized the tone of the SED attacks on the SPD as "extremely rude and aggressive."[16]

Warsaw and East Berlin were united in their firm opposition to NATO's plan to arm West Germany with atomic weapons, however. In May, the Poles initiated meetings between Czesław Wycech, Zdenek Fierlinger, and Johannes Dieckmann, the leaders of the Polish, Czechoslovak, and East German parliaments. Although earlier in the year the Polish government had rejected a joint declaration denouncing West German rearmament, now the Poles agreed to a statement protesting the stationing of atomic weapons in West Germany.[17] Ambassador Piotrowski thought the conference had resolved some of recent misunderstandings between Warsaw on the one hand and East Berlin and Prague on the other. He repeated that Poland would not risk isolation from the socialist camp for the sake of relations with the West, and above all with West Germany.[18]

The East Germans interpreted the meeting as support for their stepped-up campaign against West German militarism, imperialism, and monopoly capitalism.[19] The Polish press, however, gave little coverage to the creation of the Common Market and Euratom in 1957. In the words of one East German diplomat, these institutions were "a strong threat to peace and gave the German imperialists and militarists the possibility of producing atomic weapons." The East German Embassy was thoroughly dissatisfied with Poland's propaganda campaign and compared it unfavorably to Czechoslovakia's; the embassy recommended raising these issues with the Poles at the high-level meetings scheduled for June.[20]

During the Ninth Plenary Session of the PZPR Central Committee in May 1957, the SED waited expectantly for confirmation that the PZPR was rethinking its "anti-Marxist" foreign and domestic policies. New East German Ambassador Josef Hegen filed a typically pessimistic report, however. He said that Gomułka had tried to keep the ideological debate with the "Marxist-Leninist wing" of the party out of public view so that the party would appear unified behind his program. Hegen reported that the party leadership had failed to stress the leading role of the CPSU, and that Yugoslavia was the model for the PZPR's independent foreign policy.[21]

Although Ulbricht had serious doubts about Gomułka's foreign policy, he was gaining confidence that the GDR would play an important role in the future of Germany. The East German economy was functioning as well as or better than any in Eastern Europe, and the GDR was now an important supplier of machinery for the entire Soviet bloc. The GDR's sense of political importance was greatly increased by the integration of the NVA into the Warsaw Pact in 1957; East Berlin thought that the East German army would enable it to play a central role in German reunification.

The Warsaw Pact's fighting readiness was seriously undermined by the bad blood between the Polish and East German armed forces. Propaganda extolling the unity of the new "working class" armies had little effect on morale; the Poles were highly suspicious of German militarism, even to the point of complaining that East German army uniforms resembled the old Wehrmacht muster.[22]

A rancorous confrontation between Polish and East German sailors took place in May while the crew of the Polish ship *Bałtyk* was on shore leave in the East German port of Sassnitz. The head of the East German Navy, Vice Admiral Waldemar Verner, was shocked by the Poles' "negative and hostile attitude" toward the Soviet Union, and by their attacks on socialism in general. To his surprise, the Poles interpreted the Poznań strikes in June 1956 as a genuine workers' revolt rather than a fascist provocation. The Polish officers maintained that Poles had lived much better under capitalism before the war. They said that Soviet concentration camps had been much worse than Hitler's, and that Stalin was a criminal who had exploited the Polish economy. The Poles were proud they had removed Soviet advisors and political officers from the Polish army. One Polish sailor concluded that socialism was "shit." The Polish sailors had some particularly unflattering things to say about the GDR: They told Verner that the East German government was "too communist" and that it merely aped Moscow's policies. They called Ulbricht a "Stalinist" and wondered why he and Grotewohl had not been removed from power.[23]

The Polish sailors displayed no signs of the politically correct behavior that the East German communists had come to expect from their Warsaw Pact partners. According to the East Germans, the Polish sailors did not address each other as "comrade," and were more concerned about finding prostitutes than in "friendship meetings" to discuss Marxism. The Poles made fun of the SED's strict control over Western influences, such as the party's ban on "rock and roll" dancing; they boasted that they could smoke American-made Lucky Strike and Camel cigarettes whenever they wanted.[24]

From this confrontation, the East German officers formed real doubts about the loyalty and fighting capability of the Polish armed forces. One officer concluded that the Poles had no interest in the Warsaw Pact, and that an East German soldier sitting in a foxhole with a Pole had better be prepared "to get a knife in the ribs." Another officer observed that if high-ranking Polish officers behaved in such a way, Poland was not an asset to the Warsaw Pact. One East German officer called the Polish officers "a very reactionary bunch," and accused them of "spitting on the

Warsaw Pact." He said that had the East Germans known what a bunch of "heinis" the Polish sailors were, they would have beaten them up.[25] The SED Central Committee was quickly informed of the incident.[26]

The SED Tightens Controls on Tourism

The Polish sailors' behavior at Sassnitz confirmed the wisdom of SED's strict policy of controlling personal contacts between East Germans and Poles. Polish and East German exchanges dropped dramatically in early 1957. East Germany sent fifty-six delegations of technical and scientific experts to Poland in 1955 and forty-one in 1956, but none in the first quarter of 1957. Polish delegations to East Germany numbered 123 in 1955, 109 in 1956, but only 13 in the first quarter of 1957.[27]

East German officials were concerned about the increasing tourist traffic between Poland and Western Europe. Poles still appeared to be more interested in developing personal connections with West Germans than with East Germans. In April 1957, Florin registered a complaint with the Polish authorities about thirty-four Polish architects who had arrived unannounced at the Leipzig Trade Fair and sought out West German architects for financial support. The Polish architects had also tried to sell gold on the black market.[28]

East German officials were exceptionally annoyed whenever the Polish government afforded West Germans preferential treatment; for example, the SED district office in Magdeburg reported that West Germans had to wait only about three weeks to get a visa to Poland, but East Germans had to wait thirteen weeks.[29] In one instance, an East German called the Polish Embassy about receiving his visa by mail, but was rudely informed that "you can wait until you are blue in the face, but you will have to pick it up yourself." In another case, an East German woman asked the Polish Embassy whether she could get her visa in time to attend a wedding in Poland. She was told that she "should write Poland that the wine should be put in the cellar and the meat should be frozen for about eight weeks; that is how long it will take to process your visa application."[30] When the East Germans lodged a formal protest, Polish diplomats explained that there was normally an eight-week wait for all visas.[31]

East German journalist Suzanne Drechsler reported that Warsaw was actually encouraging Western tourists to come to Poland, especially West Germans. She warned that the "Western tourists not only bring hard currency, but act as imperialist recruiters and agents." As usual, Drechsler's answer to the problem was more propaganda: "Can't we and the other socialist countries do our best to send Poland reliable comrades with the most wide range of expertise so that they can speak with the Polish comrades and create ideological clarity [in the PZPR]?"[32]

In the fall of 1957, the East German Embassy reported that 36,000 tourists had visited Poland in 1956, and that 33,000 had already come in the first half of 1957. Of those, 7,000 were West Germans, many of whom the Polish authorities encouraged to visit their old homes in Poland. The embassy thought that these visits were hurting both countries: "We determined in all of the discussions [with the remaining Germans in Poland] that arguments against the GDR and against the PRP are best spread through the tourist traffic. After every transport new rumors reemerged against the GDR and the PRP." When the GDR began to restrict the passage of tourist busses from West Germany and West Berlin to the Polish border at Frankfurt/Oder, the Polish government re-routed them through Czechoslovakia. East German diplomats recommended holding talks with Prague to stop this traffic and suggested that the government encourage more East German tourism to Poland to replace the West Germans.[33]

But Ulbricht had already decided that casual contacts between East Germans and Poles were dangerous, and again he did not act on the recommendation. Later that fall, the East German government informed the Poles that Americans of Polish heritage would not be allowed to take busses from West Germany to Poland through the GDR. The contrast between West and East Germany's tourist policies made Poles wonder which country was their Warsaw Pact ally.[34]

Gomułka Meets Ulbricht

At the end of May 1957, the SED published an article by Heinz Pahl in which he traced the Polish people's growing disappointment in the Gomułka régime to the bureaucratization of state and economic agencies. This was an ironic criticism coming from a party that was aiming for total control over East German politics and society. Pahl blamed Gomułka for developing a "cult of personality, which led to particularly serious mistakes in Poland." He commented on the great ideological confusion in the party and among Poles in general, and accused the party of promoting "bourgeois-capitalist democracy." Pahl claimed that "these forces promote their revisionist position under the banner of the struggle with 'Stalinism.'" He alluded to ongoing problems in Poland concerning anti-Semitism, food production, and the growing influence of the Catholic Church. Pahl concluded that the majority of Poland's communists were aware that revisionism was contradictory to the interests and goals of the working class, but he was skeptical whether the Gomułka régime had the will to stamp it out.[35]

Ulbricht had a chance to get a better sense of Gomułka's intentions during their meetings in Berlin that June. It was their first meeting face-to-face since Gomułka's election as first secretary of the PZPR the previous October. They had an abiding dislike for each other, although they had some personal similarities: Both were loyal followers of Lenin, lived relatively modest lives, and spent most of their time on official matters. Neither was charismatic, but both were devoted to the communist cause and convinced of the rightness of their respective policies. Their main disagreement was over the general applicability of Stalin's model of socialism.

Cyrankiewicz and Foreign Minister Adam Rapacki accompanied Gomułka, and Ulbricht, Grotewohl, and Bolz headed the East German delegation. The perfunctory lead headline in *Neues Deutschland* proclaimed their socialist solidarity: "Fraternally United in the Struggle for a Permanent Peace and the Victory of Socialism." Subsequent issues did not mention the heated debates that had brought the parties to the breaking point in 1956.[36]

The atmosphere surrounding the meetings was, in the words of one East German official, "stiff and reserved."[37] That the two sides were still far apart in their conceptions of socialism was immediately apparant. The Poles asked the East Germans to declare their agreement with the resolutions of the Eighth and Ninth Plenary Sessions of the PZPR Central Committee, but the East Germans refused on the grounds that the resolutions were not based on Marxist-Leninist principles.[38] The Poles baited Ulbricht and the other East German hard-liners by asking them whether there was really a "fully free and unconstrained atmosphere" in the SED, in contrast to the democratization of the PZPR. The East Germans thought that Gomułka was naively underestimating the dangers of class conflict in Poland, and that his policies were not promoting Marxist-Leninist social, economic, and political development; they severely criticized Gomułka's agricultural policies and tolerance of the "reactionary and counterrevolutionary" Polish Catholic Church.[39]

A sharp exchange ensued when Ulbricht accused the Poles of passing top secret East German documents to Western governments. Gomułka called it a "serious reproach," and asked for proof of the allegations. Ulbricht replied that some Poles who had inside information on the GDR had fled to the West; Cyrankiewicz reminded Ulbricht that many East German officials had defected as well. Grotewohl tried to end the conversation by saying that they should not return to the past. Gomułka agreed and added that if there was no proof of the charges, the Poles would ignore them.[40]

The Poles also raised the contentious issue of the two countries' competing harbors on the East Sea, Szczecin and Rostock. In 1950, Ulbricht had asked for greater access to the port at Szczecin,[41] but the East Germans eventually decided to expand the Rostock harbor. During the "East

Sea Week" celebrations that June, one Pole implied that the GDR would probably not exist after German reunification, in which case Rostock would lose its economic importance. He told the East Germans to orient themselves to the unity of Germany by using the port at Hamburg instead.[42] Gomułka and Ulbricht agreed to study the use of Szczecin for the transit in and out of the GDR,[43] but the East Germans went ahead anyway with plans to expand the Rostock harbor. [44]

They also discussed trade relations, which appeared to be on the upswing. Recent agreements called for a 17 percent increase in trade in 1957.[45] The East German government projected that Poland's share of East German trade would soon return to the 1954 level of 14 percent.[46] In an interview with *Trybuna Ludu* shortly before the summit, Ambassador Hegen declared that "the very close economic relations between both countries found their natural expression in the trade agreements."[47]

Ulbricht was in fact deeply dissatisfied with Warsaw's trade policies, which he blamed for jeopardizing key elements of the GDR's economic plan.[48] Polish negotiators insisted that a new trade agreement include a clause stipulating that East Germany's negative trade balance be paid in gold or convertible currency. One member of the East German delegation wrote Grotewohl that such a clause was unacceptable, and "contradicts the common practice between socialist countries." He called the Polish negotiators "obstinate."[49]

A month before the summit, the PZPR informed an SED delegation from Frankfurt/Oder that Poland did not want to export more coal to the GDR.[50] Ulbricht took his case to Comecon, which was meeting in Warsaw that June. There he blamed the shortage of raw material imports for the GDR's failure to meet its Five-Year Plan.[51] The Polish representatives to Comecon made no direct concessions to the East Germans, but the Soviets, Hungarians, Czechoslovaks, and Bulgarians agreed to hold bilateral talks with the Poles to develop joint ventures with the Polish coal industry.[52]

Ulbricht was unable to persuade Gomułka to deliver more coal unless the East Germans paid for it in hard currency. The Poles acknowledged that they could not export as much coal to the socialist countries because, as Ulbricht suspected, they were trading it for essential imports from capitalist countries. The Poles said that their ongoing negotiations with British, French, and Swedish firms would help Poland build locomotives and electrify Polish railways; these deals, they asserted, would eventually free coal for export. The Poles also asked the East Germans for more investment credits.[53] Desperate for Poland's higher quality of coal, the East Germans eventually agreed to another 100 million ruble credit for the Polish brown coal industry.[54]

On the last day of the conference, Ulbricht, Gomułka, and Cyrankiewicz exchanged heated words over Poland's exports to West Berlin. The GDR was supplying some of the same goods to West Berlin, such as cement. The Poles argued that they were not only contractually obligated to make the deliveries, but were $40 million in debt to West Germany. When Gomułka maintained that this trade was strictly an economic matter, not a political one, Ulbricht countered that Poland's trade with West Berlin was indeed a major political problem for the GDR. Although the East Germans had earlier insisted that Poland include trade with West Berlin in agreements with West Germany, they now told the Poles not to consider West Berlin as a part of West Germany, but as a part of a greater Berlin situated in the heart of East Germany. Ulbricht acknowledged that the SED wanted to keep the "political and economic pressure on West Berlin." He said that his government would not allow Poland to compete for West Berlin cement contracts. Ulbricht pointed out that West Berlin would not be as economically and politically dependent on East Germany if it did not get its cement from the GDR.. Gomułka replied that "if [our trade agreements] are not fulfilled, it will leave the impression that discord exists between Poland and the GDR. Everything should be done to manifest unity." He then suggested that the East Germans pay hard currency for Polish cement and ship it to West Berlin themselves. The East Germans said that they would study the proposal, but they expected the Poles to acquiesce on matters regarding West Berlin.[55]

Gomułka and Ulbricht agreed to periodic meetings of their foreign ministers to discuss their outstanding problems. The SED promised to foster better personal ties between Poles and East Germans by expanding technical, scientific, educational, and cultural exchanges. Ulbricht also agreed to open an East German cultural and information center in Warsaw. The two sides agreed to work on a long-term trade deal, including Polish coal deliveries and East German exports of consumer goods.[56] In spite of all of the hard bargaining, the East Germans concluded that the talks had confirmed the principle of socialist economic cooperation.[57]

In an effort to stabilize the political and economic situation in Poland before the PZPR Congress scheduled for December, the East Germans offered to host two PZPR delegations—one to examine the SED's industrial and agricultural policies and another to study Marxist-Leninist principles at an East German university. They also proposed sending more publications and lecturers to Poland to promote socialism and alert Poles to the dangers of Western imperialism and militarism. Last, the East Germans promised to invite Polish workers to visit East German enterprises. The SED maintained tight control over these exchanges, however, and insisted that they answer to their respective central committees or foreign ministries. As a result, exchanges did not significantly increase in the next few years.[58]

Gomułka and Ulbricht could not agree on a final joint communiqué because the Poles were unwilling to support the SED's aggressive propaganda campaign against the United States and West Germany. One line in the Polish proposal for the communiqué read, "The unity of the socialist camp based on the principle of the internationalism of the proletariat is developing." Ulbricht demanded that the Poles change "developing" to "exists and is still developing." The Poles said no, arguing that they did not want to make grandiose claims that would be rejected by Western public opinion and solidify the capitalist camp.[59] The Poles also objected to wording directly attacking West German and American imperialism,[60] as well a line stating that the imperialist powers were preparing for a nuclear war. The East Germans complained that the Polish draft of the joint declaration did not use the word "aggressive" to characterize Western policies, and that the draft referred to "Poland" instead of the "Peoples' Republic of Poland."[61]

The talks confirmed the East Germans' perception that the Poles were conducting policies "on the basis of a certain great power chauvinism." The Poles refused to recognize the leading role of the CPSU and ignored Ulbricht's warnings of West German and American militarism and imperialism. One SED report predicted that Poland would try to capitalize on Cold War tensions to bargain for more credits from the West.[62]

The delegations hid their many differences from public view. As usual, the East Germans issued statements exaggerating their friendly relations and the complete unity of the two parties. Grotewohl declared that "the meetings that we held with you, dear Polish friends, brought our agreement on all questions raised." In his statement to the press, however, Gomułka substituted "clarification" for "agreement": "The talks contributed to a deepening of our solidarity, to clarification of many questions that relate to the building of socialism in our countries, as well as to better mutual understanding." Ulbricht claimed that the SED now had "complete trust" in the PZPR and Gomułka, which was obviously at variance with his personal doubts about Gomułka's foreign and domestic policies.[63]

The meetings did allay East German fears that Gomułka would emulate Tito or Nagy and take Poland out of the Warsaw Pact. East German officials now seemed more disposed to engage the Poles. At a reception at the Polish Embassy following the talks, Jakubowski commented on the East Germans' cordiality and willingness to discuss issues more frankly. He reported that Politburo members Erich Mückenberger and Erich Honecker had expressed their "complete trust in the domestic and foreign policies of the PRP." Rudolf Agsten, head of the LDP, told Jakubowski that the SED had indeed lost confidence in the PZPR for a time, but that the talks had done much to clear the air.[64]

The Aftermath of the Summit

The Gomułka-Ulbricht summit did not result in significant improvement in East German-Polish relations, however. At a press conference in Berlin in July, Hermann Matern told reporters that the SED was still nervous about developments in Poland and had to watch them closely. Matern said that the situation in Poland was "far from stabilized," and warned that "dangerous trends" still existed.[65]

Again and again East German officials turned up examples of the PZPR's patently unsocialist policies and reluctance to clamp down on political deviants. That summer, the Polish Embassy distributed some unauthorized political pamphlets to the SED's regional and district offices. Among the authors were the prominent Polish economist Oskar Lange and high-ranking trade official Stefan Jędrychowski. The East German lodged a formal protest alleging the tracts contained revisionist thinking and criticisms of the excessive bureaucratization and centralism in some socialist states, including the GDR. The SED ordered its offices to return the pamphlets to the Polish Embassy on the grounds that the SED did not want a public discussion of these issues. The SED also informed Polish diplomats that they would have to check with the SED's Department of Foreign Affairs before they could distribute other materials.[66] Polish diplomat Józef Czesak acknowledged that there were problems with the content of the pamphlets, but he termed the SED's reaction "demonstrative and inappropriate."[67]

Polish officials also reported that there was no discernable change in East German policy toward Poland in the last half of 1957. The Polish Foreign Ministry characterized the June talks as acrimonious,[68] and Polish officials told the West Germans that the atmosphere had been "very cool."[69] The Polish Embassy in Berlin filed numerous reports confirming that the East German communists still had serious doubts about the future of socialism in Poland. The embassy thought that Gomułka's visit had done nothing to change the rampant anti-Polish attitudes in East Germany: "The malicious criticisms by the German comrades are not decreasing, especially concerning our economic situation."[70]

Polish diplomats observed that East German journalists, especially *Neues Deutschland*'s Warsaw correspondents, generally ignored Polish subjects; the Poles even doubted the sincerity of complimentary stories about Poland.[71] The Polish Foreign Ministry complained that the East German press was still publishing articles with a "tone of sharp polemics." The ministry mostly objected to two articles in *Einheit*, one in which Politburo member Fred Oelssner had inveighed a Polish professor for attacking "Luxemburgism," and another by Kurt Langendorf accusing Lange of promoting "bourgeois economic policy."[72]

Ulbricht tried in vain to convince Gomułka of the pitfalls of close relations with the West, above all with the FRG. The SED thought that Poland's continued requests for loans and grants from the West was a dangerous policy for Poland and for the unity of the Warsaw Pact; the East Germans assumed that the money Poland received would be linked to political concessions. They tried to persuade the Polish government not to accept $500,000 from the Ford Foundation, but Polish officials argued that the grant was a way for Polish scientists to gain access to the world scientific community. The Poles pointed out that Poland would receive the money through UNESCO, to which they paid annual dues of $300,000. East German diplomats even criticized the building of a UNESCO-House in Warsaw because they saw it as a symbolic challenge to the monstrous new Palace of Culture and Science, which had been built with Soviet help.[73]

The summit also left the controversy over tourist traffic unresolved. There was a significant increase in cultural exchanges between Poles and West Germans that fall,[74] and the GDR continued to harass the visitors. In one case, the East German authorities refused to grant transit visas to a group of Polish artists and architects intending to travel by boat through East German waters to West Germany, Holland, Belgium and France.[75] Winzer told Piotrowski that over thirty of the architects wanted to go to West Berlin; he said that the East German government had to control travel to and from Western Europe because of the GDR's complicated geographical and political position. Winzer informed Piotrowski that "Western governments and their agents are spending millions to corrupt our students and intellectuals when they travel to West Germany."[76] Piotrowski later apologized to Bolz for the architects' improper travel documents,[77] but the Polish government did nothing to discourage Poles from travelling to the West. Ambassador Hegen reported that the Polish press was silent on the damages that this tourist traffic was doing to the socialist states, and even encouraged it.[78]

East Germans visiting Poland were genuinely surprised to find so many Westerners there. One East German university delegation to Poland that fall charged that the Westerners were treated better than they were. The Polish Minister for Higher Education gave the East German delegation a quick thirty-minute reception, but threw a party for the British delegation that lasted late into the night. One East German in the delegation was astonished that the Polish authorities allowed the Westerners to do and say what they wanted:

During a visit to the student club at the Technical Academy in Warsaw, where "rock and roll" was being danced in dim light, we determined that student delegations from England, France, and other countries were there, moving about without any supervision at all, and, as I could hear because of my own knowledge of English, met with each other for exchanges of information. The band left the club at ten o'clock to play for dollars at the American embassy. The [PZPR] party secretary did not find anything unusual about it.[79]

Workers at *Trybuna Ludu* told this same East German delegation that the imprisonment of East German writer Wolfgang Harich was a mistake. According to the East Germans, two PZPR university administrators said that they hated Ulbricht and Khrushchev, and that Ulbricht "does not have any of his own ideas, but is just a parrot of Khrushchev." The delegation was shocked to discover that only 30 out of the 12,000 students at the Technical Academy in Warsaw were members of the PZPR's youth organization. On their trip of over 800 kilometers through Poland, the East Germans reported that they had not seen one Soviet soldier, and had heard the name Bierut mentioned once; this was enough evidence for the delegation to conclude that the PZPR was doing little to combat the prevailing revisionist, nationalist, and anti-Semitic attitudes in Poland.[80]

The East Germans also faulted the PZPR for not basing the development of rural Poland on Marxist principles: East German delegations criticized Polish collective managers and workers for their complete lack of political awareness. One delegation concluded that the Poles had "no idea about the systematic construction of socialism in the countryside."[81] The East German Embassy in Warsaw suggested that the Polish government needed "moral help" from the SED to develop better propaganda on the merits of collectivization.[82]

The embassy appeared not to see that the PZPR was generally satisfied with its accommodation of private farming; indeed, agricultural production in Poland was on the rise.[83] Polish agricultural experts viewed their policy not as a retreat similar to Lenin's short-lived NEP in the early 1920s but as a new direction in socialist agricultural policy.[84]

Every East German exchange with Poland had an underlying political agenda—namely, to promote the East German version of socialism. East German Foreign Ministry officials admitted as much; in one case they invited the PZPR to send a comrade from Koszalin to Rostock "in order to influence him politically." The PZPR repeatedly rejected East German demands for more central control over delegation exchanges, and in a thinly veiled admonition to stop criticizing the PZPR's domestic policies,

Polish officials said they could not and would not try to control the foreign relations of the other communist parties.[85] During the election campaign in the FRG that fall, the East Germans again expressed their deep
dissatisfaction with the PZPR's tepid support of their propaganda campaign against West German imperialism and militarism. The East Germans suspected that Warsaw did not want to risk its trade relations with
Bonn, or jeopardize its slim chances of establishing formal diplomatic
ties. It appeared, too, that Poland wanted to circumvent the GDR in negotiations with the FRG. West German sources alleged that some high-
level officials in the East German Foreign Ministry hoped that diplomatic
contacts between Bonn and Warsaw would benefit the GDR, but only if
Poland promoted the East German cause.[86]

Most East German officials did not trust the Gomułka régime to do
that. Hegen filed another discouraging report in September: "[The PZPR]
is still underestimating the role and importance of the GDR as the basis
for a peaceful democratic German state." Hegen said that the Polish
press never presented the problem of German reunification from an East
German, or working-class, standpoint. He added that there was strong
sentiment in Poland for friendly relations with the capitalist countries,
and notably with West Germany. Hegen thought that many issues had to
be resolved between East Berlin and Warsaw before the Poles even
thought about opening diplomatic relations with Bonn.[87]

With the exception of East Germany, West Germany had more exchanges with Poland than with any other Warsaw Pact country. The West
German Foreign Ministry reported that Poland was the only socialist
country that allowed its student groups to come for extended visits, and
characterized the Poles as "open-minded" and cognizant of the disparity
between communist propaganda and what life was really like in West
Germany.[88] After a visit of Polish scientists to the FRG in November, one
West German scientist said that the Poles did not really care about relations with the GDR, and that Poland's relations with the FRG held the
key to Poland's independence from Moscow.[89]

Relations at the End of 1957

The Tenth Plenary Session of the PZPR Central Committee met in October 1957, a year after Gomułka's return to power. Former East German
Ambassador Stefan Heymann, now back in the Foreign Ministry, confirmed that the PZPR was making some progress against revisionism, although many party members were still attacking the dogmatists and demanding greater freedom of expression.[90] One Soviet envoy told an East
German diplomat that the PZPR was not committed at all to eliminating
anti-Soviet attitudes in the party or in the population as a whole.[91]

Gomułka's relations with the Soviet Union gained some traction in the last half of 1957, however. Following Khrushchev's purge of Molotov and Georgi Malenkov in June, the CPSU and the PZPR began a slow reconciliation. Gomułka began to rethink many of the reforms he had called for the previous October. Much to Khrushchev's satisfaction, Gomułka tried to marginalize the revisionists in the party rather than the right-wing Natolin group.[92]

Gomułka's visit to Moscow in November for the fortieth anniversary of the Bolshevik Revolution solidified his relationship with Khrushchev, who again confirmed the PZPR's course. The East German hard-liners still harbored lingering doubts; the East German Foreign Ministry issued a report that the Marxist-Leninist wing of the PZPR was asserting itself again, but had not yet succeeded in suppressing "decadent ideas."[93] The head of the SED's press department, Horst Sindermann, told a group of Polish journalists in November that "despite a general improvement in relations between Poland and the GDR, it is difficult to expect the GDR press to trust in Poland, because they [Polish journalists] charge the SED of 'Stalinism.'" He accused the Poles of avoiding closer ties with the GDR in deference to West Germany.[94]

The Ulbricht-Gomułka summit in June had failed to normalize relations. The SED's year-end report on Poland reiterated earlier criticisms of the PZPR for ignoring ideological and political propaganda, for underestimating the dangers of German imperialism and militarism, and for waging a half-hearted campaign against revisionism. Although the GDR had established diplomatic relations with Yugoslavia in October 1957, the report criticized Warsaw for favoring connections to Belgrade and the West over ties to the Soviet bloc countries. The East Germans also faulted the Poles for refusing to declare the Soviet Union the "first and the mightiest" socialist state. According to the report, the Polish communists also misjudged the "role and character of the GDR." In contrast to the cooperative attitude of the Czechoslovak communists, the East Germans found it impossible to conduct ideological discussions with the Polish communists about the basic foundations of Marxism-Leninism. The East Germans accused the Poles of arrogance, although it was usually the East Germans who bragged about their superior economic and political development.[95] Foreign Minister Adam Rapacki's proposal that fall to create a nuclear-free zone in East Central Europe caused yet another rift.

Notes

1. Polish Embassy report for March 15 to August 31, 1957, MSZ, 10/371/41.

2. Kopa to the Polish Foreign Ministry, undated, ca. December 1956, MSZ, 10/378/42.

3. From *Tagesspiegel*, November 15, 1956, in BRD AA, Department 2, vol. 438.

4. Glückauf to Ulbricht, February 1, 1957, SED ZK, Walter Ulbricht Papers, NL 182/1249.

5. Ibid.

6. *Trybuna Ludu*, November 24, 1956, p. 4.

7. *Neues Deutschland*, December 8, 1956, p. 1.

8. Analysis of Polish political leadership by Dr. G. Rhode of the Herder Institute, October 31, 1956, BRD BfGDF, B137/1282.

9. Jerzy Wiatr, "Kryzys internacjonalizmu?" (International crisis?), *Nowe Drogi* 10, no. 11–12 (November-December 1956), pp. 114–115.

10. Winiewicz notes of a meeting with Heymann on December 18, December 19, 1956, MSZ, 23/57/7.

11. *Trybuna Ludu*, December 21, 1956, p. 2; see also *Neues Deutschland*, December 22, 1956, p. 1.

12. Winiewicz notes of a meeting with Seyfert, December 28, 1956, MSZ, 23/57/7.

13. Schwab to Ulbricht, January 28, 1957, SED ZK, Walter Ulbricht Papers, NL 182/1249.

14. Heinz Wolff report on a fishing trip to Gdynia, November 30, 1956, SED ZK, Walter Ulbricht Papers, NL 182/1247.

15. Piotrowski notes of meeting with Bolz and Kundermann, March 29, 1957, MSZ, 10/309/36.

16. Polish Embassy report for October 1, 1956, to March 15, 1957, MSZ, 10/371/41.

17. *Neues Deutschland*, May 12, 1957, p. 1.

18. Piotrowski to the Polish Foreign Ministry, May 17, 1957, MSZ, 10/383/43.

19. *Neues Deutschland*, May 10, 1957, p. 1.

20. Lugenheim to the SED Central Committee, June 6, 1957, SED ZK, microfilm FBS 339/13495.

21. Hegen to the GDR Foreign Ministry, May 29, 1957, DDR MfAA, HA/I Secretariat, A38.

22. Schwanz to the SED Central Committee, March 20, 1957, SED ZK, microfilm FBS 339/13489; Wollweber to Honecker, March 30, 1957, SED ZK, microfilm FBS 339/13489; and Florin to the PZPR Central Committee, April 15, 1957, SED ZK, microfilm FBS 339/13489.

23. Verner to Stoph, May 9, 1957, SED ZK, Walter Ulbricht Papers, NL 182/1249.

24. Ibid.

25. Ibid. "Heini" is a derogatory term for a soldier, or an "ass."

26. Major General Borufka to the SED Central Committee, Department of Security, May 15, 1957, SED ZK, Walter Ulbricht Papers, NL 182/1249.

27. Memo from the State Planning Commission on Technical and Scientific Cooperation with Poland, June 8, 1957, SED ZK, microfilm FBS 339/13492.

28. Schwanz to the SED Central Committee, March 20, 1957, SED ZK, microfilm FBS 339/13489; Wollweber to Honecker, March 30, 1957, SED ZK, microfilm FBS 339/13489; and Florin to the PZPR Central Committee, April 15, 1957, SED ZK, microfilm FBS 339/13489.

29. Anheyer to the Headquarters of German Folk-Policy in Berlin (Hauptverwaltung Deutsche Volkspolitik), September 28, 1956, SED ZK, microfilm FBS 339/13488.

30. SED Central Committee report on the unification of families from Poland to the GDR and FRG, unsigned, undated, ca. December 1956, SED ZK, microfilm FBS 339/13493.

31. Report on visas to Poland, unsigned, September 28, 1956, SED ZK, microfilm FBS 339/13488.

32. Drechsler report, March 14, 1957, SED ZK, Walter Ulbricht Papers, NL 182/1249.

33. Report on the tourist traffic between Poland and West Germany, unsigned, undated, ca. fall, 1957, DDR MfAA, M. B. König File, A17151.

34. Beling notes of meeting between Winzer and Czeczyk, November 21, 1957, DDR MfAA, HA/I Secretariat, A38.

35. Translation of Pahl article from *Aus der internationalen Arbeiterbewegung* (From the International Workers' Movement), May 31, 1957, in MSZ, 10/448/47.

36. *Neues Deutschland*, June 21, 1957, p. 1.

37. Kopa notes of meeting with Haid on July 2, July 4, 1957, MSZ, 10/379/42.

38. Florin to Grotewohl, June 20, 1957, SED ZK, Otto Grotewohl Papers, NL 90/483.

39. Report of the Polish and GDR government and PZPR and SED party meetings, June 20, 1957, SED ZK, microfilm FBS 339/13423.

40. Record of the discussions of party and government delegations in Berlin from June 18 to June 20, June 29, 1957, MSZ, 10/309/36.

41. Ulbricht to Izydorczyk, July 14, 1950, SED ZK, Walter Ulbricht Papers, NL 182/1247.

42. SED District Office in Rostock to Ulbricht, July 25, 1958, SED ZK, Walter Ulbricht Papers, NL 182/1250.

43. Report of the Polish and GDR government and PZPR and SED party meetings, June 20, 1957, SED ZK, microfilm FBS 339/13423.

44. *Neues Deutschland*, October 26, 1957, p. 1.

45. "Joint Declaration of the Governments of the GDR and PRP," June 20, 1957, SED ZK, Otto Grotewohl Papers, NL 90/485.

46. Report on the trade relations between the GDR and Poland, June 7, DDR MfAuIH, DL-2, file 2392. The following is Poland's share of all East German trade: 1947, 3 percent; 1949, 9 percent; 1951, 13.6 percent; 1953, 14.5 percent; 1954, 14.1 percent; 1955, 13.3 percent; 1956, 11.8 percent; and 1957, 14 percent.

47. Cited in *Neues Deutschland*, May 10, 1957, p. 5.

48. König notes on Gomułka's visit to Moscow, May 31, 1957, SED ZK, Otto Grotewohl Papers, NL 90/485.

49. Grotewohl to Schmidt, June 4, 1957, SED ZK, Otto Grotewohl Papers, NL 90/485.

50. Blankenhagen report on a delegation visit to Zielona-Góra, May 6, 1957, SED ZK, Walter Ulbricht Papers, NL 182/1249.

51. Information on the Comecon meeting in Warsaw from June 18–22, June 27, 1957, SED ZK, Walter Ulbricht Office, J IV 2/202/195.

52. Communiqué on the Comecon meeting from June 18–20, June 22, 1957, SED ZK, Walter Ulbricht Office, J IV 2/202/195.

53. Information on the Comecon meeting in Warsaw from June 18–22, June 27, 1957, SED ZK, Walter Ulbricht Office, J IV 2/202/195.

54. Report on the Polish and GDR government and PZPR and SED party meetings in Berlin from June 18–20, June 20, 1957, SED ZK, microfilm FBS 339/13423.

55. Record of the discussions of party and government delegations in Berlin from June 18–20, June 29, 1957, MSZ, 10/309/36.

56. Report on the Polish and GDR government and PZPR and SED party meetings in Berlin from June 18–20, June 20, 1957, SED ZK, microfilm FBS 339/13423.

57. *Neues Deutschland*, October 9, 1957, 1; and report on political development in the Soviet zone in September, October 8, 1957, BRD BfGDF, B137/1473. Atomic power was an alternative source of energy for the GDR, and work began in October 1957 on a nuclear power plant north of Berlin. Poland and East Germany agreed to cooperate in the development of nuclear energy.

58. Report of the Polish and GDR government and PZPR and SED meetings from June 18–20, June 20, 1957, SED ZK, microfilm FBS 339/13423.

59. Record of the party and government discussions from June 18–20, June 29, 1957, MSZ, 10/309/36.

60. Florin to Grotewohl, June 20, 1957, SED ZK, Otto Grotewohl Papers, NL 90/483.

61. Notes on the Polish draft of the joint declaration, unsigned, undated, ca. June 20, 1957, SED ZK, Otto Grotewohl Papers, NL 90/483.

62. Report of the Polish and GDR government and PZPR and SED party meetings, June 20, 1957, SED ZK, microfilm FBS 339/13423.

63. See *Neues Deutschland*, June 19, 1957, pp. 1, 3, and June 22, 1957, p. 2.

64. Jakubowski notes of a reception at the Polish Embassy on June 20, June 21, 1957, MSZ, 10/379/42.

65. Foreign Ministry report on the GDR press, unsigned, undated, MSZ, 10/464/48.

66. Florin to SED Politburo members, August 2, 1957, SED ZK, Walter Ulbricht Papers, NL 182/1249.

67. Report on the meeting of the heads of the SED and PZPR Foreign Affairs Departments, October 2, 1957, SED ZK, Walter Ulbricht Papers, NL 182/1249.

68. Record of the party and government discussions from June 18–20, June 29, 1957, MSZ, 10/309/36.

69. Joachim Görlich report, "Germans in Poland," October, 1957, in BRD BfGDF, B137/1246.

70. Polish Embassy report from March 15 to August 31, 1957, MSZ, 10/371/41.

71. Ibid.

72. Foreign Ministry report on the GDR press, unsigned, undated, MSZ, 10/464/48.

73. Schmidt to the GDR Foreign Ministry, July 23, 1957, SED ZK, Walter Ulbricht Papers, NL 182/1249.

74. Foreign Ministry report on Polish-West German student exchanges, November 30, 1958, DDR MfAA, Department of Neighboring Countries, C781/73, ZR/1892/73.

75. Grosse notes of a meeting between Winzer and Piotrowski, September 12, 1957, SED ZK, Walter Ulbricht Papers, NL 182/1249.

76. Grosse notes of a meeting between Winzer and Piotrowski, September 18, 1957, SED ZK, Walter Ulbricht Papers, NL 182/1249.

77. Winzer notes on a meeting between Bolz and Piotrowski, January 18, 1958, SED ZK, Otto Grotewohl Papers, NL 90/485.

78. Hegen to Winzer, October 25, 1957, DDR MfAA, HA/I Secretariat, A14759.

79. Schilde report on a university delegation visit to Poland from September 21–28, 1957, SED ZK, Walter Ulbricht Papers, NL 182/1249.

80. Ibid.

81. Report on the cooperation between the SED district office in Frankfurt/Oder with the PZPR district office in Zielona Góra, April 8, 1958, SED ZK, microfilm FBS 339/13422.

82. GDR Embassy in Warsaw to the GDR Foreign Ministry, August 1957, SED ZK, microfilm FBS 339/13489.

83. Ungarn-Sternberg notes on relations between the FRG and the [Soviet] satellite states, November 6, 1957, BRD AA, Department 7, vol. 77.

84. Wolfgang Schneider to Hans Globke on a visit of Polish scientists, November 24, 1957, BRD BKA, B136/6717.

85. Florin report on the meetings of the SED and PZPR Foreign Affairs Departments from September 25–27, 1957, SED ZK, microfilm FBS 339/13422.

86. Report on the political development in the Soviet zone of Germany, October 8, 1957, BRD BfGDF, B137/1473.

87. Hegen to Winzer, September 25, 1957, DDR MfAA, Warsaw Embassy, A3755.

88. Notes on relations between the BRD and the [Soviet] satellite states, undated, ca. January 1958, BRD AA, Department 7, vol. 77.

89. Wolfgang Schneider to Hans Globke on a visit of Polish scientists, November 24, 1957, BRD BKA, B136/6717.

90. Heymann to the GDR Foreign Ministry, October 29, 1957, HA/I Secretariat, A38.

91. Seyfert notes of a meeting with Stiepanow (First Secretary of the Soviet Embassy in Warsaw), November 12, 1957, SED ZK, Walter Ulbricht Papers, NL 182/1249.

92. The Natolin group was named for the building in which they met.

93. Report on cultural relations with Poland in 1957, unsigned, undated, DDR MfAA, Minister's Office, A15156.

94. Polish Foreign Ministry report on the GDR press, undated, ca. December 1958, MSZ, 10/464/48. Ulbricht's demotion in early 1958 of SED veterans such as Fred Oelssner, Karl Schirdewan, Ernst Wollweber, and Paul Wandel indeed had a certain Stalinist taste.

95. Report on the results of cooperation between the regional offices of the SED and counties in Poland, undated, ca. December 1957, SED ZK, IV 2/20/31.

10

The Rapacki Plan and the German Question, 1957–1959

We are exclusively and finally responsible for what concerns relations with West Germany. There every socialist country cannot go its own way.

—*Walter Ulbricht*[1]

In 1957, NATO began serious deliberations on stationing nuclear weapons in West Germany. U.S. President Dwight Eisenhower hoped to extricate U.S. troops from Europe, and even considered putting nuclear forces under West German control.[2] The idea sent shock waves through the Polish and East German régimes. Grotewohl dusted off his 1952 proposal for a confederation of the two German states, this time with a provision that neither would station or produce atomic bombs. The FRG and GDR would end obligatory military service, leave NATO and the Warsaw Pact, and all foreign troops would leave German soil. The Adenauer government immediately rejected the plan.[3]

The former Polish ambassador to the GDR, Jan Izydorczyk, told the Polish Parliament that a confederation was a just and sensible solution to the German problem,[4] but the Polish government did not throw its full diplomatic weight behind Grotewohl's proposal. Most Poles were wary of a united German state, regardless of its composition, and a change in the status quo could jeopardize Poland's claim to the Oder-Neisse border.[5] Although Warsaw had limited options in its foreign policy regarding the German question, the Gomułka régime was determined not to wait for the Soviet Union or the GDR to dictate Poland's foreign policy toward West Germany.[6] Instead of fully supporting East Berlin's proposal, the Polish government developed its own plan to preempt the nu-clearization of Central Europe.

The idea for a nuclear-free zone appeared in the Polish journal *Świat a Polska* in the spring of 1957. Unaccustomed to diplomatic initiatives from its Warsaw Pact partners, the Soviet government was slow to respond to the Polish proposal,[7] but in September, the Soviet Chargé d'affaires in Poland told Polish Deputy Foreign Minister Marian Naszkowski that the Soviet government supported it.[8] The Polish plan eventually took the name of its foreign minister, former PPS member Adam Rapacki; it called for a nuclear free zone in Germany, Poland, and Czechoslovakia. After receiving formal approval from the Warsaw Pact, Rapacki and Czechoslovak Foreign Minister Vaclav David presented the plan to the United Nations on October 2.[9]

The Rapacki Plan was an important confidence-builder for the Polish government. Polish officials thought it would reduce tensions between NATO and the Warsaw Pact and encourage the other smaller countries of Europe to conduct more independent foreign policies. The Poles were proud of their initiative. As the editor of the weekly journal *Polityka*, Mieczysław Rakowski, later wrote,

> [the Rapacki Plan was] a good testimonial of her diplomacy. . . . [Poland] had worked out the idea contained in the plan to the minutest detail. Among the many projects put forward by various states in the initial phase of European detente, Poland's initiative for many years occupied the chief place. . . . The discussion of the Rapacki Plan helped make Poland known throughout the world.[10]

The East German Foreign Ministry immediately informed Stanisław Kopa that the Rapacki Plan "makes an important contribution to solving the German problem."[11] On October 6, *Neues Deutschland* carried a long article on the proposal, including Bolz's telegram to the U.N. declaring the GDR's support.[12] The East Germans, however, were reluctant to let Poland play a key role in German affairs. After the October 6 issue, *Neues Deutschland* virtually ignored the Rapacki Plan, choosing instead to pub-licize the Soviet Union's disarmament proposals.[13] In early 1958, the Pol-ish Foreign Ministry expressed disappointment that the SED leadership was not showing much interest in the plan: "Except for a concise sum-mary of Minister Rapacki's declaration and marginal mention in speeches by Ulbricht and Grotewohl, there were few attempts at a sincere commentary on the initiative."[14] One East German diplomat recalled that the Soviet Union and the GDR reacted to the plan with "great mistrust and did everything to let the initiative peter out."[15]

The East German leaders were indifferent to the Rapacki Plan in part because it did not include guarantees for the continued existence of the GDR. East Berlin preferred bilateral negotiations with Bonn on issues that affected the fate of East Germany. Grotewohl demanded that the two German states sign a nuclear-free agreement; such an agreement would mean the FRG recognized the GDR.[16]

The East Germans were kept in the dark about the details of Poland's negotiations on the Rapacki Plan. In December, Rapacki finally informed Ambassador Hegen about Poland's ongoing talks with Great Britain, France, Austria, and Sweden. Rapacki said that the latter two neutral countries were very supportive of the proposal.[17] Sensing that the Rapacki Plan was contributing to tensions between East Berlin and Warsaw, Czechoslovak diplomats asked Hegen about it at a reception at the East German Embassy celebrating the eighth anniversary of the founding of the GDR.[18] Hegen said that he was offended that neither Cyrankiewicz nor Gomułka had bothered to attend, and added that he still had serious doubts about Poland's political and economic stability.[19]

Official West German sources alleged that Ulbricht told Soviet Ambassador Puschkin that "the Rapacki Plan is endangering the 'GDR's' fight against 'West German imperialism' and the stationing of atomic weapons there, and therefore is weakening the solidarity of the 'socialist camp.'" Puschkin supposedly responded that the Rapacki Plan was in line with Soviet foreign policy.[20] According to another West German source, the Soviets gave the Poles a free hand to pursue the Rapacki Plan, which "purposely went around the 'GDR'."[21] During the Warsaw Pact meetings in Moscow in November, the other communist parties rebuked the SED for its harsh criticism of the PZPR in the past year, and for the failure of its own propaganda campaign against the FRG.[22]

The Poles were incensed that the East Germans would not give them credit for the Rapacki Plan.[23] The East Germans characterized it instead as a joint East German-Czechoslovak-Polish idea.[24] At the end of 1958, the Polish Foreign Ministry observed that "for a long time the 'Rapacki Plan' was presented as an initiative of the GDR, 'subsequently supported by Czechoslovakia and Poland.'" The ministry noted that the East German press had not paid much attention to the plan, and when it did, emphasized the "key role" of the GDR. *Neues Deutschland* refused to call it the "Rapacki Plan," a stance that Polish diplomats blamed on its chief editor, Hermann Axen, who had been a vigorous critic of the Gomułka régime from the beginning.[25] When the chief editor of *Trybuna Ludu*, Artur Kowalski, asked *Neues Deutschland* correspondent Karl Krahn point blank whether the GDR was indifferent to the Rapacki Plan because it was a Polish proposal, Krahn had no answer.[26]

East German officials viewed the Rapacki Plan as an imitation of Grotewohl's proposal for a German confederation. In an interview for the *Suddeutsche Zeitung* (South German Newspaper), Ulbricht said that he had already proposed an atomic-free Germany in May 1956.[27] Gomułka told *The London Times* that Poland was not interested in a unified Germany, whether or not it was atomic-free: "Any attempt to link the Rapacki Plan with the question of German reunification is completely unrealistic. . . . It would be no misfortune if Germany were to remain divided for a certain time. In our view the problem of German reunification is not the most important one."[28]

In early February 1958, the East German Foreign Ministry tried to seize the diplomatic initiative by proposing a trilateral East German–Czechoslovak-Polish disarmament plan for Central Europe. In an obvious attempt to loosen West Germany's ties to NATO, Otto Winzer suggested that the four nuclear-free states (Poland, Czechoslovakia, and East and West Germany) would pledge not to develop weapons in cooperation with other countries. The Poles rejected the idea; they argued that a joint proposal with the GDR would reduce the Rapacki Plan's chance of gaining acceptance in the West. They said that many NATO countries already opposed the Rapacki Plan on the grounds that it undermined the entire concept of the Western alliance. The Poles told Winzer that Poland had to consider the interests of countries other than Germany, not Germany alone.[29]

Poland's Relations with West Germany

The success of the Rapacki Plan did not depend on the backing of Czechoslovakia or East Germany, but on whether the Soviet Union and the Western allies signed on. On February 14, 1958, the Polish government issued the Rapacki Plan in a formal diplomatic note to the Western powers.[30] The plan had three stages: an immediate freeze of nuclear arms in the four states, discussions on reducing conventional weapons, and talks on the elimination of nuclear weapons. Rapacki suggested a procedure that would spare Bonn from having to deal directly with East Berlin.[31]

Even if the plan failed to break the impasse over German rearmament, the PZPR hoped to foster connections to some of the social democratic and liberal democratic parties in Western Europe that had shown interest in it. The Polish Foreign Ministry dismissed repeated East German warnings about West German militarism and the threat of imminent war with NATO. The ministry saw more danger in the Cold War and the arms race itself: "Not only in the socialist countries, but in the capitalist countries, state policy is not governed by a conscious pursuit of war—the main practical danger of war continues to be the arms race."[32] Warsaw particularly noted positive reactions to the plan from the SPD, the French Radical Party, and even some Gaullists. The SPD viewed the Rapacki Plan as a possible step toward unifying Germany. The West German Free Democratic Party (FDP) leaned against accepting the plan, but agreed with its basic principles for disarmament, and welcomed the possibility of normalizing relations with Poland.[33]

East German officials opposed direct talks about the plan between the Polish government and West German political parties, but the Poles ignored them. In March 1958, West German Social Democrat Carlo Schmid met Naszkowski to discuss the Rapacki Plan and relations with Poland in general. Schmid hoped the FRG would soon normalize relations with Poland, just as West Germany had overcome differences with France, another old enemy. Schmid told Naszkowski that the Rapacki Plan could be a significant breakthrough in the question of German unification: "The conception of the Rapacki Plan has created the most favorable conditions for a solution of the fundamental political problems in Europe. It is important that the idea came from the Polish side." Schmid added that he recognized Poland had to play an important role not only in the socialist countries but also in East and West Europe by breaking down the barriers between them. Naszkowski reported that his meeting with Schmid was conducted in a "warm atmosphere."[34]

The Rapacki Plan was never seriously considered a basis for addressing the escalating arms race in Central Europe, however. The Western alliance went ahead with plans to station nuclear missiles in Western Europe, including West Germany. The United States was unwilling to bargain away its NATO partner for a politically and militarily nonaligned German state; in any case, the Western powers did not trust the Soviets to allow free German elections. Furthermore, Bonn was opposed to leaving NATO and the recently constituted European Common Market. In an effort to salvage the Rapacki Plan, the Polish government announced on March 27 that the proposal did not necessarily mean that West Germany had to withdraw from NATO, or that the GDR, Czechoslovakia, and Poland had to leave the Warsaw Pact.[35] This idea went nowhere.

The Polish, East German, and Czechoslovak foreign ministers met in Prague in April to discuss the Rapacki Plan and other issues related to West Germany. Earlier disagreements immediately resurfaced. Rapacki and Naszkowski refused to criticize West Germany directly for fear of jeopardizing the PZPR's efforts to develop ties to the SPD and FDP. In the final joint communiqué, Bolz insisted on calling the FRG an imperialist state. Naszkowski agreed to a general allusion to the dangers of German militarism, but he rejected references to the existence of German imperialism on the grounds that they did "not really correspond to reality." Naszkowski eventually agreed to Bolz's formulation that there was a threat of "reconstituting imperialism" in West Germany rather than an existing or "reconstituted imperialism." The Poles also let the following line stand in reference to Bonn's refusal to recognize the Oder-Neisse border: "The German Federal Republic is the only European state in which revanchism is intentionally fostered and open territorial claims are raised." Bolz suggested that the final communiqué give direct credit to the Soviet Union for leading the socialist parties in the fight for peace, but again the Poles backed off; instead, they pushed through a version that recognized the relative importance of both Poland and the Soviet Union.[36]

The controversy over the language of the final communiqué revealed yet again the ideological differences in the two parties' policies toward the capitalist countries. A few days after the conference, Bolz told Ambassador Piotrowski that he understood why the Poles had insisted on more cautious language in reference to West Germany, but he referred to the FRG's economic expansion into Africa, the Far East, the Middle East, and South America as proof of West German imperialism. Bolz said that the GDR's strategy was to vie for the support of the workers and working classes in the West, and criticized Gomułka for seeking out the leaders of West German political parties, trade unions, and intellectual circles. Bolz considered East Germany's policy a truer reflection of Lenin's theory of continuing revolution, but thought Poland's smacked of social democratic revisionism.[37]

On September 1, 1958, the SED made a perfunctory observance of Hitler's attack on Poland in 1939. In previous years, the SED had stressed its friendship with Poland and the permanence of the Oder-Neisse border, but on this occasion the East German press devoted more attention to the East German-Czechoslovak Friendship Week that was taking place at the same time. It did not go unnoticed in Warsaw that the East German press, in contrast to its scant coverage of Poland, was excessively complimentary of relations with Czechoslovakia.[38]

Rapacki made a speech in London in September praising Poland's new political and economic ties to West Germany without mentioning the GDR. The speech confirmed the SED's suspicions that Warsaw was more interested in developing closer ties to the FRG than to the GDR. Hegen repeatedly complained that the Polish press was ignoring Grotewohl's idea for a German confederation.[39] The SED's Frankfurt/Oder office reported that Polish officials did not think that a German confederation was in Poland's best interest because they did not trust the GDR as a guarantor of the Oder-Neisse border. The office wrote that "reactionary elements [in Poland] ask whether it wouldn't be better to ally with the Americans, English, and West Germans in order to solve these problems with them."[40]

East German officials were highly sensitive to the implication that the GDR was the lesser of the two German states. They criticized Gomułka's speech to the PZPR's Ninth Party Congress in October 1958 for mentioning East Germany only in the context of Poland's relations with West Germany.[41] East German officials vigorously protested when the Polish organizers of an international conference of scientists and engineers in 1958 designated the West German seat the "Federal Republic of Germany," but worded the sign for the East German contingent "Eastern Zone of Germany." The discrepancy happened again at a meeting of the Coal Commission of the U.N. Economic Commission for Europe.[42]

Two travel agencies in Warsaw issued visas for West Germany. One was called the "Travel Agency for Germany," intimating that it represented both German states. The East German Embassy protested that "this sign makes allowance for Adenauer's claim of exclusive representation [of Germany] and discriminates against the GDR." East German officials also objected to the other travel office, the "Pass Bureau to the German Federal Republic," which they thought was a diplomatic representative of the FRG. The East Germans admonished the Poles for this indirect support of the Adenauer régime, but the Poles downplayed the significance of the visa bureau as nothing more than what it was—a travel agency.[43]

Poland's persistent attempts to foster economic and cultural ties to the West was evidence to the SED of Gomułka's opportunistic foreign policy. In April 1958, the East German Embassy wrote a scathing critique of two "revisionist" articles by economist Oskar Lange in the PZPR's ideological journal *Polityka*. The embassy was particularly annoyed that Lange called for more economic and cultural exchanges with capitalist countries, yet completely ignored exchanges with the socialist camp. The embassy complained that Polish delegations and tourist groups were eager to go to West Germany; it was "un-Marxist" to pursue exchanges with the capitalist countries while ignoring dialogue with the socialist states. The embassy thought the policy was contributing to Poland's political and economic instability.[44] The East Germans were still convinced that U.S. loans to Poland were tied to political concessions.[45]

In contrast to the many cultural exchanges between Poland and the GDR that went awry, the head of a West German friendship society with Eastern Europe found the Poles remarkably open and hospitable, more so in light of what Germany had done to Poland during the war; he was surprised by the Poles' poor treatment of East Germans.[46] When a West German journalist at the Poznań Trade Fair in 1958 protested that the East Germans were circulating propaganda against the Federal Republic, no Polish journalists came to the GDR's defense.[47]

For years, East German officials had avowed their support of closer economic and cultural ties between Poland and West Germany, but their actions indicated otherwise. The Polish Embassy knew as much; it reported that "the GDR authorities are nervous about our expanding contacts with the FRG, especially with West Berlin." This was made clear in early 1958 when the East Germans informed the Poles that they would refuse visas to anyone whose main interest was going to West Berlin.[48] Some East German diplomats thought the best way to counteract the Poles' interest in going to West Germany was to open tourist traffic and increase cultural exchanges across the Oder-Neisse border. But as much as they lobbied their superiors, the SED leadership still opposed increasing unregulated contacts between Polish and East German citizens. This policy also applied to Polish journalists, who complained that they could not adequately cover developments in the GDR if they could not see them for themselves.[49]

Disregarding official protests from East Berlin, Gomułka persisted in cultivating the SPD as a conduit for better political and economic relations with the FRG.[50] Gomułka's attempts to meet SPD leader Herbert Wehner in 1958 prompted Ulbricht to warn the Poles that "we are exclusively and finally responsible for what concerns relations with West Germany. There every socialist country cannot go its own way."[51] The East Germans continued to fault the Polish press for underestimating the West German threat and for writing without a "clear class standpoint." The East Germans' sermonizing did not work.[52] In October, Piotr Ogrodziński brushed aside Winzer's warnings that the FRG was using trade deals to pry Poland away from the Soviet bloc: "We are of the opinion that our trade relations [and] the economic relations to the capitalist countries do not loosen our relations to the socialist camp."[53]

But Poland's talks with West German political parties failed to nudge the Adenauer government closer to recognizing the Oder-Neisse border; the impasse remained the major roadblock to formal diplomatic relations. Józef Czesak, the head of the PZPR's Department of Foreign Affairs, told Ambassador Hegen that he was disappointed the SPD would not recognize the border either. Czesak promised that the Polish press would sharpen its criticism of the SPD, and said that the number of West German student visits to Poland would be reduced because the exchanges had been unproductive.[54]

The Berlin Crisis

The East Germans were genuinely angry with Poland's reluctance to support their diplomatic initiatives regarding German unification. In October 1958, Ulbricht proposed the withdrawal of the occupying troops from Germany and a one-year moratorium on the deployment of atomic weapons in Central Europe. With the Rapacki Plan already on the table, the Gomułka régime ignored Ulbricht's proposal. The Poles thought that the troop withdrawal would create a disadvantage for the Warsaw Pact, and that NATO would stall negotiations on conventional arms reductions to justify its deployment of atomic weapons.[55]

On November 4, 1958, Rapacki held a press conference to unveil a new wrinkle in his plan. There were indications that Bonn was reconsidering its position, but a new Berlin crisis ended prospects for compromise.[56] Khrushchev's strategy to prevent the stationing of nuclear weapons in West Germany was to issue an ultimatum on November 27: Within six months the entire city of Berlin would fall under the jurisdiction of the GDR.[57] Ulbricht was fully behind Khrushchev's demands; the flight of East Germans through West Berlin not only embarrassed the GDR but depleted its labor force. Gomułka was stunned. The Rapacki Plan was the centerpiece of his policy to reduce tensions in East Central Europe, and now Khrushchev and Ulbricht were threatening a showdown with NATO to force its adoption.[58]

The Poles were not alone in fearing that the Berlin ultimatum would plunge the continent into war. Few people in the West wanted to fight with the West Germans for a free West Berlin. As British Prime Minister Harold MacMillan put it, why would Britain go to war "for 2 million people we twice fought wars against and who almost destroyed us?" Eisenhower and U.S. Secretary of State John Foster Dulles did not care whether the East Germans controlled the access routes to West Berlin as long as they remained open, but the United States took a firm stance about staying in West Berlin.[59]

The Berlin crisis put Gomułka in a quandary. Even if the crisis ended peacefully, his support of Khrushchev's ultimatum could jeopardize Poland's tenuous ties to the West. Gomułka feared, too, that the GDR would gain legitimacy if the Western Allies renegotiated the status of Berlin with the East German government.[60] Finally, the Potsdam agreement was still the only legal, four-power guarantee of Berlin and the Oder-Neisse border; a change in the status of Berlin or Germany could reopen the issue.

Emigré Poles suspected that Ulbricht and Khrushchev were colluding to resolve the Berlin problem and the question of German unification without regard for Polish interests. In an article in *Wiadomości* (News), a Polish journal published in the West, W. A. Zbyszewski alleged that the Soviets were ready to embrace Ulbricht as their main ally in Central Europe if the Gomułka régime pushed its national interests too far. Zbyszewski suggested that "Ulbricht is waiting for a change in the situation; he would gladly jettison the 'brotherly Peoples' Poland.' . . . After Moscow I consider Ulbricht and his group the worst enemies of Poland;

on the other hand I consider it senseless to attack Adenauer as a 'revan-chist,' 'militarist,' or 'imperialist.'"[61]

Gomułka had similar apprehensions, but he could only sit by and wait for the crisis to play itself out. In February 1959, Otto Winzer wrote Ulbricht that the Poles were no longer actively pursuing the Rapacki Plan because they did not want to divert attention from the Soviet proposal for a peace treaty with Germany.[62] When the Berlin ultimatum lapsed, however, and there was still no resolution to the question of German unification, Gomułka again raised the idea of a nuclear-free Central Europe at the U.N. General Assembly in September 1960; and again in March 1962 at a disarmament conference in Geneva. By then the Rapacki Plan was dead.[63]

The Problem of Trade with West Germany and West Berlin

By the late 1950s, Ulbricht and Gomułka had resolved some of the trade disputes that had been so contentious in 1956. Gomułka even began to call for more integration of the Comecon economies.[64] Nonetheless, the East Germans could not reconcile themselves with Poland's eagerness to trade with West Germany and West Berlin—a trade that often came at the GDR's expense.[65]

Ulbricht knew that for East Germany to compete with West Germany and maintain political stability in the GDR, the East German standard of living had to improve dramatically. In April 1958, the SED set a goal of matching the West German economy by 1965.[66] At the Fifth Party Congress in July, Ulbricht went one step further and pledged to overtake the West German economy by 1961.[67] But Ulbricht knew this was an impossible goal without increased imports of coal and oil. The Soviet Union and Czechoslovakia could meet some of these energy needs, but imports of Silesian coal were indispensable.[68]

That spring, the East Germans launched another campaign for additional economic aid and trade concessions from its Warsaw Pact partners. Ulbricht sent a letter to Khrushchev arguing that as a developing socialist state, the GDR had to out-produce capitalist West Germany. He pointed out that East Germany lagged behind West Germany in almost every economic category: "If the GDR is supposed to function as a showcase of the socialist camp to the West, the production targets for 1959 and 1960 must be raised now." Ulbricht said that for socialism to gain popular support in Germany, it was essential that East German workers had a standard of living comparable to that of workers in the FRG. Ulbricht predicted that in the next two years the GDR would have the slowest growth rate of the socialist countries, and that the GDR was the only country in the world that still had a rationing system. Ulbricht presented Khrushchev with a long list of goods that the GDR wanted from the Soviet Union in the next two years.[69]

At the Comecon meeting in Moscow in May 1958, the East Germans asked the other socialist countries to consider the GDR's economic and political predicament as the socialist German state. But the other Comecon countries refused even to discuss raising the standard of living in East Germany, which was already well above their own. The only commitment Khrushchev would make was that, if the situation warranted it, the Soviet Union would grant the GDR credits for raw materials, machines, and consumer items. The other party leaders did not directly respond to East Germany's pleas for more trade and credits, but said they would do what they could.[70]

At the end of May, Ulbricht sent a letter to Gomułka appealing for additional shipments of coal, coke, iron ore, steel, and zinc. Ulbricht asked for 400,000 more tons of coal in 1958, and a total of 4,000,000 tons annually by 1965.[71] Gomułka's position had not changed: He was unsympathetic to Ulbricht's appeals for socialist economic solidarity, and was not persuaded by the argument that the GDR had to match West German economic output. He wrote Ulbricht that he understood the importance of the economic development of the East German state and promised to help "when possible," but said that Poland was in no position to provide economic assistance. Gomułka reminded Ulbricht that Poland had been a theater of war twice in World War II, and that the German occupation of Poland had been the longest of the war. Thirty-eight percent of Poland's national wealth had been destroyed, and ruins were still evident in Warsaw and other Polish cities. Gomułka said that the GDR was outproducing Poland in most economic categories; the GDR's per capita consumption of meat was still higher than Poland's, and East Germans consumed almost four times the amount of fruit. Gomułka added that East Germans owned three times the number of cars and twice the number of motorcycles. He maintained that Poland needed its coal as much as East Germany, but nonetheless promised the GDR a credit to purchase 1 million tons of coal; he also agreed to send meat, fat, and butter.[72]

According to Ambassador Piotrowski, who personally delivered Gomułka's letter to Ulbricht, the SED leader began another one of his long monologues by saying that he fully understood Poland's economic problems; however, Ulbricht then behaved as though he had not read Gomułka's references to the damages that the Germans had inflicted on Poland in the war. Ulbricht insisted that his requests for economic assistance were motivated not by serious political or economic problems that the GDR was having but by the need to make an eventual German confederation palatable, especially to the workers in West Germany. He stressed again that East German workers had to have the same standard of living as West German workers. Ulbricht used the same old arguments about East Germany's special needs, admitting that the East German economy was lagging far behind West Germany's. He was interested in credits not for food but for coal, coke, and steel.[73]

Willi Stoph and Stefan Jędrychowski met in June 1958 to negotiate a new trade deal. Ulbricht had requested an additional 500,000 thousand tons of Polish coal in 1959 and 600,000 tons in 1960, but Jędrychowski agreed to additional exports of only 300,000 tons of coal for each of those two years. Poland promised to ship 1,500,000 tons of coal in 1961, and 2,000,000 tons by 1965. The second figure was half the one Ulbricht had proposed. Jędrychowski said that Poland could not possibly export more iron ore or steel to the GDR.[74]

Another controversy surfaced that summer when the Poles asked for a three- to four-fold increase in the railroad tolls on Soviet and East German military transports. During talks with the Poles and Soviets in June, the East Germans contended that the current fees fully covered Poland's costs.[75] The East Germans argued that they were the first line of defense for Poland and the Warsaw Pact, but their protests went in vain. The Soviet Union and the other Warsaw Pact countries eventually agreed to the tariff hike.[76]

Before the November elections in the GDR, Ulbricht made yet another appeal to Gomułka's generosity. Again Ulbricht emphasized the GDR's strategic importance for Poland: "This goal [of economic parity with the FRG] is of considerable importance for the issue of peace in Europe, because in 1961 West Germany's atomic armament will be complete."[77] Gomułka was still not swayed. Many Polish communists, especially those who remembered the war, were bitter over Poland's standard of living, which was so much lower than East Germany's.[78] After a visit to several Polish border towns that fall, an SED functionary from the Frankfurt/Oder office reported that the Poles always wanted to know about the standard of living in the GDR, and doubted they would ever achieve the same level.[79]

Gomułka's foreign economic policy was dictated in part by Poland's need for machines and technology that it could not get from the other socialist countries. Poland's trade with the West continued to rise in 1958, much to the consternation of the East Germans, who expected to receive Polish exports first. According to East German sources, the share of Poland's trade with capitalist countries increased from 37.3 percent in 1956 to about 42 percent in 1958.[80]

Poland's trade with West Berlin continued to be a divisive issue. In 1957, the new efforts launched by West Berlin firms to trade with Polish enterprises resulted in a rapid increase in trade. The East German government responded by instituting new transit and passport regulations.[81] At Warsaw's insistence, the East German government issued one-time permits for Poland to ship coal directly to West Berlin in 1958; but the East Germans prohibited deliveries of other products that West Berlin businesses had contracted to buy from Poland. Those shipments, which included pipe, building stone, and potatoes, had to be sent through Hamburg. The new regulations again caused many Polish officials to question the wisdom of closer economic ties to East Germany.[82]

Gomułka and Ulbricht had heated arguments over these restrictions on Poland's trade with West Berlin. According to Gomułka's translator, Erwin Weit, "Gomułka complained to Ulbricht about this practice, who nonetheless did not come around. For years he let this area of Polish foreign trade annoy [the Poles], in order to get the Poles to support his aggressive policies toward West Berlin and to keep them from any unilateral flirting with the Federal Republic."[83]

While Khrushchev and Ulbricht were seeking a final resolution to the Berlin problem in the fall of 1958, the GDR prohibited shipment of any more goods from Poland to West Berlin. Gomułka sent a letter to the SED Politburo in September asking that Poland be allowed to meet its contractual obligations. Gomułka argued that Poland would have a serious balance of payments problem if these deliveries were not met.[84] In October, the East German government at last allowed the Poles to make coal deliveries to West Berlin, but only until the end of the year.[85]

There was no sign of change in Poland's foreign economic policy at the Twelfth Plenary Session of the PZPR Central Committee in November 1958. Disappointed, East German diplomats criticized the PZPR for its lack of economic cooperation with Czechoslovakia, the Soviet Union, and the GDR, especially in light of Poland's raw material exports to the West.[86] East Germany had no choice but to redirect its trade toward the Soviet Union. East German exports to Poland fell by almost 10 percent from 1956 to 1958, and by 1957 East Germany had become the Soviet Union's most important trading partner.[87]

Differences over the Rapacki Plan, the future of Germany and Berlin, and Poland's trade with West Germany demonstrated that Ulbricht and Gomułka had very different conceptions of socialist foreign policy. The East Germans remained steadfast in their Marxist interpretation of the imminent threat of capitalist imperialism; the Polish communists followed a realist approach in their search for economic and political modus vivendi with the West.

The two leaders were still engaged in heated debates over domestic policy. Ulbricht's talks with Gomułka in Warsaw in December 1958 defused some of the hard feelings of the past two years, but the leaders' fundamental disagreements still precluded a closer partnership.

Notes

1. Erwin Weit, *Ostblock intern: 13 Jahre Dolmetscher für die polnische Partei—und Staatsführung* (Inside the East bloc: Thirteen years as interpreter for the Polish Party—and government leadership) (Hamburg: Hoffmann und Campe Verlag, 1970), pp. 33–34.

2. See Marc Trachtenberg, *A Constructed Peace: The Making of the European Settlement 1945–1963* (Princeton: Princeton University Press, 1999), pp. 185–188.

3. Polish Embassy report from March 15 to August 31, 1957, MSZ, 10/371/41; see also Andrei Gromyko, *Memories* (London: Hutchinson, 1989), p. 196.

4. Izydorczyk speech to the Polish Parliament, undated, ca. November, 1957, PZPR KC, group Izydorczyk, file 473/6.

5. Łobodycz to Naszkowski, September 3, 1957, MSZ, 10/359/39.

6. Heymann to the GDR Foreign Ministry, October 29, 1957, DDR MfAA, HA/I Secretariat, A38.

7. See Eberhard Schulz, "New Developments in Intra-bloc Relations in Historical Perspective," in Karen Dawisha and Philip Hanson, eds., *Soviet-East European Dilemmas: Coercion, Competition, and Consent*, 41–60 (London: Heinemann Educational Books, 1981) p. 55; and Hansjakob Stehle, *The Independent Satellite: Society and Politics in Poland since 1945* (London: Pall Mall Press, 1965), p. 222.

8. Naszkowski notes of meeting Biernow on September 18, September 19, 1957, MSZ, 23/163/14.

9. See Franz Sikora, *Sozialistische Solidarität und nationale Interessen* (Socialist solidarity and national interests) (Cologne: Verlag Wissenschaft und Politik, 1977), pp. 151–152.

10. Mieczysław Rakowski, *The Foreign Policy of the Polish People's Republic* (Warsaw: Interpress Publishers, 1975), p. 164.

11. Kopa notes of a meeting with Beling on October 11, October 16, 1957, MSZ, 10/379/42.

12. *Neues Deutschland*, October 6, 1957, p. 1.

13. *Neues Deutschland*, October 13, 1957, p. 1.

14. Polish Foreign Ministry report on the GDR press, undated, ca. February 1958, MSZ, 10/464/48; see David Stefancic, "The Rapacki Plan: A Case Study of East European Diplomacy," *East European Quarterly* 21, no. 4 (January 1988), p. 404. Stefancic claims that Ulbricht approved of the Polish proposal at the summit with Gomułka in June 1957. Even if this is true, the Poles were disappointed with the East German reaction thereafter.

15. Horst Grunert, *Für Honecker auf glattem Parkett: Erinnerungen eines DDR-Diplomaten* (For Honecker on the smooth parquet: Memoirs of a GDR diplomat) (Berlin: Edition Ost, 1995), p. 118.

16. Douglas Selvage, "Introduction" to "Khrushchev's November 1958 Berlin Ultimatum: New Evidence from the Polish Archives," *Bulletin: Cold War International History Project*, no. 11 (winter 1998), p. 200.

17. Hegen notes of a meeting with Rapacki on December 10, December 11, 1957, SED ZK, Otto Grotewohl Papers, NL 90/485.

18. Memorandum of a meeting with Koudela, Tomasek, and Cerny (Czechoslovak Embassy diplomats), unsigned, October 10, 1957, DDR MfAA, Warsaw Embassy, A3771.

19. Łobodycz notes of meeting with Koudela (Czechoslovak Embassy) on October 9, October 10, 1957, MSZ, 10/380/42.

20. Report on the political development in the Soviet zone of Germany in December, 1957, BRD BfGDF, B137/1473.

21. Report on the political development in the Soviet zone of Germany from January 1, 1958, to February 28, 1958, BRD BfGDF, B137/1473; see also James G. Richter, *Khrushchev's Double Bind: International Pressures and Domestic Coalition Politics* (Baltimore: Johns Hopkins Press, 1994), p. 114. Richter writes that Moscow lobbied hard for the Rapacki Plan by announcing troop reductions and a moratorium on nuclear testing.

22. Report on the political development in the Soviet zone of Germany, November, 1957, BRD BfGDF, B137/1473.

23. Polish Embassy report from November 1, 1957 to February 28, 1958, MSZ, 10/371/41.

24. Piotrowski to Łobodzycz, January 2, 1958, MSZ, 10/371/41.

25. Polish Foreign Ministry report on the GDR press, undated, ca. December, 1958, MSZ, 10/464/48.

26. Karl Krahn to Hermann Axen, February 17, 1958, SED ZK, microfilm FBS 339/13489.

27. Polish Embassy report from November 1, 1957 to February 28, 1958, MSZ, 10/371/41.

28. Quoted in Hansjakob Stehle, *The Independent Satellite: Society and Politics in Poland Since 1945* (London: Pall Mall Press, 1965), p. 227.

29. Record of negotiations between Piotr Ogrodziński and Piotrowski, et al., and Handke and Winzer, et al., February 7–8, 1958, DDR MfAA, HA/I Secretariat, A14759; and Polish Embassy political report from September 1, 1957 to February 28, 1958, March 11, 1958, MSZ, 10/371/41.

30. Sweden relayed a memorandum on the Rapacki Plan to the FRG.

31. Peter Bender, *East Europe in Search of Security* (London: Chatto and Windus, 1972), p. 14, footnote 5.

32. Polish Foreign Ministry memorandum to its diplomatic corps, March 5, 1958, MSZ, 23/163/14.

33. Polish Foreign Ministry memorandum to its diplomatic corps, February 8, 1958, MSZ, 23/163/14; and Polish Foreign Ministry memorandum to its diplomatic corps, March 5, 1958, MSZ, 23/163/14.

34. Naszkowski notes of meeting with Carlo Schmid on March 11, March 12, 1958, MSZ, 23/163/14.

35. Ogrodziński memorandum, undated, ca. March, 1958, MSZ, 23/163/14.

36. Protocol of the Conference of Foreign Ministers of the GDR, Poland, and Czechoslovakia, April 12, 1958, DDR MfAA, MB Schwab, A17275.

37. Piotrowski to Łobodycz, April 18, 1958, MSZ, 10/333/37.

38. Polish Foreign Ministry report on the GDR press, undated, ca. December, 1958, MSZ, 10/464/48.

39. GDR Embassy in Warsaw to the Foreign Ministry, September 18, 1958, DDR MfAA, Warsaw Embassy, A3751.

40. SED district office in Frankfurt/Oder to the SED, December 12, 1958, DDR MfAA, HA/I Secretariat, A3821.

41. Riesner report on the Ninth Party Congress of the PZPR, October 22, 1958, SED ZK, microfilm FBS 339/13490.

42. Memo on the situation in the PZPR, unsigned, undated, ca. December, 1958, SED ZK, microfilm FBS 339/13424.

43. Notes on the FRG visa bureaus in Warsaw, November 30, 1958, DDR MfAA, Department of Neighboring Countries, C781/73, ZR/1892/73.

44. GDR Embassy in Warsaw to the GDR Foreign Ministry, unsigned, April 2, 1958, DDR MfAA, Warsaw Embassy, A3771.

45. Polish Embassy report from November 1, 1957 to February 28, 1958, MSZ, 10/371/41.

46. Wolfgang Schneider to Hans Globke, April 30, 1958, BRD BKA, B136/6717.

47. Günther Wirth notes on the Trinitatis dedication, July 10, 1958, SED ZK, Department of Church Questions, IV 2/14/89.

48. Polish Embassy report from November 1, 1957 to February 28, 1958, MSZ, 10/371/41.

49. Kirschey (chief of the Wrocław consulate) notes on visits with Poles in Szczecin, Koszalin, and Poznań, May 12–16, 1958, SED ZK, microfilm FBS 339/12495.

50. Riesner (Warsaw Embassy) to the GDR Foreign Ministry, September 25, 1958, DDR MfAA, Warsaw Embassy, A3751.

51. Weit, *Ostblock intern*, pp. 33–34.

52. Riesner to the GDR Foreign Ministry, September 25, 1958, DDR MfAA, Warsaw Embassy, A3751.

53. Record of the negotiations between Ogrodziński and Winzer, et al., October 15, 1958, DDR MfAA, HA/I Secretariat, A14759.

54. Hegen notes of meeting with Czesak on September 24, September 25, 1958, SED ZK, microfilm FBS 339/13489.

55. Winzer to Ulbricht, October 25, 1958, SED ZK, Walter Ulbricht Papers, NL 182/1250.

56. See Stefancic, "The Rapacki Plan: A Case Study of East European Diplomacy," p. 409.

57. See Trachtenberg, *A Constructed Peace*, pp. 247, 251.

58. Selvage, "Khrushchev's November 1958 Berlin Ultimatum: New Evidence from the Polish Archives," p. 200.

59. See Trachtenberg, *A Constructed Peace*, pp. 261–263; and Henry Kissinger, *Diplomacy* (New York: Simon and Schuster, 1994), p. 578–579. According to Kissinger, in January 1959, Dulles hinted at possible unification through confederation, but Adenauer rejected it as "totally unacceptable."

60. See Trachtenberg, *A Constructed Peace*, p. 261.

61. Translation of an article by W. A. Zbyszewski in *Wiadomości* (News), November 23, 1958, in BRD BKA, B136/6485.

62. Winzer to Ulbricht, February 12, 1959, SED ZK, Walter Ulbricht Papers, NL 182/1250.

63. Stehle, *The Independent Satellite*, p. 220. Gomułka remarked in 1961 that "if it had been adopted, many subsequent developments could have been avoided."

64. Polish Embassy report from September 1, 1957 to February 28, 1958, MSZ, 10/371/41; and Piotrowski to Łobodycz, March 11, 1958, MSZ, 10/371/41. East

Germany was supplying approximately 40 percent of Poland's consumer goods, and at this time Poland was still second only to the Soviet Union as the GDR's most important trade partner in the Warsaw Pact.

65. Jakubowski notes of meeting with Bringmann (GDR Foreign Ministry) on December 24, December 27, 1957, MSZ, 10/379/42. East Germany had few problems trading with Czechoslovakia, as East German officials frequently reminded the Poles.

66. Notes on the development of the GDR economy, 1958–1960 and 1961–1965, April 22, 1958, SED ZK, Walter Ulbricht Office, J IV 2/202–194.

67. Melvin Croan, "Germany and Eastern Europe," in Joseph Held, ed., *The Columbia History of Eastern Europe in the Twentieth Century* (New York: Columbia University Press, 1992), p. 362.

68. Leuschner to Grotewohl, May 17, 1957, SED ZK, Otto Grotewohl Papers, NL 90/478.

69. Ulbricht to Khrushchev, May 13, 1958, SED ZK, Walter Ulbricht Office, J IV 2/202–196; see Richter, *Khrushchev's Double Bind*, p. 116.

70. Report on the Comecon meeting in Moscow from May 20–24, 1958, PZPR KC, 237/V–281.

71. Ulbricht to Gomułka, May 29, 1958, SED ZK, microfilm FBS 339/13489.

72. Gomułka to Ulbricht, June 13, 1958, SED ZK, microfilm FBS 339/13489.

73. Piotrowski to Łobodycz, June 13, 1958, MSZ, 10/385/42.

74. Ulbricht to Gomułka, May 29, 1958, SED ZK, microfilm FBS 339/13489; and Protocol on the meetings of SED and PZPR Central Committee delegations on June 18–20, 1958, SED ZK, microfilm FBS 339/13489.

75. Notes on the protocol of the meeting between the GDR, USSR, and Poland, on military transit on Polish railways, June 19, 1958, DDR MfAA, Law and Treaty Department, A5972.

76. Reasons for the SED Politburo's refusal on February 25, 1958 of the treaty with Bulgaria, Hungary, Poland, Czechoslovakia, and Romania (signed in Warsaw on November 7, 1957), by Otto Winzer, DDR MfAA, Law and Treaty Department, A5972.

77. Ulbricht to PZPR Central Committee, September 30, 1958, PZPR KC, 237/XXII/824.

78. Heyl (SED Frankfurt/Oder office) notes on exchanges with the PZPR office in Zielona Góra, December 1, 1958, DDR MfAA, HA/I Secretariat, A3821.

79. Pucher (SED Frankfurt/Oder office) to Günter Schmidt (SED Frankfurt/Oder Office), December 1, 1958, DDR MfAA, HA/I Secretariat, A3821.

80. GDR Embassy Department of Economic Policy annual report for 1958 (by Lugenheim), February 19, 1959, SED ZK, microfilm FBS 339/12495; see also Von Sechow (FRG Embassy in Copenhagen) to the FRG Foreign Ministry, September 17, 1959, BRD AA, Department 7, vol. 438. Denmark was one of Poland's most reliable customers; the value of Poland's exports to Denmark jumped almost 35 percent from 1957 to 1958, while Danish imports increased over 180 percent.

81. SED report on the situation in the PZPR, unsigned, undated, ca. December 1958, SED ZK, microfilm FBS 339/13424; and notes on GDR-Polish economic relations, November 30, 1958, DDR MfAA, Department of Neighboring Countries, C781/73, ZR/1892/73.

82. Polish Foreign Ministry report on relations between Poland and the GDR, unsigned, undated, ca. December, 1958, MSZ, 10/464/48. Polish coal was used mainly to fuel electric power plants in West Berlin. In 1957, Poland's trade with West Berlin was worth 6 million rubles.

83. Weit, *Ostblock intern*, pp. 33–34.

84. Gomułka to the SED Politburo, September 18, 1958, SED ZK, Walter Ulbricht Papers, NL 182/1244. The Poles had agreed to ship 300,000 tons of coal to West Berlin, but only 100,000 had been sent.

85. Polish Foreign Ministry report on relations between Poland and the GDR, unsigned, undated, ca. December 1958, MSZ, 10/464/48.

86. GDR Embassy report on Poland (by H. J. Müller), November 29, 1958, SED ZK, microfilm FBS 339/12495.

87. Analysis of the Polish-East German negotiations from October 16–24 in Warsaw, October 28, 1958, DDR MfAA, Minister's Office, A10089.

11

The Right Road to Socialism and Ulbricht's Visit to Poland, 1958–1959

Won't your sons, who will serve in the army some day, turn their weapons around and want to reconquer the former German territories?

—**Polish visitor to the "East Sea Week" in the GDR, July 1958**[1]

In 1958, an atmosphere of distrust still permeated Polish-East German relations at all levels.[2] Since Gomułka's return to power in 1956, the PZPR and the SED had sparred over the meaning of national communism, cultural exchanges, tourist traffic, collectivisation, and church policy. The SED contrasted the GDR's relatively smooth-running economy and stable political system with the Poland's persistent political and economic difficulties; to Ulbricht the soundness of the SED's orthodox Leninist-Stalinist policies was self-evident. At a reception at the Polish Embassy in January 1958, Ulbricht defended the SED's tight control over all aspects of East German society: "When one has a strong police then it is possible to talk about building socialism." It was a not-so-subtle hint for the PZPR to crack down on dissidents and Stalinize its economy.[3]

At the end of February 1958, the Polish Embassy observed that most East German party and government officials still did not trust the Gomułka government:

One can clearly see a double-track [policy] in relation to Poland. For domestic purposes the SED has long had a prejudice against Poland. The lower party apparatus frequently expresses the opinion that the [June 1957] talks between Polish and German party and government [officials] yielded no result, that un-socialistic policies are still practiced in Poland, [and] in regards to the Polish countryside, [Poles are] plainly hostile [to socialism]. One hears the opinion [in the SED] that the people of Poland have less and less trust in the PZPR and W. Gomułka.[4]

When the editor of *Trybuna Ludu* asked East German journalist Karl Krahn if the SED leadership really believed in the class struggle, Krahn concluded that the Polish communists had simply given up on the principles of socialism, and were nothing but opportunists.[5]

East German diplomats in Moscow eagerly reported any signs that the Kremlin was having second thoughts about the Gomułka régime. In the fall of 1958, a Soviet Foreign Ministry official told the East Germans that Jews held most of the leadership positions in the Polish Foreign Ministry and in many other state and party bureaucracies as well. He complained that the PZPR had dismissed too many "progressive and loyal officers" from the Polish army and that they were being replaced by officers loyal to the anti-communist Polish government-in-exile in London.[6]

East German Ambassador Josef Hegen called the PZPR's efforts to purge revisionists a "complete failure"[7] in his unrelenting criticism of the party's ideological inconsistency. Hegen dutifully reported statements by Polish officials that hinted of revisionism, opportunism, or criticism of the SED's policies. During a reception at the Soviet Embassy in Warsaw in March, Zenon Kliszko said that the Polish "national communists" who were in Poland during World War II (i.e., Gomułka's wing of the PZPR) had a better idea of how to rule Poland than Soviet-backed "dogmatists." Hegen took this as a direct attack on the Ulbricht régime. He reported that several times Gomułka had tried to shut Kliszko up, telling the gathering not to take Kliszko seriously because he was "completely drunk." Nonetheless, Hegen concluded that the conservative wing of the party was being marginalized.[8]

The East Germans tried again and again to convince the PZPR leadership to coordinate its political and economic policies along Marxist-Leninist lines—the SED's way. They considered the measures the PZPR adopted to curb revisionism too weak. After the Eleventh Plenary Session of the PZPR Central Committee in March, the East German Embassy reported that head of the planning commission, Stefan Jędrychowski, had ignored "clear Marxist-Leninist conceptions" in his economic plan.[9] East German diplomat Ruth Wenk wrote that the Central Committee had briefly mentioned some of the serious deficiencies in socialist development in Poland, but had not proposed consistent policies to chart a new course.[10] The East Germans leveled some of the same criticisms at the PZPR after the Ninth Party Congress in October.[11] According to West German officials, relations were still "quite cool."[12]

Cultural Relations Remain Frozen

Since the mid-1950s, the Ulbricht régime had strictly circumscribed exchanges with Poland to prevent political unrest in the GDR. The SED district offices filed so many disturbing reports in 1958 about the Poles' political unreliability that the policy remained unchanged. The Frankfurt/Oder office reported that the PZPR was reluctant to push Marxist-Leninist propaganda on workers because all they wanted a better standard of living. East German officials contrasted the poor living conditions of Polish workers with the ostentatious receptions the PZPR threw for foreign delegations.[13] Party functionaries from Cottbus complained that their Polish counterparts avoided political or ideological discussions on the leading role of the Soviet Union in the socialist camp, the significance of the GDR for German reunification, and the dictatorship of the proletariat; the Poles just wanted to talk about improving their economy. The Cottbus office also found that the Polish comrades' excessive hospitality did not reflect the "real living conditions of the Polish people."[14]

The East German Embassy in Warsaw filed numerous reports criticizing the PZPR's weak attempts to purge the party of nationalists, clergymen, revisionists, and anti-Soviets. According to the East Germans, the party's lack of a clear and consistent ideology and method of verifying members had resulted in a completely unsatisfactory character of the party membership; only 37.8 percent of the PZPR members were workers in 1958, compared with 47 percent in 1949. East German diplomats were incredulous that the PZPR leaders were unconcerned about this trend.[15]

The SED viewed the PZPR's efforts to indoctrinate Polish youth as inadequate.[16] The party reported that Polish schools were notably delinquent in promoting "the leading role of the party and the theory of class struggle."[17] East German officials warned of "bourgeois-revisionist manifestations" in Polish culture and higher education, an example being the continuation of religious instruction in schools; the SED even alleged that children of atheists faced psychological pressure and physical punishment if they chose not to participate in these classes.[18] According to East German diplomats, Polish students still had no respect for Polish professors holding Marxist-Leninist beliefs; the students often branded them as Stalinists and sometimes assaulted them physically.[19]

In the eyes of the East German communists, the PZPR's permissive cultural policies were a critical loophole in Polish socialism. The East Germans were genuinely surprised by the PZPR's lack of consistent guidelines for artists, whom the East Germans accused of producing too many works reflecting "bourgeois culture." According to one East German source, many Polish writers and intellectuals had left the PZPR in 1957, but those who remained were still allowed to propagate un-Marxist and bourgeois-capitalist ideas.[20] In one case, the East German Foreign Ministry criticized a Polish opera company for portraying "Emilia Galotti" as "a general human problem" rather than "the class struggle of the upwardly striving bourgeoisie against feudal domination." The ministry faulted Polish officials for separating art from economic and political affairs, and for allowing artists to gain their inspiration from the West; for example, one Polish theater critic said that the main objective of art was to "bring the beautiful and the humane" to the people. Much to the concern of the SED hard-liners, he made no reference to the accepted norm of Soviet art—socialist realism.[21]

The Polish authorities ignored the SED's warnings about such "decadent art." Polish officials argued that if the press criticized these artists and the party suppressed their work, the people would transform them into heroes and martyrs.[22] The Poles also showed little interest in the East Germans' drab, predictable, dogmatic art and literature. The East Germans opened the "House of GDR Culture" in Warsaw in August 1957, but, according to a West German source, few Poles visited the center despite the East German Embassy's energetic efforts to promote it.[23] Although the East Germans made numerous offers, Polish authorities were reluctant to use East German literature and films, especially propaganda films about the dangers of West German imperialism. The Poles did purchase one East German film, but cut all scenes showing the East German army.[24]

From 1956 to 1959, Poland had only 12 government-sponsored exchanges with the GDR. Poland conducted 189 exchanges with France, 97 with Great Britain, and 110 with the Soviet Union. Even Bulgaria (27) had more exchanges with Poland. All of Poland's exchanges with the GDR were in the technical, agricultural, scientific, or medical fields, but none in the more politically sensitive areas of language, humanities, and art. In contrast, almost all the French and British exchanges fell into the last three categories.[25] The Polish Foreign Ministry paid no attention to East Berlin's complaints about Poland's budding cultural exchanges with West Germany.[26]

In late 1958, the SED indicated a willingness to expand cultural ties with Poland, but only if they were strictly regulated. The party proposed to resurrect the German-Polish "Friendship Week" as a way to inculcate the Polish communists with the SED's brand of socialism.[27] The PZPR agreed, but the Polish communists still thought that spontaneous exchanges of delegations and citizens were a better way to encourage genuine friendships.[28]

The Poles were right. The positive effects of the official cultural exchanges were ephemeral, and many exchanges confirmed old prejudices. During the "East Sea Week" in Rostock in July, for example, the SED's district office reported that whenever party members tried to discuss socialist development with the Polish delegation, the Poles "felt insulted and emphasized that they had very deep national feelings." The delegation rejected an East German proposal for a joint declaration stressing class conflict, the role of the working class in building socialism, or the struggle against anti-Soviet attitudes. The East Germans said that Tito's Yugoslavia served as a model for the Poles, not the Soviet Union.[29]

One woman in the Polish delegation told the East Germans that she could not speak her mind while in the GDR, but in Poland she would tell them her honest opinion of the Soviets. Other Polish visitors alleged that the Soviet Union was granting East Germany substantial economic aid, yet exploited Poland as though it were a colony. Several Polish students characterized the GDR as "a complete dictatorship," and proudly defended the freedoms they enjoyed in Poland. One Polish student commented that there were too many workers in the East German Parliament: "One cannot govern a country with workers, because in their stupidity they would agree to every decision." Rostock officials also complained that the Polish athletes at the festival were trying to make connections with West Germans; Polish officials had even allowed their yachtsmen to attend a party aboard a West German sailboat.[30]

One East German journalist at the East Sea Week was genuinely surprised by the Poles' deep mistrust of Soviets and East Germans. One Pole asked him, "Won't your sons, who will serve in the army some day, turn their weapons around and want to reconquer the former German territories?" Another Pole told him that "the Soviet Union once had great influence in Poland, but once Stalin was six feet under, it doesn't have any more." The Rostock office considered it their duty to inform the PZPR leadership of these "revisionist manifestations," although the Polish authorities took them less seriously.[31] One Polish politician observed that the festival had created as much enmity as good will.[32]

Other official exchanges in 1958 yielded similar results. Polish visitors to the GDR continued to make disparaging remarks about the Soviet Union and Ulbricht, and persisted in their efforts to make connections to West Germany. The East Germans repeatedly chastised the Poles for conducting cultural events that catered to West European artists.[33] Responding to the visit of Polish engineers to a power plant in Leipzig that fall, one SED functionary commented that "it is incomprehensible to me that socialist countries delegate such un-political people to a friendly socialist state." He added that this delegation would not contribute to "building socialism in the world."[34]

The SED Criticizes PZPR Church Policy

The SED had no confidence in Gomułka's resolve to check the power of the Polish Catholic Church. Organized religion in the GDR fell under the strict control of the East German authorities; they knew that a rival ideology would inevitably undermine socialist beliefs. The régime's compromise with the Evangelical Church in the GDR was a tactical and temporary retreat before the eventual victory of socialism. The East Germans repeatedly alerted Polish officials to the dangers of religious freedom, and to the "reactionary activity" of the West German Catholic Church.[35] The East German Embassy warned that the Polish Catholic Front (PAX) in the Polish Parliament was opposed to socialism and rejected the class struggle as a foundation for state policy.[36]

When Gomułka began to crack down on the independence of the Church in 1958,[37] the East Germans took some credit for it. Willi Barth, the head of the SED's Department of Church Questions, reported that he had "the impression that the [Polish] comrades attach great importance to the experiences of our party in the ideological struggle against political clericalism." The Polish authorities agreed to coordinate their efforts to counteract the agitation of the West German churches in Poland,[38] but a year later the East Germans alleged that West German agents were the inspiration for a demonstration by Catholic priests in Zielona Góra. In their denial, the Poles shrugged off the accusation that these incidents were the result of the PZPR's inconsistent church policies.[39]

After the Twelfth Plenum of the PZPR Central Committee in the fall of 1958, the East German Embassy again expressed disappointment with the party's feeble attempts to reduce the power of the Catholic Church. According to East German diplomats, the ZSL, in alliance with Polish "clerics, kulaks, and reactionaries," had secured its political influence in the countryside.[40] Blinded by their own ideological zeal, the East Germans ignored the deep roots of Catholicism in Poland and advised the PZPR Central Committee to purge the party of all churchgoers.[41]

East German officials were even more concerned about the links between the small Lutheran Church in Poland and the German Lutheran Church. In April 1958, Barth reported that the president of the Polish Lutheran Church, Reverend Michaelis, had recently visited West Germany without contacting the so-called "progressive representatives of the churches in the GDR."[42] The SED's Department of Church Questions alerted the SED leadership that Michaelis wanted to develop ties between the German and Polish Protestants as a means to draw the two countries together. The East Germans were also critical of the financial assistance afforded the Polish Protestant churches by congregations in Europe and the United States.[43] They were even suspicious of the relief packages that the Catholic and Lutheran Churches in West Germany were sending Polish congregations; the East Germans saw this as part of a coordinated effort to subvert the socialist states.[44]

That summer, Michaelis invited church leaders from West Germany, the United States, and other Western countries to the dedication of the

Trinitatis Church in Warsaw. Michaelis also invited two clergymen from West Berlin, but Barth protested that they intended to agitate among the Germans in Poland to show their solidarity with "Christians from the German homeland." The issue appeared to have resolved itself when the Polish Embassy in Berlin refused to grant visas to the West Berliners on the grounds that Michaelis had not followed proper application procedures.[45] Nonetheless, Florin sent a letter to the PZPR protesting the invitations. He called the West Berlin clergymen "representatives of the NATO-wing [sic] in the Evangelical Church hierarchy."[46]

Leaders from the World Council of Churches and Lutheran World Federation were among those invited to the dedication. Barth gave the Poles this warning: "The goal of the appearance of these reactionary men of the World Council of Churches is . . . to undermine the policies of the peoples' democracies and of the GDR in particular. As is known the World Council of Churches takes the position that there is only one German state, namely the German Federal Republic."[47] After the dedication ceremonies on June 22, the SED chastised Michaelis and the Bishop of Hanover, Hans Lilje, for making statements critical of the GDR. Lilje had also contrasted the Poles' hospitality with the cool receptions he had previously received from East German officials: "How exquisitely I have been received *here*!"[48]

The December Summit

In the weeks leading up to Ulbricht's trip to Warsaw in December, the SED began to see some positive political and economic developments in Poland. Although East Germany had recently slipped from Poland's second-largest to its third-largest trading partner, the SED predicted that the volume of trade between the two countries would increase 11 percent from 1957 to 1958. The East Germans were gratified that the Poles had recently named four enterprises and schools after Wilhelm Pieck. The SED also noted that the government was removing the crucifixes that had reappeared in schools in 1956.[49]

The East Germans were encouraged by a subtle shift in Poland's policy toward West Germany. In November 1958, the Polish Foreign Ministry began to restrict the number of visas for student delegations going to the FRG; the SED interpreted this as a significant policy reversal.[50] The East German press reported that the PZPR was publishing more complete information about the GDR, and was silencing revisionism in the party.[51] The SED district office in Frankfurt/Oder wrote an unusually positive report on relations with the PZPR office in Zielona Góra, commenting that their Polish comrades now were more receptive to advice on the right way to build socialism.[52]

Some Polish officials also thought that relations had taken a turn for the better, especially in the economic sphere. Polish diplomats were pleased with the terms of a new trade agreement signed in February, and with the increased volume of East German goods handled by Polish ports and merchant ships.[53] In a briefing prepared for the meetings in December, the Polish Foreign Ministry applauded the convergence of the two countries' foreign policy objectives that had taken place since the last high-level meetings in June 1957; it cited as evidence several new economic and cultural agreements that the two countries had signed in the last year and a half.[54]

These reports noted unresolved issues, however. The Poles viewed the GDR's recent suspension of Polish exports to West Berlin not only as a political decision but as an attempt to eliminate Polish competition for West Berlin markets. The embassy also pointed out that the East Germans had chosen closer economic relations with Czechoslovakia rather than with what the East Germans referred to as "the unreliable Polish partner."[55] The Polish Foreign Ministry filed several reports contrasting the East German journalists' extensive coverage of the Soviet Union and Czechoslovakia with their indifference to Poland's political and economic developments. The Poles also suspected that the East German press seldom mentioned the Oder-Neisse border because the SED, in anticipation of a breakthrough on Germany reunification, was rethinking its recognition of the border. Polish officials were angered by the East German practice of censoring all speeches, articles, and other information sent from Poland; they thought the average East German was receiving a "one-sided" and "warped sense" of what was going on in the country.[56]

Before the December meetings, the Polish Foreign Ministry confirmed its opposition to trilateral Czechoslovak-East German-Polish initiatives directed against the West. The ministry also reiterated its objections to bilateral agreements with East Germany that compromised Poland's national interests. The ministry recommended periodic consultations with the East Germans about Poland's relations with West Germany, but left no doubts that policy would be made in Warsaw, not in East Berlin.[57]

Shortly before summit, Ambassador Hegen wrote Winzer that Polish officials wanted to avoid taking the East German delegation to a collective farm, probably because the SED had attacked the PZPR so often for its "bourgeois" agricultural policies. Hegen added that the Poles intended to show the East Germans a Polish port in hopes that Ulbricht would rethink his decision to expand Rostock harbor.[58] The Poles had first voiced their opposition to the expansion of the harbor during the Ulbricht-Gomułka summit over a year earlier. In late November, Polish trade officials told the East Germans that Rostock was a direct competitor to the Polish ports of Szczecin, Gdańsk, and Gdynia, harbors the Polish government had just enlarged at great expense. They maintained that only 40 percent of these harbors' capacity was being used.[59] Jędrychowski questioned the high cost of expanding Rostock's harbor and argued that the East Germans could use the money saved to develop such industries as the East German chemical industry. The head of the PZPR's Gdańsk office said that the Polish harbors should dominate the Baltic seaboard, but added this indelicate caveat: "In this question the PRP must avoid kicking the socialist brother countries in the behind." The East German Foreign Ministry characterized this official as an "outspoken revisionist who frequently expressed his antipathy for the Soviet Union. Today he is still a propagandist of October 1956."[60]

The East Germans planned to confront Gomułka about reducing the cost of transporting goods through Poland to the Soviet Union. During trade talks in November, East German negotiators scolded the Poles for requesting 350 million rubles annually for this transit. The East Germans would have to increase exports to Poland to cover these costs, an action they were not prepared to take. The Poles ignored appeals to expand the capacity of Polish inland waterways; the East German Foreign Ministry suspected that the Poles were making more money on rail transit and wanted to keep it that way.[61]

Ulbricht and Grotewohl led the East German delegation to Warsaw. As usual, the East Germans included workers and farmers in an effort present the SED as the true representative of the working classes. The Polish delegation had none. Gomułka's translator, Erwin Weit, remembered that "right from the start Ulbricht, with his wooden vocabulary, set himself up as the school master."[62]

Economic cooperation took center stage. In an exchange that had repeated itself many times before, the Poles rejected Ulbricht's argument that the GDR was, in his words, the "shop window of socialism" to West Germany, and therefore deserved special trade concessions. Gomułka pointed out that the Polish economy was having difficulty because of a recent fall in coal prices. When the Poles pressed Ulbricht to allow more Polish exports to West Berlin, he replied that the Khrushchev's ultimatum on Berlin would soon resolve that issue.[63]

Once again, the Poles complained about the treatment of Polish visitors to the GDR and the persistent harassment Poles suffered when traveling through East Germany to Western Europe. Earlier in the year, East German border guards had confiscated some West German brochures on home building and machinery from an SD functionary; the guards admonished, "What do you have this for; would you like to have another October in Poland again?" Polish officials maintained that the brochures contained nothing controversial and could easily be obtained by mail. They said it was natural for Poles to compare West German border guards' friendly treatment with this kind of harassment by the East Germans.[64]

Some Poles had to wait up to five months for visas to East Germany, if they got them at all. Polish officials pointed out that it was easier for a Pole to obtain a visa to West Germany than to the GDR. Ulbricht and Bolz tried to conceal the real basis for this policy, which was intended to limit contacts between East Germans and Poles, and Poles and Westerners. They would admit only that some bureaucratic mistakes had been made. Cyrankiewicz responded that Poles faced the same travel restrictions as Westerners. He said that Poles could not comprehend why a supposedly friendly socialist country conducted such a policy. Cyrankiewicz also hinted that the East German authorities used visa restrictions on Western travelers through the GDR to limit the success of the Poznań Trade Fair; he pointed out that Westerners had no problems obtaining visas for the Leipzig Trade Fair.[65]

Ulbricht denied it. He said that the strict visa controls on Westerners were imperative because NATO agents were trying to spy on the GDR; East German security forces wanted Poles and Westerners to travel by train so that they could be more carefully watched. A frustrated Cyrankiewicz concluded that it was a good thing the Poznań fair took place in June; the two sides still had time to resolve the problem.[66]

When Cyrankiewicz and Gomułka complained that the East German authorities were harassing Polish truck traffic as well, Ulbricht angrily replied that if Poland would support his policies toward West Germany and West Berlin, all these problems would be solved. Ulbricht then warned the Poles against cultivating ties to the SPD, especially to Wehner, whom he called a leading revisionist. Gomułka retorted that "for us Wehner is no problem at all," and that if it was in Poland's interest to pursue Wehner and other Social Democrats, he would do it.[67]

Ulbricht's public appearances in Poland that December did not resonate with the Polish people. In a speech to the workers at the "Rosa Luxemburg" light bulb factory in Warsaw, Ulbricht boasted of the GDR's enormous economic progress in the past few years. Given East German workers' higher standard of living, this was not what Polish laborers wanted to hear. Ulbricht also made a pointed reference to the SED's allegedly successful collectivization program, implying that the PZPR's agricultural policy not only was unsuccessful but was un-Marxist: "The higher growth rate of production in the collective farms proves their superiority and attests to the rightness of the Socialist Unity Party's struggle against opportunistic and revisionist conceptions about the development of agriculture in the transition period from capitalism to socialism." Ulbricht praised the PZPR's recent efforts to increase production in the collectives, and encouraged the party to continue the policy.[68]

The debate over the final joint communiqué was as contentious as it had been at the Berlin summit a year and a half earlier. As always, the East Germans wanted to lavish praise on the Soviet Union, proclaim the superiority of collectivized agriculture, criticize the churches, attack West German militarism and imperialism, and issue a warning that the FRG was planning to attack the GDR. The Poles agreed only to general statements about the development of socialism in East Germany and Poland's support for some sort of German confederation. Gomułka refused to issue a joint statement warning of an imminent West German attack.[69] Ulbricht was reduced to slipping this line into a toast at the reception following the talks: "The aggressive plans of German militarism show that peace for the Polish people and the defense of the Oder-Neisse border is guaranteed only by the struggle with German imperialism."[70] Weit later gave this frank appraisal of the meetings: "Ulbricht and Gomułka had serious differences."[71]

The Polish press maintained that, in contrast to the coverage of other meetings between Polish and East German officials in the past few years, this one was more productive. *Trybuna Ludu* declared that the meetings had "punched a wide breach in the wall of distrust." According to an East German source, Polish press releases on the summit "reflect the positive results of the visit. The most important tenor of their content is undoubtedly the perception that on the essential questions complete agreement existed between the GDR delegation and the Polish people."[72] The Polish Embassy in Berlin reported that "the visit and the atmosphere in which it unfolded will be treated by the [East German] populace as a manifestation of the coming together of the PRP and the GDR and the thawing of what was essentially an 'embargo' of the Polish problem that existed up till now."[73]

The Polish Foreign Ministry noted that the East German press was now refraining from "harsh polemics" and "critical opinions of particular aspects of evolutionary process in Poland."[74] At the beginning of 1959, the East German diplomats in Warsaw saw some encouraging signs that the PZPR was adopting policies consistent with the East German version of socialism. They concluded that their lobbying efforts were at last bearing fruit.[75]

No Consensus on Germany or the Border

Although the December summit appeared to have begun a reconciliation between the two communist leaders, this second meeting with Gomułka failed to change Ulbricht's doubts about the reliability of the PZPR, more so in regard to the German question. Ulbricht's agents warned him that Polish diplomats and journalists were still sending Warsaw "unreliable" and "misleading" reports about the GDR.[76]

With time running out on Khrushchev's six-month Berlin ultimatum, tensions between the West and the Soviet Union remained high in early 1959. The SED refused to countenance Polish interference in this issue; the party had ample evidence that Warsaw was disregarding East German interests in West Germany and West Berlin. Despite repeated protests from the East German government, the Polish Military Mission in West Berlin continued to refer to that half of the city as part of the FRG.[77] Polish diplomat Ludwik Gronowski had the temerity to ask Heymann whether Ulbricht's unpopularity was causing so many East Germans to leave the GDR through West Berlin. Heymann replied that the number of West Germans coming to the GDR was about equal to the number of East Germans leaving for the FRG, an assertion that was patently untrue.[78] Relations were still so fragile in 1959 that the Polish Foreign Ministry reprimanded Gronowski for posing the question, and advised its diplomats not to mention the embarrassing exodus of East Germans.[79]

The East Germans remained highly sensitive about being treated as the junior German state.[80] That spring, Grotewohl wrote Cyrankiewicz protesting *Trybuna Ludu*'s designation of the East German representatives to the Geneva Conference of Foreign Ministers as a "consultative group" rather than a "government delegation."[81] Polish officials were equally perturbed about the East Germans' persistent references to the GDR as "Middle Germany," as though Poland's Western Territories constituted "East Germany." In May, Piotrowski wrote Łobodycz that, according to *Neues Deutschland*, Ulbricht himself had recently used the expression.[82] At first, Heymann told Polish diplomat Leon Szybek that the newspaper's report was an editorial error, and that he was "surprised and perplexed" by the mix-up. But when Szybek later showed him a copy of the speech, Heymann tried to explain that Ulbricht was referring to a workers' revolt near Halle in the 1920s that had been called the "middle German uprising."[83] The Poles remained unconvinced. The Polish Foreign Ministry advised Piotrowski to inform the East German Foreign Ministry that Polish public opinion was strongly opposed to the term.[84]

Polish officials suspected that the SED referred to the GDR as "Middle Germany" to pander to the East German settlers from Poland; these émigrés still expected to recover their land. A functionary in the SED's propaganda section, Horst Heinrich, told Polish diplomat Stanisław Kopa that "the view is rather widespread of the necessity to revise the border drawn in the Potsdam agreement. . . . Recognition of the right of Germans to return to these areas is justified mainly by the difficulties Poland has had in administering them."[85] The SED felt pressured by the constant West German propaganda calling for a revision of the Oder-Neisse border. The party's one indirect way of questioning the border was to reject historical justification for Poland's acquisition of the territories.[86] East German journalists told Polish diplomat Janusz Rachocki that they knew Poland had controlled the area in the Middle Ages, but that they refrained from talking about it for fear of evoking anti-Soviet sentiments among the German émigrés from Poland. Rachocki reported that East German educators sometimes taught that old Poland included the Western Territories, but that propaganda intended for the adult population did not.[87]

The press attachés from the European communist countries met in Berlin in June. According to Rachocki, the Soviet, Hungarian, and Yugoslavian attachés agreed that the Oder-Neisse border was the most troublesome issue for the SED because a majority of East Germans remained unreconciled to it. The Soviet attaché said that even the younger generation in the GDR did not accept the Oder-Neisse border, but he declared that Poland had resolved lingering questions about its ability to govern the Western Territories.[88]

The SED interpreted Khrushchev's visit to East Berlin in March 1959 as a sign that the Soviets approved of their political and economic program, rather than Gomułka's reform movement.[89] To avoid the impression in the West that there was a rift with Gomułka, however, Khrushchev agreed to attend the fifteenth anniversary celebration of the People's Republic of Poland in July.[90] Gomułka was effusive in his praise of Khrushchev; he ended one speech with "Long live our dear Soviet guest."[91] Gomułka even made some unusually generous comments about the GDR, but he avoided the ritual praise that typified the SED's propaganda: "We entertain good relations with it [the GDR]. We are developing mutual cooperation, we are united through a common ideology and common goals, together we belong to the Warsaw Pact."[92]

A SED report on Khrushchev's visit to Poland praised new developments in the PZPR—for instance, the party's renewed efforts to eliminate "revisionists" and return to central economic planning and collectivisation. The report concluded that Khrushchev's visit would further cement this "Marxist-Leninist development" in the PZPR.[93] Even Ambassador Hegen, who was a verbose critic of the Gomułka régime, publicly declared that "there are no controversial issues between Poland and the GDR .... The fifteen-year existence of the People's Poland shows that the friendship of Poland with the GDR is indissoluble."[94]

By 1959, Gomułka was in greater control of the political situation. He moved Jerzy Morawski off the Politburo and demoted Jerzy Albrecht and Władysław Matwin. Gomułka curbed the relatively free ideological debate in the PZPR that had been going on since 1956, and began to challenge the power of the Catholic Church.[95] A turning point in Gomułka's increasingly repressive policies was the removal of the young revisionist scholar Leszek Kołakowski from the editorship of *Studia filozoficzne* (Philisophic Studies) in the spring of 1959. That fall,

Gomułka sacked his old comrade Władysław Bieńkowski as Minister of Higher Education, and charged Jarosław Iwaszkiewicz with bringing ideological conformity to the Polish Writers' Union.[96] When Gomułka called on the old Stalinist Eugeniusz Szyr to head the central planning commission, Hegen predicted that Szyr would employ consistent "Marxist-Leninist principles of socialist command economy" to help the stagnant economy recover.[97]

The East Germans were obviously relieved that Gomułka had not tried to follow Tito out of the Soviet bloc, and that he was asserting greater party control over the Polish press, economy, and Catholic Church. Mired in self-delusion about the success and popularity of their own socialist system, however, the East German communists interpreted the Polish people's growing disappointment with Gomułka as a result of his political and economic liberalization, not his increasing political repression and limited economic successes. After a decade of building a relatively successful socialist system in the GDR, the East German communists encouraged Gomułka to adopt the SED's model of communism.

Notes

1. Rostock office to Ulbricht, July 25, 1958, SED ZK, Walter Ulbricht Papers, NL 182/1250.

2. Duscheck report on the visit of a Polish party delegation in the GDR, February 5, 1958, SED ZK, microfilm FBS 339/13489.

3. Piotrowski to Rapacki, January 8, 1958, MSZ, 23/77/9.

4. Polish Embassy report from November 1, 1957 to February 28, 1958, MSZ, 10/371/41.

5. Krahn to Hermann Axen, February 17, 1958, SED ZK, microfilm FBS 339/13489; and Krahn to Brandt (*Neues Deutschland* editor), February 24, 1958, SED ZK, microfilm FBS 339/13489.

6. Rossmeisl notes of meeting with an unidentified Soviet Foreign Ministry official, September 12, 1958, SED ZK, Otto Grotewohl Papers, NL 90/485.

7. Report on the situation in Poland, unsigned, January 24, 1958, SED ZK, microfilm FBS 339/13489.

8. Report on the Eleventh Plenary of the PZPR Central Committee, unsigned, March 5, 1958, SED ZK, microfilm FBS 339/13489.

9. Report on the Eleventh Plenary of the PZPR Central Committee, unsigned, March 12, 1958, DDR MfAA, Warsaw Embassy, A3771.

10. Wenk notes on the Eleventh Plenary of the PZPR Central Committee and the Fourth Trade Union Congress, undated, ca. May 1958, DDR MfAA, Warsaw Embassy, A3771.

11. Lugenheim report on the Ninth Party Congress of the PZPR, October 22, 1958, SED ZK, microfilm FBS 339/13490.

12. Political development in the Soviet zone of Germany from May 1–31, 1958, June 6, 1958, BRD BfGDF, B137/1473.

13. SED report on cooperation between the district office in Frankfurt/Oder and the PZPR in Zielona Góra, April 8, 1958, SED ZK, microfilm FBS 339/13422.

14. Leicht (SED office in Cottbus) to the SED Central Committee, April 10, 1958, SED ZK, microfilm FBS 339/13422.

15. Püschel to the GDR Foreign Ministry, July 15, 1958, SED ZK, microfilm FBS 339/13489.

16. Wenk notes of a meeting with Tönnies and Lipinski, June 19, 1958, DDR MfAA, Warsaw Embassy, A3771.

17. SED district office in Frankfurt/Oder report on exchanges with the PZPR office in Zielona Góra for the second half of 1958, December 19, 1958, SED ZK, microfilm FBS 339/13422.

18. SED report on the situation in the PZPR, unsigned, undated, ca. December 1958, SED ZK, microfilm FBS 339/13424; SED country report on Poland, November 30, 1958, SED ZK, Otto Grotewohl Papers, NL 90/485; and report for the delegation to Poland in December, November 30, 1958, DDR MfAA, Department of Neighboring Countries, C781/73, ZR/1892/73.

19. GDR Embassy in Warsaw to the SED Department of Foreign Affairs, August, 1957, SED ZK, microfilm 339/13489.

20. SED Department of Foreign Affairs report on Poland, February, 1959, SED ZK, Alfred Kurella Office, IV 2/ 2.026/16.

21. Report on an SED delegation visit to Zielona Góra, unsigned, November 30, 1958, DDR MfAA, Warsaw Embassy, A3821.

22. Report by Stropp, Püschel and Wenk of their trip to the Wrocław area from June 2–4, 1958, DDR MfAA, Warsaw Embassy, A3771.

23. Joachim Görlich report on the Germans in Poland, October, 1956, BRD BfGDF, B137/1246.

24. Riesner in Warsaw to the GDR Foreign Ministry, September 25, 1958, DDR MfAA, Warsaw Embassy, A3751.

25. PZPR Department of Science and Education report on educational exchanges with foreign countries, 1956–1959, PZPR KC, 237/V–442.

26. Notes on relations between Poland and the GDR, unsigned, undated, ca. December, 1958, MSZ, 10/464/48.

27. Wiese notes of a meeting with Kałróżny (Polish Ministry of Culture) on October 30, November 1, 1958, SED ZK, microfilm FBS 339/12495. The friendship week had been discontinued in 1956.

28. Proposal for a German-Polish Friendship Week in 1959, November 30, 1958, DDR MfAA, Department of Neighboring Countries, C781/73, ZR/1892/73.

29. Rostock office to Ulbricht, July 25, 1958, SED ZK, Walter Ulbricht Papers, NL 182/1250.

30. Ibid.

31. Ibid.

32. Michał Grendys to Józef Czesak, October 1, 1958, PZPR KC, 237/XXII–824.

33. Spielhagen notes on his visit to Warsaw, October 17, 1958, SED ZK, Otto Grotewohl Papers, NL 90/485.

34. Fliegner (GDR Planning Committee) to the SED Central Committee, August 20, 1958, SED ZK, Walter Ulbricht Papers, NL 182/1250.

35. Wenk notes of meeting with Wiese, April 20, 1959, DDR MfAA, Poland Section, A1798.

36. Riesner to the GDR Foreign Ministry, August 5, 1958, SED ZK, microfilm FBS 339/13489.

37. Werner Eggerath report on Polish church/state relations, December 8, 1957, SED ZK, Otto Grotewohl Papers, NL 90/478; and notes on the activities of the Catholic Church in Poland, unsigned, September 10, 1958, SED ZK, Department of Church Questions, IV 2/14/89; see also M. K. Dziewanowski, *The Communist Party of Poland: An Outline of History* (Cambridge: Harvard University Press, 1976), p. 295. In September 1958, the government decreed that no members of religious orders could give school instruction unless they were fully qualified as teachers. There was to be no religious symbols in the schools. Religious instruction in schools was abolished in 1961.

38. Politburo Working Group on Church Questions report on meetings with the Stachelski (Polish Minister of Church Affairs), June 1, 1959, SED ZK, Department of Church Questions, IV 2/14/90.

39. Püschel notes of meeting with Lech, June 20, 1959, SED ZK, Department of Church Questions, IV 2/14/90.

40. Lugenheim to the GDR Foreign Ministry, November 8, 1958, SED ZK, microfilm FBS 339/13490.

41. Riesner notes of a meeting with Szewczuk (Director of the Foreign Department of the PZPR Central Committee) on August 2, August 6, 1958, SED ZK, microfilm FBS 339/13489.

42. Willi Barth to Ulbricht, April 8, 1958, SED ZK, Walter Ulbricht Papers, NL 182/1250.

43. Notes on Michaelis and the meeting of the World Council of Churches, unsigned, September 22, 1958, SED ZK, Department of Church Questions, IV 2/14/89.

44. Politburo Working Group on Church Affairs report on meetings with Stachelski, June 1, 1959, SED ZK, Department of Church Questions, IV 2/14/90. The East German government estimated that there were about 3,000 German members of the Evangelical Church in Poland.

45. SED Department of Foreign Affairs to the PZPR Central Committee, May 31, 1958, ZK SED, microfilm FBS 339/13489; Viebig (GDR Foreign Ministry) notes of a meeting with Weise and Dressler (Department of Church Questions) May 3, 1958, DDR MfAA, Poland Section, A1804; and Hegen notes of meeting with Stachelski (Polish Minister of Church Affairs), May 19, 1958, DDR MfAA, Poland Section, A1804.

46. Florin to the PZPR Central Committee, May 31, 1958, PZPR KC, 237/XXII–824.

47. Wirth notes, June 9, 1958, SED ZK, Department of Church Questions, IV 2/14/89.

48. Wirth notes on the Trinitatis dedications, July 10, 1958, SED ZK, Department of Church Questions, IV 2/14/89.

49. SED country report on Poland, November 30, 1958, SED ZK, Otto Grotewohl Papers, NL 90/485; and report for the delegation to Poland in December,

November 30, 1958, DDR MfAA, Department of Neighboring Countries, C781/73, ZR/1892/73. The East Germans had only two schools named for Polish communists, one for Bolesław Bierut and one for Julian Marchlewski.

50. GDR Foreign Ministry report on contacts between West German and Polish students, November 30, 1958, DDR MfAA, Department of Neighboring Countries, C781/73, ZR/1892/73.

51. SED report on the activity of the SED Press Department, unsigned, undated, ca. December 1958, SED ZK, microfilm FBS 339/12495.

52. Report by the SED Frankfurt/Oder office on exchanges with the PZPR office in Zielona Góra for the second half of 1958, December 19, 1958, SED ZK, microfilm FBS 339/13422.

53. Polish Embassy report on economic relations with the GDR from 1956–1958, November 18, 1958, MSZ, 10/385/42.

54. Topics for the discussions with the GDR party and government delegation in December, unsigned, undated, ca. December, 1958, MSZ, 10/464/48.

55. Polish Embassy report on economic relations with the GDR from 1956–1958, November 18, 1958, MSZ, 10/385/42; and briefing paper for the discussions with GDR party and government delegation in December, unsigned, undated, ca. December, 1958, MSZ, 10/464/48. Polish exports to West Berlin were essential to balance the trade deficit that Poland was running with West Germany, which by 1958 amounted to almost DM 100 million. The Polish Foreign Ministry argued that West Berlin's dependence on trade with the entire Soviet bloc made political sense.

56. Polish Foreign Ministry report on the GDR press, unsigned, undated, ca. December, 1958, MSZ, 10/464/48.

57. Topics for the discussions with the GDR party and government delegations, unsigned, undated, ca. December 1958, MSZ, 10/464/48.

58. Hegen to Winzer, November 20, 1958, SED ZK, Otto Grotewohl Papers, NL 90/483.

59. Notes on GDR-Polish economic relations, November 30, 1958, DDR MfAA, Department of Neighboring Countries, C781/73, ZR/1892/73.

60. GDR Foreign Ministry report on the political situation in the PZPR leadership, November 30, 1958, DDR MfAA, Department of Neighboring Countries, C781/73, ZR/1892/73.

61. Notes on GDR-Polish economic relations, November 30, 1958, DDR MfAA, Department of Neighboring Countries, C781/73, ZR/1892/73.

62. Erwin Weit, *Ostblock intern: 13 Jahre Dolmetscher für die polnische Partei—und Staatsführung* (Inside the East bloc: Thirteen years as interpreter for the Polish Party—and government leadership) (Hamburg: Hoffmann und Campe Verlag, 1970), p. 39.

63. Record of meetings between the PZPR and SED, December 9–14, 1958, SED ZK, microfilm FBS 339/13424.

64. Michał Grendys to Józef Czesak, October 1, 1958, PZPR KC, 237/XXII–824.

65. Record of meetings between the PZPR and SED, December 9–14, 1958, SED ZK, microfilm FBS 339/13424.

66. Ibid.

67. Ibid.

68. Ulbricht speech to Warsaw workers, undated, SED ZK, Walter Ulbricht Papers, NL 182/577.

69. Weit, *Ostblock intern*, pp. 39, 42–45. A few days after the meetings, another summit meeting was supposed to take place in Warsaw on the fortieth anniversary of the founding of the KPP. Khrushchev was planning to attend, but when Ulbricht said he would not stay in Poland, Khrushchev sent Mikojan. Ulbricht sent Honecker.

70. Ulbricht toast at a reception thrown by the PZPR Central Committee, December 9, 1958, SED ZK, Walter Ulbricht Papers, NL 182/577.

71. Weit, *Ostblock intern*, p. 39.

72. Hackel report on the Polish press reports of the party and government meetings in Warsaw, December 23, 1958, SED ZK, microfilm FBS 339/13424.

73. Polish Embassy report for February 1, 1958 to February 28, 1959, MSZ, 10/372/41.

74. Polish Foreign Ministry report on the GDR press, unsigned, undated, ca. December, 1958, MSZ, 10/464/48.

75. Wiese report on the activities of the GDR Embassy Department of Culture in 1958, undated, ca. February, 1959, SED ZK, microfilm FBS 339/12495.

76. Winzer to Ulbricht, February 12, 1959, SED ZK, Walter Ulbricht Papers, NL 182/1250.

77. Stropp (GDR Embassy in Warsaw) to the GDR Foreign Ministry, March 2, 1959, DDR MfAA, Warsaw Embassy, A3750.

78. Ludwik Gronowski notes of meeting with Heymann on July 2, July 3, 1959, MSZ, 10/346/38.

79. Łobodycz to Piotrowski, July 9, 1959, MSZ, 10/346/38.

80. Püschel (GDR Embassy in Warsaw) report, September 12, 1959, SED ZK, microfilm FBS 339/13423.

81. Łobodycz notes of meeting with Wiese, April 18, 1959, MSZ, 10/383/42.

82. Piotrowski to Łobodycz, May 17, 1959, MSZ, 10/383/42.

83. Leon Szybek notes of discussions with Heymann on May 19 and May 27, May 29, 1959, MSZ, 10/383/42.

84. Łobodzycz to Piotrowski, May 18, 1959, MSZ, 10/383/42.

85. Kopa notes of meeting with Horst Heinrich, February 11, 1959, MSZ, 10/346/38.

86. Ludwik Gronowski notes of meeting with Brinkmann and Wenk, April 25, 1959, MSZ, 10/381/43.

87. Janusz Rachocki notes of meeting with the editors of *BZ am Abend*, May 28, 1959, MSZ, 10/381/43.

88. Łobodycz to A. Gwiżdż (Polish Parliament), July 13, 1959, MSZ, 10/310/36.

89. See Franz Sikora, *Sozialistische Solidarität und nationale Interessen* (Socialist solidarity and national interests) (Cologne: Verlag Wissenschaft und Politik, 1977), pp. 152–153.

90. Tadeusz Gede notes of meeting with Khrushchev, March 3, 1959, MSZ, 23/58/7.

91. Quoted in Dziewanowski, *The Communist Party of Poland*, p. 290.

92. SED Department of Foreign Affairs report on Khrushchev's visit to Poland, July 29, 1959, SED ZK, microfilm FBS 339/12495.

93. Notes on relations between the CPSU and the PZPR, unsigned, undated, ca. July, 1959, SED ZK, Otto Grotewohl Papers, NL 90/485.

94. Hegen quoted in *Neues Deutschland*, July 22, 1959, in a Polish Foreign Ministry memorandum, July 28, 1959, MSZ, 10/381/43.

95. See R. F. Leslie, et al., *The History of Poland Since 1863* (Cambridge: Cambridge University Press, 1980), pp. 369–373.

96. See Dziewanowski, *The Communist Party of Poland*, p. 290. Iwaszkiewicz had served as deputy chairman in the early 1950s.

97. Hegen to König, October 30, 1959, SED ZK, Walter Ulbricht Papers, NL 182/1250.

12

The GDR as a Model for Polish Socialism, 1959–1961

The [East] Germans act as if they were the master people here, [they] drink and eat their fill and cost the Polish state too much. . . . Those East Germans who spend a year in Poland and still can't speak Polish are nationalists and should be shot.

-Polish engineer on the East German workers at a Polish factory in Turów[1]

By the end of the 1950s, relations had rebounded from their nadir in 1956. Political, ideological, and trade disputes were less contentious now. After a two-year postponement, the Third PZPR Congress convened in March 1959. There, Gomułka put a brake on the reforms of the past three years when he explained that the Polish October had nothing to do with revolution, but rather with "renewal" and "changing our methods of work."[2]

Gomułka's harder line seemed to vindicate the SED's consistent rejection of liberalization. East German officials repeatedly held up the SED's domestic and foreign policies as a template for the PZPR. The tone of their critiques were often patronizing and self-satisfied, and whenever the PZPR adopted a policy that the SED had been advocating, the East Germans took credit for it.

The East German Embassy's report on the Fourth Plenary Session of the PZPR Central Committee in early February 1960 was complementary of the PZPR for reaffirming its commitment to the Soviet bloc parties. The embassy was encouraged by the party's desire to expand all types of exchanges with the GDR. Nonetheless, the embassy identified glaring weaknesses in the new program, including the absence of a definite plan to mobilize the masses for socialism. The embassy criticized the PZPR for exaggerating the role of the intelligentsia in building socialism rather than stressing the Marxist education of the working class. Furthermore, the embassy found that the PZPR still allowed too many Western influences to creep into the country, for instance, the U.S. public and private funds for U.S. films, books, magazines, and newspapers, which, according to the East Germans, led to "holes in the ideological front."[3] After the Fifth Plenary Session in June, East German diplomats again faulted the PZPR for failing to inspire the Polish working class to work harder for socialism.[4]

The SED hounded the PZPR to adopt its supposedly superior political and economic structure. The East German communists encouraged the PZPR to adopt stronger measures against the Catholic Church and to reassert party control over agriculture, although the SED's own collectivization program was still fraught with problems. The party claimed to be committed to a voluntary program of socialist agriculture, but most East German farmers had been forced to join a collective. By the end of the decade, few private farms were left in the GDR.[5]

The SED had long been critical of Gomułka's indifference to socialist agricultural development. Ulbricht thought there was no socialism without the collectivization of agriculture. In early 1958, Hegen concluded that the PZPR had "renounced in part its leading role" in setting agricultural policy.[6] The Soviets were also troubled by the dismantling of Polish collectives; of the approximately 10,000 collectives in Poland before October 1956, only 1,800 remained by 1959.[7]

At first, the SED was optimistic that the new Polish Agricultural Minister in 1959, former party chief Edward Ochab, would speed up re-collectivization; but during a visit to an agricultural exhibition in Leipzig in June-July, Ochab defended the PZPR's past agricultural policies. He said that the Poles did not want to make the same disastrous mistakes with collectivisation that Stalin had made—to force the peasants into collectives. He pointed out that Poland was a much poorer country than the GDR, and that because Poland had suffered greater war damages it had to build its industrial base first. Ochab ended with a scathing criticism of the East Germans' false propaganda asserting that West German private farming was a failure; he said that in reality West German agriculture was a great success, and that West German visitors to the Leipzig exhibition would be offended by such blatant distortions of the truth.[8] The East German Embassy in Warsaw concluded simply that "there is a lack of a Marxist-Leninist assessment of the situation in the [Polish] countryside."[9]

In any case, Polish farmers were not receptive to the East Germans' lectures on socialist agricultural policy. One Polish farmer told an East German delegation that the GDR, which was under Soviet occupation, had no choice but to collectivize.[10] Poles often told the East Germans that eliminating private farming in Poland was impossible because the independent-thinking Polish farmer was simply not suited to collectivized agriculture.[11] At an agricultural exhibition in the East German town of

Markkleeburg in 1960, Polish officials said that they would wait for Polish farmers to form collectives voluntarily. The Poles even praised private farmers for producing agricultural goods that were of superior quality and salable in the West.[12]

Some East German officials thought that if Polish officials could see for themselves the smooth-running collective farms in the GDR, they would change their agricultural policies. With that goal in mind, Florin advised Ulbricht to increase regional cooperation between the SED district offices along the Oder-Neisse border and their PZPR counterparts in the former German areas.[13] The SED's Department of Propaganda also urged Ulbricht to allow more exchanges, especially to increase the Poles' awareness of the dangers of West German militarism and revanchism. As usual, Ulbricht shelved these requests.[14]

When the Comecon countries met in February 1960 to discuss the mounting agricultural crisis in the entire Soviet bloc, Ulbricht recommended more collectivization.[15] The PZPR made no move in that direction, however; it calculated that its compromises to private farming and private land ownership would prevent the Catholic Church from openly opposing the régime.[16] *Trybuna Ludu* made no mention of the collectives in its reporting on the Sixth Plenary Session of the PZPR in September 1960.[17]

The SED continued to criticize the PZPR for accepting U.S. aid for private farming and agricultural research, although that aid was relatively small.[18] In January 1961, Winzer told Ulbricht that a new $20 million investment credit from the United States was a means for the Americans to steer Polish agriculture away from collectivization, and would make Polish agriculture dependent on the West.[19]

The SED argued that the dominant position of the Catholic Church in rural Poland was yet another reason to collectivize. The SED was somewhat encouraged by the PZPR's crackdown on the Catholic Church in 1960; religious instruction was banned from middle schools, business schools, and trade schools, although about half of the elementary schools still had it.[20] But several religious demonstrations against the PZPR that year revealed the party still had a serious church problem. In April, an estimated 25,000 to 30,000 people from Nowa Huta demonstrated against the PZPR for building a school on the site where the party had promised to build a church. Eighteen police officers were hurt when the protest turned violent—some seriously.[21] At the end of May, 2,500 people in Zielona Góra massed to protest the state's confiscation of a church building for the local symphony. Over 300 people were arrested and 156 police were injured. According to East German sources, the demonstrators were heard yelling, "Kill the communists, kill the Jews, cut the police to pieces. . . . You are like the fascists, you are just like the Gestapo, you are just like the Cheka." The head of the SED district office in Frankfurt/Oder, Edvard Götzl, concluded that the demonstrations were symptomatic of the PZPR's lack of control over the Catholic Church, especially in the rural areas. He promised that his office would "exert with all circumspection our political influence on the [Polish] comrades, in order to help them to follow a correct Marxist-Leninist policy."[22]

Ongoing Problems in Cultural Affairs

In some ways, the slight thaw in relations between the PZPR and the SED in 1959 made it more difficult for the Polish communists to swing Polish opinion around to support the German socialist state. As average Poles became more disgruntled with their government, they had even less interest in the official, contrived efforts to bring East Germans and Poles together. The SED repeatedly claimed that it had the support of the East German people, but the SED's close surveillance over them belied this claim. The East Germans expected the Polish authorities, who governed an even more recalcitrant populace, to silence political dissent.

At a meeting in Berlin in June 1959, the press attachés from the East European embassies all complained about the lack of cooperation from the East German Foreign Ministry's Press Department. They agreed that it was virtually impossible to persuade the East Germans to print anything about their countries, except news of official events. Polish diplomats said that the behavior of some East German press officials lacked "basic decency."[23] The Poles had complained for several years about the GDR's unenthusiastic commemoration of Hitler's attack on Poland on September 1, 1939. On the twentieth anniversary of the attack in 1959, Polish diplomats again criticized the East German press for its limited coverage, and reported that the East Germans were reluctant to attend the ceremonies. Polish diplomat Ludwik Gronowski concluded that "knowledge of Polish issues in the GDR is very limited," and that the SED was not doing much about it.[24]

Over ten years of communist propaganda extolling Polish-East German friendship had failed to change peoples' negative stereotypes. Many cultural and economic exchanges still flared into unpleasant confrontations. That fall, the head engineer of a Polish factory in Turów castigated the East Germans working there for their arrogant and chauvinistic attitudes: "The Germans act as if they were the master people here, [they] drink and eat their fill and cost the Polish state too much. . . . Those East Germans who spend a year in Poland and still can't speak Polish are nationalists and should be shot." One Polish locksmith complained that whenever he was on a bus full of these East German workers, "the German pigs sit and the Poles have to stand." The East Germans also overheard the Poles saying that the German workers were taking away their bread. One East German engineer at the plant concluded that working with the Poles was bringing no positive results.[25]

The SED's files were also rife with reports of politically damaging exchanges; for instance, in 1959, the SED sent a protest note to the PZPR about the questionable behavior of Professor Knebel from the PZPR party school in Warsaw, who was visiting Weimar University. Knebel had allegedly criticized the SED's economic and social policies, and suggested that the SED's agricultural policies were making farmers so unhappy that they were leaving in droves for the FRG. Knebel also reproached the SED for its "narrow-minded" youth policies and for granting privileges to party functionaries. The report concluded that Knebel simply did not understand "the use of Leninism and the experiences of the CPSU in the GDR."[26]

In 1960, the SED district office in Gera hosted a group of Polish officials whom the East Germans found completely lacking in socialist sensibilities. At one dinner, the Poles asked why Soviet flags had to be placed on the table between the Polish and the East German colors. The Poles doubted the sincerity of the East Germans' references to the Russians as their "friends"; after all, the Russians had defeated the Germans in the war, and had treated them harshly ever since. The East Germans were also shocked when the Poles tried to deal for East German currency to buy East German cameras and other goods. These were harmless business transactions to the Poles, but to the East Germans, such corrupt capitalist practices subverted the socialist state and the socialist economy, not to mention socialist minds.[27]

In light of these and other similar incidents, the SED would not loosen its tight controls on Polish tourists. The SED denied permission for delegations or individuals visiting the GDR to go to West Berlin or West Germany, and it became nearly impossible for Poles traveling to West Berlin or West Germany to obtain a transit visa through the GDR.[28] The Polish Foreign Ministry still received numerous complaints from Poles about the thorough searches and unlawful confiscation of their property by East German border guards.[29]

For several years, the East Germans had disparaged the Poles for their great interest in cultivating contacts with Western capitalists. For that reason alone, the top SED leaders remained opposed to easing restrictions on personal connections between Polish and East German citizens. Of the 57,000 visitors to Poland in 1959, 42,000 came from capitalist countries; 21,500 Poles visited other countries, 19,000 of them to the Soviet bloc countries and 2,500 to capitalist countries. The majority of Polish tourists went to the Soviet Union, in part because that was all they could afford. The East Germans criticized the Polish government for allowing

2,500 more Poles to visit Western countries in 1960, most of them to France, Denmark, Greece, and to Italy for the Olympic Games in Rome. The tourist traffic between Poland and East Germany in 1959 was relatively light, but as usual, the Polish government allowed many more Poles to travel to the GDR than the GDR allowed Germans to visit Poland; in 1959, 144 East Germans visited Poland, but 2,700 Poles went to the GDR. The majority of all of the visits were to the Leipzig and Poznań Trade Fairs.[30] East German authorities also kept a watchful eye on the sharp increase in Polish tourists to Yugoslavia and the United States.[31] Winzer informed Ulbricht that the Rockefeller Foundation and the Ford Foundation were funding 650 Poles to study in the West, and he warned of the "negative ideological effects" of the study-abroad program.[32]

In May 1960, the East German Foreign Ministry once again recommended an increase in cooperative efforts with Poland to help familiarize the Polish people with the GDR.[33] Ulbricht was still hesitant, being particularly concerned about the state of Polish art and literature. According to the Polish diplomats in Berlin, relations between the East German and Polish Writers' Congresses were still "stiff and cool. . . . In the area of art the German comrades have grave reservations about our contemporary creations."[34]

The conduct of the Polish Writers' Congress in Wrocław that May was so unsettling to the East German leadership that Alfred Kurella, the head of the SED's Commission for Cultural Affairs, asked two East German writers, Jan Koplowitz and Alfred Schulz, for a full account of the proceedings.[35] Koplowitz and Schulz were dissatisfied with the PZPR's lack of organization and oversight of the congress. They found it inexplicable that the Poles virtually ignored socialist realism as the foundation of Marxist writing. They reported that Polish writers lacked ideological consistency, and, which was worse, rejected all censorship.[36]

In his speech to the congress, Koplowitz said that West German writers had told him they were "in ideological coexistence" with Polish writers. The chairman of Polish Writers' Congress, Jarosław Iwaszkiewicz, stood up in protest and said, "I'm not taking part in this any more."[37] Koplowitz and Iwaszkiewicz later argued bitterly over the latter's suggestion that East German literature was in decline, in part because of its mechanical adherence to socialist realism.[38]

The head of the PZPR district office in Wrocław, Roman Werfel, accused Koplowitz of bringing unnecessary confusion into the congress. He defended the PZPR's policies because Poland was in a "special situation." Koplowitz countered that the GDR was in an even more precarious position with West Germany on its western border. Werfel agreed that the GDR had, in his words, its "rabid wolf Adenauer." When Koplowitz replied that Poland faced the same danger from West Germany, Werfel's response stunned him: "I have enough to do to prove to the people here that Walter Ulbricht is not the rabid wolf."[39]

Koplowitz and Schulz concluded that the Polish writers were not interested in East German literature, but were "well informed" about West German publications. One writer told them that she was learning German to read the West German magazine *Spiegel*, and another said that his good and bad experiences with Germans during the war now enabled him to distinguish between West and East Germans in the same way— and he liked the West Germans more.[40]

The two East German writers observed that their Polish counterparts were proud of promoting the Polish road to socialism, which afforded them greater freedom than writers in the GDR. The Poles criticized the East Germans for their strict dogmatism and blind loyalty to the Soviet Union. Koplowitz reported that "the Polish colleagues reproached us because we simplify everything in the GDR too much and do not come to grips with the various intellectual currents that exist in the world." Egon Naganowski, one of Poland's most noted literary critics, admonished Koplowitz and Schulz for the SED's crude propaganda, for instance, the unfounded claim that East German farmers had gone into collectives voluntarily: "You don't believe that yourselves; we know, of course, how one effects such a thing [collectivization], we experienced that already and thank God [we] liquidated [them] again. Furthermore, we read every day in the West German press how many thousand farmers leave [the GDR], and that really says everything."[41]

When the East German delegation asked to check with their superiors in East Berlin before signing a friendship agreement, the Poles speculated that the East German Writers' Congress was unwilling to put itself on record as recognizing the Oder-Neisse border. Although there was truth to this accusation, the East Germans could not or would not acknowledge it. In typically condescending fashion, Koplowitz and Schulz urged the SED to provide "fraternal help" for the few true Marxist Polish writers.[42]

East German officials tried to give Polish filmmakers and actors "fraternal help" as well. That summer, East German artist Ursula Hafranke denounced a "bourgeois" Polish cinema and theater exhibition that was touring East Germany. She said that both the form and the content of the Polish works were influenced by "Western decadent drama." She singled out one Polish film—*Two Men with the Trunk from the Sea*—for not sending a political message. Rather than extolling the bright socialist future of the world, the film depicted man's alienation, which to the East German communists was a decadent bourgeois concept. Hafranke wrote, "At the end of the film the two disappointed men pulled their trunk back with them into the sea from which they came (into a better world? Or where to?)." Because some East German artists had reacted positively to the film, she worried about the political impact of such exhibitions. Hafranke called for more vigilance in screening the content of foreign performances in the GDR: "In principle I do not think that it is right for a representative of a friendly socialist state to travel around our country and to exhibit cultural maxims that are completely inimical to ours."[43] Although Hafranke's report was sharply critical of the exhibition, Kurella characterized it as "obviously somewhat softened up."[44]

Defending the Oder-Neisse Border

The inability of the SED and the PZPR to resolve their ideological differences, or to bring their two peoples together in genuine cultural exchanges, represented a serious problem for the Warsaw Pact's cohesiveness on its strategic western front. Given the failure of cultural programs to engender real friendships, the reliability of the East German and Polish soldier to the common defense of the two countries was questionable. Polish diplomat Stanisław Kopa reported that many East German soldiers were opposed to a peace treaty that maintained the present borders of Germany, especially without input from the German people. [45]

In June 1959, East German army officer Fritz Surkau presented Polish diplomat Janusz Rachocki with a long list of criticisms of the PZPR's foreign and domestic policies, notably the party's distrust of the working classes and feeble efforts to purge reactionaries. Surkau said that the SED and the other Soviet bloc parties had their doubts about the future of socialism in Poland under the present PZPR leadership. Surkau alleged that the Polish army was permeated with nationalist and anti-Soviet sentiment, and that the party was doing little to combat it.[46]

The tenth anniversary of the 1950 Zgorzelec agreement on the Oder-Neisse border was an opportunity to trumpet the solidarity of the two peoples, but differences immediately surfaced over the site of the celebration. Rapacki proposed a summit and a large demonstration at Zgorzelec in support of the Oder-Neisse border, but the East Germans told the Poles that they wanted to avoid giving the West the impression that Poland and the GDR needed to reconfirm their recognition of the border. In reality, the East German communists wanted no part of a big public show of support for a border that was still unpopular among the East German people. Furthermore, the SED wanted to keep celebrations under tight control. Bolz suggested to Ulbricht that they make an immediate counterproposal to preclude small changes in the original Polish plan; he recommended a smaller ceremony in Magdeburg that would be devoted to condemning West German revanchism. The East Germans saw symbolic importance in holding the commemoration on the Elbe and not on the Oder; they wanted tacit Polish agreement that an attack on the GDR's western border would be considered an attack on Poland.[47] Polish

Ambassador Piotrowski reluctantly agreed to the Magdeburg demonstration, and said that Cyrankiewicz would speak at the event.[48]

As usual, the East Germans were much more effusive in their praise of the ceremony as a symbol of cooperation between the two peoples. *Neues Deutschland* hailed the event with the headline "Shoulder to Shoulder on the Peace Watch on the Elbe."[49] Grotewohl declared that "this demonstration confirms once again that the GDR and PRP are true friends and will always remain true friends." Cyrankiewicz criticized German militarism and imperialism in general terms, but much to the disappointment of the East Germans, did not attack Adenauer or other West German leaders.[50] Nonetheless, the East German Foreign Ministry was generally satisfied with Poland's propaganda campaign, which they again credited to East Germany's persistent lobbying efforts.[51]

The SED and Gomułka's Policy Toward the West

Gomułka's retreat from the reform program of October 1956 gradually put Poland's relations with the Soviet bloc back on solid ground. The Polish Embassy in Berlin speculated that the PZPR's Thirteenth Party Congress in March 1959 and Khrushchev's visit to Warsaw in July were restoring the confidence of the CPSU and the SED in the PZPR.[52] But Gomułka's invitation of U.S. Vice President Richard Nixon to visit Poland in early August again alerted the SED to the dangers of a rapprochement with Poland.[53] The East German Embassy speculated that by inviting Nixon, Gomułka was trying to enhance Poland's prestige in the West and expand trade with the United States. By now, the East German diplomats were more confident that U.S. schemes to lure Poland away from the Warsaw Pact would fail;[54] but they concluded that the PZPR was practicing "a certain form of bourgeois secret diplomacy," which included improving relations with neutral countries, Yugoslavia, and Western social democratic parties. The embassy interpreted Nixon's visit as consistent with a policy that had its roots in the "un-Marxist [PZPR] platform of 1956–1957." The East Germans also speculated that the United States was using Yugoslavia to woo Poland away from the Soviet bloc.[55]

While Nixon was in Poland, the SED directed its press agency to launch a propaganda campaign against U.S. foreign policy. The East Germans denounced Washington's anti-communism, coercive trade and financial policy, use of spies against Poland and the other socialist states, and deployment of nuclear weapons in West Germany.[56] Ulbricht approved of this measure, and recommended starting a new attack campaign against the FRG to expose the "subversive activity of West German revanchists from West Berlin against the Peoples' Republic of Poland."[57]

Poles on the street gave Nixon an enthusiastic welcome. Accustomed to choreographing all public demonstrations, East German officials charged foreign agents and Polish dissident groups with inciting the crowds.[58] The East German diplomats in Warsaw warned of anti-socialist and revisionist forces in Poland. They thought that the PZPR still had a long way to go to "establish the moral-political unity of the Polish people." They concluded that Nixon's visit would encourage the United States to renew its efforts to undermine Poland's connections to the Warsaw Pact.[59]

The SED's cool reaction to Nixon's visit prompted the Polish Embassy in Berlin to file this report:

> It seemed as if the GDR leadership had problems with this event [Nixon's visit]. [They] withheld information about the meetings and official talks with Nixon until the moment came when the Polish leaders drew Nixon's attention to the dangers coming from the remilitarization of West Germany. From this example it can be seen that our policy toward the West has still not found complete understanding in the SED.[60]

The Poles were understating the extent of East Berlin's displeasure with Warsaw's policy toward the West; the SED was convinced that Polish officials were ignorant of the dangerous political game that West Germany and its allies were playing. Ulbricht did not doubt that Gomułka would sell out the GDR should the opportunity present itself. These fears were confirmed again that fall when the Polish government considered accepting a West German proposal for a nonaggression pact. The West Germans had rebuffed a similar East German proposal, and East Berlin was firmly opposed to Bonn's attempt to differentiate between East Germany and its Warsaw Pact partners. Gomułka eventually rejected the proposal on the grounds that Bonn would not recognize the Oder-Neisse border, but the whole affair unnerved the East Germans.[61]

By this time, Gomułka recognized that his attempt to balance political and economic relations between the capitalist and socialist countries had left Poland dangerously isolated; East German Foreign Ministry officials were pleased when he began to strengthen Poland's ties to the Soviet bloc countries in 1960.[62] In January, Hegen told Naszkowski that his government had taken note of Gomułka's recent declarations condemning the influence of fascism, militarism, and revanchism in West Germany, and his emphasis on the progressive role of the GDR in the German question. The East Germans again took some credit for this shift in the PZPR's policy, even though it had more to do with the limited success of Warsaw's overtures toward Bonn.[63] The East German Embassy in Warsaw also reported that the Polish Foreign Ministry was slowly overcoming reservations about confiding in East German diplomats.[64]

There were still unresolved issues that stood in the way of a closer coordination of their foreign policies, however. Several minor incidents confirmed East German suspicions that Gomułka had not ended his dalliance with the West.[65] The East Germans cited one case in which the Dutch government asked the Polish Embassy in the Netherlands to stop issuing visas on behalf of the GDR, because France and Great Britain had lodged protests. Rather than offend these Western countries, the Poles complied. Naszkowski told Hegen that an "open conflict with the Dutch would not be in our interest nor in the interest of the GDR." French President Charles de Gaulle's support of the Oder-Neisse border was one more reason for the Poles not to press the issue.[66]

Rapacki addressed the German problem in an article in the January 1960 issue of *Nowe Drogi*, but the East German Embassy criticized him for overlooking the role of the GDR and the danger West Germany posed to the Warsaw Pact.[67] A month later, Rapacki declared that "Poland stands in the center of the present system of international relations and actively influences it." The East German Embassy viewed this as a typical exaggeration of Poland's importance in European affairs, and accused the Poles of failing to consult with the Soviet Union on important diplomatic initiatives. The embassy also faulted Gomułka for not supporting East German proposals to bolster the defense of the GDR.[68] The GDR Foreign Ministry renewed its efforts to convince the Gomułka régime of East Germany's key political and economic role in the socialist camp, and even the GDR's part in helping to develop socialism in Poland.[69] The ministry was still unsure about the long-term political stability of the Gomułka régime.[70]

Rapacki and Bolz met in Berlin at the end of May. Bolz reminded Rapacki that the SED and the GDR, not the West German SPD, would guarantee peace in Germany, and that the development of the East German economy was the best way to influence the working class in West Germany to support socialism.[71] According to Bolz's account of the meeting, they agreed to work harder to combat West German remilitarization and revanchism, and to coordinate their foreign policies toward the Asian and African countries. Rapacki also promised to strengthen Poland's representation of the GDR in international organizations and in Scandinavia.[72]

The East Germans were noticeably pleased with the results of this meeting: The Poles, it appeared, were at last recognizing the GDR as the only legitimate German state. At the Poznań Trade Fair in June, for instance, the Polish authorities confiscated West German literature that used the term *East Zone* for the GDR, and maps that did not show the Oder-Neisse border. In contrast to previous years, the Poles also limited the number of West Germans allowed to travel outside of Poznań.[73]

The Polish government remained opposed to compromises of their important political or economic interests in West Germany and West Berlin, however. In its refusal to make direct attacks on the West German government, the Polish Foreign Ministry instructed its diplomats around the world to stress instead the general danger of "revanchist elements" in

West Germany.[74] The East German Foreign Ministry had repeatedly asked the Poles not to send representatives to international conferences in West Berlin, but when the Poles did not comply, Bolz raised the issue during meetings with Polish Foreign Ministry officials in August 1960. Once again, the Poles refused. They agreed to represent East German political and economic interests in the Third World, but only if it did not jeopardize Poland's relations with these countries. Satisfied with the outcome of the conference, Bolz declared that "our interests are the same." Rapacki's account of the meetings was not so optimistic, but he acknowledged that they had contributed to the better coordination of foreign policy.[75]

The Warsaw Pact communist parties watched closely as Sino-Soviet relations worsened in 1960. The Gomułka régime feared that this rift, along with greater East-West tensions after the cancellation of the U.S.-Soviet summit in Paris in May, would prompt Moscow to clamp down on Poland's tenuous ties to the West. Ulbricht, planted himself firmly behind the CPSU against the Chinese, however, to prove that the GDR was Moscow's most trusted ally.

That fall, after the Warsaw Pact meetings in Bucharest and the Sixth Plenary Session of the PZPR Central Committee, East German officials worried that the PZPR's open discussion of the Sino-Soviet confrontation would upset the fragile stability that the Polish communists had established in the last few months. East German diplomats reported that "revisionist forces" in the PZPR were taking advantage of the Sino-Soviet split to advance their cause against "dogmatism." The embassy also criticized the Polish press for its scant coverage of the Bucharest conference and the Warsaw Pact's declarations on disarmament and peaceful coexistence.[76]

East German diplomats reproached the Polish communists for subordinating the "leading role of the socialist system as a defining element for the course and direction of international development," and chided the PZPR for nationalist deviations from Marxist-Leninist principles of foreign policy.[77] At a reception at the Polish Embassy in Moscow in late September, an East German diplomat noted that of the guests from Mongolia, North Korea, North Vietnam, the Peoples' Republic of China and Albania, he was the only one to raise a toast to the unity of the socialist camp under the leadership of the CPSU.[78]

The East Germans also watched Poland's relations with Yugoslavia, especially Belgrade's consultations with Warsaw on Berlin and German unification. East German diplomat Ewald Moldt told Łobodycz that the Yugoslavs did not fully comprehend the danger of West German militarism, nor did they realize the seriousness of the West Berlin problem to the GDR. Moldt said that it was essential that Yugoslavia accept East German sovereignty over West Berlin. He pointed out that Yugoslavia was prepared to sign a peace treaty with the GDR only if there was no possibility of an agreement with the FRG on German unification. Moldt suggested that the Poles try to convince the Yugoslavs to rethink their policy.[79]

The Polish government would not cooperate on this front, either. East German officials informed Ulbricht that the Poles would not support Soviet and East German diplomacy in Central Europe, more so regarding West Germany. The East German Foreign Ministry repeatedly criticized the Poles for not stressing the importance of the GDR in the context of the German question, and added that the propaganda the Poles published to this end was insufficient. In December 1960, Moldt reported that in a recent article on West Germany in *Nowe Drogi*, Łobodycz had not mentioned the important work of the KPD in West Germany. Moldt attacked Łobodycz for failing to emphasize the supposedly positive influence on the FRG of East Germany's "peace policy." He determined that it was impossible to convince the Polish communists to coordinate their German policy with the GDR.[80]

A month later, Winzer informed Ulbricht that the head of the PZPR Press Department, Artur Starewicz, had advised Polish journalists not to repeat Warsaw Pact declarations on "American imperialism and Yugoslavian revisionism." Winzer also accused the Polish press of giving the false impression that U.S. policy toward Poland benefited Poles; he viewed U.S. policy as subversive and coercive, but he could not persuade the Poles that good relations with the United States was a hindrance, not a help, in building socialism.[81]

Toward Détente in 1961

Despite these problems, the SED noted several positive trends in Poland's foreign policy in 1961. At the Seventh Plenary Session of PZPR Central Committee in January, Gomułka stressed that Poland's relations with the FRG could not be expanded without the Adenauer government's recognition of the Oder-Neisse border.[82] The East German Foreign Ministry reported that for the first time the Polish government was taking "an open and unmistakable position against the militarism and revanchism in West Germany."[83] To the satisfaction of East German officials, Polish authorities also decided to permit fewer Poles to visit West Germany because they were being recruited as agents there. The PZPR informed Moldt that they would lobby the West Germans harder for a peace treaty and recognition of the Oder-Neisse border; however, the Poles indicated that they would not compromise their economic connections to the FRG by putting too much pressure on Bonn to resolve these political issues.[84]

Later that month, a West German industrialist told Cyrankiewicz that the Adenauer government was ready to sign a three-year trade agreement and another accord on cultural exchanges. He said that Bonn was also prepared to talk about an exchange of trade consulates as a possible bridge to diplomatic recognition. Cyrankiewicz stressed that Poland wanted improved economic and cultural relations, but he stipulated that the Adenauer government recognize the Oder-Neisse border first before his government would talk about diplomatic ties or interim trade consulates.[85] The Adenauer government refused, however, and in February Cyrankiewicz told East German officials that his government would never compromise the present border for diplomatic relations with the FRG.[86]

In February, the SED issued a report on Warsaw Pact relations that was unusually complimentary of the PZPR's policy toward West Germany, even acknowledging that Poland's trade with the FRG was not tied to political concessions. The report found that the PZPR was cultivating closer ties to East German government and party officials, but that the PZPR still had a long way to go to realize the same close cooperation that the SED had with the CzCP, especially at the regional level.[87]

A month later, Gomułka declared that "any attack on the GDR and Czechoslovakia would be an attack on Poland." The statement came as a surprise to the East Germans. Moldt called Gomułka's recognition of the importance of the GDR "remarkable." Moldt also praised Foreign Minister Rapacki for instructing the Polish press to stress the role of the GDR in resolving the German question. Moldt added that Łobodycz had counseled the Polish press to change its nationalistic bias against the GDR.[88] Gomułka also rejected Adenauer's offer of a nonaggression pact on the grounds that Bonn was trying to isolate the GDR. Gomułka argued that the only benefactor of such a pact would be the FRG: "That cannot happen. The security of the GDR is the security of Poland."[89]

The East German Embassy complimented the PZPR for the way it conducted the April elections. The embassy claimed that "democracy" had prevailed in Poland, and that the people had expressed their satisfaction with party and government policies.[90] Another SED report observed that Western influence on the elections had been less than in years past.[91] Although East German officials were wrong about the PZPR's popularity among the Polish people, which was declining, the Polish communists were slowly reconfirming their ties to the Warsaw Pact.

Warsaw's reaction to a new Berlin crisis in 1961 was indicative of Gomułka's new course. Gomułka had opposed Khrushchev's first Berlin ultimatum in 1958 because of his fears that it might lead to war between the Warsaw Pact and NATO. But when the Berlin Wall went up in August 1961, Gomułka resigned himself to supporting it.

Notes

1. Kornisch (chief engineer at VEB Kohlenanlagen Leipzig) to the secretary of the German-Polish Commission, September 23, 1959, SED ZK, Walter Ulbricht Papers, NL 182/1250.

2. Krystyna Kersten, "1956—The Turning Point," in Odd Arne Westad, Sven Holtsmark, and Iver B. Neumann, eds., *The Soviet Union in Eastern Europe, 1945–1989* (New York: St. Martin's Press, 1994), p. 59.

3. GDR Embassy report on the Fourth Plenary of the PZPR, February 10, 1960, SED ZK, microfilm FBS 339/13491; see also Hansjakob Stehle, *The Independent Satellite: Society and Politics in Poland Since 1945* (London: Pall Mall Press, 1965), p. 209–210. Polish movie houses showed mostly foreign films from the West; in 1960, twenty-nine films from the United States were shown, but only seven made in East Germany.

4. Lugenheim notes on Fifth Plenary of the PZPR Central Committee, July 30, 1960, SED ZK, microfilm FBS 339/13491.

5. Hans Rodenberg to Ulbricht, January 30, 1960, SED ZK, Walter Ulbricht Papers, NL 182/1250; and Croan, "Germany and Eastern Europe," p. 362.

6. Report on the situation in Poland, unsigned, January 24, 1958, SED ZK, microfilm FBS 339/13489.

7. Rossmeisl notes of meeting with an unidentified Soviet Foreign Ministry official, September 12, 1958, SED ZK, Otto Grotewohl Papers, NL 90/485.

8. Mückenberger to Ulbricht, July 15, 1959, SED ZK, Walter Ulbricht Papers, NL 182/1250.

9. GDR Embassy report, October, 1959, SED ZK, microfilm FBS 339/13490.

10. ADN press representative in Warsaw to the SED Central Committee, April 26, 1960, SED ZK, microfilm FBS 339/13491.

11. Paul Rost report on a visit of Polish tourists to Gera, November 7, 1960, SED ZK, microfilm FBS 339/13492.

12. Fuchs notes on the Polish pavilion at the agricultural exhibition in Markkleeburg, June 15, 1960, SED ZK, microfilm FBS 339/12495.

13. Florin to Ulbricht, November 11, 1959, SED ZK, microfilm FBS 339/13423.

14. SED Department of Agitation and Propaganda to Ulbricht, December 23, 1959, SED ZK, Walter Ulbricht Papers, NL 182/1244.

15. Carola Stern, *Ulbricht: A Political Biography* (New York: Frederick Praeger, 1965), p. 207.

16. Rodenberg to Ulbricht, January 30, 1960, SED ZK, Walter Ulbricht Papers, NL 182/1250.

17. Lugenheim (GDR Embassy) report on the Sixth Plenary of the PZPR, September 20, 1960, SED ZK, microfilm FBS 339/12495.

18. E. Plachy (Director of the German Academy of Agricultural Science) to Mückenberger, November 9, 1959, SED ZK, Walter Ulbricht Papers, NL 182/1250; see M. K. Dziewanowski, *Poland in the 20th Century* (New York: Columbia University Press, 1977), p. 188. From 1957 to 1960 Poland received approximately $365 million from the West.

19. Winzer to Ulbricht, January 10, 1961, SED ZK, Walter Ulbricht Papers, NL 182/1250.

20. Püschel notes of meeting with Lech, September 22, 1960, DDR MfAA, Warsaw Embassy, A3725.

21. Günter Pöggel (from *Die Arbeit*) report on his visit to Poland on April 27–28 April, May 9, 1960, SED ZK, Walter Ulbricht Papers, NL 182/1250.

22. Götzl (Frankfurt/Oder district office) to Ulbricht, June 23, 1960, SED ZK, Walter Ulbricht Papers, NL 182/1250.

23. Rachocki notes of a meeting with the press attachés from the socialist countries in Berlin on June 24, June 26, 1959, MSZ, 10/346/38; and Łobodycz to A. Gwiżdż (Polish Parliament), July 13, 1959, MSZ, 10/310/36.

24. Ludwik Gronowski memorandum, September 25, 1959, MSZ, 10/381/43.

25. Kornisch (chief engineer at VEB Kohlenanlagen Leipzig) to the secretary of the German-Polish Commission, September 23, 1959, SED ZK, Walter Ulbricht Papers, NL 182/1250.

26. SED Central Committee Department of Foreign Affairs to the PZPR Central Committee Department of Foreign Affairs, July 8, 1959, SED ZK, microfilm FBS 339/13490.

27. SED district office in Gera to Ulbricht, December 6, 1960, SED ZK, Walter Ulbricht Papers, NL 182/1250.

28. Guidelines for the PZPR-SED/PRP-GDR delegation exchange, undated, ca. December 1959, SED ZK, microfilm FBS 339/13423.

29. Polish Foreign Ministry report, "Unlawful Confiscations on the Border of the PRP-GDR," undated, MSZ, 10/384/42.

30. Bienert (Embassy attaché) notes of meeting with Marczak (Director of the Polish travel agency Orbis), March 4, 1960, DDR MfAA, Warsaw Embassy, A3725.

31. Bienert notes of meeting with Cerny (Czechoslovak Embassy) February 12, 1960, DDR MfAA, Warsaw Embassy, A3725.

32. Winzer to Ulbricht, January 10, 1961, SED ZK, Walter Ulbricht Papers, NL 182/1250.

33. Proposal for the improvement of relations with Poland, May 4, 1960, DDR MfAA, Twelfth Foreign Ministry Council Meeting on May 4, LS-A369.

34. Polish Embassy report, September 15, 1959, MSZ, 10/372/41.

35. Kurella (head of the Commission for Cultural Affairs) to Koplowitz, May 19, 1960, SED ZK, Alfred Kurella Office, IV 2/ 2.026/16.

36. Kirschey (GDR Embassy) report on the Polish Writers' Congress, May 11, 1960, SED ZK, microfilm FBS 339/12495.

37. Ibid.

38. Alfred Schulz and Jan Koplowitz report on their visit to the Polish Writers' Congress in Wrocław, undated, ca. May 1960, SED ZK, Alfred Kurella Office, IV 2/ 2.026/16.

39. Kirschey (GDR Embassy) report on the Polish Writers' Congress, May 11, 1960, SED ZK, FBS 339/12495.

40. Schulz and Koplowitz report on their visit to the Polish Writers' Congress in Wrocław, undated, ca. May 1960, SED ZK, Alfred Kurella Office, IV 2/ 2.026/16.

41. Ibid.

42. Ibid.

43. Ursula Hafranke report on an exhibition of Polish film and theater on June 20 in the GDR, June 28, 1960, SED ZK, Alfred Kurella Office, IV 2/2.026/16.

44. Kurella to Florin, August 2, 1960, SED ZK, Alfred Kurella Office, IV 2/ 2.026/16.

45. Kopa notes of meeting with Colonel Grünberg, April 10, 1959, MSZ, 10/346/38.

46. Rachocki notes of meeting with Fritz Surkau, June 29, 1959, MSZ, 10/381/43.

47. Bolz to Ulbricht, June 11, 1960, SED ZK, Walter Ulbricht Papers, NL 182/1250.

48. Grunert notes of meeting between Bolz and Piotrowski, June 22, 1960, SED ZK, Walter Ulbricht Papers, NL 182/1250.

49. *Neues Deutschland*, July 6, 1960, p. 1.

50. Grotewohl and Cyrankiewicz speeches in Magdeburg on the tenth anniversary of the Görlitz agreement, July 7, 1960, BRD BKA, B136/6718.

51. Wenk to the GDR Foreign Ministry, September 26, 1960, DDR MfAA, Warsaw Embassy, A3751.

52. Polish Embassy report, September 15, 1959, MSZ, 10/372/41.

53. Riesner (GDR Embassy in Warsaw) notes of meeting with Czyrek (Polish Foreign Ministry), August 8, 1959, SED ZK, Walter Ulbricht Papers, NL 182/1250.

54. König to Grotewohl, August 7, 1959, SED ZK, Otto Grotewohl Papers, NL 90/485.

55. GDR Embassy report, August 14, 1959, SED ZK, microfilm FBS 339/13425.

56. Gunter Kohrt (Department of Foreign Affairs) to Ulbricht, July 27, 1959, SED ZK, Walter Ulbricht Papers, NL 182/1250.

57. Ulbricht to Kohrt, July 28, 1959, SED ZK, Walter Ulbricht Papers, NL 182/1250.

58. König to Grotewohl, August 4, 1959, SED ZK, Otto Grotewohl Papers, NL 90/485.

59. GDR Embassy in Warsaw report, August 14, 1959, SED ZK, microfilm FBS 339/13425.

60. Polish Embassy report, September 15, 1959, MSZ, 10/372/41.

61. Czyrek to Winiewicz, August 10, 1959, MSZ, 10/383/42.

62. Foreign Ministry proposal for the improvement of relations with Poland, May 4, 1960, DDR MfAA, Twelfth Foreign Ministry Council Meeting of May 4, LS-A369.

63. Naszkowski notes of meeting with Hegen, January 25, 1960, MSZ, 23/58/7; Moldt to the GDR Foreign Ministry, January 26, 1960, DDR MfAA, Warsaw Embassy, A3751; see also Christoph Royen, "Osteuropaische Staaten" (East European states), in Hans Adolf Jacobsen, Gerd Leptin, Ulrich Scheuner, and Eberhard Schulz, eds., *Drei Jahrzehnte Aussenpolitik der DDR*, 599–619 (Munich: R. Oldenbourg Verlag, 1979), p. 607.

64. Seyfert notes of meetings with the Polish Foreign Ministry Department of International Organizations, August 24, 1960, SED ZK, microfilm FBS 339/13491.

65. Bruno Baum to Florin, February 2, 1960, SED ZK, Walter Ulbricht Papers, NL 182/1250.

66. Naszkowski notes of meeting with Hegen, January 25, 1960, MSZ, 23/58/7.

67. Moldt to the GDR Foreign Ministry, February 2, 1960, DDR MfAA, Warsaw Embassy, A3751.

68. Moldt report on Polish Parliamentary meetings of February 16–17, February 23, 1960, SED ZK, microfilm FBS 339/12495.

69. Foreign Ministry proposal for the improvement of relations with Poland, May 4, 1960, DDR MfAA, Twelfth Foreign Ministry Council Meeting of May 4, LS-A369.

70. Protocol of the Twelfth Foreign Ministry Council Meeting on May 4, May 5, 1960, DDR MfAA, Twelfth Council Meeting of May 4, LS-A369.

71. Rapacki notes of meetings with Bolz on May 31-June 1, June 15, 1960, MSZ, 23/58/7.

72. Bolz notes of meetings with Rapacki from May 31-June 1, 1960, SED ZK, Walter Ulbricht Papers, NL 182/1250.

73. Krahn to the SED, June 21, 1960, SED ZK, Walter Ulbricht Papers, NL 182/1250.

74. Weise notes of meeting with Łobodycz, June 15, 1960, DDR MfAA, Warsaw Embassy, A3725.

75. Stenographic record of the meetings between the Polish and East German Foreign Ministries in Berlin from August 4–8, 1960, DDR MfAA, Minister's Office, A17670.

76. Hegen to Fischer (SED Department of Foreign Affairs), November 25, 1960, SED ZK, microfilm FBS 339/13423.

77. GDR Embassy report on the Sixth Plenary of the PZPR on September 13–14, 1960, October 3, 1960, SED ZK, microfilm FBS 339/12495.

78. Professor Abraham notes of a reception at the Polish Embassy in Moscow, September 28, 1960, SED ZK, Walter Ulbricht Papers, NL 182/1250.

79. Łobodycz notes of meeting with Moldt, November 25, 1960, MSZ, 23/167/14.

80. Moldt to Seyfert, December 20, 1960, DDR MfAA, Warsaw Embassy, A3751.

81. Winzer to Ulbricht, January 10, 1961, SED ZK, Walter Ulbricht Papers, NL 182/1250.

82. Report of the Session of Main Council of the Society for the Development of the Western Territories on February 19, 1961, PZPR KC, group Izydorczyk, 473/17; and Baum (SED district office in Potsdam) to Florin, February 7, 1961, SED ZK, Walter Ulbricht Papers, NL 182/1250. In February, Baum told Cyrankiewicz that after the disputes at the Moscow Conference in 1960, Gomułka had unequivocally taken the Soviet side in the Sino-Soviet dispute.

83. Annual GDR Embassy report for 1960 (by Bechner) to the GDR Foreign Ministry Poland Section, February 14, 1961, DDR MfAA, Poland Section, A1780.

84. Moldt notes of meeting with Szewczyk (PZPR Department of Foreign Affairs), January 6, 1961, DDR MfAA, Warsaw Embassy, A3751.

85. Hegen to König on a meeting between Beitz (Krupp Steel Company) and Cyrankiewicz, January 24, 1961, SED ZK, Walter Ulbricht Papers, NL 182/1250.

86. Baum to Florin, February 7, 1961, SED ZK, Walter Ulbricht Papers, NL 182/1250.

87. Report on relations with the communist and workers' parties in the socialist countries, February 17, 1961, SED ZK, Department of Foreign Affairs, IV 2/20/31.

88. Moldt to König, March 21, 1961, SED ZK, Walter Ulbricht Papers, NL 182/1250.

89. Quoted in Peter Raina, *Gomułka: Politische Biographie* (Gomulka: Political biography) (Cologne: Verlag Wissenschaft und Politik, 1970), p. 130.

90. Littke memorandum on the Polish elections of April 1961, April 28, 1961, SED ZK, microfilm FBS 339/13424.

91. SED Department of Foreign Affairs information on the Polish Parliamentary and National Council elections, June 6, 1961, SED ZK, microfilm FBS 339/13491.

13

The Berlin Wall and the Détente in Polish–East German Relations, 1961–1962

To us there is no doubt that great changes have been made in the People's Republic of Poland, that the Poland of 1962 differs fundamentally from the Poland of 1956.

—*SED report on Poland, December 1962*[1]

Unlike the Berlin ultimatum of 1958, which was Khrushchev's answer to U.S. plans to nuclearize West Germany, Ulbricht was the driving force behind the new Berlin crisis in 1961. The thousands of East Germans who left the GDR through the open city left behind a depleted labor force and a country deprived of its best minds. Approximately one-sixth of the Soviet zone's population had fled to the West since 1945; 144,000 left in 1959, and another 200,000 in 1960. About 1,000 a day were leaving in the summer of 1961.[2]

Prosperous West Berlin undermined East German propaganda promoting socialism as Germany's future. East German citizens could go to West Berlin and see the fruits of capitalism, which were obviously more bountiful than anything the GDR had to offer. It was most embarrassing to the SED that many East Berliners preferred to work in West Berlin for better wages. The SED's claims that East Germany equalled and even surpassed West Germany's standard of living could not stand the comparison.

Ulbricht's position was strengthened by East Germany's economic importance to the Soviet Union and the NVA's integration into the military structure of the Warsaw Pact. After relations with Beijing broke down in 1960, Khrushchev was determined to stay on good terms with the satellites in Eastern Europe, more so with the GDR. In January 1961, East

Berlin tested the limits of its diplomatic freedom by issuing a unilateral warning to the Western Allies to stop their aggressive actions in Berlin. Surprised by the move, Khrushchev told Ulbricht not to do it again.[3] With his economy in trouble, Khrushchev could not risk economic sanctions from the West by challenging their presence in West Berlin.[4]

Ulbricht at last convinced Khrushchev of the need for a wall to divide the city. The two leaders no longer believed in their grandiose claims that the GDR would soon surpass West Germany's economic output. Khrushchev later recalled that he did not want the exodus of East Germans to cause a labor shortage that the Soviets would have to resolve: "We didn't want our workers to clean their toilets."[5]

For years the Ulbricht régime had tried to persuade Warsaw to coordinate its Berlin policy with the GDR. The East German Foreign Ministry suspected that the Poles were reluctant to support Ulbricht in Berlin because they still doubted the long-term viability of the GDR.[6] When Polish organizers of the Poznań Trade Fair sent West Berlin firms New Year's greetings addressed to "West Berlin, Federal Republic of Germany," the East Germans informed Khrushchev that the West German press was playing up the incident.[7] The East Germans were also disappointed with the lack of Polish press coverage of the fifteenth anniversary of the founding of the SED in April 1961, more so because they had supplied the Polish authorities with plenty of propaganda to publicize the event.[8] A few months later, when the Polish press incorrectly translated a statement that Ulbricht had made in reference to the German question, Ulbricht appeared to have questioned the GDR's commitment to the Oder-Neisse border.[9]

On July 21, Gomułka declared that if the Western powers did not want to make peace with both German states, then Poland, the Soviet Union, and the other socialist states would sign one with the GDR. He said that this was not the best option, however: "Of course this will be the worse solution, but it is unavoidable. . . . The Soviet Union and other socialist countries are determined to conclude a peace treaty and turn West Berlin into a free city by the end of the year." Ulbricht vehemently objected that a peace treaty with the GDR alone was a "worse solution," and to the suggestion that Berlin become a "free city" rather than a city fully integrated into the GDR.[10]

At the Vienna summit between Khrushchev and new U.S. President John F. Kennedy in June, Khrushchev issued a new six-month ultimatum on Berlin. The Kennedy administration, embarrassed by the failed invasion of Cuba and the Soviets' successful manned space flight, was determined to take a hard stand on West Berlin. Many Polish communists worried that if steps were taken to halt traffic between East and West Berlin, rioting would break out in the GDR capitol; if this happened, West

Germany, armed with nuclear weapons, would be compelled to intervene. Khrushchev assured the Warsaw Pact countries that NATO would
not force an armed confrontation in Berlin. Gomułka believed him, although, until the Warsaw Pact meetings in Moscow that August, he was
unaware of the plans to build a wall.[11]

On August 13, 1961, the Soviets and East Germans halted traffic between East and West Berlin. *Trybuna Ludu* commented that the GDR and
the Soviet Union were trying to prevent Western provocations in the city
and to regulate the anomalous situation of West Berlin's being situated in
the middle of the GDR.[12] The newspaper called the decision to put up the
wall "correct and necessary."[13] According to one SED source, most PZPR
members recognized that West Berlin was creating too many political
and economic problems for the GDR.[14] In language that seemed more
suited to the crude propaganda of Stalin's era, Polish diplomats told East
German officials that the wall helped the Polish people understand that
East Germany and the entire Soviet camp had to contain the "West German war mongers."[15]

News of the division of Berlin sent the Polish people into a panic. Food
shops quickly sold out as nervous Poles laid in supplies; soldiers in the
Polish army were convinced they were going to war.[16] One East German
journalist in Warsaw reported that the Poles, including many party members, thought the Germans were all the same and would do something to
cause a new war, whether it was Adenauer's atomic weapons or Ulbricht's Berlin Wall.[17]

At first, Gomułka reacted cautiously to the crisis. The Czechoslovak
and Hungarian governments issued official declarations in support of
the Berlin Wall, but Gomułka did not elaborate on the Warsaw Pact's
joint communiqué justifying the move.[18] Gomułka could no longer afford
to alienate the other Soviet bloc countries, however. After years of court-
ing the West, Gomułka had failed to gain significant diplomatic or economic results. His tacit acceptance of the Berlin Wall marked a turning
point in Polish-East German relations; in September, Gomułka announced that he would not sign a nonaggression treaty with West Germany. Much to the satisfaction of East Berlin, Gomułka declared unam-
biguously that "the security of the GDR is the security of Poland."[19]
Cyrankiewicz said that it was time to sign a peace treaty with both German states, and promised his government's support of the GDR's efforts
to resolve the Berlin problem, including the problem of the Berlin Wall.[20]

Polish press coverage of the GDR increased in the fall of 1961, and Polish journalists were generally more sympathetic to East Germany's struggle with West Germany than they had been in the past.[21] One SED report
was unusually positive about the change in official Polish policy toward
the GDR: "The measures of our government were supported uncondi-

tionally and widely publicized in the [Polish] press."[22] The East German Embassy in Warsaw praised Poland's foreign policy, especially the PZPR's support of East Germany in the Berlin crisis. Even Poland's relations with Yugoslavia now appeared to parallel those of the rest of the Warsaw Pact countries.[23] In contrast to past years, the SED characterized recent meetings between SED and PZPR regional offices in the Oder-Neisse region as "sincere and open."[24] East German officials noticed that Poles were even willing to discuss political and ideological questions, having conspicuously avoided them before. The East Germans credited their own propaganda for this change in attitude.[25]

Soviet diplomats in Warsaw were also impressed with Gomułka's newfound willingness to cooperate with the Warsaw Pact; one described the political situation in Poland as "absolutely healthy."[26]

The Border and Germany

The deep distrust that the Ulbricht and Gomułka régimes had developed over the years could not be overcome overnight, however. The two parties could not find common ground on various ideological issues, although they now kept the debates out of public view. The main problem, as it had been for the entire postwar period, was the SED's refusal to recognize Poland's historical claim to German territory. The SED would not budge from this position. The Poles suspected that the SED wanted to keep its options open for a border revision should Germany be reunified.

The controversy resurfaced in June 1961, when the Poles criticized Ulbricht for ignoring Poland's historical claims and adhering instead to the old SED line that Hitler had merely gambled away the eastern territories.[27] A year later, the East German government issued a document that made a positive reference to German General Hans von Seekct's support of the Treaty of Rapallo between Weimar Germany and the Soviet Union in 1922. The document cited Rapallo as part of the tradition of friendly Soviet-German relations—which the GDR was now perpetuating—and blamed German monopoly capitalists and wealthy land owners for fighting Hitler's war and losing German territory.[28]

For years, Polish officials had expressed their objection to positive references to Rapallo; they interpreted the Treaty of Rapallo as a precedent to the Nazi-Soviet Pact of 1939. They were especially angered by the East German government's document because Seekct was a confirmed enemy of Poland.[29] Gomułka cited as proof Seekct's declaration that "the existence of Poland is intolerable, irreconcilable with the conditions of the life of Germany. Poland must disappear and will disappear."[30] A sharp critique of the document by Dr. Wirginia Grabska, the head of the German department of the Polish Institute for International Relations, prompted one East German diplomat to write that "her words left the perception that the GDR was going back on its recognition of the Oder-Neisse border." East German diplomats tried to explain that the publication was for West German consumption, but one Polish official responded that the price for this kind of propaganda was too high: "Poland feels hit on the head by it. Whom does that help?"[31]

The document added to Polish perceptions that should a German confederation become a reality, East Berlin would work with Bonn to revise the Oder-Neisse border. The PZPR still doubted that the SED was trying to eradicate revanchism in East Germany. The members of one PZPR delegation to the GDR in the spring of 1962 repeatedly expressed their distrust in the East German people and questioned the SED's commitment to the border.[32] Speaking to a crowd in Gdańsk in July, Gomułka intentionally cited Poland's historical presence along the Baltic Sea, and notably in Gdańsk, to justify Polish claims to the former German territories.[33]

Over five years had passed since the formation of the Warsaw Pact, but Soviet commanders still held serious doubts about whether the East German and Polish armies would fight together to defend the Oder-Neisse border. Neither the Polish communists nor the Polish people in general trusted the loyalty of the East German army in a war against West Germany and NATO.[34] Gomułka was reluctant to allow the East German army to participate in Warsaw Pact maneuvers in Poland; he knew that Poles would shudder at the sight of a German army marching around the countryside and German military convoys rolling down Polish roads. Gomułka asked Ulbricht why East German soldiers had to wear uniforms that were so similar to the old Wehrmacht issue. Ulbricht acknowledged that it was a compromise to East German feelings of nationalism: "We give the people their uniforms, [which is] perhaps a compromise, but in this way we win them over and can more easily raise them to be good communists."[35]

Trybuna Ludu wrote that it was important for Poles to know what East German soldiers thought was their mission and what they knew about Poland.[36] Polish officials chided the East Germans for allowing nationalist and anti-Polish elements to play a significant role in East German military, political, and economic affairs, and for coddling former Nazi and neofascist elements in the army, party, government, and intelligentsia.[37] Polish officials even told the East Germans that they were glad that the Soviet army was stationed in the GDR.[38] A year after the Berlin Wall went up, party functionaries were still telling the East Germans that the Polish people feared the decision to divide Berlin might lead to war.[39]

No matter which policy the PZPR conducted in regard to the German question, it rarely seemed to satisfy the dogmatic East German communists. For example, in September 1961, SED Politburo member Erich

Mückenberger spoke in Warsaw for the twenty-second anniversary of Hitler's attack on Poland. For several years the Poles had criticized the SED's lackadaisical observances of this event, but now the East German Embassy faulted the Poles for not promoting Mückenberger's speech and for not mentioning that many former Wehrmacht officers held high positions in the West German army.[40] The embassy concluded that in general "East Germany's peace proposals, the German peace plan, and other special actions and initiatives of the GDR are still not propagated enough."[41]

The East Germans alleged that Poles had serious misconceptions about German reunification, and repeatedly faulted the PZPR for not promoting the GDR's socialist system as Germany's future.[42] In February 1962, a SED report found that Polish attitudes toward the two German states had not changed much over the past few years; even many PZPR members downplayed the importance of the GDR. The SED branch office in Neubrandenburg wrote that "many [Poles] are of the opinion that the West will not begin a war; or that it [life] is much better in the West than [it is] here."[43] Although East German officials could not understand the reason their Polish comrades had more trust in the West Germans, the Poles knew that Bonn conducted a more honest, if hostile, policy toward Poland, and that East Berlin feigned friendship.[44]

Unresolved Policy Differences

In the early 1960s, Gomułka began to turn the clock back to 1955, if not to 1953. His régime took on some of the trappings of Stalinism—becoming increasingly intolerant of dissent and more rigid in its foreign and domestic policies. Gomułka surrounded himself with obsequious yes-men, and, according to one biographer, became "a rigid, narrow-minded, authoritarian, petty tyrant. . . . He developed fits of rage, became moody, capricious, and morbidly preoccupied with his prestige. He could stand no criticism."[45]

Although his régime began to look more like Ulbricht's, Gomułka could abide no criticism from the East German communists. The East Germans were highly critical of the PZPR's constant references to October 1956 as the beginning of Poland's political and economic renewal.[46] The Polish cultural scene remained much more open than any other in the bloc, and the PZPR still tolerated private farming and some private enterprise. The SED kept up its relentless attacks on Poland's private farming sector and the influence of the Catholic Church in the countryside; for years, Ulbricht had maintained that socialism in Poland had no future without absolute control over religious affairs and the reactionary Polish clergy— which the East Germans thought was infiltrated by Western agents. The SED criticized the PZPR for its half-baked policy of weakening peoples' religious beliefs to the point of indifference to Catholicism and socialism.[47]

In March 1962, a delegation of women from East German collective farms confirmed what the SED leadership had been saying for years— that there was little PZPR presence in the rural areas. The East German delegation urged Polish officials to collectivize immediately.[48] Later that spring, East German officials confronted Zenon Kliszko with a long list of the PZPR's failed domestic policies: the party's inadequate efforts at propaganda, lack of economic planning, and bankrupt agrarian policies.[49] A few months later, East German officials lectured another delegation of Polish agricultural experts on the superiority of collective agriculture. The Poles were still not listening to these tired old refrains. Although the PZPR was interested in the East Germans' agricultural technology, the party maintained its position that the Polish farmer could not be forced to collectivize, but had to find his own way of socializing agriculture.[50]

Khrushchev also had his differences with Gomułka over the lack of collectivized farming in Poland, but, unlike Ulbricht and the SED, Khrushchev did not press the matter. He later wrote that "the organization of farmlands was an internal matter for Poland, and we never took Comrade Gomułka to task for it. If we ever raised questions at all, it was only to inform ourselves about how their system of agriculture worked." Khrushchev acknowledged that Polish agriculture was more productive than that of most of the other Comecon countries;[51] he ridiculed Ulbricht for importing Polish potatoes at the same time the SED was bragging about the superiority of its collectivized farms.[52]

East German officials were still unhappy with the PZPR's tolerance of ideologically unreliable elements, more so in literature and art. The East German Foreign Ministry called it too much "modernist" influence.[53] The East German communists could never wholeheartedly embrace their Polish comrades until the PZPR tightened censorship. In January 1961, Alexander Abusch, the East German Minister of Culture, visited Poland for discussions on expanding official cultural exchanges. In Abusch's opinion, Polish officials were reluctant to discuss ideological issues for fear of exposing their weakness on this front. Edward Ochab said that the Polish Writers' Congress was more politically reliable now, but Abusch and Hegen thought that he was overlooking various ideological contradictions in cultural life in Poland.[54]

The East German Embassy warned that "the cultural scene [in Poland] shows that the enemy is still very strong,"[55] adding that "there is no clear party line in the question of the Marxist aesthetic."[56] The Polish Minister of Culture and Art, Tadeusz Galinski, told an East German Foreign Ministry official that it was up to Polish artists to decide how to achieve the "realization of the social function of art." The East Germans quickly responded that Polish artists were allowed far too much latitude. Without socialist realism as the main criteria for evaluating art, they argued, Polish artists would continue to create decadent, bourgeois works.[57]

The SED still belittled the PZPR for failing to inculcate Polish youth with socialist ideas, or to change Polish prejudices against East Germans.[58] In contrast to the FDJ's allegedly comprehensive and successful indoctrination of East German youth, the SED blamed the PZPR's youth organization, the ZMS, for failing to promote the construction of a socialist society.[59] At one "friendship meeting" between Polish and East German youth groups in Görlitz, the Poles jeered FDJ members and asked them such questions as, "Why are you hiding yourselves behind the [Berlin] Wall?" The meeting ended in a fist fight.[60]

Such incidents hardened the SED leaders' disinclination for closer relations with Poland. Until the PZPR and the Polish people proved their Marxist credentials, Ulbricht was reluctant to expand cultural relations and tourist exchanges, in spite of repeated entreaties from his diplomats and lower-level party members to do so.[61] At the Leipzig Trade Fair in March 1962, Cyrankiewicz proposed a freer exchange of tourists, but the East Germans did not respond.[62] According to SED reports, Polish tourists on vacation in East Germany usually tried to avoid reminders of work, a situation zealous East German officials viewed as more proof of the PZPR's inadequate propaganda efforts.[63]

Chronic Economic Disputes

West European economic recovery in the late 1950s marginalized the importance of imports from Poland. Western Europe was meeting more of its demand for coal, and oil was replacing it as the main energy source. Poland had few other products that the West wanted to buy. By the end of the decade, Gomułka began to shift trade back to the Warsaw Pact countries and to support Khrushchev's call for more joint ventures.[64]

A widespread belief in Poland held that East Germany was enjoying too many economic concessions from the Soviet Union, and that trade with the GDR and the Warsaw Pact in general was to Poland's disadvantage. Envious of the East Germans' higher standard of living, Polish officials thought that if any country should be receiving trade concessions, it was Poland.[65] Gomułka's frequent requests for economic aid caused Khrushchev to comment that "Gomułka had a way of turning these matters into a national issue." Khrushchev accused the Poles of "selfishness," and of trying to take advantage of him.[66]

The difference between the relative prosperity of the GDR and poverty in Poland was an embarrassment for both governments. In the early

1960s, East Germany's per capita income and personal consumption was at least 50 percent higher than Poland's.[67] Polish officials from Gdańsk told one East German delegation that the GDR standard of living was 60 percent higher than Poland's.[68] The Poles frequently reminded the East Germans that Poland had been the victim of German aggression less than a generation ago.

The Gomułka régime knew that the disparity in standards of living would confirm East German stereotypes about the inability of the Poles to run an efficient economy.[69] For example, many Poles blamed a shortage of flour in 1962 on Poland's exports to East Germany. When one East German visitor to Poland was asked about the availability of flour in East German stores, he boasted that, if they wanted, East Germans could buy a car-full. Polish officials observed that such arrogant behavior contributed to a common belief that the East Germans were no different from the Germans in Hitler's Reich, and certainly no better than those in the FRG.[70] Polish officials were also sensitive to implications that Poland had only coal and food to sell, but the more technologically advanced East German economy produced manufactures for export. Polish officials criticized the East German press for contributing to peoples' impression that unprofitable trade with Poland was responsible for the GDR's economic problems.[71]

Reintegrating the two economies after the numerous trade disputes of the past several years was difficult. By the time Gomułka tried to rekindle economic connections to the GDR, the East German government was less interested; after all, Poland had not been a reliable supplier.[72] The rapid increase in the GDR's trade with the Soviet Union in 1959 and 1960 resulted in a drop in East German food exports to Poland and forced Poland to buy foodstuffs from the United States and Canada at higher prices.[73]

The GDR was in a much stronger economic position in the 1960s than it had ever been before. East Germany supplied about one-third of the machines for the entire Soviet bloc, and was Comecon's most important chemical exporter. But the East German economy was still dependent on the Warsaw Pact for raw materials and steel. The GDR had to import approximately 30 percent of its steel, iron ore, and copper; 50 percent of its coke; 70 percent of its coal; and all of its oil. Chronic shortages of raw materials, Polish coal especially, prevented East Germany from exporting more manufactured goods. The Soviet Union replaced some of the Polish imports, but not enough to satisfy the GDR's needs.[74] The SED estimated that to catch up to the West German economy by 1965, it would have to import an additional 400,000 tons of coal in 1958, 800,000 tons in 1959, and 800,000 in 1960. Total imports of coal had to reach 8,300,000 tons in 1961, and 9,800,000 tons in 1962.[75]

After the Berlin Wall went up in 1961, the East German leaders tried to increase trade with Poland, but on their own terms. The Politburo resolved to end the "one-sided character of its economic relations with Poland."[76] That fall, Bruno Leuschner, the deputy chairman of the GDR Council of Ministers, went to Warsaw to make direct requests for an increase in coal, steel, and chemical deliveries. Leuschner argued that the GDR was now in a delicate political and economic situation because of the economic division of Berlin and the FRG's refusal to negotiate a new trade agreement. He requested an additional 500,000 tons of coal for 1961, and a total of 3 million tons of coal and 300,000 tons of coke in 1962. Polish negotiators agreed to send an additional 100,000 tons of coal above the amount agreed to in the plan for 1961, and an extra 150,000 tons of coal in 1962, but no more coke. The Poles also agreed to handle an extra 11.6 million tons of Soviet exports to the GDR on Polish railways in 1962. The Poles had to accept a reduction in East German imports in 1961 and 1962, among them 64 million convertible złotys worth of consumer goods. The Poles also waived a promised credit for the purchase of East German machines and equipment for a factory in Turoszów, and granted the GDR a credit of 100 million convertible złotys for technology projects. The Poles rejected such other East German proposals as the one asking for a total of 4.5 million tons of Polish coal in 1962. This was 1.5 million more tons than Leuschner had requested. One Polish trade official called this request "completely incomprehensible." The Poles also denied the East Germans a credit to cut transit costs in half, and refused to enter into negotiations on reducing the cost of the coal. Polish trade officials demanded to know when East Germany would meet its obligations to ship machines and industrial equipment, but Leuschner said that until the GDR was sure of its own imports it could promise anything.[77]

After some hard bargaining, Leuschner was able to sign a new trade agreement that fall. But the SED was still not satisfied that Poland was doing all it could to export steel, coal, coke, and phosphorus to the GDR, or to provide credits to buy these and other goods. The East Germans were incensed that the Poles would not increase their "completely insufficient" steel exports to the GDR because of Poland's export obligations to West Germany. They were also unsympathetic to Polish demands for machines and consumer goods to make up the GDR's trade deficit, and more so when the Poles refused to reduce transit costs through Poland.[78]

By late October 1961, the two sides were already blaming each other for not making the deliveries called for in the agreement.[79] According to Polish sources, Poland fulfilled 101.1 percent of its export obligations to East Germany in 1961, and the GDR fulfilled 97.2 percent of its obligations. One Polish official thought that trade with the GDR was "generally disadvantageous for Poland," notably the shortfall in East German machines for the Polish chemical industry. By the spring of 1962, about one-third of these deliveries were still delinquent.[80]

At the end of 1961, the East German Embassy characterized the progress of trade negotiations with Poland as "limited," and recommended new efforts to convince the Poles of the complex problems facing the GDR economy. For years, the East Germans had tried to persuade the Poles that the health of the East German economy was in the interest of Poland and the entire Soviet bloc.[81] With the East German economy outperforming most of the other socialist economies in the early 1960s, Poland and the other Comecon countries were still not persuaded by this argument. At the Comecon meeting in Warsaw in December 1961, Polish Deputy Premier Stefan Jędrychowski angrily criticized some "undisciplined" countries for not keeping their export promises. According to East German diplomat Karl Mewis, the other Comecon representatives shouted, "That's right, the GDR!" Mewis concluded, "I don't have any more illusions; what concerns the [economic] plan for 1962 there is only one motto: We must help ourselves."[82]

With the exception of a few staunch Marxists, Polish officials were painfully aware that the socialist economies would never be a match for the West. They ridiculed the East Germans for predicting that the GDR would equal and then surpass the West Germans' per capita consumption by 1962.[83] The Polish government was certainly not going to help the East Germans to achieve that goal, anyway. In the early 1960s, about 60 percent of Poland's trade was with the Comecon countries (30 percent with the Soviet Union), the smallest percentage of any Soviet bloc country.[84] Trade with Poland comprised only 10 percent of all East German trade with the Comecon countries in 1960, and only 7 percent of East German trade as a whole. Five years later, these figures had not changed, and did not fluctuate much for the rest of the decade.[85]

West Germany was Poland's most important capitalist trading partner, doing $151.1 million in business in 1959. In April 1960, Poland and West Germany signed a new trade agreement to raise each country's deliveries by DM 150 million. In a shift from years past, the East German government now objected to the inclusion of trade between West Berlin and Poland in the agreement because of the implication that West Berlin was a part of the FRG.[86] In 1961, Poland's exports to West Germany increased 15.2 percent over 1960, but West German exports to Poland dropped 6.2 percent, leaving the Poles with a positive trade balance of about DM 70 million.[87] By 1961, Great Britain had replaced the FRG as Poland's most important trading partner in the West, but that trade represented only 6.5 percent of Poland's total trade.[88]

The Adenauer government assumed that Ulbricht's push for greater economic cooperation with the Soviet Union would cause Poland to expand its economic ties to the West, but when the Common Market countries signed an agreement in January 1962 to cut the price of their agricultural products, Poland's exports were squeezed out. Agricultural goods made up over half of Poland's trade with West Germany. Talks on a new trade deal stalled,[89] and in the first half of 1962, trade between Poland and West Germany dropped 10 percent.[90] In October 1962, the Polish government predicted that trade with West Germany would fall 20 percent that year.[91]

East German trade officials knew that Poland was in dire need of machines and consumer goods in 1962, and they drove a hard bargain for a new trade deal. Polish officials often commented that it was much easier to do business with the Czechoslovaks.[92] The Poles were reluctant to accept a significant East German trade deficit or to provide a credit to cover it, but they eventually agreed to let the GDR run a 30-million ruble deficit, less than half the original East German proposal.[93] Poland covered about 45 percent of its imports from the GDR in 1962 with transit charges, but the East Germans were trying to reduce those costs by expanding the Rostock harbor, other water routes, and pipelines.[94] There was also an impasse over a new deal on waterway traffic; the East Germans argued that a simple extension of the 1954 agreement was inequitable now because the Poles could use a new network of waterways that extended throughout the GDR, and Poland's waterways still connected only the northern and western parts of the country.[95]

Polish representatives to the Comecon meetings in July 1962 called for an intensification of economic cooperation with the GDR,[96] but the Poles and the Romanians would not accept the East German and Czechoslovak recommendations for a division of labor in Comecon that would assign Poland and Romania the job of exporting raw materials. The Poles and Rumanians rejected arrangements that would compromise their own industrial development.[97]

In September, East German diplomat Moldt concluded that the Polish government's stronger political support of the GDR "is not finding its equivalent expression in the economic sphere." Moldt contrasted the problems with Poland with the GDR's close economic cooperation with Czechoslovakia, and even with West Germany and West Berlin.[98] Moldt concluded that Poland's unwillingness to increase agricultural exports to East Germany was proof that Polish exports to the capitalist countries had priority.[99]

At the behest of the East Germans, Leuschner again went to Warsaw on September 10 to meet Eugeniusz Szyr. Leuschner acknowledged that the historical legacy of German exploitation was partly responsible for the difference in Polish and East German economic standards and that his government would keep that in mind during the negotiations. The

PZPR blamed the SED's lack of a concrete economic plan for the stalemate, but Leuschner laid out a series of precise propositions for closer economic cooperation. The Poles denied Leuschner's allegations that Poland was charging 80 percent more for coal and coke than the capitalist countries. A PZPR report concluded that, given the relatively short distance from Silesia to the GDR, Polish coal was cheaper. Unable to convince the Poles to lower the price, the East Germans began to charge more for some of its exports to Poland.[100]

Leuschner stood his ground during the negotiations. Not only was the East German economy outproducing Poland's, but Poland was running an overall trade deficit, in part because of the falling price of coal on the world market.[101] The East Germans were aware that the Polish government would have to cut investment plans by approximately 60 billion złotys in 1962.[102]

Although the Poles were reluctant to tie themselves to long-term agreements that would force them to import East German machines after they became obsolete, they had little choice by now. From 40 to 50 percent of Poland's imports from East Germany consisted of machines and industrial equipment; chemical products made up 35 percent, and consumer goods comprised from 15 to 20 percent. That Poland could no longer cover the cost of East German goods through exports and East German transit payments made matters worse, and in 1964, Poland's credits from the GDR were to come due.[103]

Szyr and Leuschner could not break the impasse, however, although Szyr agreed to increase cooperative efforts in the coal and chemical industries.[104] The talks were unsuccessful in part because Szyr thought that Poland was in a stronger negotiating position. The Polish Foreign Ministry doubted that the GDR would fulfill its economic plan for 1962, and was facing shortages of potatoes, corn, and grain. The ministry observed that the economic downturn was creating considerable dissatisfaction among East Germans, who had assumed that the Berlin Wall was temporary. The ministry warned that "a rather strong materialist attitude reigns in GDR society. This affects a significant part of the [East German] youth as well."[105]

In a briefing paper for the meetings between Gomułka and Ulbricht in October, the East German Embassy in Warsaw observed that the Polish government had not lived up to the promise Cyrankiewicz had made at the Leipzig Trade Fair earlier in the year—namely, to give the GDR "maximum economic support." The embassy recommended adopting a hard negotiating position to reduce transit costs, increase imports of Polish steel, and ensure punctual deliveries of coal and coke.[106] An annual SED report on trade with Poland concluded that the annual increase in the volume of trade was still "insufficient."[107]

From left to right: Jósef Cyrankiewicz, Władysław Gomułka, and Walter Ul-
bricht at the East German People's Parliament in Berlin on October 19, 1962.
(Photo courtesy Stiftung Archiv der Parteien und Massenorganisationen der
DDR im Bundesarchiv, reprinted with permission)

The Third Gomułka-Ulbricht Summit

The summit between Ulbricht and Gomułka in October was shaping up
to be more productive than their two previous encounters. One SED
briefing paper for Ulbricht was optimistic about Poland's recent political
development, especially the PZPR's assertion of its leading role in Polish
society. The SED observed that Poland's official policy on the German
question was paralleling the GDR's; it praised the Polish press for "un-
covering the militarist and revanchist policy of the Adenauer government." The report even complimented Poland for its economic cooperation. The rest of the report was still critical of the Gomułka régime for
ideological inconsistencies, however, and for erratic cultural and agricultural policies. According to the SED, the PZPR was not doing enough to
promote the accomplishments of the GDR, and was not acting in tandem
with the Soviet Union to ostracize China and Albania.[108]
   The East German Embassy in Warsaw suggested that Ulbricht lobby
Gomułka for more support of the GDR against West Germany, including
more Polish press coverage on the dangers of West German militarism
and imperialism. The embassy reported that "at forums and other discussions we still see the reservations of the Polish people toward the pol-

From left to right: Władysław Gomułka, Jósef Cyrankiewicz, and Walter Ulbricht reviewing East German troops at the Brandenburg Gate, October 19, 1962. (Photo courtesy Stiftung Archiv der Parteien und Massenorganisationen der DDR im Bundesarchiv, reprinted with permission)

itics, the organs, and the actions of the GDR." The East Germans charged that the average Pole could not distinguish between the East and West German flags.[109] Karl Krahn, the East German correspondent in Warsaw, warned Ulbricht that dangerous revisionist forces were still lurking in the PZPR. He blamed these elements for their unfounded allegations that Polish security forces had pushed a Polish journalist out of a window to his death. Krahn considered the journalist politically unreliable anyway. Krahn reported that well over 300 high-level party and government officials, intellectuals, and journalists, all of whom he characterized as "revisionists," had attended the reporter's funeral. Nonetheless, Krahn thought that Gomułka's position in the party was strong enough to combat all rivals.[110]

A comprehensive briefing report for the Polish delegation raised a number of outstanding issues. The Poles were still apprehensive about the political reliability of the East German army and the lingering nationalism of the SED *nomenklatura*, who frequently used the nationalist term *fatherland* in reference to Germany. Polish officials thought that East German propaganda employed too many references to the traditions and leaders of the old Prussian-German army. The report also blamed the East German government for the failure of several cooperative efforts in the chemical and machine industries. The Poles noted that the SED was now more interested in exchanges in the scientific field, but that exchanges were still too one-sided; many more Polish scientists, professors, and students went to the GDR.[111]

The Polish report cited new problems in tourist traffic with East Germany. More East German emigrés from the former German territories were now visiting Poland, in part because the Berlin Wall had cut them off from West Berlin and West Germany. The East German authorities, however, made it more difficult for the emigrés to go to Poland by increasing the visa fee. The Poles could not help but contrast this situation with the growth in tourism between East Germany and Czechoslovakia.[112]

The briefing also found problems with cultural exchanges, such as the East German government's indifference to popularizing Polish art and literature. Sixteen Polish books appeared in East Germany in 1961, but 92 East German titles circulated in Poland. The East Germans had not performed a single Polish dramatic work in the past few years, but the Poles had performed six East German plays. Polish officials criticized the SED for rejecting theater pieces that did not promote socialist realism.[113]

Gomułka and Cyrankiewicz led the Polish delegation to East Berlin on October 15, 1962, just as the Cuban missile crisis was unfolding. Highlighting the visit was Gomułka's speech to the East German Parliament, which marked the first time in history that a Polish leader had appeared in front of a German legislative body. Gomułka thanked the East Germans for the warm reception, and expressed his satisfaction with the SED's educational efforts to change East German attitudes toward Poland. He contrasted the optimistic mood of this summit with the cool atmosphere that had surrounded the meetings in Berlin over five years earlier. He said that Western attempts to drive a wedge between the SED and the PZPR had failed: "This propaganda about cold relations between the PZPR and the SED was calculated to create the impression in GDR society that the SED was fencing itself off from the PZPR—and vice versa—was calculated to isolate the SED from its own people." Even though the SED had conducted such a policy toward the PZPR, Gomułka said that the visit was a turning point in the history of relations between Poland and East Germany because now the two governments were coming together on their own volition.[114]

The tone of the talks was indeed friendlier than usual, and largely devoid of the acrimony that had punctuated previous encounters. At the top of the agenda was the improvement of trade relations and scientific and technological cooperation. Gomułka admitted that "economic cooperation between our countries is very limited," and pointed out that the GDR and Czechoslovakia had much closer economic ties. Ulbricht said that the GDR was facing serious economic problems because of the division of Berlin, and he seconded Gomułka's call for a wider range of economic exchanges. The two sides agreed on the construction of an oil and gas pipeline from the Soviet Union through Poland to the GDR, cooperative efforts to expand Polish brown coal production, joint industrial ventures, and a general increase in trade.[115]

The talks elicited favorable commentary from Polish journalists; they told one East German reporter that the meetings had exceeded beyond their expectations.[116] Ulbricht declared that "the unbreakable friendship between the German Democratic Republic and the Peoples' Republic of Poland lives!"[117] Ulbricht had made such grandiose statements before, but his confidence in Gomułka was growing. An annual SED report on the state of relations with Poland was unusually optimistic about the country's socialist future: "To us there is no doubt that great changes have been made in the People's Republic of Poland, that the Poland of 1962 differs fundamentally from the Poland of 1956."[118] Even the West German government conceded that the October summit had been a success and that the chances of drawing Poland out of the Soviet sphere were now slim. The West German Foreign Ministry called the talks a significant step in bringing Poland and East Germany together on several political and economic issues. The ministry also observed that the Polish government was becoming more hostile toward the FRG, especially concerning propaganda about the imminent West German threat to the Oder-Neisse border.[119]

The SED and the PZPR were pleased with the results of the talks. In early January 1963, *Trybuna Ludu* assessed the last three months of relations with the GDR as "particularly fruitful."[120] East German diplomats in Warsaw blunted their earlier criticism of the PZPR and its policies when they reported an improvement in their personal relations with Polish officials. One East German diplomat reported that, contrary to previous meetings, exchanges with Polish officials now contributed to a better atmosphere.[121]

The embassy was pleasantly surprised by the new direction of the West Institute in Poznań, which for years had leaned toward studies of West Germany; the institute was now paying more attention to East German affairs.[122] East German diplomats also praised such Polish journals as *Nowe Drogi* and *Sprawy Międzynarodowe* (International Affairs) for their extensive coverage of the GDR in connection with Gomułka's visit. The East Germans were particularly pleased with the stronger statements that PZPR members were making about the GDR's importance to Poland's political and economic future.[123]

The SED's satisfaction with Gomułka was directly related to the PZPR's increasingly repressive policies. Although Gomułka tried to steer a course between the revisionists and the dogmatists in the party in the early 1960s, most of his purges came at the expense of his old supporters, namely, former Minister of Education Władysław Bieńkowski and Warsaw University philosophy professor Leszek Kołakowski, who was expelled from the party in 1966.[124] After testing the limits of Poland's national sovereignty for half a decade, Gomułka knew that the fate of communist Poland ultimately depended on closer political and economic cooperation with the Soviet Union. Khrushchev later claimed that, with each passing year, Polish-Soviet relations continued to improve: "While he [Gomułka] and I still differed in our approach to certain specific issues, our personal relations couldn't have been better."[125]

Gomułka's loyalty to Moscow was dictated in part by his long-standing fear of Germany. Khrushchev remembered Gomułka's telling him, "You know what our intelligentsia fears most of all? The Germans. And the Germans will become a threat to the Poles if our friendly relations with the Soviet Union are ruined."

Gomułka did not differentiate between East and West Germans.[126] Both Khrushchev and Gomułka had benefited politically from de-Stalinization. This was not true of Ulbricht, who remained a staunch supporter of Stalin's legacy and practitioner of his political and economic policies. But Gomułka had to learn to cohabit with the GDR. As one Polish journalist now wrote, "Whatever could threaten [the existence of the GDR]— will affect our country. Today a common destiny ties us to the neighbor on the other side of the Oder."[127] As true as this was, most East Germans and Poles did not like it. The two communist parties did not really believe in their common destiny, either, but in the end they had no choice but to accept it.

Notes

1. Information on the policies of the "fraternal parties" of the socialist countries, December 21, 1962, SED ZK, IV 2/20/31.

2. John Lewis Gaddis, *We Now Know: Rethinking Cold War History* (Oxford: Clarendon Press, 1997), pp. 138, 143, 147.

3. Ibid., p. 144.

4. Douglas Selvage, "Introduction" to "Khrushchev's November 1958 Berlin Ultimatum: New Evidence from the Polish Archives," *Bulletin: Cold War International History Project,* no. 11 (winter 1998), p. 218.

5. Quoted in Gaddis, *We Know Now*, p. 149.

6. Annual report for 1960 by Bechner (Department of Cultural Policy) to the Poland Section of the GDR Foreign Ministry, February 14, 1961, DDR MfAA, Poland Section, A1780.

7. Hain and Seyfert notes of meeting with Karkut (Polish Embassy), January 16, 1961, DDR MfAA, Warsaw Embassy, A3751.

8. Röse (GDR Embassy) report on the celebrations in Poland of the SED's fifteenth anniversary, May 2, 1961, SED ZK, microfilm FBS 339/13496.

9. Röse report, June 19, 1961, SED ZK, microfilm FBS 339/13496.

10. Winzer to Ulbricht, July 24, 1961, SED ZK, Walter Ulbricht Papers, NL 182/1250.

11. Peter Raina, *Gomułka: Politische Biographie* (Gomulka: Political biography) (Cologne: Verlag Wissenschaft und Politik, 1970), pp. 130–131: See Selvage, "Khrushchev's November 1958 Berlin Ultimatum: New Evidence from the Polish Archives," p. 219.

12. *Trybuna Ludu*, August 12, 1961; and August 14, 1961, p. 2.

13. *Trybuna Ludu*, August 15, 1961, p. 2.

14. Olivier to the SED Central Committee, August 22, 1961, SED ZK, microfilm FBS 339/13496.

15. Notes of meeting between Seyfert (GDR Foreign Ministry) and Tomala (Polish Embassy) on September 8, September 11, 1961, DDR MfAA, Warsaw Embassy, A3751.

16. Tönnies (GDR Embassy) report on his visit to Poznań from August 13–15, August 23, 1962, SED ZK, microfilm FBS 339/13422; see also Raina, *Gomułka*, pp. 131–132.

17. Olivier to the SED Central Committee, August 22, 1961, SED ZK, microfilm FBS 339/13496.

18. Moldt to König, August 29, 1961, DDR MfAA, Warsaw Embassy, A3750.

19. Raina, *Gomułka*, p. 130; see also *Nicholas* Bethell, *Gomułka, His Poland and His Communism* (London: Longmans, Green and Co., 1969), p. 243.

20. *Trybuna Ludu*, October 6, 1961, p. 1.

21. See, for example, *Trybuna Ludu*, October 7, 1961, p. 1, October 8, 1961, p. 2, and subsequent issues.

22. Information on the relations with the "fraternal parties" of the socialist camp and with the League of Yugoslav Communist Party in 1961, February 24, 1962, SED ZK, IV/2/20/31.

23. Norbert Kalusche (GDR Embassy) to the GDR Foreign Ministry, December 20, 1961, SED ZK, microfilm FBS 339/13491.

24. SED report on delegation exchanges between the Polish-GDR border areas, April 1, 1962, SED ZK, microfilm FBS 339/13422.

25. SED report on exchanges of delegations with Szczecin, Koszalin, and Gdańsk in 1961, February 7, 1962, SED ZK, microfilm FBS 339/13422.

26. Röse notes of a meeting with Soviet press attaché Scharykin on November 16, November 17, 1961, SED ZK, microfilm FBS 339/13424.

27. Röse to the GDR Foreign Ministry, September 25, 1961, SED ZK, microfilm FBS 339/13496.

28. Mieszław Tomala notes of a meeting with Helmer, undated, ca. April 1962, PZPR KC, 237/XXII–1103.

29. Stenographic summary of a meeting with East German officials on the issue of the GDR and the future of Germany, May 16, 1962, PZPR KC, 237/XXII–1103.

30. Observations on the document "The History of the GDR and the Future of Germany," undated, ca. May 1962, PZPR KC, 237/XXII–1103.

31. Hilmar Schumann report, May 22, 1962, SED ZK, microfilm FBS 339/13496.

32. East German translator (for the Polish delegation to the GDR from May 17–19) to the SED Central Committee Department of Affairs, unsigned, May 22, 1962, SED ZK, microfilm FBS 339/13422.

33. GDR Embassy report on the state holiday in Poland on July 22, July 31, 1962, SED ZK, microfilm FBS 339/13496.

34. Schumann report on his visit to Łódz, August 27, 1962, SED ZK, microfilm FBS 339/13496.

35. Quoted in Franz Sikora, *Sozialistische Solidarität und nationale Interessen* (Socialist solidarity and national interests) (Cologne: Verlag Wissenschaft und Politik, 1977), p. 161.

36. *Trybuna Ludu*, February 28, 1962, p. 1.

37. PZPR evaluation of the situation in the GDR, unsigned, undated, ca. fall 1961, PZPR KC, 237/XXII–1102.

38. Püschel notes of meeting between Reissig and Wichlacz, et al., on January 11, 1962, January 16, 1962, SED ZK, microfilm FBS 339/13496.

39. Tönnies report on his visit to Poznań from August 13–15, August 23, 1962, SED ZK, microfilm FBS 339/13422.

40. Schumann to the GDR Foreign Ministry, September 5, 1961, SED ZK, microfilm FBS 339/13496.

41. GDR Embassy report on Poland for 1961, December 22, 1961, SED ZK, microfilm FBS 339/13496.

42. Information on the relations with the "fraternal parties of the socialist camp and with the League of Yugoslav Communist Party in 1961, February 24, 1962, SED ZK, IV/2/20/31.

43. SED report on exchanges of delegations with Szczecin, Koszalin, and Gdańsk in 1961, February 7, 1962, SED ZK, microfilm FBS 339/13422.

44. Schumann report on his visit to Łódz, August 27, 1962, SED ZK, microfilm FBS 339/13496.

45. Quoted in Bethell, *Gomułka, His Poland and His Communism*, p. 254.

46. GDR Embassy report on the Twenty-Second Congress of the CPSU, November 20, 1961, SED ZK, microfilm FBS 339/13424.

47. Püschel notes on the PZPR's relationship with the Catholic Church, January 8, 1961, SED ZK, microfilm FBS 339/13491.

48. Thilde Scheibe report on the visit of her delegation to Poland from March 21–27, April 9, 1962, SED ZK, microfilm FBS 339/13492. By this time virtually all East German farming was collectivized.

49. Report on the visit of the PZPR delegation to Berlin from May 17–19, May 23, 1962, SED ZK, microfilm FBS 339/13422.

50. Hans Engmann report on a visit of a Polish agricultural delegation to the GDR, September 18, 1962, SED ZK, microfilm 339/13492.

51. Khrushchev, *Khrushchev Remembers: The Last Testament*, pp. 211, 213.

52. East German Ambassador Dölling note on the discussion between Khrushchev and Ulbricht," February 26, 1962, in *Bulletin: Cold War International History Project*, no. 11 (winter 1998), p. 226.

53. GDR Foreign Ministry Department of Culture annual report for 1960 (by Bechner), February 14, 1961, DDR MfAA, Poland Section, A1780.

54. Abusch to Ulbricht, February 1, 1961, SED ZK, Walter Ulbricht Papers, NL 182/1250; and memorandum on Abusch's visit to Poland, unsigned, January 31, 1961, DDR MR, DC–20, file 700.

55. Weise (GDR Embassy) to the SED Central Committee Department of Foreign Affairs, March 14, 1961, SED ZK, microfilm FBS 339/12495.

56. GDR Embassy report on Poland for 1961, December 22, 1961, SED ZK, microfilm FBS 339/13496.

57. Tautz (GDR Foreign Ministry Cultural Department) to Walter (Department of Foreign Affairs), August 20, 1962, SED ZK, Department of Literature and Art, microfilm FBS 277 (IV 2/906/77).

58. Sikora, *Sozialistische Solidarität und nationale Interessen*, p. 161.

59. Olivier to the GDR Foreign Ministry, November 13, 1961, SED ZK, microfilm FBS 339/13424.

60. Wolf Oschlies, "Aktionen der DDR-Reaktionen in Osteuropa" (Actions of the GDR-reactions in Eastern Europe), in Gerd Leptin, ed., *Die Rolle der DDR in Osteuropa* (The role of the GDR in Eastern Europe), 103–121 (Berlin: Duneker und Humboldt, 1974), p. 108.

61. GDR Embassy report on Poland for 1961, December 22, 1961, SED ZK, microfilm FBS 339/13496.

62. Report on the situation in the GDR, unsigned, March 31, 1962, PZPR KC, 237/XXII–1103.

63. See, for example, Gunttmann report on the visit of PZPR members to the GDR from June 1–29, July 6, 1962, SED ZK, microfilm FBS 339/13422.

64. Michael Kaser, *Comecon: Integration Problems of the Planned Economies* (London: Oxford University Press, 1967), p. 15.

65. Wiese notes of meeting with Borkowski (Second Secretary of the Wrocław Party Committee), October 6, 1960, DDR MfAA, Warsaw Embassy, A3725.

66. Nikita Khrushchev, *Khrushchev Remembers: The Last Testament* (Boston: Little, Brown, 1974) p. 211–214.

67. Kaser, *Comecon*, pp. 135–136.

68. Püschel notes of conversation between Reissig and Wichlacz, et al., on January 11, 1962, January 16, 1962, SED ZK, microfilm FBS 339/13496.

69. Report on the situation in the GDR, unsigned, March 31, 1962, PZPR KC, 237/XXII–1103.

70. Gunttmann report on the visit of PZPR members to the GDR from June 1–29, July 6, 1962, SED ZK, microfilm FBS 339/13422.

71. Report on the GDR, March 31, 1962, PZPR KC, 237/XXII–1103; and Helmer notes of meeting between König and Baranowski on July 14, July 16, 1962, SED ZK, microfilm FBS 339/13424.

72. See Christoph Royen, "Osteuropaische Staaten" (East European states), in Hans Adolf Jacobsen, Gerd Leptin, Ulrich Scheuner, and Eberhard Schulz, eds., *Drei Jahrzehnte Aussenpolitik der DDR*, 599–619 (Munich: R. Oldenbourg Verlag, 1979),p. 607.

73. Sieger report on Soviet-Soviet Zone trade, July 11, 1961, BRD AA, Department 7, vol. 439.

74. Sikora, *Sozialistische Solidarität und nationale Interessen*, p. 175.

75. Observations on the development of the GDR economy, 1958–1960, and 1961–1965, April 22, 1958, SED ZK, Walter Ulbricht Office, J IV 2/202–194.

76. Kaser, *Comecon*, p. 105; and Selvage, "Khrushchev's November 1958 Berlin Ultimatum: New Evidence from the Polish Archives," p. 219.

77. F. Zeiler (Central Committee Department of Machine Manufacturing and Metallurgy) notes on trade negotiations with Poland, September 1, 1961, SED ZK, Walter Ulbricht Papers, NL 182/1250; notes of the meeting of Polish and East

German delegations, August 14, 1961, PZPR KC, 237/V–379; Poland-GDR trade proposal, August, 1962, PZPR KC, 237/V–379; Piotr Jaroszewicz to Gomułka, August 16, 1961, PZPR KC, 237/V–379; Zeiler and Carl Eckloff (Deputy Minister for Foreign and Intra-German Trade) report on trade negotiations with Poland, August 25, 1961, SED ZK, Walter Ulbricht Papers, NL 182/1250; and GDR Embassy report on Poland for 1961, December 22, 1961, SED ZK, microfilm FBS 339/13496. According to this SED report, the price of Polish coal was nearly twice the cost of coal from the capitalist countries.

78. Ebersbach report on Polish economic assistance for the GDR, April 2, 1962, SED ZK, microfilm FBS 339/13491.

79. SED Central Committee Department of Trade, Supply, and Foreign Trade report on a meeting with Kopczynski (Polish trade official), October 30, 1961, SED ZK, Walter Ulbricht Papers, NL 182/1250.

80. Record of the completion of the Comecon plan, and protocols on foreign trade with the socialist countries for 1961, April 25, 1962, PZPR KC, 237/V–348.

81. GDR Embassy report on Poland for 1961, December 22, 1961, SED ZK, microfilm FBS 339/13496.

82. Karl Mewis to Ulbricht, December 21, 1961, SED ZK, Walter Ulbricht Papers, NL 182/967.

83. Olivier to the SED Central Committee, August 22, 1961, SED ZK, microfilm FBS 339/13496.

84. Sieger report on the political and economic situation in Poland and German-Polish economic relations, May 18, 1962, BRD AA, Department 7, vol. 438.

85. From *Statistisches Jahrbuch der DDR, 1976, 1978* (Statistical Yearbook of the GDR, 1976, 1978), in Phillip J. Bryson, "Rat für gegenseitige Wirtschaftshilfe" (The Council of Mutual Economic Assistance), in Hans Adolf Jacobsen, Gerd Leptin, Ulrich Scheuner, and Eberhard Schulz, eds., *Drei Jahrzehnte Aussenpolitik der DDR* (Munich: R. Oldenbourg Verlag, 1979), p. 578.

86. Lugenheim to the GDR Foreign Ministry, June 20, 1960, DDR MfAA, Warsaw Embassy, A3751.

87. Naszkowski briefing for a delegation visit to the GDR, October 12, 1962, PZPR KC, 237/V–379.

88. Sieger report on the political and economic situation in Poland and on German-Polish economic relations, May 18, 1962, BRD AA, Department 7, vol. 438. Trade with the West Germany amounted to about 5 percent of Poland's trade.

89. Sieger report on the political and economic situation in Poland and German-Polish economic relations, May 18, 1962, BRD AA, Department 7, vol. 438.

90. Moldt to the GDR Foreign Ministry, September 24, 1962, SED ZK, microfilm FBS 339/13496.

91. Naszkowski report for the delegation to the GDR (including a Central Committee briefing report), October 12, 1962, PZPR KC, 237/V–379. West Germany's trade with Poland represented a relatively insignificant 0.7 percent of the FRG's total trade.

92. Adam (SED Central Committee Department of Foreign Affairs) report on the trade negotiations with Poland in 1962, April 3, 1962, SED ZK, microfilm FBS 339/13491.

93. Notes of meeting with Leucht, undated, unsigned, ca. early 1962, SED ZK, microfilm FBS 339/13491.

94. Naszkowski report for the delegation to the GDR (including a Central Committee briefing report), October 12, 1962, PZPR KC, 237/V–379.

95. Kolmar (*Neues Deutschland* correspondent) to Florin, November 27, 1962, SED ZK, microfilm FBS 339/13496.

96. Sikora, *Sozialistische Solidarität und nationale Interessen*, p. 155.

97. FRG Foreign Ministry report on developments in Bulgaria, Czechoslovakia, Poland, Romania, and Hungary, April 1-October 31, 1962, November 20, 1962, BRD AA, Department 7, vol. 438.

98. Moldt report on PZPR policies, September 5, 1962, SED ZK, microfilm FBS 339/13424.

99. Moldt to the GDR Foreign Ministry on the current state of Polish-West German relations, September 24, 1962, SED ZK, microfilm FBS 339/13496.

100. Naszkowski report for the delegation to the GDR (including a Central Committee briefing report), October 12, 1962, PZPR KC, 237/V–379.

101. Kolmar to Florin, November 27, 1962, SED ZK, microfilm FBS 339/13496.

102. Viebig notes of meeting with Pasko on December 13, December 21, 1962, SED ZK, microfilm FBS 339/13496.

103. Sikora, *Sozialistische Solidarität und nationale Interessen*, pp. 173–175.

104. Documents of the 116th Meeting of the Presidium of the Council of Ministers, November 8, 1962, DDR MR, DC–20, I/4 634.

105. Naszkowski report for the delegation to the GDR (including a Central Committee briefing report), October 12, 1962, PZPR KC, 237/V–379; and notes on the present situation in the GDR, unsigned, undated, ca. October, 1962, PZPR KC, 237/XXII–1103; see also Sikora, *Sozialistische Solidarität und nationale Interessen*, p. 157.

106. GDR Embassy recommendations for the Polish party and government delegation visit to the GDR, undated, ca. September, 1962, SED ZK, microfilm FBS 339/13424.

107. Information on the policies of the "fraternal parties" of the socialist countries, December 21, 1962, SED ZK, IV 2/20/31.

108. Report on the policies of the Polish communist party, unsigned, undated, ca. October 1962, SED ZK, Walter Ulbricht Papers, NL 182/1251.

109. GDR Embassy recommendations for the Polish party and government delegation visit to the GDR, undated, ca. September, 1962, SED ZK, microfilm FBS 339/13424.

110. V. Guttmann (SED Department of Foreign Affairs) to Ulbricht, October 10, 1962, SED ZK, Walter Ulbricht Papers, NL 182/1251.

111. Naszkowski report for the delegation to the GDR (including a Central Committee briefing report), October 12, 1962, PZPR KC, 237/V–379.

112. Ibid.

113. Ibid.

114. Protocol of the discussions between the GDR and Polish delegations, October 18, 1962, PZPR KC, 237/XX–1103; see also Sikora, *Sozialistische Solidarität und nationale Interessen*, p. 158.

115. Protocol of the discussions between the GDR and Polish delegations, October 18, 1962, PZPR KC, 237/XX–1103.

116. Kolmar report, November 4, 1962, SED ZK, microfilm FBS 339/13424.

117. SED memorandum, unsigned, October 17, 1962, SED ZK, Walter Ulbricht Papers, NL 182/678.

118. Information on the policies of the "fraternal parties" of the socialist countries, December 21, 1962, SED ZK, IV 2/20/31.

119. Foreign Ministry report on developments in Bulgaria, Czechoslovakia, Poland, Romania, Hungary, April 1-October 31, 1962, November 20, 1962, BRD AA, Department 7, vol. 438.

120. *Trybuna Ludu*, January 22, 1963, p. 2.

121. Schumann notes on relations with the Polish government, undated, ca. December 1962, SED ZK, microfilm FBS 339/13496.

122. Viebig notes on his visit to the West Institute in Poznań, November 21, 1962, SED ZK, microfilm FBS 339/13496.

123. Viebig notes on the Polish press, November 22, 1962, SED ZK, microfilm FBS 339/13496.

124. See R. F. Leslie, et al., *The History of Poland Since 1863* (Cambridge: Cambridge University Press, 1980), p. 374; and M. K. Dziewanowski, *Poland in the 20th Century* (New York: Columbia University Press, 1977), p. 188ff.

125. Khrushchev, *Khrushchev Remembers: The Last Testament*, p. 210.

126. Nikita Khrushchev, *Khrushchev Remembers: The Glasnost Tapes* (Boston: Little, Brown, 1990), p. 118.

127. From *Zagadnienia i materiały* (Problems and Materials) in Sikora, *Sozialistische Solidarität und nationale Interessen*, pp. 154–155.

Conclusion

The situation in Poland is worse than 1968 in Czechoslovakia.

—*SED Politburo, October 1980*[1]

The Berlin Wall completed the division of Germany: There would be no more crises over Berlin to threaten the peace in Europe. Until the late 1980s, neither the Kremlin nor the Western powers floated any more serious diplomatic proposals to reunite Germany. The deployment of vast arsenals of nuclear weapons in the Warsaw Pact and NATO countries in Europe virtually assured that neither side could risk war to change the status quo in Central Europe. As long as the borders of Poland remained the same, Gomułka did not oppose a Soviet deal with the West to unify Germany. Gomułka harbored no illusions about the SED's willingness to sacrifice better relations with Poland if there was a breakthrough on German unification and a change in the Oder-Neisse border.

Although the Cuban Missile crisis ushered in a more realistic approach to East-West relations,[2] the building of the Berlin Wall resulted in a change in East German-Polish relations. The Polish and East German communists reached a détente in the early 1960s, but it was a relationship dictated by Moscow and the contingencies of the Cold War, not a genuine partnership of common interests. Their own "cold war" continued.

Fundamental ideological differences between the SED and the PZPR persisted, especially in agricultural and cultural policy. The East Germans, Stalinists to the core, demanded that the PZPR collectivize, eschew capitalist loans, clamp down on the Catholic Church, and expunge all such Western cultural influences as the Western newspapers that still circulated in Poland.[3] But Polish officials recognized that the SED's dogmatic socialism and exorcism of all real or perceived bourgeois-capitalist influences would not work in Poland. Ruling a people that was deeply Catholic, anti-Soviet, and nationalistic, the PZPR took a more opportunistic, realistic approach. Just how little many Polish communists believed in Marxism was reflected in what a Polish official told an East German diplomat in late 1962: "A country can also live without perspectives."[4] This was heresy to the East German communists; to them Marxism-Leninism was an absolute blueprint for the future, not merely a justification for totalitarian dictatorship.

It was Gomułka, not Ulbricht, who had to adjust his thinking to the realities of a divided Europe. In the fall of 1956, it had looked to the East Germans as if Gomułka would follow Tito's path of independence from the Soviet Union and the other socialist countries. But Gomułka enjoyed much less latitude than Tito. Sandwiched between East Germany and the Soviet Union on the Warsaw Pact's most strategic front, Moscow was not about to let Poland go its own way. Gomułka resigned himself to the division of Europe into two armed camps and reconfirmed Poland's loyalty to the Warsaw Pact. Gomułka's domestic policies gradually became more repressive in the early 1960s, and his foreign policy began to mimic the Kremlin's.

Khrushchev's fall from power in 1964 circumscribed Gomułka's options even further. Although Gomułka's rise to power had surprised and angered Khrushchev, both had dabbled in aborted domestic reforms and risky diplomatic gambits. In the end, Khrushchev was powerless to change the status quo in Germany, and Gomułka's strategy to open Poland to the West had also largely failed him. He had no other choice but to revive Poland's political and economic partnerships with the Soviet bloc. In 1965, the editor of the weekly journal *Polityka*, Mieczysław Rakowski, correctly observed, "What nonsense it was for Western journalists to write him [Gomułka] up as a national communist, to try to pass him off as an opponent of the Soviet Union."[5]

Much to Ulbricht's satisfaction, these developments vindicated the SED's steady Marxist-Leninist-Stalinist course. With the East German economy outperforming the other Soviet bloc countries, it was the SED, not the PZPR, that now held the diplomatic upper hand. New Soviet leader Leonid Brezhnev promised a return to the normalcy of the latter years of Stalin's rule. The political situation in Central Europe stabilized, and Gomułka's policies petrified as well. When West Germany's "Grand Coalition" began to explore détente and diplomatic relations with Poland in the late 1960s, Gomułka took Ulbricht's hard-line, albeit without the SED's vituperative criticism of the FRG's new *Ostpolitik*. In light of Poland's serious economic problems at the time, Gomułka was still interested in an expansion of the trade with the FRG.[6]

The Prague Spring in 1968 posed a serious threat to this neo-Stalinist order in the Soviet bloc. As usual, Ulbricht rejected the Czechoslovak reforms, and urged Brezhnev to take military action to stop the contagion from spreading. The Prague Spring presented a bigger dilemma for

Gomułka. He had avoided a Soviet armed intervention in 1956 by assuring Khrushchev that the party would maintain its monopoly on power and keep Poland in the Warsaw Pact. The CzCP was now making the same promises. Gomułka had quietly disapproved of the Soviet invasion of Hungary, not only out of principle and the precedent that it set, but to gain public support for his new régime. Now Gomułka, with public discontent growing and party factions shaking the foundations of his power, supported a Warsaw Pact intervention into Czechoslovakia. If the Prague Spring had threatened communist rule in Poland or East Germany, undoubtedly Ulbricht and Gomułka would have supported military intervention into each other's country as well.

Brezhnev's presence at the PZPR congress in November 1968 solidified Gomułka's position within the PZPR for the time being, but worker unrest in Gdańsk led to his downfall two years later.[7] Edvard Gierek succeeded him. The Kremlin forced Ulbricht out in favor of Erich Honecker a year later, in part because of Ulbricht's stubborn rejection of SPD leader Willy Brandt's *Ostpolitik*. Gierek and Honecker did not bring the personal distrust of their predecessors to the table, and relations normalized once again in the seventies. Formal and informal exchanges now took place more frequently.

Worker revolts in Poland in 1976 and the Solidarity strikes in 1980 again alerted the SED to the dangers of close ties to Poland. Honecker closed the border to keep the Solidarity Movement from spreading to the GDR. In October 1980, the SED Politburo observed that "the situation in Poland is worse than 1968 in Czechoslovakia." Honecker ordered the East German army to mobilize in case the Soviets decided use Warsaw Pact troops against Poland.[8]

The imposition of martial law in Poland in December 1981 temporarily stabilized the political situation, but Polish-East German relations remained tense. In 1985, for instance, the GDR declared an extension of its territorial waters at Świnoujście from two to ten nautical miles, which the Polish government did not recognize. In several instances, the East German coast guard fired warning shots to scare Polish boats away.[9] And as the economic crisis paralyzed Poland in the late 1980s, more and more East Germans doubted Poland's ability ever to achieve a stable political and economic system. Many grumbled about the Poles coming across the border to buy up East Germany's precious consumer goods.

Soviet leader Mikhail Gorbachev recognized in the late 1980s that the inherent lack of trust between Poles and East Germans was a serious weakness in the Warsaw Pact. Warsaw Pact commanders knew that communist propaganda promising the allegiance of the pact's national forces to a common defense of socialism was bankrupt of the truth. Not only were Poles and East Germans reluctant alliance partners, but so too were

East Germans and Czechs, Slovaks and Hungarians, and Bulgarians and Romanians. The unity of the Warsaw Pact was a myth, a dangerous fantasy of Marxist theory, a leap of faith that Communist ideology had overcome national allegiances. Gorbachev recognized that the satellites were contributing little to Soviet security and were a drag on the Soviet economy. The relative costs of maintaining Stalin's empire were just too great.

When Gorbachev abandoned the Brezhnev Doctrine and left the communist governments in Eastern Europe to fend for themselves, the régimes quickly fell. The formation of the Polish Solidarity government in 1989 marked the first time in over forty years that a non-communist government ruled an East European country. For decades the SED had been trying to shield the GDR from the political deviations that had periodically surfaced in Poland. Now, without support from the Soviet Union, the SED was powerless to stop the rising tide of popular opposition to communist rule.

Free now to choose their own friends, the new non-communist governments in Eastern Europe immediately abandoned the Warsaw Pact and lined up to join NATO. Although there was some post–Cold War cooperation between Poland, the Czech Republic, Slovakia, and Hungary (the so-called Visegrad Four), they eschewed a joint application to NATO; each country wanted to be judged on its own merits. It was a sign that socialist internationalism had failed to overcome national differences.

The voluntary rapprochement that developed between France and West Germany during the Cold War provides an instructive comparison to East German-Polish relations within the Soviet empire. The proud and patriotic French, like the Poles, had good reason to doubt that Germany would ever become a trusted ally. The French had fought three wars with Germans within seventy-five years, losing to the Prussians in 1870, winning a Pyrrhic victory in World War I, and then capitulating again in 1940. Hitler's entry into Paris and the four-year German occupation was the ultimate humiliation for France. The Poles endured an even more brutal occupation.[10]

In contrast to relations among the communist parties in Eastern Europe, the post-war French and West German partnership was nurtured under the umbrella of what Geir Lundestad and John Lewis Gaddis have called U.S. hegemony by "invitation."[11] In the late 1940s, the Marshall Plan and NATO helped usher in a new epoch in Franco-German relations. In the 1950s, the European Coal and Steel Community and the Common Market further cemented the two countries together in unprecedented economic cooperation. The French and Germans were able to overcome their linguistic, cultural, and historic differences and find a common bond in the economic and political future of Western Europe.

The East Germans and Poles had no such opportunity. Without the presence of the Soviet army in Central Europe after World War II, the East German and Polish communist régimes would not have come to power. East Germans and Poles were subjected to illegitimate communist dictatorships imposed upon them by the Soviet Union, and relations between the régimes and the peoples in the Soviet empire did not develop naturally. Because the communist parties in Poland and East Germany never trusted the other, it is hardly surprising that there was no reconciliation between the two peoples, either.

Marxist educators confronted none of the national conflicts in a meaningful way, and communist propaganda also blurred the many conflicts between the SED and the PZPR. The East German communists could coerce their people into silent obedience to Marxist ideology. They could inculcate and brainwash, but they could not educate. No significant groundswell for Stalin's style of socialism came from the people anywhere in Eastern Europe, least of all in Poland. Repressive and authoritarian in their methods, and rigidly dogmatic and fundamentalist in their ideology, the zealous East German communists made few converts to socialist internationalism.

Gomułka's vision that the Polish people could find their own way to socialism also proved to be an illusion, but at least for a time the PZPR allowed a more open and honest debate about relations with the SED. After witnessing the recurrent upheavals in Poland in 1956, 1968, 1970, 1976, and 1980, however, the East German communists viewed the PZPR's more flexible and liberal socialism as a complete failure.

The "cold war" between the Ulbricht and Gomułka régimes was yet another division in the communist world that so many Western scholars and policymakers, especially for the first two decades after the war, perceived as a monolithic movement directed by Moscow. Polycentrism happened from the inside, regardless of whether or not the West encouraged it from the outside. Aggressive Western policies to subvert communist solidarity may have made Soviet leaders more reluctant allow the satellites the latitude that Khrushchev briefly gave them in the mid-1950s.

Given the strategic importance of East Germany and Poland to the Soviet Union, however, the Kremlin could not allow the problems in East German-Polish relations to develop into an open break. It almost came to that in 1956. There is little doubt that, if left on their own, relations between the East German and Polish communists would have gone the way of the Tito-Stalin split in the late 1940s, or the Sino-Soviet break in the early 1960s.

The strained East German-Polish relationship after the World War II provides further evidence that the communist parties of Eastern Europe could not supplant national loyalties with Marxist internationalism. Even the leadership and the rank and file of the SED and the PZPR remained staunchly nationalist. The rapid disintegration of the Warsaw Pact after 1989 and the civil wars in Yugoslavia in the 1990s reveal just how dysfunctional this socialist brotherhood really was.

Notes

1. Michael Kubina and Manfred Wilke, "Das Mosaiksteinchen Polen 1980/81. Verantwortungsgemeinschaft in Deutschland" (The Mosaic Stone Poland, 1980–81. The Responsible Community in Germany), in Klaus Schroeder, ed., *Geschichte und Transformationen des SED-Staates* (History and transformation of the SED State) (Berlin: Akademie Verlag, 1994), pp. 151–152.

2. See Marc Trachtenberg, *A Constructed Peace: The Making of the European Settlement 1945–1963* (Princeton: Princeton University Press, 1999), pp. 398. Trachtenberg wrote that "the threat of general nuclear war, which had loomed so large in 1961 and 1962, now faded into the background. The Cold War had become a different kind of conflict, more subdued, more modulated, more artificial, and above all, less terrifying"; see also John Lewis Gaddis, *We Now Know: Rethinking Cold War History*. Oxford: Clarendon Press, 1997, p. 261.

3. Viebig notes on the Polish press, November 22, 1962, SED ZK, microfilm FBS 339/13496; and Viebig report on the lectures by Bogusz and Kosicki in the GDR from December 4–14, December 27, 1962, SED ZK, microfilm FBS 339/13422.

4. Viebig notes of meeting with Pasko on December 13, December 21, 1962, SED ZK, microfilm FBS 339/13496.

5. Quoted in Nicholas Bethell, *Gomułka, His Poland and His Communism* (London: Longmans, Green and Co., 1969), p. 253.

6. Michael J. Sodaro, *Moscow, Germany, and the West from Khrushchev to Gorbachev* (Ithaca: Cornell University Press, 1990) pp. 94–98, 145.

7. Erwin Weit, *Ostblock intern: 13 Jahre Dolmetscher für die polnische Partei—und Staatsführung* (Inside the East bloc: Thirteen years as interpreter for the Polish Party—and government leadership) (Hamburg: Hoffmann und Campe Verlag, 1970), p. 187; and Konrad Syrop, *Poland in Perspective* (London: Robert Hale, 1982), p. 198.

8. Kubina and Wilke, "Das Mosaiksteinchen Polen 1980/81," pp. 151–152.

9. See Martin McCauley, "Soviet-GDR Relations under Gorbachev," *East Central Europe*, no. 14–15 (1987–1988), p. 470.

10. Certainly one cannot overlook the fact that there were significant cultural and historical differences between the Germans who ended up in the FRG, such as the Rhinelanders and Bavarians, and the Germans in the GDR, such as the Saxons and the Prussians. But as a result of communist rule, these East Germans were never given the opportunity to foster new friendships with Poles on a free and voluntary basis.

11. See John Lewis Gaddis, "The Cold War, the Long Peace, and the Future," in Geir Lundestad and Odd Arne Westad, eds., *Beyond the Cold War* (New York: Oxford University Press, 1993), p. 12.

Bibliography

Unpublished Documents

A. Archiwum Akt Nowych (Archive of Newer Records). Warsaw.
Records of the Central Committee of the Polish United Workers' Party.
People's Republic of Poland. Records of the Government Ministries.
B. Archiwum Ministerstwa Spraw Zagranicznych (Archive of the Ministry of Foreign Affairs). Warsaw.
People's Republic of Poland. Records of the Political Department.
People's Republic of Poland. Records of the Minister's Office.
C. Bundesarchiv (Federal Archive). Koblenz.
Federal Republic of Germany. Records of the Federal Ministry for All-German Questions.
Federal Republic of Germany. Records of the Chancellor's Office.
D. Bundesarchiv. Abteilung Potsdam (Federal Archive. Potsdam Department). Potsdam.
German Democratic Republic. Records of the Government Ministries.
E. Bundesarchiv. Auswärtigen Amtes der BRD (Federal Archive. Foreign Office of the Federal Republic of Germany). Bonn.
Federal Republic of Germany. Political Archive of the Foreign Office.
F. Politisches Archiv des Auswärtigen Amtes. Bestand Ministerium für Auswärtigen Angelegenheiten der DDR (Political Archive of the Foreign Office. Holdings of the Ministry of Foreign Affairs of the GDR). Berlin.
German Democratic Republic. Records of the Ministry of Foreign Affairs.
G. Stiftung Archiv der Parteien und Massenorganisationen der DDR im Bundesarchiv (Archive of the Party and Mass Organizations of the GDR in the Federal Archive). Berlin.
Records of the Central Committee of the Socialist Unity Party.

Published Documents

Kubina, Michael, and Manfred Wilke. *Hart und kompromisslos durchgriefen: Die SED contra Polen 1980/81: Geheimakten der SED-Führung über die Unterdrückung der polnischen Demokratiebewegung* (Tough and uncompromising measures: The SED against Poland, 1980–1981: Secret documents of the SED leadership about the suppression of the Polish democratic movement). Berlin: Akademie Verlag, 1995.

Krajowa Rada Narodowa. *Sprawozdanie Stenograficzne* (National People's Council. Stenographic records).

Procacci, Giuliano, ed. *The Cominform: Minutes of the Three Conferences, 1947/1948/1949.* Milan: Giangiacomo Feltrinelli, 1994.

Memoirs and Collected Works

Brandt, Heinz. *The Search for a Third Way: My Path Between East and West.* Garden City, N.Y. Doubleday, 1970.

Gniffke, Erich W. *Jahre Mit Ulbricht* (Years with Ulbricht). Cologne: Verlag Wissenschaft und Politik, 1966.

Gomułka, Władysław. *O problemie Niemieckim* (On the German problem). Warsaw: Książka i Wiedza, 1971.

Gromyko, Andrei. *Memories.* London: Hutchinson, 1989.

Grunert, Horst. *Für Honecker auf glattem Parkett: Erinnerungen eines DDR-Diplomaten* (For Honecker on the smooth parquet: Memoirs of a GDR diplomat). Berlin: Edition Ost, 1995.

Khrushchev, Nikita. *Khrushchev Remembers: The Glasnost Tapes.* Boston: Little, Brown, 1990.

_____ *Khrushchev Remembers: The Last Testament.* Boston: Little, Brown, 1974.

Lemmer, Ernst. *Manches war doch anders: Erinnerungen eines deutschen Demokraten* (Some things were really otherwise: Memories of a German democrat). Frankfurt/Main: Verlag Heinrich Scheffler, 1968.

Luxemburg, Rosa. *Gesammelte Werke. Band 1: 1893 bis 1905* (Collected works. Volume 1: 1893 to 1905). Berlin: Dietz Verlag, 1990.

Marx, Karl and Frederick Engels. *Collected Works. Volume 6: 1845–48.* Moscow: Progress Publishers, 1976.

_____. *Collected Works. Volume 8: 1848–49.* Moscow: Progress Publishers, 1977.

_____. *Collected Works. Volume 45: 1874–79.* Moscow: Progress Publishers, 1991.

Pieck, Wilhelm. *Gesammelte Reden und Schriften. Band II: Januar 1920 bis April 1925* (Collected speeches and writings. Volume 2: January 1920 to April 1925). Berlin: Dietz Verlag, 1959.

Resis, Albert, ed. *Molotov Remembers: Inside Kremlin Politics. Conversations with Felix Chuev.* Chicago: Ivan R. Dee, 1993.

Spasowski, Romuald. *The Liberation of One.* New York: Harcourt Brace Jovanovich, 1986.

Ulbricht, Walter. *Die Entwicklung des deutschen volksdemokratischen Staates, 1945–1958* (The development of the German peoples' democratic state). Berlin: Dietz Verlag, 1961.

Weit, Erwin. *Ostblock intern: 13 Jahre Dolmetscher für die polnische Partei—und Staatsführung* (Inside the East bloc: Thirteen years as interpreter for the Polish party—and government leadership). Hamburg: Hoffmann und Campe Verlag, 1970.

Winiewicz, Józef. *Co pamiętam z długiej drogi życia* (What I remember from the long road of life). Poznań: Wydawnictwo Poznańskie, 1985.

Books

Bethell, Nicholas. _Gomułka, His Poland and His Communism_. London: Longmans, Green and Co., 1969.

Bender, Peter. _East Europe in Search of Security_. London: Chatto and Windus, 1972.

Bruns, Wilhelm. _Die Aussenpolitik der DDR_ (The foreign policy of the GDR). Berlin: Colloquium Verlag, 1985.

Brzezinski, Zbigniew. _The Soviet Bloc: Unity and Conflict_. Cambridge: Harvard University Press, 1967.

Bühler, Phillip. _The Oder-Neisse Line: A Reappraisal under International Law_. Boulder: East European Monographs, 1990.

Childs, David. _The GDR: Moscow's German Ally_. London: Unwin Hyman, 1988.

Clemens, Diane. _Yalta_. New York: Oxford University Press, 1970.

Coutouvidis, John, and Jaime Reynolds. _Poland 1939–1947_. New York: Holmes and Meier, 1986.

Croan, Melvin. _East Germany: The Soviet Connection_. Beverly Hills, Calif: Sage Publishing, 1976.

Davies, Norman. _God's Playground: A History of Poland, Volume II: 1795 to the Present_. New York: Columbia University Press, 1982.

Deuerlein, Ernst, ed. _DDR 1945–1970: Geschichte und Bestandsaufnahme_ (The GDR 1945–1970: History and inventory). Munich: Deutscher Taschenbuch Verlag, 1966.

Dobrzycki, Wiesław. _Granica Zachodnia w polityce polskiej 1944–1947_ (The western border in Polish politics, 1944–1947). Warsaw: Państwowe Wydawnictwo Naukowe, 1974.

Duhnke, Horst. _Die KPD von 1933 bis 1945_ (The KPD from 1933 to 1945). Cologne: Kiepenheuer u. Witsch, 1972.

Dziewanowski, M. K. _The Communist Party of Poland: An Outline of History_. Cambridge: Harvard University Press, 1976.

_____. _Poland in the 20th Century_. New York: Columbia University Press, 1977.

Ettinger, Elżbieta. _Rosa Luksemburg: Ein Leben_ (Rosa Luxemburg: A life). Bonn: Verlag J.H.W. Dietz, 1990.

Fodor, Neil. _The Warsaw Treaty Organization: A Political and Organizational Analysis_. New York: St. Martin's Press, 1990.

Fulbrook, Mary. _Anatomy of a Dictatorship: Inside the GDR, 1945–1989_. Oxford: Oxford University Press, 1995.

Gaddis, John Lewis. _We Now Know: Rethinking Cold War History_. Oxford: Clarendon Press, 1997.

Gajda, Eugeniusz. _Polska Polityka Zagraniczna, 1944–1971: Podstawowe Problemy_ (Polish foreign policy, 1944–1971: Basic problems). Warsaw: Ministerstwa Obrony Narodowy, 1972.

Grieder, Peter. _The East German Leadership, 1946–1973_. Manchester: Manchester University Press, 1999.

Hänisch, Werner. _Aussenpolitik und internationale Beziehungen der DDR, 1949–1955_ (The foreign policy and international relations of the GDR, 1949–1955). Berlin: Staatsverlag der DDR, 1972.

Kamiński, Marek. *Polsko-Czechosłowackie stosunki polityczne 1945–1948* (Polish-Czechoslovak political relations, 1945–1948). Warsaw: Państwowe Wydawnictwo Naukowe, 1990.

Kaser, Michael. *Comecon: Integration Problems of the Planned Economies.* London: Oxford University Press, 1967.

Kissinger, Henry. *Diplomacy.* New York: Simon and Schuster, 1994.

Klafkowski, Alfons. *The Polish-German Frontier After World War Two.* Poznań: Wydawnictwo Poznańskie, 1972.

Koćwin, Lesław. *Polityczne determinanty polsko-wschodnioniemieckich stosunków przygranicznych 1949–1990* (Political determinants of Polish-East German relations on the border 1949–1990). Wrocław: Wydawnictwo Uniwersytetu Wrocławskiego, 1993.

Lehmann, Hans Georg. *Der Oder-Neisse-Konflikt* (The Oder-Neisse conflict). Munich: C. H. Beck, 1979.

Leslie, R. F., et al. *The History of Poland Since 1863.* Cambridge: Cambridge University Press, 1980.

Liczmański, Ryszard. *Adam Rapacki: Zarys biograficzny* (Adam Rapacki: Biographical sketch) Warsaw: Akademia Nauk Społecznych PZPR, 1989.

Loth, Wilfried. *Stalins ungeliebtes Kind: Warum Moskau die DDR nicht wollte* (Stalin's unwanted child: Why Moscow did not want the GDR). Berlin: Rowohlt, 1994.

Ludz, Peter C. *Die DDR zwischen Ost und West* (The GDR between East and West). Munich: Verlag C. H. Beck, 1977.

Merkl, Peter H. *German Foreign Policies, West and East: On the Threshold of a New European Era.* Santa Barbara, Calif: ABC-Clio, 1974.

Moreton, Edwina. *East Germany and the Warsaw Alliance: The Politics of Detente.* Boulder: Westview Press, 1978.

Naimark, Norman. *The Russians in Germany: A History of the Soviet Zone of Occupation, 1945–1949.* Cambridge: Harvard University Press, 1995.

Naimark, Norman, and Leonid Gibianski, eds. *The Establishment of Communist Regimes in Eastern Europe, 1944–49.* Boulder: Westview Press, 1997.

Phillips, Ann L. *Soviet Policy Toward East Germany Reconsidered: The Postwar Decade.* New York: Greenwood Press, 1986.

Rachwald, Arthur R. *Poland between the Superpowers: Security vs. Economic Recovery.* Boulder: Westview Press, 1983.

Radde, Jurgen. *Der diplomatische Dienst der DDR: Namen und Daten* (The Diplomatic Service of the GDR: Names and dates). Cologne: Verlag Wissenschaft und Politik, 1977.

Rakowski, Mieczysław. *The Foreign Policy of the Polish People's Republic.* Warsaw: Interpress Publishers, 1975.

Raina, Peter. *Gomułka: Politische Biographie* (Gomulka: Political biography). Cologne: Verlag Wissenschaft und Politik, 1970.

Richter, James G. *Khrushchev's Double Bind: International Pressures and Domestic Coalition Politics.* Baltimore: Johns Hopkins Press, 1994.

Schenk, Fritz. *Im Vorzimmer der Diktatur; 12 Jahre Pankow* (In the antechamber of the dictatorship: Twelve years Pankow). Cologne: Kiepenheuer and Witsch, 1962.

Schickel, Alfred. *Deutsche und Polen: Ein Jahrtausend gemeinsame Geschichte* (Germans and Poles: A thousand years of common history). Bergisch Gladbach, Germany: Gustav Lübbe Verlag, 1984.

Sikora, Franz. *Sozialistische Solidarität und nationale Interessen* (Socialist solidarity and national interests). Cologne: Verlag Wissenschaft und Politik, 1977.

Skowronski, Andrzej. *Polska a problem Niemiec, 1945–1965* (Poland and the German problem, 1945–1965). Warsaw: Książka i wiedza, 1967.

Sodaro, Michael J. *Moscow, Germany, and the West from Khrushchev to Gorbachev.* Ithaca: Cornell University Press, 1990.

Staritz, Dietrich, ed. *Die Gründung der DDR: Von der sowjetischen Besatzungsherrschaft zum sozialistischen Staat* (The founding of the GDR: From the Soviet Occupation Authority to the socialist state). Munich: Deutscher Taschenbuch Verlag, 1984.

_____. *Geschichte der DDR, 1949–1985* (History of the GDR, 1949–1985). Frankfurt/Main: Suhrkamp Verlag, 1985.

Steele, Jonathan. *Inside East Germany: The State that Came in from the Cold.* New York: Urizen Books, 1977.

Stehle, Hansjakob. *The Independent Satellite: Society and Politics in Poland Since 1945.* London: Pall Mall Press, 1965.

Stern, Carola. *Ulbricht: A Political Biography.* New York: Frederick Praeger, 1965.

Strobel, Georg W. *Deutschland-Polen: Wunsch und Wirklichkeit* (Germany-Poland: Wish and reality). Bonn: Edition Atlantic Forum, 1969.

Stone, Gerald. *The Smallest Slavonic Nation: The Sorbs of Lusatia.* London: The Athlone Press, 1972.

Syrop, Konrad. *Poland in Perspective.* London: Robert Hale, 1982.

Terry, Sarah. *Poland's Place in Europe: General Sikorski and the Origins of the Oder-Neisse Line, 1939–1943.* Princeton: Princeton University Press, 1983.

Trachtenberg, Marc. *A Constructed Peace: The Making of the European Settlement 1945–1963.* Princeton: Princeton University Press, 1999.

Ulam, Adam B. *Expansion and Coexistence: The History of Soviet Foreign Policy.* New York: Frederick A. Praeger, 1968.

Vierheller, Viktoria. *Polen und die Deutschland-Frage 1939–1949* (Poland and the German question 1939–1949). Cologne: Verlag Wissenschaft und Politik, 1970.

Vosske, Heinz. *Wilhelm Pieck: Biographischer Abriss* (Wilhelm Pieck: Biographical abstract). Berlin: Dietz Verlag, 1975.

Weber, Hermann. *Geschichte der DDR* (History of the GDR). Munich: Deutscher Taschenbuch Verlag, 1985.

Wiewióra, Bolesław. *The Polish-German Frontier from the Standpoint of International Law.* Poznań: Wydawnictwo Zachodnie, 1959.

Zeiger, Gottfried. *Die Haltung von SED und DDR zur Einheit Deutschlands, 1949–1987* (The attitude of the SED and the GDR toward the unification of Germany, 1949–1989). Cologne: Verlag Wissenschaft und Politik, 1988.

Zubok, Vladislaw, and Constantine Pleshakov. *Inside the Kremlin's Cold War: From Stalin to Khrushchev*. Cambridge: Harvard University Press, 1996.

Articles

Badstübner, Ralf. "Die sowjetische Deutschlandpolitik im Lichte neuer Quellen" (The Soviet policy toward Germany in light of new sources). In Wilfried Loth, ed., *Die Deutschland Frage in der Nachkriegszeit* (The German question in the post-war period), 11–28. Berlin: Akademie Verlag, 1994.

Brus, Wlodzimierz. "Economic Reforms as an issue in Soviet-East European relations." In Karen Dawisha and Philip Hanson, eds., *Soviet-East European Dilemmas: Coercion, Competition, and Consent*, 84–89. London: Heinemann Educational Books, 1981.

Bryson, Phillip J. "Rat für gegenseitige Wirtschaftshilfe" (The Council of Mutual Economic Assistance). In Hans Adolf Jacobsen, Gerd Leptin, Ulrich Scheuner, and Eberhard Schulz, eds., *Drei Jahrzehnte Aussenpolitik der DDR* (Three decades of the foreign policy of the GDR), 575–597. Munich: R. Oldenbourg Verlag, 1979.

Croan, Melvin. "East Germany." In Adam Bromke, ed., *The Communist States at the Crossroads: Between Moscow and Peking*, 126–139. New York: Frederich A. Praeger, 1965.

_____. "Germany and Eastern Europe." In Joseph Held, ed., *The Columbia History of Eastern Europe in the Twentieth Century*, 345–393. New York: Columbia University Press, 1992.

Dallin, Alexander. "Stalin and the Prospects for Post-War Europe." In Francesca Gori and Silvio Pons, eds., *The Soviet Union and Europe in the Cold War, 1943–53*, 185–190. New York: St. Martin's Press, 1996.

Di Biagio, Anna. "The Marshall Plan and the Founding of the Cominform, June-September 1947." In Francesca Gori and Silvio Pons, eds., *The Soviet Union and Europe in the Cold War, 1943–53*, 208–221. New York: St. Martin's Press, 1996.

Dziewanowski, M. K. "Poland." In Adam Bromke, ed., *The Communist States at the Crossroads: Between Moscow and Peking*, 56–70. New York: Frederich A. Praeger, 1965.

Fischer, Alexander. "Aussenpolitische Aktivität bei ungewisser sowjetischer Deutschland-Politik (bis 1955)" (Foreign policy activity in uncertain Soviet German policy to 1955). In Hans Adolf Jacobsen, Gerd Leptin, Ulrich Scheuner, and Eberhard Schulz, eds., *Drei Jahrzehnte Aussenpolitik der DDR*, 51–84. Munich: R. Oldenbourg Verlag, 1979.

Flemming, George L. "The Polish Eagle Looks West." *East Europe* 16, no. 10 (1967): 16–20.

Gaddis, John Lewis. "The Cold War, the Long Peace, and the Future." In Geir Lundestad and Odd Arne Westad, eds., *Beyond the Cold War*, 7–22. New York: Oxford University Press, 1993.

Gemkow, Heinrich. "*Gemeinsame Traditionen der revolutionären deutschen und polnischen Arbeiterbewegung 1917/18 bis 1945*" (Common traditions of the revolutionary German and Polish Workers' Movement, 1917/18 to 1945). *Beiträge zur Geschichte der Arbeiterbewegung* (Contributions to the history of the Workers' Movement) 16, no. 1 (1974): 3–30.

Gibianski, Leonid. "The Soviet-Yugoslav Conflict and the Soviet Bloc." In Francesca Gori and Silvio Pons, eds., *The Soviet Union and Europe in the Cold War, 1943–53*, 222–245. New York: St. Martin's Press, 1996.

————. "The Soviet-Yugoslav Split and the Cominform." In Norman Naimark and Leonid Gibianski, eds., *The Establishment of Communist Régimes in Eastern Europe, 1944–49*, 291–312. Boulder: Westview Press, 1997.

Görlich, Joachim G. "Kommunistische Freundschaft an der Oder und Neisse" (Communist friendship on the Oder and Neisse). *Osteuropa* 14, no. 10 (1964): 724–728.

Griffith, William E. "The Sino-Soviet Split: A Reconstructed History, 1956–64. In Adam Bromke, ed., *The Communist States at the Crossroads: Between Moscow and Peking*, 43–55. New York: Frederich A. Praeger, 1965.

Gross, Jan. "War as Revolution." In Norman Naimark and Leonid Gibianski, eds., *The Establishment of Communist Régimes in Eastern Europe, 1944–49*, 17–40. Boulder: Westview Press, 1997.

Holzer, Jerzy, "Osteuropa und die neue deutsche Staatenordnung" (Eastern Europe and the new German state order). In Werner Weidenfeld and Hartmut Zimmerman, eds., *Deutschland—Handbuch: Eine doppelte Bilanz 1949–1989* (Germany handbook: A double balance 1949–1989), 685–697. Munich: Carl Hanser Verlag, 1989.

Hübner, Christa. "Das Abkommen von Zgorzelec und die politisch-ideologische Arbeit der SED 1950/51" (The Treaty of Zgorzelec and the political-ideological work of the SED, 1950–1951). *Beiträge zur Geschichte der Arbeiterbewegung* 23, no. 1 (1981): 39–50.

Iazhborovskaia, Inessa. "The Gomulka Alternative." In Norman Naimark and Leonid Gibianski, eds, *The Establishment of Communist Régimes in Eastern Europe, 1944–49*, 123–137. Boulder: Westview Press, 1997.

Jacobsen, Hans Adolf. "Auswärtige Kulturpolitik" (Foreign cultural policy). In Hans Adolf Jacobsen, Gerd Leptin, Ulrich Scheuner, and Eberhard Schulz, eds., *Drei Jahrzehnte Aussenpolitik der DDR*, 235–260. Munich: R. Oldenbourg Verlag, 1979.

Jacobsen, Hans-Dieter. "Strategie und Schwerpunkte der Aussenwirtschaftsbeziehungen" (Strategy and the main points of foreign economic relations). In Hans Adolf Jacobsen, Gerd Leptin, Ulrich Scheuner, and Eberhard Schulz, eds., *Drei Jahrzehnte Aussenpolitik der DDR*, 293–311. Munich: R. Oldenbourg Verlag, 1979.

Kanet, Roger. "Research on East European Foreign Policy: Other Needs, Other Areas, New Directions." In Ronald H. Linden, ed., *The Foreign Policies of East Europe: New Approaches*, 311–319. New York: Frederich A. Praeger, 1980.

Kenney, Patrick. "Polish Workers and the Socialist Transformation." In Norman Naimark and Leonid Gibianski, eds., *The Establishment of Communist Régimes in Eastern Europe, 1944–49*, 139–166. Boulder: Westview Press, 1997.

Kersten, Krystyna. "1956—The Turning Point." In Odd Arne Westad, Sven Holts-
    mark, and Iver B. Neumann, eds, *The Soviet Union in Eastern Europe,
    1945–1989*, 47–62. New York: St. Martin's Press, 1994.
Kubina, Michael, and Manfred Wilke, "Das Mosaiksteinchen Polen 1980/81. Ver-
    antwortungsgemeinschaft in Deutschland" (The mosaic stone Poland,
    1980–81. The responsible community in Germany). In Klaus Schroeder, ed.,
    Geschichte und Transformationen des SED-Staates (History and transformation
    of the SED State), 149–165. Berlin: Akademie Verlag, 1994.
Krisch, Henry. "Vorstellungen von künftiger aussenpolitischer Orientierung in
    der SBZ bis 1947 und ihre Auswirkungen auf die spätere Aussenpolitik der
    DDR" (Concepts of the future foreign policy orientation in the Soviet occu-
    pation zone to 1947). In Hans Adolf Jacobsen, Gerd Leptin, Ulrich Scheuner,
    and Eberhard Schulz, eds., *Drei Jahrzehnte Aussenpolitik der DDR*, 37–49. Mu-
    nich: R. Oldenbourg Verlag, 1979.
Loth, Wilfried. "Die Historiker und die Deutsche Frage: Ein Rückblick nach dem
    Ende des kalten Krieges" (The historians and the German question: A look
    back after the end of the Cold War). In Wilfried Loth, ed., *Die Deutschland
    Frage in der Nachkriegszeit*, 11–28. Berlin: Akademie Verlag, 1994.
————. "Stalin's Plans for Post-War Germany." In Francesca Gori and Silvio
    Pons, eds., *The Soviet Union and Europe in the Cold War, 1943–53*, 23–36. New
    York: St. Martin's Press, 1996.
Marsh, Peter. "Foreign Policy Making in the German Democratic Republic." In
    Hannes Adomeit, ed., *Foreign Policy Making in Communist Countries*, 79–111.
    London: Saxon House, 1979.
Mastny, Vojtech. "'We Are in a Bind': Polish and Czechoslovak Attempts at Re-
    forming the Warsaw Pact, 1956–1959." *Bulletin: Cold War International History
    Project*, no. 11 (winter 1998): 230–250.
McCauley, Martin. "Soviet-GDR Relations under Gorbachev." *East Central Europe*
    14–15 (1987–1988): 461–482.
Mietkowska-Kaiser, Ines. "Zur brüderlichen Zusammenarbeit zwischen polnis-
    chen und deutschen Kommunisten und Antifaschisten nach dem Sieg über
    den deutschen Faschismus (1945–1949)" (On the fraternal cooperation be-
    tween the Polish and German communists and anti-fascists after the victory
    over German fascism, 1945–1949). *Jahrbuch für Geschichte der sozialistischen
    Länder Europas* (Yearbook for the history of the socialist countries of Europe)
    23, no. 1 (1979): 49–67.
Moreton, Edwina. "Foreign Policy Perspectives in Eastern Europe." In Karen
    Dawisha and Philip Hanson, eds., *Soviet-East European Dilemmas: Coercion,
    Competition, and Consent*, 172–194. London: Heinemann Educational Books,
    1981.
Morrison, James F. "The Foreign Policy of Poland." In James Kuhlmann, ed., *The
    Foreign Policies of East Europe: Domestic and International Determinants*,
    129–165. Leyden, Netherlands: A. W. Sijthoff, 1978.
Mosely, Philip E. "Introduction: Power and Ideology in the Communist States."
    In Adam Bromke, ed., *The Communist States at the Crossroads: Between Moscow
    and Peking*, 3–20. New York: Frederich A. Praeger, 1965.

Naimark, Norman. "The Soviets and the Christian Democrats, 1945–1949." In Francesca Gori and Silvio Pons, eds., *The Soviet Union and Europe in the Cold War, 1943–53*, 37–56. New York: St. Martin's Press, 1996.

Narinskii, Michail M. "The Soviet Union and the Berlin Crisis." In Francesca Gori and Silvio Pons, eds., *The Soviet Union and Europe in the Cold War, 1943–53*, 57–75. New York: St. Martin's Press, 1996.

Oschlies, Wolf. "Aktionen der DDR-Reaktionen in Osteuropa" (Actions of the GDR-reactions in Eastern Europe). In Gerd Leptin, ed., *Die Rolle der DDR in Osteuropa* (The role of the GDR in Eastern Europe), 103–121. Berlin: Duneker und Humboldt, 1974.

Pączkowski, Andrzej. "The Polish Contribution to the Victory of the 'Prague Coup' in February 1948." *Bulletin: Cold War International History Project*, no. 11 (winter 1998), 141–148.

Raack, R. C. "Stalin Plans His Post-War Germany." *Journal of Contemporary History* 28 (1993): 53–73.

Royen, Christoph. "Osteuropaische Staaten" (East European states). In Hans Adolf Jacobsen, Gerd Leptin, Ulrich Scheuner, and Eberhard Schulz, eds., *Drei Jahrzehnte Aussenpolitik der DDR*, 599–619. Munich: R. Oldenbourg Verlag, 1979.

Rupieger, Hermann-Josef. "Verpasste Chancen? Ein Rückblick auf die deutschland-politischen Verhandlungen, 1952–1955" (Missed chances? A look back at the German political negotiations, 1952–1955). In Wilfried Loth, ed., *Die Deutschland Frage in der Nachkriegszeit*, 11–28. Berlin: Akademie Verlag, 1994.

Schulz, Eberhard. "New Developments in Intra-bloc Relations in Historical Perspective." In Karen Dawisha and Philip Hanson, eds., *Soviet-East European Dilemmas: Coercion, Competition, and Consent*, 41–60. London: Heinemann Educational Books, 1981.

Selvage, Douglas. "Introduction" to "Khrushchev's November 1958 Berlin Ultimatum: New Evidence from the Polish Archives." *Bulletin: Cold War International History Project*, no. 11 (winter 1998), 200–203.

Starrels, John M., and Anita M. Mallinckrodt. "East Germany's Foreign Policy." In James Kuhlmann, ed., *The Foreign Policies of East Europe: Domestic and International Determinants*, 79–107. Leyden, Netherlands: A. W. Sijthoff, 1978.

Stefancic, David. "The Rapacki Plan: A Case Study of East European Diplomacy." *East European Quarterly* 21, no. 4 (January 1988): 401–412.

Trepte, Hans-Christian. "Polish Literature and Culture in East Germany: A Window to the West?" *The Polish Review* 16, no. 1 (1996): 63–72.

Wettig, Gerhard. "The Soviet Union and Germany in the Late Stalin Period, 1950–3." In Francesca Gori and Silvio Pons, eds., *The Soviet Union and Europe in the Cold War, 1943–53*, 357–374. New York: St. Martin's Press, 1996.

Wiatr, Jerzy. "Kryzys internacjonalizmu" (International crisis)? *Nowe Drogi* (New Paths) 10, nos. 11–12 (November-December 1956): 109–117.

Wilke, Manfred. "Kommunismus in Deutschland und Rahmenbedingungen politischer Handelns nach 1945" (Communism in Germany and the contingencies of political exchange). In Manfred Wilke, ed., *Anatomie der Parteizentrale: Die KPD/SED auf dem Weg zur Macht* (Anatomy of the central party office: The KPD/SED on the road to power), 13–48. Berlin: Akademie Verlag, 1998.

Wozniak, Peter. "Blut, Erz, Kohle: A Thematic Examination of German Propaganda on the Silesian Question during the Interwar Years." *East European Quarterly* 28 (September 1994): 319–334.

Newspapers and Periodicals

Einheit
Deutsche Volkszeitung
Głos Ludu
Neues Deutschland
Nowe Drogi
Polityka
Trybuna Ludu

Index